IO and
Global Inequality

IQ and
Global Inequality

RICHARD LYNN and TATU VANHANEN

Washington Summit Publishers

Augusta, Georgia

A National Policy Institute Book

2006

Washington Summit Publishers
P. O. Box 3514
Augusta, GA 30914-3514

Library of Congress Cataloging-in-Publication Data

Lynn, Richard, 1930-
  IQ and global inequality / Richard Lynn and Tatu Vanhanen.
    p. cm.
  "A National Policy Institute book."
  Includes bibliographical references and index.
  ISBN-13: 978-1-59368-025-1 (hard cover)
  ISBN-13: 978-1-59368-024-4 (paper back)
  1. Intellect--Social aspects. 2. Intellect--Cross-cultural studies. 3. National characteristics. I. Vanhanen, Tatu. II. Title. III. Title: Intelligence quotient and global inequality.
  BF431.L95 2006
  153.9--dc22

                                    2006024627

Printed in the United States of America

Typeset in Sabon LT Std font by L. R. Andrews, Inc.

To our wives

Joyce and Anni

Contents

Appendices

Tables

Figures

Why Isn't the Whole World Developed?

The question "Why isn't the whole world developed?" was the title of a keynote lecture delivered in 1981 at a conference of the American Economic History Association by Richard Easterlin, a distinguished development economist and the Kenan Professor of Economics at the University of Pennsylvania. His lecture was relevant for the present book because he raised the possibility that there might be differences in intelligence between the peoples of different countries and that these might explain why some are more economically developed than others. However, he rejected this possibility: "I think we can safely dismiss the view that the failure of modern technological knowledge to spread rapidly was due to significant differences among nations in the native intelligence of their populations. To my knowledge there are no studies that definitively establish differences, say, in basic IQ among the peoples of the world" (1981, p. 5). Twenty years later two other economists, Eric Hanushek of the Hoover Institution and Dennis Kimko of the American National Bureau of Economic Research, reiterated this position: "we assume that the international level of average ability of students does not vary across countries" (Hanushek and Dennis Kimbo, 2000, p. 1191).

In 2000 we decided to examine the assumption of economists that the average level of intelligence is the same in all nations. We surveyed the research on average levels of intelligence in many different countries and found that intelligence differed considerably among nations. Our conclusions were presented in our book *IQ and the Wealth of Nations* (Lynn and Vanhanen, 2002). In this we gave measured average IQs for 81 nations and found remarkable differences ranging from an average IQ of

59 in Equatorial Guinea to an average IQ of 107 in Hong Kong. The IQs were based on a mean of 100 for Britain, with a standard deviation of 15, so that there was a difference of slightly more than three standard deviations between the two extremes. Next, we examined the relation between the national IQs and national wealth (expressed as per capita income) and rates of economic growth and found substantial correlations. National IQs were correlated at 0.82 with per capita GNP (Gross National Product, 1998) and at 0.64 with the rate of economic growth from 1950-1990. Correlations of similar magnitude were present with other measures of national wealth, including per capita GNP-PPP (Gross National Product at Purchasing Power Parity, 1998, r = 0.84) and real GDP (Gross Domestic Product, 1998, r = 0.83), and at 0.60 with rates of economic growth from 1983 to 1996. These are Spearman rank correlations in the group of 81 countries. Pearson product-moment correlations are somewhat weaker. We interpreted these positive correlations as showing that national differences in intelligence are an important factor contributing to differences in national wealth and rates of economic growth.

Our theory has received a mixed reception among social scientists, with positive and negative reactions being about equally divided. For some, we had discovered a major factor that answered Easterlin's question—"Why isn't the whole world developed?" Among the positive reactions, Erich Weede and Sebastian Kampf (2002, p. 376), professors of sociology at the University of Bonn, made additional calculations and found that national IQs determine national rates of economic growth much more strongly than other measures of human capital, such as years of education. They concluded that "there is one clear and robust result: average IQ does promote growth." Edward Miller (2002, p. 522), professor of economics at the University of New Orleans, wrote that "the theory helps significantly to explain why some countries are rich and some poor." Marcus Richards (2002, p. 175), a psychologist at University College, London, wrote that "it is impossible to overlook the central finding of a positive association between IQ and national wealth, and the authors have gathered an impressive sweep of evidence in its support." J. Philippe Rushton (2003, p. 367), professor of psychology at the University of Western Ontario, wrote that the book "systematically documents a stunningly straightforward and yet greatly overlooked thesis." Gunnar Adler-Karlsson (2002), the founder of the Capri Institute of International Social Philosophy, said about our book that "it may, indeed, give us the deepest cause behind the world's economic gaps and so-called injustices." Michael Palairet (2004), a professor of economic and social history at the University of Edinburgh, comes to the conclusion that "Lynn and Vanhanen have launched a powerful challenge to economic historians and development economists who prefer not to use IQ as an analytical input."

But several reviewers reacted negatively to our thesis. Astrid Ervik (2003, pp. 406–408) of the University of Cambridge asked "are people in rich countries smarter than those in poorer countries?" and concluded that "the authors fail to present convincing evidence and appear to jump to conclusions." Thomas Volken (2003, p. 412), a German sociologist, contended that our study is "neither methodologically nor theoretically convincing." Thomas Nechyba (2004, p. 220) of Duke University wrote of "relatively weak statistical evidence and dubious presumptions." Susan Barnett and Wendy Williams (2004), two psychologists at Cornell University, went so far as to assert that our cross-country comparisons are "virtually meaningless."

Thus, it is evident that our theory that the IQ of the population is an important determinant of national differences in per capita income and economic growth failed to convince a number of critics. We have therefore returned to the problem in the present book.

We address the following questions. First, in Chapter 1, we review the major theories of economic growth that have been developed since this problem was considered by Charles de Montesquieu and Adam Smith in the eighteenth century, and introduce the 192 countries of this study. In Chapter 2 we define and describe what is meant by intelligence. In Chapter 3, we summarize work showing that intelligence is a determinant of incomes and related phenomena (educational attainment and socioeconomic status) among individuals in a number of countries; this is the basis of our theory that the intelligence of national populations is likely to be a determinant of per capita incomes among nations. Chapter 4 describes how we have collected and quantified the IQs of nations and presents new IQ data for a further 32 nations. This brings the total number of nations for which we have measured IQs to 113. In addition, national IQs are estimated for 79 other countries so that we have IQs for all countries with populations of more than 40,000. In Chapter 5, five measures of the quality of human conditions and their composite index (QHC) are introduced as well as 12 alternative variables that measure human conditions from different perspectives. In Chapter 6, the hypothesis on the positive relationship between national IQ and the quality of human conditions is tested by empirical evidence on PPP GNI (Gross National Income at Purchasing Power Parity) per capita in 2002, the adult literacy rate in 2002, the tertiary enrollment ratio, life expectancy at birth in 2002, and the level of democratization in 2002. Chapter 7 focuses on the relationship between national IQ and the composite index of the quality of human conditions (QHC). The results are analyzed at the level of single countries on the basis of regression analyses. The results are checked by exploring the impact of latitude and annual mean temperature on human conditions through national IQ. Chapter 8 shows that national IQ is correlated also with many other variables that measure differences in human conditions from different perspectives. Twelve alternative variables are used in these analyses. Chapter 9 discusses the contributions of genetic and environmental determinants to national differences in intelligence and concludes that the racial identity of the population is the major factor. Chapter 10 considers the causal interactions between our most important measures. Chapter 11 (Criticisms and Rejoinders) discusses and responds to the criticisms made of our theory by reviewers. Finally, we summarize the results and conclusions of this study in Chapter 12 and discuss policy implications.

Five appendices complement the text. In Appendix 1, the calculation of national IQs for 113 countries is presented and documented. Appendix 2 includes documented empirical data on the adult literacy rate in 2002, the gross enrollment ratio at the tertiary level of education, PPP GNI per capita in US dollars in 2002, and the life expectancy at birth in 2002 for the total group of 192 countries. Appendix 3 provides documented data on the measures of democracy, of the calculated values of the Index of the Quality of Human Conditions (QHC), and of latitude and annual mean temperature. Appendix 4 includes residuals of regression analyses of the five components of QHC on national IQ for single countries in the group of 192 countries. Appendix 5 provides estimated data on per capita GDP derived from Maddison (2003) for 1500 and 2000 in a group of 109 countries.

CHAPTER 1

Theories about Economic and other Global Inequalities

The problem of human inequalities and disparities has been recognized and discussed since time immemorial. Disparities within and between nations have been described in innumerable studies. Most explanations have focused on historical, cultural, and various proximate factors, especially on social structures and conditions, but sometimes explanations have been sought also from human nature and the innate characteristics of people. We do not try to review at length the history of such studies, but we want to summarize some ideas and explanations presented in the previous research literature, because they constitute the theoretical background for our own attempt to examine this problem and the ultimate causes of global economic and other inequalities in the contemporary world.

1. Classical Studies

We can start with Aristotle, who noticed that in every city "the people are divided into three sorts: the very rich, the very poor, and those who are between them" (*The Politics of Aristotle*, 1952, Book IV: Chapter XI; see also Aristotle, 1984). Aristotle's observation is still valid everywhere in the world. He recognized these and many other disparities in human societies and discussed their political consequences, but he did not explain why these exist, although he seems to be aware that there are differences in the innate characteristics of people and that these differences are reflected in social and political structures and institutions.

In the eighteenth century, Montesquieu discussed global disparities in his book *De L'Esprit des Lois* (1748). He observed that rich nations tend to lie in temperate latitudes and poor nations in the tropics and semi-tropics and concluded that climate must be in some way associated with these differences. Montesquieu traced the origin of global disparities to climatic differences and their impact on human nature and through it on political and other human conditions (see also Lowenthal, 1987, pp. 526–529). Montesquieu's ideas have been discussed and re-examined in some contemporary studies (see Parker, 2000; Firebaugh, 2003).

Rousseau was one of the first philosophers who attempted to explain the origin of inequalities. The question proposed by the Academy of Dijon ("What is the origin of inequality among men, and is it authorized by natural law?") which he answered in his *Discourse on the Origin and Basis of Inequality Among Men* (1754) is still discussed, and concerns the main subject of this book. Rousseau sought the origin of the differences that exist among men from changes in the human constitution (Rousseau, 1974, p. 138). He argued that inequality was almost negligible in the state of nature when people lived without any significant personal possessions. Later the inventions of metallurgy and agriculture led to the emergence of private property and inequalities in organized societies. It is interesting to note that Rousseau traced the origin of inequalities to differences in innate abilities of people. He wrote: "Things in this state might have remained equal if abilities had been equal...," but they were not equal.

> The strongest did more work; the most skillful turned their efforts to better advantage; the most ingenious found ways to shorten their labor.... Those who were excluded from ownership, who because of weakness or indolence had acquired nothing, became poor without having lost anything, because while everything around them was changing, they themselves had not changed (pp. 180–182).

Rousseau can be regarded as a precursor of our study.

Adam Smith explored the nature and causes of the wealth of nations in his book *The Wealth of Nations* (1776), and came to the conclusion that the principal factors responsible for economic development were human skills, specialization and the division of labour, and the existence of markets. Smith was not particularly concerned with the gap between rich and poor, or with economic inequalities within and between nations. He attributed economic development and the growth of wealth to special skills and talents, education, and appropriate economic and political institutions needed to use available opportunities. He took into account the difference in natural talents of different people, but emphasized that the "difference between the most dissimilar characters, between a philosopher and a common street porter, for example, seems to arise not so much from nature, as from habit, custom, and education" (Smith, 1976 Volume One, pp. 19-20; see also Cropsey, 1987a). So he stressed the importance of environmental factors in the development of talents. The scope of his study is global.

Thomas Robert Malthus argued in his book on population, the first edition of which was published in 1798, "that poverty and misery observable among the lower classes of people in every nation" is principally caused by the constant tendency of population to increase more than the means of subsistence. As a consequence, very powerful checks are needed to keep the number of people on a level with the means of subsistence. The main checks are moral restraint, vice, and misery (Malthus, 1960, pp. 147–165). He illustrated his theory of the impact of population growth on poverty and misery by extensive evidence from many countries around the world.

Alexis de Tocqueville (1835) was impressed by the general equality of conditions in America and wrote "that this equality of condition is the fundamental fact from which all others seem to be derived...." (Tocqueville, 1963, p. 3). The general equality of conditions had produced democracy and powered the drive for even more complete equality, but Tocqueville also noted that the democratic revolution had not resolved the eternal struggle between the rich and the poor. He emphasized that appropriate laws and institutions had furthered equality in America, but he was not particularly concerned with the problem of the social and economic disparities, although he seemed to connect the survival of disparities to the fact that equality did not extend to intellectual capacity. According to Marvin Zetterbaum (1987, pp. 763, 769), Tocqueville acknowledges that "even with the advent of the most extreme equality of conditions the inequality of intellect will remain as one of the last irksome reminders of the old regime.... All cannot be raised to the level of the great, for differences of ability originate from God, or from nature." Tocqueville emphasized the significance of appropriate laws and institutions.

Karl Marx and Friedrich Engels argued that the private ownership of productive resources was the basic cause of the great economic and social disparities within societies, especially in capitalist societies, but they did not explain why the means of production are unequally distributed among people in all societies. They assumed that it would be possible to end the class struggle and economic disparities by abolishing the private ownership of the means of production and to establish a classless communist society based on the principle: from each according to his ability, to each according to his needs (see Cropsey, 1987b; cf. Marx and Engels, 1969). It is true that in his book *The Origin of the Family, Private Property, and the State* (1884) Engels explains the origin of private property by the theory of a patriarchal takeover sometime in the past, but it does not provide any explanation for the unequal distribution of private property. The Marxist theory of communism has been tested extensively in practice since the 1917 Bolshevik takeover in Russia, but all attempts to establish communist societies have failed. We think that those experiments in many countries of the world have failed because Marxist theory contradicts the basic principle of evolutionary theory, according to which the genetic diversity of individuals and the scarcity of the means of livelihood make the struggle for existence inevitable and permanent in all species. Consequently, it has been impossible to realize the communist utopia anywhere in our world.

The arguments and ideas presented in these classical works concern some aspects of the problem of global disparities in human conditions. Aristotle's observation about the existence of great economic inequalities and their political significance is nowadays as valid as it was more than 2,000 years ago. Montesquieu explained global disparities by the impact of geographical and climatic differences on human nature. Rousseau traced the origin of inequalities ultimately to differences in innate abilities of people. Adam Smith emphasized the significance of economic and political institutions and education. Malthus argued that poverty is causally related to the pressure of population to increase more rapidly than the means of subsistence. Tocqueville stressed that the general equality of condition can lead to significant decrease of various inequalities, although it cannot remove all of them. The failure of Marx and Engels' communist utopia shows that the malleability of human nature is not unlimited.

2. Alternative Contemporary Explanations

Contemporary theoretical explanations for economic and other disparities in human conditions within societies and between nations are relatively rare compared to the number of studies which describe inequalities and disparities from different perspectives. In our previous book *IQ and the Wealth of Nations* (Lynn and Vanhanen, 2002, Chapter 2), we reviewed several types of contemporary theoretical explanations for economic development and for the gap between rich and poor countries. Our discussion covered climate theories, geographical factors, modernization theories, psychological theories, cultural explanations, dependency and world system theories, neoclassical theories, and some multi-causal theories. These theories and studies provide alternative and partly contradictory explanations for global disparities.

In a recent review of the problem, James Gwartney and Robert Lawson (2004, p. 28) differentiate among three alternative theories of growth. The neoclassical theory argues that growth is a result of expansion in the supply of productive inputs and improvements in technology. Investment in physical and human capital is assumed to explain differences in economic growth. Geographic theory argues that climatic conditions and access to major markets are the primary determinants of growth. A hot tropical climate is unfavorable for economic development. The institutional approach stresses the importance of appropriate institutional and policy environment.

Neoclassical and institutional theories trace the differences in economic growth and development to the market economy, savings and capital formation, private initiative, and deregulation of governmental controls. The so-called Washington consensus recommends export promotion and a market-oriented development strategy for the Third World countries. The poverty of Third World countries is assumed to be causally related to various errors of state policy, which consist of excessive government interference in the economy, corruption, and the failure to develop free markets (see, for example, Solow, 1956; Olson, 1996; Nafziger, 1997; Weede, 1998; Ayittey, 1999; Todaro, 2000; Seligson and Passé-Smith, 2003). These theories are concerned with the means to further economic growth; they do not discuss the origin of global economic disparities and they do not pay any attention to human diversity. It may be erroneous to assume that the same policies and institutional arrangements could be introduced with equal success to all countries.

Climate theories are based on the idea that climatic differences provide the fundamental theoretical explanation for economic development differences between the countries of the tropics and the countries of the temperate zones (cf. Kamarck, 1976). Some researchers have added to climate several other geographical factors that affect economic development and cause global disparities in human conditions such as the presence of navigable rivers (see Diamond, 1998; Landes, 1998; Parker, 2000; Firebaugh, 2003).

Gerhard Lenski's (1970) ecological-evolutionary approach offers a different explanation. According to him, the scarcity of resources makes conflict between societies inevitable and leads to the elimination of weaker societies and to sociocultural diversification. Technologically more advanced societies and social groups have better chances to succeed in this competition than less advanced societies and groups. In this connection he refers to racialist explanations based on the idea that Europeans are genetically superior, but he does not accept the explanations based on intelligence tests (p. 106). He is satisfied to explain domestic and global disparities in wealth and development by various proximate factors, especially by differences in technology, but he does not make it clear why there are such great global differences in technological development (see also Lenski and Lenski, 1987).

Sociologists have described stratification and social inequalities extensively, but they have not yet found any coherent theoretical explanations for the origin of the great inequalities in the world. Their explanations have been limited to various environmental factors and other social variables (see, for example, Bendix and Lipset, 1969; Giddens, 1995). David B. Grusky notes:

> The human condition has so far been a fundamentally unequal one; indeed, *all* known societies have been characterized by

inequalities of some kind.... The task of contemporary stratification research is to describe the contours and distribution
of inequality and to explain its persistence despite modern
egalitarian or anti-stratification values (Grusky, 1994, p. 3).

Our purpose in this study is to explain its persistence by seeking
its origin in human diversity of intelligence.

Many researchers have used cultural factors to explain developmental differences and especially economic growth (see, for example,
Landes, 1998; Harrison and Huntington, 2000). The problem with
cultural explanations is that they start from the existence of cultural
differences; they do not explain the origin of such differences. P.T.
Bauer (1981) approaches the origin of cultural and developmental
differences when he notes that "economic differences are largely the
result of people's capacities and motivations" (Bauer, 1981, p. 19).
This is the closest admission we have found from an economist that
human abilities contribute to economic development.

Dependency and world system theories propose that the capitalist
world system is responsible for the poverty of underdeveloped countries.
The rich core countries have been able to exploit the peripheral countries
in Latin America, Asia, and Africa. These theories have been derived from
Marxist ideas and Lenin's theory of imperialist capitalism's exploitation
of economically underdeveloped countries (see, for example, Frank, 1967;
Santos, 1970; Wallerstein, 1975 and 2004; Roberts and Hite, 2000). The
problem with these theories is that they do not explain the origin of
developmental differences between the capitalist core countries and
the underdeveloped parts of the world. Many researchers have rejected
the basic arguments of the dependency theory (see, for example, Bauer,
1981; Chisholm, 1982; Weede, 1998).

It is common for these theoretical explanations that they are more
concerned with the means to further economic and social development
or to mitigate existing inequalities than with attempts to seek original
causes of global economic and other disparities. Our research question
concerns the ultimate causal factors that are responsible for the emergence
of global inequalities in human conditions. It is also common for these
theoretical explanations, with some exceptions, that they do not pay any
serious attention to human diversity, to the possibility that significant differences in the characteristics of human populations might be responsible
for the emergence of economic and other inequalities and disparities. In

our previous book *IQ and the Wealth of Nations* (2002), national IQ is used as the fundamental explanatory variable. In other words, we seek the origin of domestic and global inequalities namely in human diversity, in the variation of people's mental abilities. Thus the nature of our principal explanatory factor differentiates our theory from all other explanations given for domestic and global inequalities and disparities.

3. Human Capital Theory

A number of economists have developed the concept of "human capital" as a factor contributing to earnings within national populations and between nations. There is no consensus definition among economists on the precise definition of human capital, but it is generally taken to mean the skills and abilities that contribute to efficient work and which command higher incomes. These skills are generally considered to be acquired through education and are measured by various measures of educational inputs (e.g., expenditures on education, primary or secondary rates of school enrollment, or years of education) and educational outputs (e.g., scores on tests of mathematics and science, and literacy rates). Economists have shown that all of these are related to earnings within and between nations and argued that these differences in "human capital" are an important factor contributing to differences in national wealth. For instance: "human capital, particularly that attained through education, has been emphasised as a critical determinant of economic progress" (Barro and Lee, 2001, p. 541); "it is well accepted that human capital is the source of long-run growth, as human capital engenders technological innovation" (Zak and Park, 2002, p. 1); "human capital has taken a central role in the theory of economic growth, with formal education often considered the primary conduit for human capital accumulation" (Blackenau and Simpson, 2004, p. 601); "changes in growth rates between countries are assumed to be primarily due to changes in the rates of human capital accumulation" (Engelbrecht, 2003, p. S40). The missing element in these formulations is the failure to recognize that intelligence is an important determinant of educational attainment and therefore of human capital. The economists who work in this area apparently believe that while there are large national differences in educational attainment that are clearly related to rates of economic growth and per capita incomes, there are no national differences in intelligence. Given the magnitude of the correlations between educational attainment and intelligence within and between nations, this is exceedingly improbable. The correlation between educational attainment and intelligence within nations (reviewed in Chapter 3) typically lies between 0.6–0.7, while the correlation between educational attainment and intelligence across nations (reviewed in Chapter 4) is even higher at between 0.79 and 0.89 (Table 4.4). With such high correlations, the measures of educational attainment used by economists and shown to be related to economic growth must be largely functions of differences in intelligence among national populations. The human capital theory of economic growth is close to our own theory insofar as it recognizes the contribution of human abilities to economic development. The crucial link missed by economists working in this field is the strong association between human capital and intelligence.

4. Recent Studies on Global Inequalities and Poverty

The theories reviewed above may not explain the origin of global economic and other disparities, but they can help to explain some parts of the variation in the wealth of nations, and they indicate factors that further or hamper economic and social development. The results of our 2002 study showed that national IQ is the most powerful single explanatory variable, but because the explained part of variation does not rise higher than 40–60 percent, this explanation leaves room for other explanatory factors. Therefore it is useful to review some recent studies on economic growth, social inequalities, poverty, and the quality of life in order to see what kinds of variables have been used to explain global disparities and how they are related to our argument about the significance of the differences in national IQs.

At the 1995 World Summit for Social Development, representatives of 185 governments declared their determination to eradicate world poverty. The United Nations Development Program (UNDP) made the eradication of poverty its overriding priority. UNDP Administrator James Gustave Speth (1997) says in the Forward to *Human Development Report 1997* that "poverty is no longer inevitable. The world has the material and natural resources, the know-how, and the people to make a poverty-free world a reality in less than a generation." This is an extremely optimistic statement in light of the fact that until now there have been rich and poor in all countries of the world (cf. Aristotle, 1952, Book IV: Chapter XI).

UNDP's *Human Development Report 1997* reviews the challenge to eradicate poverty from the human development perspective and discusses strategies to reduce poverty. The report claims that the time "has come to eradicate the worst aspects of human poverty in a decade or two—to create a world that is more humane, more stable, more just" (p. 106). The concept of human poverty refers to many types of global disparities. Human poverty is measured by a new human poverty index (HPI), which takes into account "the percentage of people expected to die before age 40, the percentage of adults who are illiterate, and the overall economic provisioning in terms of the percentage of people without access to health services and safe water and the percentage of underweight children under five" (p. 14). This index distinguishes human poverty from income poverty (measured by GNP or by GDP [PPP$]), which represents another dimension of poverty. Data on HPI are published in *Human Development Reports* (see UNDP, 2000–2004). They make it possible to follow to what extent the target to eradicate human and income poverty has been achieved.

At the United Nations General Assembly in 2000, heads of state and governments adopted the United Nations Millennium Declaration, in which they set specific goals for development and poverty eradication, to be achieved by 2015: (1) to halve the proportion of the world's people living on less than $1 a day, (2) to halve the proportion of the world's people suffering from hunger, (3) to halve the proportion of the world's people without access to safe drinking water, (4) to achieve universal completion of primary schooling, (5) to achieve gender equality in access to education, (6) to reduce maternal mortality ratios by three-quarters, (7) to reduce under-five mortality rates by two-thirds, and (8) to halt and begin to reverse the spread of HIV/AIDS, malaria, and other major diseases (UNDP 2001, pp. 21–25; cf. UNDP 2002, pp. 16–30; UNDP 2003, pp.1–13). These are extremely ambitious goals.

Global disparities in human conditions are discussed and documented extensively in each issue of the World Bank's *World Development Report*. In the Foreword to the 2000/2001 report, James D. Wolfensohn, then President of The World Bank, says that the report "seeks to expand the understanding of poverty and its causes and sets out actions to create a world free of poverty in all its dimensions" (Wolfensohn, 2001,

p. V). Causes of poverty are discussed briefly in the report, but unfortunately the report does not provide any theoretical explanation for poverty and global differences in poverty. Causes of poverty are traced to the poor people's lack of income and assets to attain basic necessities, to their sense of voicelessness and powerlessness in the institutions of state and society, and to their vulnerability to adverse shocks, linked to an inability to cope with them (World Development Report 2000/2001, p. 34; cf. UNDP Poverty Report 1998). We think that these characteristics describe the nature of poverty, but do not explain the causes of poverty. The report notes that in East Asia the number of people living on less than $1 a day has decreased dramatically, whereas in Latin America, South Asia, and sub-Saharan Africa their numbers have been rising. The report argues that "if some countries can make great progress toward reducing poverty in its many forms, others can as well" (p. 5). We suspect that this is not so because of the significant differences in the average mental abilities of the populations that we document in Chapter 4 (see also World Development Reports, 2002–2004; World Development Indicators, 2003, 2004).

Nancy Birdsall (1998) says that inequality is nobody's fault and cannot be fixed in our lifetime: "Understanding its causes helps to determine what can be done about it and what might actually make it worse" (p. 10). So what are the causes? She refers to historical inheritances. In Latin America, for example, the extreme concentration of land ownership perpetuates inequality. Another source of inequality lies in predictable human behavior. For example, the rich and educated marry each other, as do the poor and uneducated, which widens family income gaps. "The most avoidable and thus most disappointing sources of inequality are," according to Birdsall, "policies that hamper economic growth and fuel inflation" (p. 11). These and other factors discussed by Birdsall can explain contemporary inequalities, but they do not explain the origin of these differences.

Robert J. Barro's (1999) book *Determinants of Economic Growth* covers roughly one hundred countries observed from 1960 to 1990. The results of his analysis support the main arguments of the neoclassical theory, but he broadens the concept of capital to include human capital in the forms of education, experience, and health, and stresses the importance of government policies that maintain property rights and free markets. Barro comes to the conclusion that the data reveal a pattern of conditional convergence. The speed of convergence is increased when the starting level of human capital is high. In fact, this conclusion is in harmony with our prediction that the "best chances for strong economic growth are for countries with large negative residuals, which indicate that the country has not fully utilized its population's mental abilities" (Lynn and Vanhanen, 2002, p. 196; cf. Barro, 1999, pp. 42-47). Mancur Olson (2000) emphasized in his book on power and prosperity the significance of government policies and appropriate institutions. From the perspective of economic growth, it is crucial that private property rights are secured, that the enforcement of contracts is impartial, and that the government is not predatory.

Adrian Leftwich (2000) emphasizes the primacy of politics in development and argues that the nature of the state matters. The "developmental state" provides the best chances for development. His concept of the "developmental state" refers to states "whose *politics* have concentrated sufficient power, autonomy, capacity, and legitimacy at the centre to shape, pursue, and encourage the achievement of explicit developmental objectives," whether by promoting the conditions of economic growth in the capitalist developmental state or by organizing it directly in the socialist developmental state. A combination of capitalist and socialist developmental states would also be possible (p. 155). Leftwich admits that such states are not common (for India, see Drèze and Amartya Sen, 2002).

Poverty and Development into the 21st Century (2000), edited by Tim Allen and Alan Thomas, is an interesting book from the perspective of explanatory theories. It is stated in the Preface that the book is mostly about explanations of global poverty and different ways of analyzing and viewing the world, but it is difficult to find any theoretical explanation for global poverty in this book. In fact, the book is confined to descriptions of various dimensions of global poverty and the relationship between poverty and development. In the case of development, Thomas (2000) refers to the main theories of development, including neo-liberal views derived from Adam Smith and Marxism and dependency theory. He comes to the conclusion that the main theoretical perspectives on development have failed "to deliver major improvements in living conditions to the world's poorest individuals and communities" (p. 48).

William Easterly (2002) says in his book *The Elusive Quest for Growth* that fifty years ago economists began their quest "to discover the means by which poor countries in the tropics could become rich like the rich countries in Europe and North America" (p. XI) and claims that all the policies recommended by economists have failed. His list of panaceas that did not work as promised includes investment, foreign aid, education, population control, and debt forgiveness. His central idea is that people respond to incentives and that those panaceas failed because they provided wrong incentives. His statistical analysis shows that "there is no evidence that investment is either a necessary or a sufficient condition for high growth" (p. 40). Several sub-Saharan African countries turned out to be growth disasters despite high initial investment and high subsequent aid, whereas real superstars like Singapore, Hong Kong, Thailand, Malaysia, and Indonesia grew rapidly despite low initial investment and subsequent aid (pp. 42–44). He claims that unconditional "aid will not cause its recipients to increase their investments; they will use aid to buy more consumption goods" (p. 38; see also Kayizzi-Mugerwa, 2003).

Surjit S. Bhalla (2002) investigates global poverty from the perspective of the number of people, not of the number of countries, and comes to the conclusion that the Millennium Development Goal in poverty reduction has already been achieved and that the process of convergence is taking place. So he challenges the conventional wisdom, according to which inequalities have increased, not declined during the past 20 years. However, it should be noted that his results are mainly due to the decrease of the number of poor people in China, and to a lesser degree in India. In the Middle East, North Africa, and Latin America changes have been small, and in sub-Saharan Africa the number of poor people significantly increased in the period 1960–2000 (pp. 141–147; cf. World Development Indicators 2004, pp. 2–4). For Bhalla, globalization is the major factor causing equalization in the contemporary world, and growth is sufficient for poverty reduction. He does not explore the origin of global inequalities, although he refers briefly to the fact that labor is differentiated by education and differences in ability (p. 189; see also *The Economist*, August 23rd 2003, p. 56, "If you consider people, not countries, global inequality is falling rapidly").

Glenn Firebaugh (2003) presents similar arguments. His major argument is that global inequality has most likely already peaked and that "many more people live in poor nations that are catching up (largely in Asia) than in the poor nations that are falling farther behind" (p. 122). This conclusion is principally due to the difference between East Asia and sub-Saharan Africa. He notes that "in recent decades East Asia in particular has experienced robust economic growth while sub-Saharan Africa has languished" (p. 141). Firebaugh emphasizes the significance of physical geography and climate in the connection of the diffusion of industrialization, which tends to reduce inequality across nations. Geographical distances and climatic differences matter. He refers to studies which show that "per capita income is strongly positively associated with a nation's distance from the equator" (p. 180). Philip Parker (2000) refers to Montesquieu and claims that "some seventy percent of the variances in income per capita across countries can be explained by absolute latitude" (p. VIII). He regards latitude as a principal explanatory factor, but fails to note the association between latitude and intelligence.

Francois Bourguignon and Christian Morrison (2002) investigate also world inequality among individuals rather than countries over the period 1820–1992. In some respects, the results of their analysis differ from those of Bhalla. Their analysis shows that world inequality worsened over the last two centuries and that this result was mainly due to a dramatic increase in inequality across countries or regions of the world. The rapid enrichment of the European population during the first century and a half after the beginning of the industrial revolution caused divergence in the world economy. Poverty was largely an Asian problem until just after World War II, but now it is fast becoming an African problem. They note that the increasing concentration of world poverty in some regions of the world, especially in Africa, is worrying, but they do not have any explanation for this phenomenon. In addition to the distribution of income, they use life expectancy to measure another dimension of world inequality.

Angus Maddison's (1995, 1999, 2001, 2003) historical datasets on the levels of GDP per capita and economic growth rates extend to 1820 and partly to the year 1. He discusses causal factors of economic growth and argues that four main causal influences go a long way to explain economic growth. These are: (1) technological progress; (2) accumulation of physical capital; (3) improvement in human skills, education, organising ability; and (4) closer integration of individual national economies. According to him, technological progress has been the most fundamental element of change (Maddison, 1995, p. 33). However, these factors can be regarded as proximate factors of change. They do not explain why they have functioned quite differently in different parts of the world. In a later study, *The World Economy: A Millennial Perspective* (2001), Maddison says that the purpose of his book is to identify the forces which explain the success of the rich countries and to explore the obstacles which hindered advance in regions which lagged behind. He explains economic performance over the past millennium by referring to three interactive processes: (1) conquest or settlement of relatively empty areas; (2) international trade and capital movement; and (3) technological and institutional innovation (Maddison 2001, p. 18).

In the WIDER (The World Institute for Development and Economics Research) conference on inequality, poverty, and human well-being held in Helsinki, 2003, many papers were presented on different aspects of inequality, poverty, and human well-being, but it is remarkable that causes of great global inequalities were not discussed in any of these papers (see WIDER, 2003).

None of these studies consider the possibility that global disparities in human conditions might be caused by differences in mental abilities within societies and between nations. The list of explanatory factors discussed in these studies includes economic growth, globalization, the nature of economic systems, human capital, governmental policies, historical legacies, institutions, investment, and technological change. It is quite possible that all of these factors can explain some part of global disparities, although it has been difficult to operationalize these variables and to measure their explanatory power. It is characteristic of these studies that researchers have not investigated the origin of the differences in their explanatory variables, or they have explained it with some other contemporary social and environmental factors. Our argument is that it would be worthwhile to seek the ultimate explanation for many types of contemporary global inequalities in human diversity, which has preceded all contemporary economic, social, and political disparities in human conditions by thousands of years.

5. Roots of Global Inequalities in Human Diversity

The fact that significant disparities in human conditions have existed since time immemorial and that they have reappeared over and over again in different forms in all known human societies implies that their ultimate causes are, at least to some extent, older than any contemporary social circumstances which have been used to explain poverty and other inequalities in human conditions within societies and across nations. This observation about the persistence of inequalities in human conditions, which is supported by ample historical evidence (see, for example, Herodotus, 1972; Aristotle, 1984; Montesquieu, 1989; Mann, 1986; Gernet, 2002), makes it reasonable to consider the possibility that some characteristics of evolved human nature might provide the ultimate explanation for the persistence of human inequalities. One significant characteristic of human nature is human diversity in the sense that all individuals (except identical twins) are genetically unique.

Human diversity is an inevitable consequence of sexual reproduction, which may have emerged because it increased variability and thus the chances for individuals to survive in varying environmental conditions. The existence of two sexes makes possible sexual reproduction, which recombines genetic elements through the meiotic and crossing-over processes. The benefit of sexual reproduction resides in recombination, which reshuffles the genes in such a way that a new individual is not genetically identical to either parent. Every individual has a unique genotype (Daly and Wilson, 1983, pp. 1–14, 59–75; cf. Dobzhansky et al., 1977; Ritter, 1981, pp. 9–13; Whitehouse, 1992). Human diversity is a fact of life that we cannot change.

All individuals differ genetically to some extent from each other, except for identical twins, who differ only slightly. It has been estimated that each "human shares 99.9% of its DNA with any other human, which means, nevertheless, that there are approximately three million differences in the complete DNA sequence between any two people" (Cole, 1999, p. 61). Most of these three million variations are in regions of the "junk" DNA, which neither codes for protein nor regulates gene expression, but approximately 1%, or 30,000 variations, may be in our genes. Francis S. Collins notes that the "remaining 0.1% is very interesting because it accounts for all the variability in our species." All genetic differences between individuals are due to these 30,000 variants (Collins, 1999, pp. 46, 52–53). They measure genetic diversity within the human population. One could argue that 0.1% is not much, but it should be remembered that the "genome of chimpanzees is 99% identical with ours; yet the differences between humans and chimps are profound" (Cole, 1999, p. 61). It is justified to assume that many types of physical, mental, and behavioral differences between individuals are due to this genetic diversity of the human species. As David Botstein says, "Everything that makes one of us different from the other—ignoring, for now, environmental influences—is in the genes that are on our chromosomes" (Botstein, 1999, p. 33; for genetic diversity, see also Dobzhansky et al., 1977, pp. 45–56; Ritter, 1981; Lewontin, 1982; Jones, 1992; Wilson, 1992; Rushton, 1995; Bouchard, 1997; Jensen, 1998).

Human diversity at the level of individuals is a biological fact that is generally accepted. All individuals within a population are genetically to some extent different, and these differences affect both morphological characteristics, like facial features and skin color, and behavior. Edward O. Wilson (1978) says that the "question of interest is no longer whether human social behavior is genetically determined; it is to what extent" (p. 19). He refers to similarities between human and chimpanzee social behavior and argues that human social behavior rests on a genetic foundation; it is "organized by some genes that are shared with closely related species and others that are unique to the human species" (p. 32). According to him, "evidence is strong that a substantial fraction of human behavioral variation is based on genetic differences between individuals" (Wilson, 1978, p. 43). Sir Walter Bodmer (1995) says that studies in twins clearly indicate genetic components to behavior, although it does not mean that "there are specific genes for particular human behaviors, such as for high moral quality, for musical and mathematical ability, or for achievement in sport." This means, he continues, that "there will be genetic differences that affect the probability of an individual's having certain behavior, depending on the environmental stimuli" (Bodmer, 1995, p. 421; see also, for example, Barkow et al., 1992; Hass et al., 2000).

Genetic differences between individuals can now be identified at the DNA level, but it has been much more difficult to find out whether there are, as a consequence of natural selection, some genetic differences between populations, too, and what is their significance. Bodmer (1995, p. 422) notes that studies "of the distribution of classical marker polymorphisms in different populations have already told us that most genetic variation can be found within any population and, in comparison, the genetic differences between populations are relatively minor" (see also Lewontin, 1982; Ritter, 1981).

We have empirical data on genetic differences between populations in *The History and Geography of Human Genes* (1994) of L. Luca Cavalli-Sforza, Paolo Menozzi, and Alberto Piazza. Their extensive study of gene frequencies (120 alleles) in 42 aboriginal populations that were in place before intercontinental travel began around A.D. 1500 shows that there are genetic distances between populations and that they vary. They divided the 42 populations into nine major clusters: Africans (sub-Saharan), Caucasoids (European), Caucasoids (Asian and North African), Northern Mongoloids (excluding Arctic populations), Arctic populations, Southern Mongoloids (mainland and insular Southeast Asia), New Guineans plus Australians, inhabitants of minor Pacific islands, and Native Americans. The first division took place between Africans and all non-Africans, which means that the greatest genetic distance is between Africans and all other populations. The next major division separated the New Guinean and Australian, Pacific Islander, and Southeast Asian clusters from Mongoloids and Caucasoids. Later on the two Caucasoid clusters separated from Mongoloids (pp. 77–83). They speak of geographical populations and assert that clusters cannot be identified with races. Variation between clusters is gradual. All population clusters overlap "when single genes are considered, and in almost all populations, all alleles are present but in different frequencies." Therefore, they come to the conclusion that "there is no discontinuity that might tempt us to consider a certain level as a reasonable, though arbitrary, threshold for race distinction" (Cavalli-Sforza et al., 1996, pp. 19–20; see also Cavalli-Sforza and Cavalli-Sforza, 1995; Oppenheimer, 2003). It is certainly true that genetic variation between populations and population clusters is gradual and without any clear discontinuity, but, on the other hand, the genetic distances between Africans, Mongoloids, and Caucasoids discovered by Cavalli-Sforza and his colleagues are in harmony with the traditional classifications of the existence of the three major racial groups: Negroids, Mongoloids, and Caucasoids (cf. *The New Encyclopaedia Britannica*, Vol. 18, *Macropaedia*, 1985, pp. 967–979; Jensen, 1998, pp. 428–432, 517–518; Rushton, 2000, pp. 85–89).

It is evident that there is some genetic variation between populations, although it seems to be small compared with variation within population clusters (see Lewontin, 1982, pp. 120–23; Cavalli-Sforza et al., 1996, p. 19). Because a substantial part of the variation in morphological features, behavior, and mental abilities at the level of individuals is based on genetic differences between individuals, it is reasonable to assume that there are similar differences also between populations that differ genetically from each other. The origin of such differences is in natural selection. In the continual struggle for existence and scarce resources, natural selection has favored the survival and reproduction of individuals that have been best or at least sufficiently well adapted to existing environmental conditions. In the struggle for existence, people tend to use all their abilities. It is reasonable to assume that mental abilities have played a significant role in this struggle. Those with better mental abilities or intelligence have had better chances to get and keep scarce resources for their own use. Our theoretical argument that there must be a causal relationship between intelligence and various social achievements is derived from this assumption on the role of mental abilities and intelligence in the struggle for existence.

Because people have lived in greatly varying environmental conditions (geographical and climatic conditions in particular), it is quite probable that to some extent different kinds of morphological and behavioral characteristics have been helpful in different environmental conditions. As a consequence, there are some differences between geographical populations and especially between the major racial groups of Negroids, Mongoloids, and Caucasoids in their morphological features but probably also in their mental abilities (cf. Lynn, 1991a, 1991b, 2003, 2005; Itzkoff, 2000). It would be difficult to argue that mental abilities of all geographical populations have remained the same, although they differ from each other in many other characteri·tics that are based on small genetic differences between populations. It is more reasonable to assume that in significantly different environmental conditions different mental abilities have been helpful in the struggle for existence.

Empirical evidence shows that within societies differences in mental abilities measured by IQ are clearly related to differences in social stratification. Usually, although not always, people with high IQ have been able to achieve a higher social position and better living conditions than people for whom IQ is low. Of course, family background and other differences in environmental conditions also affect a person's social status, income, and wealth, but even when these factors are controlled, there seems to be a strong relationship between IQ and indicators of social stratification (see Herrnstein and Murray, 1994). We argue that the same hypothesis about the positive relationship between the level of mental abilities and social, economic, and educational achievements can be extended from the level of individuals to the level of nations and applied to global disparities in the wealth of nations and also to other human conditions.

We have already tested this hypothesis in our book *IQ and the Wealth of Nations* (2002), in which we correlated various indicators of per capita income and economic growth rates with national IQs. The results show that a moderate or strong positive correlation exists and has existed at least since 1820. Large differences in national IQs explain, for example, the enormous difference in economic development between East Asia and sub-Saharan Africa. In this book, our intention is to extend the study to cover some other types of global inequalities in human conditions on the basis of the following hypothesis:

The quality of human conditions tends to be the higher, the higher the average level of mental abilities (intelligence) of a nation.

This hypothesis can be tested by empirical evidence to the extent that it is possible to measure the hypothetical concepts "mental abilities" and "quality of human conditions" by operationally defined indicators. It is clear that operational variables can measure only some aspects of hypothetical concepts. We shall measure variation in mental abilities by data on national IQs as in our previous study. The concept of intelligence and the construction of the "national IQ" variable will be discussed and defined in later chapters. The indicators intended to measure some aspects of the variation in "the quality of human conditions" are formulated and defined in Chapter 5.

Our argument is that the same theory can be used to explain both domestic and global inequalities and disparities in human conditions, but in this study we refer only briefly to domestic inequalities. We focus on global inequalities and try to explore to what extent it is possible to explain global disparities in the quality of human conditions by national IQ. We do not expect this relationship to be complete, but our theoretical argument about the significance of mental abilities both within societies and between societies presupposes that global differences in human conditions are more strongly related to national IQ than to any other possible explanatory factor.

6. Units of Analysis

Our previous study, *IQ and the Wealth of Nations*, covered 185 contemporary countries. Only the smallest countries, with populations less than 50,000, were excluded. In this study, we shall use as the units of analysis 192 contemporary countries. The group includes 185 independent countries whose population was 40,000 or more in 2000, six self-governing territories from which data on intelligence tests are available (Bermuda, the Cook Islands, Hong Kong, New Caledonia, the Northern Mariana Islands, and Puerto Rico), and Taiwan. Consequently, only the tiny states like the Holy See (Vatican City), Liechtenstein, Monaco, Nauru, San Marino, Tuvalu, and several small colonies and self-governing territories are excluded from the study. Compared to our *IQ and the Wealth of Nations*, this study includes three new independent countries (Andorra, Bosnia and Herzegovina, and Timor-Leste) and four new self-governing territories (Bermuda, the Cook Islands, New Caledonia, and the Northern Mariana Islands). Serbia and Montenegro have replaced the former Yugoslavia.

CHAPTER 2

The Concept of Intelligence

1. Historical Conceptions of Intelligence

The fact that people differ in their intelligence has been recognized since the beginnings of civilization. In the fourth century BC the concept of intelligence was expressed in classical Greece by the term *nous*. Plato in his *Republic* planned for three types of people: artisans characterized by their good workmanship, soldiers characterized by their martial qualities, and rulers characterized by their *nous* or intelligence. Plato also recognized that *nous* is largely inherited, since he envisaged that in his *Republic* the rulers would be bred for it by selectively breeding from couples who had the most *nous*.

About the same time differences in intelligence were recognized in China. In the Sui dynasty, tests of ability were used about the year 500 BC to select applicants for the administrative class of mandarins who governed the provinces of the empire. These tests, normally in mathematics, astronomy, Chinese literature, and Chinese history, continued to be used up to the twentieth century (Wang, 1993).

In more recent times, in the sixteenth century the Spanish physician Juan Huarte (1575) discussed the nature of intelligence (*ingenios*) in his book *Examen de Ingenios,* which is concerned with the different kinds of intelligence required for success in law, medicine, the church, the army, and administration. Huarte's book was translated into English in 1594 with the title *A Triall of Wits* or *The Examination of Men's Wits*— "wits" being the term used in English in the sixteenth century for what has become known as *intelligence*, and whose sense is still preserved in the expression "having our wits about us."

In the seventeenth century the concept of differences in wits appears in Thomas Hobbes' (1651) *Leviathan*. Here he wrote:

> Virtue generally, in all sorts of subjects, is somewhat that is valued for eminence, and consisteth in comparison. For if all things were equal in all men, nothing would be prized. And by 'virtues intellectual' are always understood such abilities of the mind as men praise, value and desire should be in themselves; and go commonly under the name of a "good wit" (pp. 38–39).

Hobbes proposed the concept of "natural wit" which "is gotten by use only and experience; without method, culture or instruction" (p. 39) and he is distinguishing here between intelligence and educational attainment. He proposed further

> this *natural wit* consisteth in two things, *celerity of imagining,* that is swift succession of one thought to another, and *steady direction* to some approved end. A slow imagination maketh that defect or fault of mind that is commonly called *dullness, stupidity,* and sometimes by other names that signify slowness of motion (p. 39).

In the nineteenth century the concept of intelligence was developed further in England by Francis Galton (1869) in his *Hereditary Genius* and subsequent publications. Galton argued that intelligence is a single entity rather than a number of independent aptitudes, that it is largely genetically determined, that the intelligence of a people is the major determinant of their level of civilization, and that there are differences in the average intelligence of the races. He quantified these by the numbers of geniuses they produced in relation to the size of their populations. His conclusion was that the Greeks of classical Athens were the most intelligent people, followed in descending order by the lowland Scots, the English, the Africans, and the Australian Aborigines.

2. Charles Spearman and the Discovery of General Intelligence

Early in the twentieth century a significant advance in the theory of intelligence was made by Charles Spearman (1904). Spearman showed that all cognitive abilities are positively inter-correlated, such that people who do well on some tasks tend to do well on others. He invented the statistical method of factor analysis to show that the efficiency of performance on all cognitive tasks is partly determined by a common factor. He designated this common factor g for "general intelligence." To explain the existence of the common factor, Spearman proposed that there must be some general mental power determining performance on all cognitive tasks and responsible for their positive inter-correlation. However, he also found that the correlations between tests of different abilities are not perfect. To explain this he proposed that in addition to g, there are a number of specific abilities that determine performance on particular kinds of tasks, over and above the effect of g.

By the end of the twentieth century Spearman's basic theory had become virtually universally accepted in the academic discipline of differential psychology. The principal elaboration of the theory has been the development of what is called the hierarchical model of intelligence. This consists of a hierarchical structure in which there are numerous narrow specific abilities at the base, eight "second order" or "group" factors consisting of verbal comprehension, reasoning, memory, spatial, perceptual and mathematical abilities, cultural knowledge, and cognitive speed in the middle of the structure, and a single general factor—Spearman's g—at the apex. This model is widely accepted among contemporary experts such as the American Task Force chaired by Ulrich Neisser (1996), Jensen (1998), Mackintosh (1998), Carroll (1994), Deary (2000), and many others.

The most recent extensive expositions of g and its heritability, biology, and correlates have been presented by Jensen (1998) and Deary (2000). Jensen in his book *The g Factor* describes g as a factor that he defines as "a hypothetical variable that 'underlies' an observed or measured variable" (p. 88). It is not possible to measure g directly, but the scores obtained from intelligence tests and expressed as IQs (intelligence quotients) are approximate measures of g.

3. Alfred Binet Constructs the Intelligence Test

About the same time as Spearman advanced the theory of *g*, Alfred Binet in France constructed the first intelligence test (Binet, 1905). His test consisted of a number of different kinds of mental tasks including verbal reasoning ("hand is to glove as foot is to ?"), non-verbal reasoning entailing the solution of reasoning problems in design or pictorial format, mental arithmetic, vocabulary, verbal comprehension, perceptual, spatial, and memory abilities. In the early tests the IQ was measured by the use of the concept of mental age. This was defined as the level of ability of the average child of any particular chronological age. Thus, a mental age of eight was defined as the tests that were passed by the average 8-year-old. The IQ was then calculated by the formula Mental Age divided by Chronological Age multiplied by 100 = IQ. Hence, a child with a chronological age of 4 years who could pass the tests of the average 4-year-old but not any of the harder tests for older children, would have a mental age of 4 years, and would have an IQ of 100 (4 divided by 4 multiplied by 100 = 100). An adolescent with a chronological age of 16 who functioned at the same mental level of the average 8 year old would have an IQ of 50. This formula for the calculation of IQs is not used in more recent tests, which transform the scores obtained on tests to a metric with the mean set at 100 and the standard deviation at 15. However, it remains a useful approximate method for estimating IQs and understanding what they mean.

A number of intelligence tests provide IQs for several primary factors such as reasoning, verbal, spatial, and other abilities. These IQs are invariably substantially intercorrelated, normally at a magnitude of around 0.6 to 0.7. The reason for these high inter-correlations is that all these tests are largely measures of *g*. The IQs of primary abilities are normally aggregated to give a single IQ, and this is almost entirely a measure of *g* (Jensen, 1998).

The scores obtained on intelligence tests are expressed in a metric in which the mean IQ of a representative sample of a national population is set at 100 and the standard deviation is set at 15. Thus approximately 96 percent of the population have IQs in the range of 70 to 130. Approximately 2 percent of the population have IQs below 70 and are regarded as mentally retarded or as having learning difficulties. Another 2 percent have IQs above 130 and are considered as gifted. The maximum IQs ever recorded using the mental age formula are around 200, but the maximum IQ given on most contemporary tests is about 160.

When intelligence is conceptualized as general ability (*g*) and a number of group factors and specific abilities, it has been found that *g* is by far the most important determinant of task performance. Group and specific abilities make virtually no contribution to the efficiency of performance over and above the effect of *g*. For instance, in a study carried out for the United States Air Force, 78,049 trainees were given the Armed Services Vocational Aptitude Battery, a test with ten components consisting of arithmetic reasoning, numerical operations, verbal comprehension of paragraphs, vocabulary, perceptual speed (a coding test), general science, mathematics knowledge, electronics information, mechanical information, and automotive shop information. The *g* extracted from this battery of tests correlated 0.76 with attainment on job training courses. The remaining non-g portion of the test variance had a correlation of an additional 0.02 (Ree and Earles, 1994). Thus for practical purposes *g* is the only useful predictor of attainment on the training program. For particular areas of expertise, *g* is a more important predictor of performance than a test of ability in the area. For instance, performance on a test of mechanical aptitude is more strongly determined by *g* than by mechanical ability (Ree and Earles, 1994).

4. Contemporary Consensus on Intelligence

By the end of the twentieth century a wide degree of consensus had emerged on intelligence. A useful definition of intelligence was provided by a committee set up by the American Psychological Association in 1995 under the chairmanship of Ulrich Neisser. The committee consisted of eleven American psychologists whose mandate was to produce a consensus view of what is generally known and accepted about intelligence. The definition of intelligence proposed by the Task Force was that intelligence is the ability "to understand complex ideas, to adapt effectively to the environment, to learn from experience, to engage in various forms of reasoning, to overcome obstacles by taking thought" (Neisser, 1996, p. 1).

A similar definition was advanced by Linda Gottfredson and 52 leading experts, and published in the *Wall Street Journal* in 1994:

> Intelligence is a very general mental capacity which, among other things, involves the ability to reason, plan, solve problems, think abstractly, comprehend complex ideas, learn quickly, and learn from experience. It is not merely book learning, a narrow academic skill, or test taking smarts. Rather, it reflects a broader and deeper capability for comprehending our surroundings—"catching on," "making sense" of things, or "figuring out" what to do (Gottfredson, 1997, p. 13).

More recently Schmidt and Hunter (2004, p. 162) have taken stock of the results of a century's research on intelligence: "the accumulated evidence has become very strong that general intelligence is correlated with a wide variety of life outcomes, ranging from risky health-related behavior to criminal offenses, to the ability to use a bus or a subway system." Among the numerous tasks that intelligent people do more effectively than less intelligent people is to acquire complex skills and work more proficiently. This enables them to command higher incomes, as we shall see in detail in the next chapter. These studies are the foundation for our thesis that differences in intelligence contribute to the differences in incomes between nations.

CHAPTER 3

Intelligence as a Determinant of Earnings and Achievement

In this chapter we review the evidence showing that intelligence is a determinant of earnings among individuals. This is the foundation of our thesis that the intelligence of national populations is a major determinant of national per capita incomes and rates of economic growth. We also review the evidence showing that intelligence is a determinant of trainability and job proficiency which explains why those at higher levels of intelligence are able to secure higher earnings.

1. Effects of Intelligence on Earnings

Because we are concerned with the relationship between IQs and earnings among nations, it is important to begin by establishing that intelligence is a determinant of earnings among individuals. There have been a number of studies showing that this is so. Some of these studies have measured intelligence in childhood or adolescence and related these to earnings in adulthood, while others have measured intelligence in adulthood at the same time as earnings. Several studies have shown that intelligence assessed in childhood from the age of about 8 years and above is fairly stable over the life span and is correlated at about 0.7 to 0.8 with intelligence in adulthood (McCall, 1977; Li, 1975). The longest span of time over which a high stability of IQ has been demonstrated is 66 years. This was shown in a study by Deary et al. (2000) in which children intelligence tested in 1932 at the age of eleven were tested again in 1998 at the age of 77. The correlation between the two scores was 0.77. It does not therefore make much difference for studies of the relation between intelligence and earnings whether IQs are assessed in childhood or adolescence and shown to predict future earnings, or whether IQs and earnings are assessed simultaneously among adults. Since intelligence is fairly stable from around the age of eight, both methodologies imply that intelligence predicts earnings obtained in adulthood.

The results of the major studies of the relationship between intelligence and earnings are summarized in Table 3.1. Row 1 to 4 gives data from the Netherlands for a sample whose IQs were tested at the age of 12 years and whose earnings were obtained at the ages of 43 and 53. Rows 1 and 2 give results for men and show that IQs were correlated at 0.17 with earnings at age 43 and 0.19 with earnings at age 53. Rows 3 and 4 give the corresponding data for women and show that IQs were correlated at 0.03 with earnings at age 43 and 0.19 (the same as men) with earnings at age 53. Probably the low correlation between IQ and earnings for women at age 43 is because many women were rearing children and had little or no earnings, but by the age of 53 the women had resumed work and the correlation between IQ and earnings become exactly the same as for men. Row 5 gives data from Norway for a sample whose IQs were tested at age 18 years and whose IQs were correlated at 0.33 with earnings ascertained subsequently (age not given). Rows 6 through 13 give data from Sweden for a sample born in 1928 in Malmo and intelligence tested at the age of 10 years and again at the age of 20 years while doing military service. Earnings were ascertained at the ages of 25, 30, 35, and 43. Rows 6 through 9 give the correlations between IQs at age 10 and adult earnings and show that these were negligible (0.08) at the age of 20 but become statistically significant and increasingly large from the age of 25 until they reach 0.40 at the age of

43. Rows 10 through 13 give the corresponding correlations between IQs at age 20 and adult earnings and show the same trend with the correlation reaching 0.50 at the age of 43. The correlations between IQs and earnings are higher when IQs are measured at the age of 20 than at age 10, probably because the IQs at age 20 are more valid.

Rows 14 through 29 give data for the relationship between intelligence and earnings in the United States. Row 14 gives the results of the first study by Duncan (1968) who presented data from the 1964 Current Population Survey carried out by the National Opinion Research Center (NORC) on a sample of white males with an average age of 30 (range 24–35). Their IQs were obtained from the AFQT (Armed Forces Qualification Test) taken from their military records and showed that their IQ was correlated at 0.31 with their earnings (the size of the sample is not given). Rows 15 through 18 give data for a sample from New England. The age at which the IQs were obtained is not given. The correlation between the IQs and earnings at the age of 19 was 0.15 and increased progressively as the sample grew older up to 0.49 at the age of 34. This confirms the results obtained by Fagerlind (1975) in Sweden showing that the correlation between the IQs and earnings increases with age. Row 19 gives a correlation of 0.26 between the IQs of a sample in Wisconsin and earnings at the age of 25.

Rows 20 through 23 (Brown and Reynolds, 1975) are derived from a study of the relation between the IQ of males measured in early adulthood and earnings approximately 12 years later for samples of 24,819 whites and 4,008 blacks. The correlations of IQ and earnings are 0.24 and 0.33 for whites at the approximate ages of 30 and 36, and 0.08 and 0.13 for blacks at the same ages. The explanation for the lower correlations for blacks is not clear. Row 24 (Murray, 1998) is derived from the National Longitudinal Study of Youth, a nationally representative American sample of 12,686 males intelligence tested in 1980 between the ages of 14 and 23 and whose incomes were recorded in 1992 at the average age of 30; the correlation between IQ and income is 0.37. Row 25 gives data for 1943 sibling pairs from the NLSY sample and shows a correlation between IQ and income of 0.35. The point of using pairs of siblings is that it is possible to estimate the heritability of income, calculated in this study at 0.42. Row 26 gives the highest correlation (0.53) in the table between IQ at age 12 and income at the age of 45.

Rows 27 and 28 (Nyborg and Jensen, 2001) give data obtained from samples of white and black men who had served in the United States Armed Forces in the Vietnam war, of whom 62% were draftees

Table 3.1. Correlations between IQ and earnings

	Country	Number	Sex	Age	Age	r	Reference
1	Netherlands	835	M	12	43	0.17	Dronkers, 1999
2	Netherlands	819	M	12	53	0.19	Dronkers, 1999
3	Netherlands	350	F	12	43	0.03	Dronkers, 1999
4	Netherlands	237	F	12	53	0.19	Dronkers, 1999
5	Norway	1,082	M/F	18	-	0.33	Tambs et al., 1989
6	Sweden	346	M	10	25	0.08	Fagerlind, 1975
7	Sweden	460	M	10	30	0.22	Fagerlind, 1975
8	Sweden	631	M	10	35	0.34	Fagerlind, 1975
9	Sweden	707	M	10	43	0.40	Fagerlind, 1975
10	Sweden	312	M	20	25	0.10	Fagerlind, 1975
11	Sweden	410	M	20	30	0.22	Fagerlind, 1975
12	Sweden	532	M	20	35	0.43	Fagerlind, 1975
13	Sweden	585	M	20	43	0.50	Fagerlind, 1975
14	USA	-	M	18	30	0.31	Duncan, 1968
15	USA	345	M	-	19	0.15	Hause, 1971
16	USA	345	M	-	24	0.29	Hause, 1971
17	USA	345	M	-	29	0.45	Hause, 1971
18	USA	345	M	-	34	0.49	Hause, 1971
19	USA	4,388	M	17	25	0.26	Hauser et al., 1973
20	USA-whites	24,812	M	18	30	0.24	Brown & Reynolds, 1975
21	USA-whites	24,812	M	18	36	0.33	Brown & Reynolds, 1975
22	USA-blacks	4,008	M	18	30	0.08	Brown & Reynolds, 1975
23	USA-blacks	4,008	M	18	36	0.13	Brown & Reynolds, 1975
24	USA	12,686	M/F	18	30	0.37	Murray, 1998
25	USA	1,943	M/F	18	30	0.35	Rowe et al., 1998
26	USA	-	M	12	45	0.53	Judge et al., 1999
27	USA-whites	3,484	M	19	37	0.36	Nyborg & Jensen, 2001
28	USA-blacks	493	M	19	37	0.37	Nyborg & Jensen, 2001
29	USA	1,448	M	17	27	0.22	Murnane et al., 2001

and 38% were enlisted. Their IQs were obtained in 1967 at the age of 19 and their earnings were obtained at the age of approximately 37. In this sample the correlations between IQs and earnings were virtually identical for whites (0.36) and blacks (0.37), unlike the results in rows 18 and 19 where the correlations are greater for whites. These correlations will be a little lower than would be obtained for a fully representative sample of the population because those with IQs below the tenth percentile are not accepted into the armed services. The final row gives a correlation of 0.22 between IQs at the age of 17 and income at the age of 27.

Looking at the results as a whole, it is apparent that all of them show positive correlations between IQs obtained in childhood or adolescence and earnings in adulthood. These studies show that IQ is a determinant of income because IQs are established quite early in childhood and predict income achieved in adulthood (e.g., Duncan, 1968; Duncan, Featherman, and Duncan, 1972; Jencks, 1972; McCall, 1977; Jensen, 1998). It might be supposed that the family environment is the common cause of children's intelligence and their subsequent adult earnings, but this is improbable because it has been shown by Duncan, Featherman, and Duncan (1972) and by Jencks (1972) that the positive relation between childhood IQ and adult income is present when parental socioeconomic status is controlled. Furthermore, among pairs of brothers who have been raised in the same family and have experienced the same environment, the brother with the higher IQ in childhood has the greater earnings in adulthood (Jencks, 1972; Murray, 1998; Waller, 1971).

The median correlation between IQ and earnings at the age of the thirties and forties is 0.36. The effect of a correlation of 0.36 between intelligence and earnings is to produce substantial differences in the earnings of high and low IQ groups. As Jencks (1972, p. 222) noted, men inducted in the Korean War who had been tested and scored above the 80th percentile for intelligence, representing IQs of 110 and over, had personal incomes when they returned to civilian life 34 percent above the national average. Conversely, the military inductees who scored below the 20th percentile on intelligence, representing IQs of below 90, had personal incomes when they returned to civilian life approximately 34 percent below the national average.

It will be noted that the results set out in Table 3.1 show that the correlations between IQ and earnings are quite low in early adulthood but become larger among older age groups in their thirties and forties. In Fagerlind's (1975) Swedish data IQ and earnings are correlated at only 0.08 among 25-year-olds but at 0.40 among 43-year-olds. Similarly, in Hause's American data IQ and earnings are correlated at only 0.15 among 19-year-olds but at 0.49 among 34-year-olds. This age effect has been usefully illustrated by Murray (1997) for the National Longitudinal Study of Youth sample. He divides the sample into five IQ groups from 65–75 up to 125+ and gives their average earnings at the ages of 18, 26, and 32 years. His results are shown in Table 3.2.

At the age of 18, the middle IQ group (IQs 90–109) have the highest average earnings ($8,000), while the earnings of the highest IQ group (IQs 125+) are quite low ($3,000). By the age of 26, the earnings of the groups have become sorted by IQ but the highest IQ group earns only marginally more ($21,000),than the next highest IQ group ($20,000). By the age of 32, the differences in the earnings of the groups have become greater, with the highest IQ group earning substantially more ($36,000) than the next highest IQ group ($27,000), and some seven times more than the lowest IQ group ($5,000). There are two major explanations for these differences. First, in late adolescence and early adulthood, most of the high IQ groups are at school or in college so they do not earn as much as the middle IQ group who are mainly working. Second, the earnings of all the groups increase as they get older, but the earnings of the higher IQ groups increase more than those of the lower IQ groups. The reason for this is that everyone acquires skills as they get older, but the higher IQ groups acquire more skills than the lower IQ groups because intelligent people can learn skills that less intelligent people are unable to learn.

Table 3.2. Relation between IQ and earnings (US dollars) at ages 18, 26, and 32

	125+	110-124	90-109	75-89	60-75
18	3,000	8,000	8,000	5,000	2,000
26	21,000	20,000	16,000	10,000	3,000
32	36,000	27,000	20,000	12,400	5,000

2. High IQs and High Earnings

The general relationship between IQ and earnings holds for those with exceptionally high IQs who have been found to have exceptionally high earnings, as well as exceptionally high lifetime achievement judged by other criteria. The classical study showing this was begun about the year 1920 by Lewis Terman and his colleagues at Stanford University. They began by intelligence testing a large number of children in California. From these were selected 1528 (857 boys and 671 girls) with IQs of 135 and above. The minimum IQ of 135 represents approximately the top one percent of the population. The average IQ of the total sample was 151 (Terman, 1925). The sample was followed up when they were in their early forties. By this age the authors concluded that "the superior child, with few exceptions, becomes the able adult, superior in nearly every respect to the generality" (Terman and Oden, 1959, p. 143). It was found that 70 percent had graduated from college; two fifths of the men and three fifths of the women had gone through graduate school. Of the men, 86 percent were in the two highest socioeconomic categories of the professions and management. None were in the lowest socioeconomic category of unskilled workers, as compared with 13 percent of the male population at this time. 70 of the men were listed in *American Men of Science* and three had been elected to the National Academy of Sciences. Thirty-one were listed in *Who's Who in America*. Between them, they had produced nearly 2000 scientific papers, some 60 books in the sciences, 230 patents, and 33 novels. Fourteen percent of the men did not fulfil the promise of their high IQs and failed to obtain the top two socioeconomic class occupations. These were almost all impaired by psychiatric problems or lack of motivation. Among the women, most of them became housewives and mothers and consequently did not have such visible achievements. Nevertheless, seven were listed in *American Men and Women of Science* and two in *Who's Who in America*. Between them, they had produced 32 scholarly books, five novels, more than 200 scientific papers, and five patents.

A more recent study finding similar results has been carried out by Lubinski, Benhow, Webb, and Bleske-Rechek (2005). They searched the United States for children below the age of 13 years who tested very highly talented in verbal reasoning and mathematical abilities as measured by the Scholastic Aptitude Test (SAT) (these abilities are highly correlated with intelligence: see below, Section 4). These children were given the SAT, normally taken by 18-year-olds for college entrance, and were included in the sample if they scored in the top 1 per 10,000 of the general population. For this they would have to have had an IQ of approximately 160. They were followed up at the age of 33 years. At this age they were exceptionally successful and had exceptionally high earnings. Half of them had doctorates, compared with 1 percent of the general population. 37 percent of the men and 21 percent of the women had annual incomes of $100,000 and above, while 8 percent of the men and 2 percent of the women had annual incomes of $250,000 and above. In addition, 26 percent of the sample had taken out at least one patent, compared with 1 percent of the general population of this age. This confirms the high earnings commanded by the highly intelligent and their exceptional contribution to national economic development as shown by their numerous patents.

3. Economists' Studies of Effects of IQ on Earnings

The studies summarized in Table 3.1 have been largely conducted by psychologists and sociologists. The effects of intelligence on earnings have also been studied by economists. Typically, they avoid the term *intelligence*. They prefer terms like *cognitive ability* (Cawley, Heckman, and Vytlacil, 2001) or *intellectual capacity* (Zax and Rees, 2002). Economists do not normally express the relationship between *cognitive ability* or *intellectual capacity* as a correlation coefficient. They generally prefer to express it as the effect of an increase of one standard deviation of intelligence on the percentage increase in earnings. The results of nine studies are summarized in Table 3.3. Row 1 gives Crouse's (1979) estimate derived from a sample in Kalamazoo whose IQs were obtained in sixth grade between 1928 and 1952, and whose earnings were obtained as adults of various ages. His estimate was that an increase of one standard deviation of intelligence produces a 15 percent increase in earnings. Row 2 gives Bishop's (1989) estimate derived from a national American sample whose IQs and earnings were obtained as adults aged 25–64 in 1971. His estimate was that an increase of one standard deviation of intelligence produces a 19 percent increase in earnings.

Rows 3 and 4 give the results of a national sample (the National Longitudinal Study of Youth) that was born between 1961 and 1964 and intelligence tested between the ages of 15–18 with the AFQT

Table 3.3. Effects of IQ on earnings

	Country	Number	Sex	Age	Age	%Effect on	Reference
1	USA	692	M	12	-	15	Crouse, 1979
2	USA	1,774	M	25–64	25–64	19	Bishop, 1989
3	USA	1,593	M	15–18	19–34	17	Neal & Johnson, 1996
4	USA	1,446	F	15–18	19–32	23	Neal & Johnson, 1996
5	USA	1,448	M	17	27	19	Murnane et al., 2001
6	USA	2,959	M	17	35	11	Zax & Rees, 2002
7	USA	2,264	M	17	53	21	Zax & Rees, 2002
8	Sweden	3,404	M	12	34	10	Zetterberg, 2004
9	Sweden	3,277	F	12	34	11	Zetterberg, 2004

(Armed Forces Qualification Test). The results show that a one standard deviation advantage in IQ produces a 17 percent increase in earnings for men at the age of 19 to 32 and a 23 percent increase in earnings of women. These results are unusual in finding that intelligence is more strongly related to earnings in women than in men. Row 5 gives the results of a sample of boys whose ability was measured by a math test at the age of 17 and which found that a one standard deviation advantage in ability produced a 19 percent increase in earnings for men at the age of 27.

Rows 6 and 7 give the results of a sample of boys in Wisconsin whose IQs were measured at the age of 17 and whose earnings were ascertained at the ages of 35 and 53. The results show that a one standard deviation advantage in IQ produces an 11 percent increase in earnings for men at the age of 35 and a 22 percent increase in earnings at the age of 53. These figures are an underestimate of the effects of intelligence on earnings in the population of the United States because of restriction of range. The sample does not include high school drop-outs and has very few blacks and Hispanics, all groups that have lower IQs and lower adult earnings. Nevertheless, the effect of IQ on earnings is substantial. Furthermore, IQ has twice as large an effect in middle age as in the mid-thirties. The effect of IQ on earnings evidently increases over the course of the life span. The effect is like a marathon. In the early stages all the runners are bunched together and there is not much difference between the good runners and the poor runners. Later in the race, the gap between the good runners and the poor runners becomes greater. The authors conclude that their results show "that earnings depend heavily on innate ability" (p. 606).

Rows 8 and 9 show similar data for Sweden. The IQs of a representative sample of 6,681 12–13-year-olds in Gothenburg were obtained in 1979/80. The test had three sections measuring reasoning, verbal, and spatial abilities, which were summed to give IQs. The sample has been followed up and earnings obtained at the age of 34. The data presented show that for men a one standard deviation increase in IQ produced on average 10 percent higher earnings, while for women a one standard deviation increase in IQ produced on average 11 percent higher earnings. For males this estimate is of similar magnitude to the one reported in Zax and Rees (2002) (11 percent) but is lower than the estimates reported in Neal and Johnson (1996) (18 percent) and Murnane et al (2001) (19 percent). A possible explanation for the (on average) smaller effect of intelligence on earnings in Sweden is that earnings differentials are in general more equalised in the Swedish labour market.

While these correlations show that intelligence is a significant determinant of earnings, it is not of course the only determinant. It is generally considered in psychology that the other principal determinants are the strength of motivation for achievement and opportunity. These determinants have been expressed in the formula IQ x Motivation x Opportunity = Achievement (Jensen, 1980). The algebraic terms indicate that if any of the three variables is low or zero, the achievement output will be low or zero. Thus, an individual with high IQ and strong motivation reared in an environment lacking in opportunity will not achieve much. Nor will an individual with high intelligence and reared in an environment with high opportunity, but deficient in motivation. Nor, finally, will an individual with strong motivation reared in an environment with high opportunity but with low intelligence.

4. Intelligence and Educational Attainment

IQs also predict educational and occupational achievement. Typically IQs measured in childhood or adolescence predict subsequent educational achievement at a magnitude of a correlation of around 0.5 to 0.7. The results of a number of major and typical studies are summarized in Table 3.4.

The first column gives the country, the second column gives the number in the sample, the third gives the age at which intelligence was measured, the fourth gives the age at which educational attainment was measured, the fifth gives the measure of educational attainment assessed by tests in an academic subject, the years of education, or the level reached. The sixth gives correlation between intelligence and educational attainment. The correlations range between 0.41 and 0.74 with a median of 0.62. Note that IQ measured in childhood or adolescence predicts not only scores obtained on

Table 3.4. Correlations between intelligence and educational tainment

	Country	N	Age	Age	Subject	r	Reference
1	Canada	208	13	13	General	0.55	Gagne & St. Pere, 2002
2	England	85	5	16	English	0.62	Yule et al., 1982
3	England	85	5	16	Math	0.72	Yule et al., 1982
4	Great Britain	8,699	11	21	Years	0.70	Thienpont & Verleye, 2003
5	Great Britain	20,000	11	16	GCSE	0.74	Deary, 2004
6	N. Ireland	701	16	16	GCSE	0.65	Lynn et al., 1984
7	N. Ireland	451	16	23	Level	0.40	Cassidy & Lynn, 1991
8	Norway	1,082	18	18	Years	0.50	Tambs et al., 1989
9	Sweden	570	20	20	Years	0.53	Fagerlind, 1975
10	USA	-	-	-	General	0.71	Walberg, 1984
11	USA	455	13	13	Reading	0.68	Lloyd & Barenblatt, 1984
12	USA	-	18	18	Math	0.66	Lubinski & Humphreys, 1996
13	USA	1,943	17	31	Years	0.63	Rowe et al., 1998
14	USA	3,484	19	37	Years	0.59	Nyborg & Jensen, 2001
15	USA-blacks	493	19	37	Years	0.41	Nyborg & Jensen, 2001
16	Switzerland	82	11	11	Math	0.45	Tewes, 2003

educational tests but also the number of years and the level of education. The main reason for this is that children with high IQs do well at school and find school rewarding, so they opt to remain in education longer than those with lower IQs who tend to find school unrewarding.

Row 1 gives a correlation of 0.55 between IQ measured with the Otis-Lennon Test and the average of the mean of scores in French, English, Math, and History for a sample of 208 13-year-old girls at a secondary school in Montreal. Rows 2 and 3 come from a study in England in which IQs were obtained for 85 children at the age of 5 years and were found to be correlated with grades obtained in the public examinations in English (0.61) and mathematics (0.72) taken at the age of 16 years. Row 4 gives a correlation of 0.74 for a British sample for IQs obtained at the age of 11 and marks in the public GCSE (General Certificate of Education) examination at the age of 16 years. Row 5 gives a correlation of 0.70 for a British sample for IQs obtained at the age of 11 and years of education by age 21. Row 6 gives a correlation of 0.65 for a sample in Northern Ireland for IQs obtained at the age of 16 and marks in the public GCSE/GCE (General Certificate of Secondary Education) examination obtained approximately 8 months later. Row 7 gives a correlation of 0.40 for the same sample between IQs at 16 and level of education at the age of 23. Rows 8 and 9 give similar results for Norway and Sweden. Rows 10 through 15 give six similar results from American studies, and row 16 gives a further similar result from Switzerland.

It will be seen that all the correlations between intelligence and educational attainment are substantial and lie in the range between 0.44 and 0.74. It makes little difference whether intelligence is measured early in childhood or among young adults. One of the highest correlations (0.72) is between intelligence measured at the age of 5 years and educational attainment in mathematics at the age of 16 years.

It has sometimes been argued that the correlation between intelligence and educational attainment is not a causal one but arises through the common effects of the socioeconomic status of the family on both intelligence and educational attainment. Thus, middle class families produce children with high intelligence, either through genetic transmission or by providing environmental advantages, and also ensure that their children have a good education. This explanation cannot be correct because the correlation between parental socioeconomic status and their children's educational attainment obtained from a meta-analysis of almost 200 studies is only 0.22 (White, 1982). Such a low correlation could not account for much of the higher association between children's IQs and their educational attainment. In addition, it has been found that among pairs of brothers brought up in the same family, there is a correlation of approximately 0.3 between IQ and educational attainment (Jencks, 1972). This shows that correlation between IQ and educational attainment remains, although it is reduced, even when family effects are controlled. The only reasonable explanation of the correlations shown in Table 3.4 is that intelligence has a direct causal effect on educational attainment. It does this because IQ determines the efficiency of learning and comprehension of all cognitive tasks. The correlations between IQ and subsequent educational attainment are not perfect because educational attainment is partly determined by motivation, interests, compliance, and the effectiveness of teaching. Nevertheless the correlations are substantial and show that intelligence tests measure real cognitive abilities that are also expressed in educational attainment.

5. Intelligence and Socioeconomic Status

Further evidence that intelligence is a determinant of earnings comes from studies showing that intelligence is a significant determinant of socioeconomic status, which is itself strongly associated with earnings. The major studies are summarized in Table 3.5. Row 1 gives data from Britain showing a correlation of 0.39 between IQs measured at the age of 11 years and earnings at the age of 42. Row 2 gives data from Northern Ireland showing a correlation of 0.24 for a sample whose IQs obtained at the age of 16 and whose socioeconomic status was obtained at the age of 23. Row 3 gives data from Norway showing a correlation of 0.33 for a sample whose IQs were obtained at the age of 18; the age at which the socioeconomic status was obtained is not given. Rows 4 through 7 give data from Sweden from a study that began by obtaining IQs for a sample of 10-year-olds in Malmo in 1928. Socioeconomic status was ascertained at the ages of 25, 30, 35, and 43. Rows 8 through 11 give data from the same study in which the men were IQ tested again at the age of 20 while doing military service (the correlation between the two IQs was 0.75). Notice that the correlations become increasingly large from the age of 25 onwards and that the correlations are higher for the IQs obtained at the age of 20 than at age 10. The reason for this is probably that the IQs at age 20 are more valid.

Rows 12 through 19 give data for correlations between intelligence and socioeconomic status in the United States. Row 12 shows a correlation of 0.45 derived from a sample of white men enlisted into the Armed Forces during World War Two and their occupational status, whose IQs and SES were assessed simultaneously on joining the Armed Forces. Row 13 shows a correlation of 0.45 derived from a sample whose IQs were assessed at age 18 and whose socioeconomic status was obtained at age 30.

Table 3.5. Correlations between intelligence and socioeconomic status

	Country	N	Sex	Age	Age	r	Reference
1	Britain	5,038	M	11	42	0.39	Nettle, 2003
2	N. Ireland	451	M/F	16	23	0.24	Cassidy & Lynn, 1991
3	Norway	1,082	M	18	.	0.33	Tambs et al., 1989
4	Sweden	346	M	10	25	0.28	Fagerlind, 1975
5	Sweden	460	M	10	30	0.35	Fagerlind, 1975
6	Sweden	631	M	10	35	0.35	Fagerlind, 1975
7	Sweden	707	M	10	43	0.40	Fagerlind, 1975
8	Sweden	312	M	20	25	0.40	Fagerlind, 1975
9	Sweden	410	M	20	30	0.48	Fagerlind, 1975
10	Sweden	532	M	20	35	0.50	Fagerlind, 1975
11	Sweden	585	M	20	43	0.53	Fagerlind, 1975
12	USA	81,553	M	-	-	0.45	Stewart, 1947
13	USA	-	M	18	30	0.45	Duncan, 1968
14	USA	437	M	11	45	0.46	Bajema, 1968
15	USA	4,388	M	17	26	0.36	Sewell et al., 1970
16	USA	408	M	17	36	0.41	Sewell et al., 1980
17	USA	330	F	17	36	0.33	Sewell et al., 1980
18	USA	131	M	16	-	0.57	Waller, 1971
19	USA	170	M	13	-	0.50	Waller, 1971
20	USA	-	M	12	45	0.47	Judge et al., 1999
21	USA-whites	3,484	M	19	37	0.38	Nyborg & Jensen, 2001
22	USA-blacks	493	M	19	37	0.31	Nyborg & Jensen, 2001

Row 14 gives a correlation of 0.46 derived from a sample in Kalamazoo whose IQs were obtained in sixth grade in 1928 from the Terman Group Test and whose SES was obtained by the NORC prestige scale at the age of 46 in 1952. Row 15 gives results for a sample of men in Wisconsin born in 1939 and shows that IQ at age

17 tested with the Henman-Nelson Test predicts SES measured with the Duncan scale at age 24 at a correlation of 0.36. Rows 16 and 17 show a reduced number from the same sample whose SES was obtained at the age of 36 for whom the correlation was 0.41. This study also included women, for whom the correlation between IQ and SES at age 36 was a little lower (0.33) than men (0.41). Rows 18 and 19 give correlations of 0.38 for whites and 0.31 for blacks for samples whose IQs were assessed at age 19 and whose socioeconomic status was obtained at age 37.

6. Intelligence and Trainability

There are two major explanations for the positive association between IQ and income and socioeconomic status. These are: first that people with high IQs can be trained to acquire more complex skills that command higher incomes and enable them to achieve higher socioeconomic status; and second, that people with high IQs work more proficiently than those with low IQs and this makes them more productive and able to earn higher incomes and achieve higher socioeconomic status. In this section we consider studies of the relation between IQ and trainability. These studies come from the United States and Europe and are summarized in Table 3.6.

Rows 1 through 3 give the results of a meta-analysis of American studies that combines 425 individual studies to produce an overall result. The jobs are categorized into high, medium, and low complexity, and the results show that intelligence is correlated substantially more highly with trainability for high complexity occupations (0.58) than for low complexity occupations (0.25). Rows 4 and 5 give the results from a study of the relation between intelligence and training success in American military training schools. All recruits to the American military are given an intelligence test, the AFQT (Armed Forces Qualification Test). They are then sent to training schools. At the end of training, they are assessed for how well they have done on the course by tests assessing job performance, knowledge, and skills. The results based on a sample of 472,539 military personnel have been analyzed by Hunter (1986), who presents the correlations between IQ and training success for five types of training, namely: Mechanical, Clerical, Electronic, General Technical, and Combat. These correlations are shown in Table 3.6.

It will be seen that all the correlations are substantial and lie between 0.45 and 0.67. The magnitude of the correlations depends on the cognitive complexity of the skills assessed. The highest correlation is for Electronics (0.67), which is the most cognitively demanding. Correlations for Mechanical and Technical are a little lower at 0.62. The correlation for Clerical comes next at 0.58. The lowest correlation is for Combat, which is the least cognitively demanding and for which success is heavily dependent on physical skills, but even for

Table 3.6. Correlations between intelligence and trainability

	Country	Complexity	r	Reference
1	United States	High	0.58	Hunter & Hunter, 1984
2	United States	Medium	0.40	Hunter & Hunter, 1984
3	United States	Low	0.25	Hunter & Hunter, 1984
4	United States	Electronics	0.67	Hunter, 1986
5	United States	Mechanical	0.62	Hunter, 1986
6	United States	Technical	0.62	Hunter, 1986
7	United States	Clerical	0.58	Hunter, 1986
8	United States	Combat	0.45	Hunter, 1986
9	Europe	High	0.29	Salgado et al., 2003
10	Europe	Medium	0.29	Salgado et al., 2003
11	Europe	Low	0.23	Salgado et al., 2003

this the correlation of 0.45 is appreciable. Rows 9 through 11 give the results of a meta-analysis of 69 European studies that adopts the same categorization into high, medium, and low complexity. The results confirm the American studies in showing that intelligence is correlated more highly with trainability for high complexity occupations (0.29) than for low complexity occupations (0.23), although the correlations in the European studies are rather lower than in the United States.

7. Intelligence and Job Proficiency

The second explanation for the positive association between IQ and income and socioeconomic status is that people with high IQs work more proficiently than those with low IQs, and this makes them more productive and able to earn higher incomes and achieve higher socioeconomic status. Studies of the relation between IQ and job proficiency are summarized in Table 3.7. Rows 1 through 3 give the results of a review of American studies carried out by Ghiselli (1966). His conclusions were that virtually all studies found some positive correlation between IQs and ratings of job proficiency and that the magnitude of the correlation depended on the complexity of the job. For the least complex jobs, such as sales, service occupations, machinery workers, packers, and wrappers, the correlations between intelligence and job proficiency lay in the range between 0 and 0.19. For jobs of intermediate complexity, such as supervisors, clerks, and assemblers, the correlations lay in the range between 0.20 and 0.34. For the most complex jobs, such as electrical workers and managerial and professional occupations, the correlations lay in the range between 0.35 and 0.47. Rows 4 through 7 give the results of the second major American study consisting of the meta-analysis by Hunter and Hunter (1984) of 425 studies which have used the General Aptitude Test Battery (GATB), a test of general intelligence, for the prediction of job proficiency. The results confirmed Ghiselli's (1966) conclusion that when jobs are classified according to their complexity, IQ correlates more highly for complex jobs, at a correlation of 0.57, than it does for jobs of low complexity, for which the correlations are between 0.23 and 0.40. Row 8 gives the results

Table 3.7 Correlations between intelligence and job proficiency

	Country	Complexity	r	Reference
1	United States	High	0.42	Ghiselli, 1966
2	United States	Medium	0.27	Ghiselli, 1966
3	United States	Low	0.15	Ghiselli, 1966
4	United States	High	0.57	Hunter & Hunter, 1984
5	United States	Medium	0.51	Hunter & Hunter, 1984
6	United States	Low-general	0.40	Hunter & Hunter, 1984
7	United States	Low-industrial	0.23	Hunter & Hunter, 1984
8	United States	All	0.51	Schmidt & Hunter, 1998
9	Europe	All	0.25	Salgado et al., 2003

of a more recent synthesis of American studies reported from the 1920s through the mid-1990s showing an overall correlation of 0.51 between IQ and job proficiency. They conclude that "the conclusion from this research is that for hiring employees without previous experience in the job the most valid predictor of future performance is general mental ability." Row 9 gives the results of a meta-analysis of 69 European studies. The results confirm the American studies in showing that intelligence is positively correlated (0.25) with job proficiency, although the correlation is rather lower in the European studies than in the United States.

In this chapter we have seen that there are a large number of studies from several different countries showing that intelligence is positively and causally related to incomes and to the associated variables of educational attainment and socioeconomic status. We are now ready to examine whether intelligence is also related to incomes between nations.

CHAPTER 4

The Measurement of the Intelligence of Nations

Binet's test provided the model for many intelligence tests that were constructed during the course of the twentieth century. Most of these have been developed in the United States and Britain. These tests have subsequently been administered to samples of the populations in many other countries throughout the world. A number of these tests have been standardizations for use in different countries, while others have been administered to samples for various reasons such as, for instance, to see whether nutritional supplements have any advantageous effect on increasing intelligence. From these studies we found it possible in our *IQ and the Wealth of Nations* to calculate the mean IQs of the populations of 81 nations.

1. Measured IQs of 113 Nations

In our present study we have obtained IQs for a further 32 nations, bringing the total to 113. In nearly all the studies from which these national IQs are derived, the intelligence tests have been constructed in the United States or Britain and then administered to samples in other countries. In calculating national IQs we have set the mean IQ in Britain at 100 with a standard deviation of 15 and the mean IQs of other nations have been calculated in relation to this standard. The method is to obtain the sample's raw score on the test and calculate the corresponding British IQ. There are 65 countries for which we have two or more IQs. Where there are two IQs we have taken the mean and where there are three or more IQs we have used the median. The results of these calculations are given in Table 4.1.

Table 4.1. IQs of 113 nations

Country	National IQ	Country	National IQ	Country	National IQ
Argentina	93	Hong Kong	108	Poland	99
Australia	98	Hungary	98	Portugal	95
Austria	100	Iceland	101	Puerto Rico	84
Barbados	80	India	82	Qatar	78
Belgium	99	Indonesia	87	Romania	94
Bermuda	90	Iran	84	Russia	97
Bolivia	87	Iraq	87	Serbia	89
Brazil	87	Ireland	92	Sierra Leone	64
Bulgaria	93	Israel	95	Singapore	108
Cameroon	64	Italy	102	Slovakia	96
Canada	99	Jamaica	71	Slovenia	96
Central African Republic	64	Japan	105	South Africa	72
Chile	90	Jordan	84	South Korea	106
China	105	Kenya	72	Spain	98
Colombia	84	Kuwait	86	Sri Lanka	79
Congo-Brazzaville	64	Laos	89	St. Lucia	62
Congo-Zaire	65	Lebanon	82	St. Vincent	71
Cook Islands	89	Lithuania	91	Suriname	89
Croatia	90	Madagascar	82	Sudan	71
Cuba	85	Malaysia	92	Sweden	99

Country	National IQ	Country	National IQ	Country	National IQ
Czech Republic	98	Malta	97	Switzerland	101
Denmark	98	Mariana Islands	81	Syria	83
Dominica	67	Marshall Islands	84	Taiwan	105
Dominican Republic	82	Mauritius	89	Tanzania	72
Ecuador	88	Mexico	88	Thailand	91
Egypt	81	Morocco	84	Tonga	86
Equatorial Guinea	59	Mozambique	64	Turkey	90
Estonia	99	Netherlands	100	Uganda	73
Ethiopia	64	Nepal	78	United Kingdom	100
Fiji	85	New Caledonia	85	United States	98
Finland	99	New Zealand	99	Uruguay	96
France	98	Nigeria	69	Venezuela	84
Germany	99	Norway	100	Vietnam	94
Ghana	71	Pakistan	84	Western Samoa	88
Greece	92	Papua New Guinea	83	Yemen	85
Guatemala	79	Paraguay	84	Zambia	71
Guinea	67	Peru	85	Zimbabwe	66
Honduras	81	Philippines	86		

Technical details of the tests used in each study, the size and age of the samples, and of how these calculations have been made are given in Appendix 1. It should be noted that the figures given for IQs should not be regarded as accurate to 1 IQ point. When we presented similar figures in *IQ and the Wealth of Nations*, some critics demanded to know why the IQ in Belgium was 99 while the IQ in France was only 98. These small differences should be regarded as sampling errors and not as real differences.

2. Estimation of IQs for 192 Nations

There are 192 nations in the world with populations over 40,000. IQs have been given for 113 of these in Section 1. It would be useful to have

IQs for the remaining 79 nations, because this would make it possible to examine the relation between national IQs and per capita income, rates of economic growth, health and other factors for the totality of nations. To estimate IQs for the 79 nations for which we do not have data, we have estimated the IQs on the bases of neighboring countries. Inspection of the empirically derived national IQs given in Table 4.1 will show that neighboring countries typically have closely similar IQs. For instance, in Western Europe, the IQ is 98 in France, 99 in Belgium and Germany, 100 in Britain, 101 in the Netherlands, and 101 in Switzerland. Similarly, in West Africa the IQ is 64 in Cameroon, the Central African Republic and Congo-Brazzaville, and 65 Congo-Zaire. We have assumed that the countries for which we do not have IQs would likewise have similar IQs to those of neighboring countries. We can test the validity of this assumption in the following way. In *IQ and the Wealth of Nations* we used the method of estimating the IQs of countries for which we had

Table 4.2. Comparison of estimated and measured IQs in 25 countries

Country	Estimated IQ	Measured IQ	Country	Estimated IQ	Measured IQ
Bolivia	85	87	Malta	95	97
Central African Republic	68	64	Mauritius	81	89
Chile	93	90	Mozambique	72	64
Dominica	75	67	Pakistan	81	84
Dominican Republic	84	82	Papua New Guinea	84	83
Estonia	97	99	Sri Lanka	81	79
Honduras	84	81	St. Lucia	75	62
Iceland	98	101	St. Vincent	75	71
Jordan	87	84	Syria	87	83
Kuwait	83	86	Venezuela	89	84
Laos	89	89	Vietnam	96	94
Lithuania	97	91	Yeman	83	85
Madagascar	79	82			

no evidence from the IQs of neighboring countries, and we have now obtained measured IQs for 19 of these. We can therefore compare our previously estimated IQs with the measured IQs.

This comparison is shown for the 25 countries in Table 4.2. It can be seen that the estimated IQs are close to the measured IQs. The correlation between the two data sets is 0.913. Such a high correlation shows that national IQs can be estimated from those of neighboring countries with considerable accuracy.

We have adopted the same method as used previously to estimate the IQs of the countries for which we do not have direct evidence based on intelligence tests: for these, we have estimated the IQs on the basis of the arithmetic means of the measured IQs of neighboring countries. These estimates are given in Table 4.3. In each case, the comparison countries and their national IQs are indicated in the table. Decimal points are rounded to the nearest whole number, 0.5 upwards.

Table 4.3. National IQs for 192 countries based on the results of intelligence tests and estimated national IQs (marked by *) based on the IQs of neighboring or other comparable countries

	Country	National IQ	Comparison Countries
1	Afghanistan	84*	Iran 84, Pakistan 84
2	Albania	90*	Greece 92, Serbia 89, Turkey 90
3	Algeria	83*	Morocco 84, Egypt 81
4	Andorra	98*	France 98, Spain 98
5	Angola	68*	Congo-Zaire 65, Zambia 71
6	Antigua & Barbuda	70*	Dominica 67, St. Lucia 62, St. Vincent 71, Barbados 80
7	Argentina	93	
8	Armenia	94*	Russia 97, Turkey 90
9	Australia	98	
10	Austria	100	
11	Azerbaijan	87*	Iran 84, Turkey 90
12	Bahamas	84*	Cuba 85, Dominican Republic 82
13	Bahrain	83*	Iran 84, Kuwait 86, Qatar 78
14	Bangladesh	82*	India 82
15	Barbados	80	

	Country	National IQ	Comparison Countries
16	Belarus	97*	Russia 97
17	Belgium	99	
18	Belize	84*	Guatemala 79, Mexico 88
19	Benin	70*	Ghana 71, Nigeria 69
20	Bermuda	90	
21	Bhutan	80*	India 82, Nepal 78
22	Bolivia	87	
23	Bosnia and Herzegovina	90*	Croatia 90, Serbia 89
24	Botswana	70*	South Africa 72, Zambia 71, Zimbabwe 66
25	Brazil	87	
26	Brunei	91*	Indonesia 87, Malaysia 92, Vietnam 94
27	Bulgaria	93	
28	Burkina Faso	68*	Ghana 71, Nigeria 69, Sierra Leone 64
29	Burundi	69*	Congo-Zaire 65, Tanzania 72
30	Cambodia	91*	Laos 89, Thailand 91, Vietnam 94
31	Cameroon	64	
32	Canada	99	
33	Cape Verde	76*	Guinea 67, Morocco 84
34	Central African Republic.	64	
35	Chad	68*	Central African Republic 64, Nigeria 69, Sudan 71
36	Chile	90	
37	China	105	
38	Colombia	84	
39	Comoros	77*	Madagascar 82, Tanzania 72
40	Congo-Brazzaville.	65	
41	Congo, Republic	64	
42	Cook Islands	89	
43	Costa Rica	89*	Argentina 93, Colombia 84
44	Côte d'Ivoire	69*	Ghana 71, Guinea 67
45	Croatia	90	
46	Cuba	85	
47	Cyprus	91*	Greece 92, Turkey 90

	Country	National IQ	Comparison Countries
48	Czech Republic	98	
49	Denmark	98	
50	Djibouti	68*	Ethiopia 64, Sudan 71
51	Dominica	67	
52	Dominican Republic	82	
53	Ecuador	88	
54	Egypt	81	
55	El Salvador	80*	Guatemala 79, Honduras 81
56	Equatorial Guinea	59	
57	Eritrea	68*	Ethiopia 64, Sudan 71
58	Estonia	99	
59	Ethiopia	64	
60	Fiji	85	
61	Finland	99	
62	France	98	
63	Gabon	64*	Cameroon 64, Congo-Brazzaville 64
64	Gambia	66*	Sierra Leone 64, Guinea 67
65	Georgia	94*	Russia 97, Turkey 90
66	Germany	99	
67	Ghana	71	
68	Greece	92	
69	Grenada	71*	Barbados 80, St. Lucia 62, St. Vincent 71
70	Guatemala	79	
71	Guinea	67	
72	Guinea-Bissau	67*	Guinea 67
73	Guyana	87*	Brazil 87, Suriname 89, Venezuela 84
74	Haiti	67*	Jamaica 71, St. Lucia 62, Dominica 67
75	Honduras	81	
76	Hong Kong	108	
77	Hungary	98	
78	Iceland	101	
79	India	82	
80	Indonesia	87	

	Country	National IQ	Comparison Countries
81	Iran	84	
82	Iraq	87	
83	Ireland	92	
84	Israel	95	
85	Italy	102	
86	Jamaica	71	
87	Japan	105	
88	Jordan	84	
99	Kazakhstan	94*	Russia 97, Turkey 90
90	Kenya	72	
91	Kiribati	85*	Marshall Islands 84, Tonga 86
92	Korea, North	106*	China 105, South Korea 106
93	Korea, South	106	
94	Kuwait	86	
95	Kyrgyzstan	90*	Turkey 90, Iran 84, Russia 97
96	Laos	89	
97	Latvia	98*	Estonia 99, Russia 97
98	Lebanon	82	
99	Lesotho	67*	South Africa 72, Mozambique 64, Zimbabwe 66
100	Liberia	67*	Ghana 71, Guinea 67, Sierra Leone 64
101	Libya	83*	Egypt 81, Morocco 84
102	Lithuania	91	
103	Luxembourg	100*	Belgium 99, Netherlands 100
104	Macedonia	91*	Bulgaria 93, Greece 92, Serbia 89
105	Madagascar	82	
106	Malawi	69*	Mozambique 64, Tanzania 72, Zambia 71
107	Malaysia	92	
108	Maldives	81*	India 82, Sri Lanka 79
109	Mali	69*	Guinea 67, Ghana 71
110	Malta	97	
111	Marshall Islands	84	
112	Mauritania	76*	Guinea 67, Morocco 84
113	Mauritius	89	
114	Mexico	88	

	Country	National IQ	Comparison Countries
115	Micronesia	84*	Marshall Islands 84
116	Moldova	96*	Romania 94, Russia 97
117	Mongolia	101*	China 105, Russia 97
118	Morocco	84	
119	Mozambique	64	
120	Myanmar (Burma)	87*	India 82, Thailand 91
121	Namibia	70*	South Africa 72, Zambia 71, Zimbabwe 66
122	Nepal	78	
123	Netherlands	100	
124	New Caledonia	85	
125	New Zealand	99	
126	Nicaragua	81*	Guatemala 79, Colombia 84, Honduras 81
127	Niger	69*	Nigeria 69
128	Nigeria	69	
129	Northern Mariana Islands	81	
130	Norway	100	
131	Oman	83*	Iraq 87, Qatar 78
132	Pakistan	84	
133	Panama	84*	Colombia 84
134	Papua New Guinea	83	
135	Paraguay	84	
136	Peru	85	
137	Philippines	86	
138	Poland	99	
139	Portugal	95	
140	Puerto Rico	84	
141	Qatar	78	
142	Romania	94	
143	Russia	97	
144	Rwanda	70*	Congo-Zaire 65, Tanzania 72, Uganda 73
145	Saint Kitts & Nevis	67*	Dominica 67, Saint Lucia 62, St. Vincent 71

	Country	National IQ	Comparison Countries
146	Saint Lucia	62	
147	Saint Vincent/ Grenadines	71	
148	Samoa (Western)	88	
149	Sao Tome & Principe	67*	Cameroon 64, Nigeria 69
150	Saudi Arabia	84*	Iraq 87, Kuwait 86, Qatar 78
151	Senegal	66*	Guinea 67, Sierra Leone 64
152	Serbia and Montenegro	89	
153	Seychelles	86*	Mauritius 89, India 82
154	Sierra Leone	64	
155	Singapore	108	
156	Slovakia	96	
157	Slovenia	96	
158	Solomon Islands	84*	Papua New Guinea 83, Marshall Islands 84
159	Somalia	68*	Ethiopia 64, Kenya 72
160	South Africa	72	
161	Spain	98	
162	Sri Lanka	79	
163	Sudan	71	
164	Suriname	89	
165	Swaziland	68*	Mozambique 64, South Africa 72
166	Sweden	99	
167	Switzerland	101	
168	Syria	83	
169	Taiwan	105	
170	Tajikistan	87*	Iran 84, Turkey 90
171	Tanzania	72	
172	Thailand	91	
173	Timor-Leste	87*	Indonesia 87
174	Togo	70*	Ghana 71, Nigeria 69
175	Tonga	86	
176	Trinidad & Tobago	85*	Suriname 89, Barbados 80

	Country	National IQ	Comparison Countries
177	Tunisia	83*	Egypt 81, Morocco 84
178	Turkey	90	
179	Turkmenistan	87*	Iran 84, Turkey 90
180	Uganda	73	
181	Ukraine	97*	Russia 97
182	United Arab Emirates	84*	Iraq 87, Kuwait 86, Qatar 78
183	United Kingdom	100	
184	United States	98	
185	Uruguay	96	
186	Uzbekistan	87*	Iran 84, Turkey 90
187	Vanuatu	84*	Papua New Guinea 83, Marshall Islands 84
188	Venezuela	84	
189	Vietnam	94	
190	Yemen	85	
191	Zambia	71	
192	Zimbabwe	66	

3. Reliability of National IQs

Several critics of the national IQs given in our *IQ and the Wealth of Nations* questioned the reliability of the figures. For instance, Astrid Ervik (2003, p. 408) wrote that there are "large disparities in test scores for the same country" and "the authors fail to establish the reliability of intelligence (IQ) test scores." Susan Barnett and Wendy Williams (2004) make a similar criticism: "It turns out that the samples used to estimate the national IQs on which the book's argument is based are, in many cases, not representative of the countries from which they are derived. When more than one sample is used to estimate a national IQ, it is unsettling how great the variability often is between samples from the same country." If samples from which the IQs are derived are unrepresentative and if different measures from the same country give widely differing results, the IQ figures will have low reliability, as Ervik and Barnett and Williams assert.

The *reliability* of a psychometric test means the extent to which the score it provides can be replicated in a further study. The reliability of a test is best assessed by using it to make two measurements of an individual or set of individuals and examining the extent to which the two measurements give the same results. Where the two measurements are made on a set of individuals the correlation between the two scores is calculated to give a measure of the degree to which they are consistent. The resulting correlation coefficient is a measure of the reliability and is called the *reliability coefficient.*

In our *IQ and the Wealth of Nations* we examined the reliability of the measures by taking 45 countries in which the intelligence of the population has been measured in two or more independent investigations. This is the same procedure that is used to examine the reliability of tests given to sets of individuals. We reported that the correlation between two measures of national IQs is 0.94, showing that the measures give highly consistent results and have high reliability. This reliability coefficient is closely similar to that of tests of the intelligence of individuals, which typically lies in the range between 0.85 and 0.90 (Mackintosh, 1998, p. 56). In the present study we have 71 countries and sub-categories within countries for which there are two or more scores. The correlation between the two extreme IQs (i.e., the highest and lowest) is 0.92 and is highly statistically significant. This method underestimates the true reliability because it uses the two extreme values. An alternative method is to exclude the two extreme scores and use the next lowest and highest scores. The change concerns the 15 countries for which we have five or more IQ scores (Brazil, China, Congo-Zaire, Germany, Greece, Hong Kong, India, Israel, Jamaica, Japan, Kenya, Morocco, South Africa-blacks, South Africa-Indians, and Taiwan). Using this method, the correlation between the two scores is 0.95. This figure establishes that the national IQs have high reliability.

4. Validity of National IQs

The validity of intelligence tests is the extent to which they measure what they purport to measure. A test cannot be valid if it has low reliability, but a test with high reliability (in the sense that repeated measures give closely similar results—as in the case of our tests of national IQs) need not necessarily be valid. The national IQs purport to be measures of the cognitive abilities of national populations. But it can be argued that intelligence tests are biased against some national populations because these lack experience of the kinds of problems presented in the tests. According to this view, the peoples of sub-Saharan Africa whose IQs average around 70, are just as intelligent as the peoples of Europe, whose IQs average around 100, and the peoples of East Asia, whose IQs average around 106. This criticism of our data on national IQs has been voiced by Barnett and Williams (2004) who argue that the tests are not valid measures of the intelligence of peoples in many economically developing nations.

The problem of the validity of intelligence tests has long been recognized because it is also present for individuals in western countries. We may find that one child has an IQ of 130 while another has an IQ of 70. But critics have questioned whether these differences have any meaning beyond the ability to solve the problems in intelligence tests. This question has been addressed by examining whether IQs predict earnings, educational achievement, and socioeconomic status. We showed in Chapter 3 that they do, and in particular that in eighteen countries IQs predict educational achievement with a median correlation of 0.63 (Table 3.4). We have used the same methodology to assess the validity of the IQs of nations. If the IQs are valid as measures of national IQs, they will be correlated with measures of national educational attainment, just as they are among individuals. To examine whether this is the case, national scores on mathematics and science have been obtained from the International Studies of Achievement in Mathematics and Science. These are a series of studies carried out between the mid-1960s and 1994 in which representative samples of primary and secondary school students from a number of countries have been given tests of mathematics and science. Some results are available for a total of 53 countries but not all countries participated in all the studies, so there is quite a lot of missing data. Five data sets of national scores on mathematics and science have been used here and are given in Table 4.4.

Column 1 gives the nations' IQs. Column 2 gives the data from the first two International Studies of Achievement in Mathematics and Science Scores carried out between the mid-1960s and 1982 and combined by Hanushek and Kimko (2000) to give a single score for each nation set on a mean of 50 and standard deviation of 10. The figure for Swaziland is taken from Baker and Jones (1993). Columns 3, 4, 5, and 6 give, respectively, results for 10- and 14-year-olds in mathematics

Table 4.4. National IQs and attainments in Math and Science

Nations	IQ	Math & Science 1964-86	Math 1994 Age 10	Math 1994 Age 104	Science 1994 Age 10	Science 1994 Aged 14
Australia	98	48.13	546	530	562	545
Austria	100	-	559	539	565	558
Belgium	99	53.25	-	-	546	511
Brazil	87	33.91	-	-	-	-
Bulgaria	93	59.28	-	-	-	565
Canada	99	47.57	532	527	549	531
China	105	59.28	-	-	-	-
Chile	90	26.30	-	-	-	-
Colombia	84	-	-	385	-	411
Cyprus	85	-	502	474	475	463
Czech Republic	98	-	567	564	557	574
Denmark	98	53.48	-	-	-	478
Finland	99	48.76	-	-	-	-
France	98	54.15	-	-	538	498
Germany	99	59.03	-	-	-	531
Greece	92	-	492	484	-	497
Hong Kong	108	56.93	587	588	533	522
Hungary	98	53.85	548	537	532	554
Iceland	101	-	474	487	505	494
India	82	21.63	-	-	-	-
Iran	84	20.75	429	428	416	470
Ireland	92	47.59	550	527	539	538
Israel	95	51.29	531	522	505	524
Italy	102	44.59	-	-	-	-
Japan	105	60.65	597	605	574	571
Jordan	84	39.38	-	-	-	-
Kuwait	86	-	400	392	401	430
Latvia	98	-	525	493	512	485
Lithuania	91	-	-	477	-	476

Nations	IQ	Math & Science 1964-86	Math 1994 Age 10	Math 1994 Age 104	Science 1994 Age 10	Science 1994 Aged 14
Mozambique	64	24.26	-	-	-	-
Nigeria	69	34.15	-	-	-	-
Netherlands	100	56.84	577	541	557	560
New Zealand	99	52.44	499	508	531	525
Norway	100	49.60	502	503	530	527
Philippines	86	34.35	-	-	-	-
Portugal	95	50.28	475	454	480	480
Romania	94	-	-	-	-	486
Russia	97	-	-	-	-	538
Singapore	108	56.51	625	643	547	607
Slovakia	96	-	547	544	-	-
Slovenia	96	-	552	541	546	560
South Africa	72	-	354	326	-	326
South Korea	106	56.21	611	607	597	565
Spain	98	49.40	-	-	487	517
Swaziland	68	32.00	-	-	-	-
Sweden	99	47.41	-	-	-	535
Switzerland	101	57.17	-	545	-	-
Taiwan	105	56.28	-	-	-	-
Thailand	91	39.83	490	522	473	525
Turkey	90	41.52	-	-	-	-
United Kingdom	100	53.98	513	506	551	552
United States	98	43.43	545	500	-	534
Correlations with IQ	-	0.81	0.86	0.89	0.79	0.81

and science in the Third International Mathematics and Science Study carried out in 1994. The data for these are given by Beaton, Mullis, Martin, Gonzales, Kelly, and Smith (1996) and Beaton, Martin, Mullis, Gonzales, Smith, and Kelly (1996).

The bottom row gives the correlations between national IQs and the scores on educational attainment. The correlations range between 0.79 and 0.89 and are all statistically significant at the 1 per cent level. These correlations are reduced from their true values by measurement error. In fact the average of the intercorrelations among the five measures of educational attainment is 0.78 and is lower than the average of the correlations (0.83) between the IQs and the five measures of educational attainment. Correction for the unreliability of these measures (correction for attenuation), adopting reliability coefficients of 0.95 for IQs and 0.83 for educational attainment, gives a true correlation of 1.0 between national IQs and national educational attainment. This validates the national IQs and shows that they measure important cognitive abilities that are expressed in the ability to perform well in tests of math and science as well as in intelligence tests.

5. The IAEP Study of Math and Science

A further study of educational attainment in mathematics and science in fifteen countries was carried out in 1990 in the International Assessment of Educational Progress. The results given by Heyneman (1997) are shown in Table 4.5. The tests were given to representative samples of 13-year-olds. Both the mathematics and science were in three parts dealing with conceptual understanding (knowledge of facts and concepts), procedural knowledge (solution of routine problems according to standard procedures), and problem solving (ability to apply several skills to a unique situation). The national scores on these three components are consistent and have been combined to single figures of percentages of correct answers. There is only one country in this data set that does not appear in Table 4.4 This is Scotland, where the IQ is 97 in relation to a British IQ of 100 (Lynn, 1979). The validity of national IQs can be considered further by examining their relation with these new data sets on educational attainment in mathematics and science. It can be seen by inspection that there is broad correspondence. South Korea and Taiwan have the highest IQs and the highest scores on mathematics and science. The twelve European nations together with Canada and the United States fall in the middle, while Jordan has the lowest IQ and the lowest mathematics and science scores. The correlations between national IQs and the scores on educational attainment are 0.83 for mathematics and 0.89 for science scores and are statistically significant at the 1 per cent level. These results provide further evidence for the validity of the national IQs.

Table 4.5. National IQs and attainments in Math and Science in 15 nations

Nations	IQ	Math	Science
Canada	99	61	70
France	98	65	70
Hungary	98	68	73
Ireland	92	60	65
Israel	95	62	70
Italy	102	63	71
Jordan	84	39	57
Russia	97	70	72
Scotland	97	60	69
South Korea	106	73	76
Spain	98	56	67
Slovenia	96	59	72
Switzerland	101	71	73
Taiwan	105	73	75
United States	98	55	67

6. The PISA Studies

In the years 2000 and 2003 the OECD carried out studies of the mathematical and science abilities of representative samples of 15-year -olds in a number of countries (40 in 2000 and 39 in 2003). The studies are known as the Program for International Student Assessment (PISA). The results for mathematics are given by OECD on its website (see Helsingin Sanomat, December 7, 2004) and further results for mathematics and science for the 2000 study are given by De Bertoli and Creswell (2004). The mean scores of the participating nations for the two years are given in Table 4.6. Also shown are the IQs of the nations. The scores are based on a mean of 500 for all the countries and standardization of 100.

Looking first at the results for the year 2000, it will be seen that once again there is a general correspondence between the scores in mathematics and science and national IQs. The three countries with the highest math and science scores are Japan, Hong Kong, and South Korea, and these are

Table 4.6. National IQs and attainments in Mathematics in the PISA studies

Nations	National IQ	Math 2000 Age 15	Science 2000 Age 15	Math 2003 Age 15
Albania	90	370	375	-
Argentina	93	380	395	-
Australia	98	533	525	524
Austria	100	515	520	506
Belgium	99	520	495	529
Brazil	86	330	375	356
Bulgaria	93	430	448	-
Canada	99	533	530	532
Chile	90	375	410	-
China (Macao)	105	-	-	527
Czech Republic	98	498	508	516
Denmark	98	514	515	514
Finland	99	536	540	544
France	98	517	500	511
Germany	99	490	480	503
Greece	92	447	455	445
Hong Kong	108	550	540	550
Hungary	98	488	498	490
Iceland	101	514	515	515
Indonesia	82	360	395	360
Ireland	93	503	510	503
Israel	95	435	438	-
Italy	102	457	475	466
Japan	105	557	550	534
Latvia	97	465	455	483
Luxembourg	100	446	445	493
Macedonia	91	370	400	-
Mexico	88	387	420	383
Netherlands	101	-	-	538
New Zealand	99	537	575	523

Nations	National IQ	Math 2000 Age 15	Science 2000 Age 15	Math 2003 Age 15
Norway	100	499	500	495
Peru	85	295	335	-
Poland	99	470	475	490
Portugal	95	452	455	466
Russia	97	480	455	468
Serbia	89	-	-	437
Slovakia	96	-	-	498
South Korea	106	547	550	542
Spain	98	476	485	485
Sweden	100	510	508	509
Switzerland	101	529	495	527
Thailand	91	430	440	417
Tunisia	83	-	-	359
Turkey	90	-	-	423
United Kingdom	100	529	535	-
United States	98	493	500	483
Uruguay	96	-	-	422
Correlations with IQ	-	0.876	0.833	0.871
Number	-	40	40	39

also the three countries with the highest IQs. The three countries with the lowest math and science scores are Peru, Brazil, and Indonesia, and these are also the countries with the lowest IQs. The correlations between national IQs and scores in mathematics and science are 0.876 and 0.833, respectively. The magnitude of the national differences in mathematics is broadly similar to that of the national differences in intelligence. For instance, Japan scores higher than Britain by $0.28d$ (standard deviation units) on mathematics and by $0.47d$ on IQ, while Greece scores lower than Britain by $0.88d$ (standard deviation units) on mathematics and by $0.47d$ on IQ.

Looking now at the 2003 results, it will be seen that once again there is a general correspondence between the scores in mathematics and national IQs. The highest score was obtained by Hong Kong, followed by Finland, South Korea, the Netherlands, and Japan. Macao, representing China, scores a little lower at 527. Thus, the four East Asian nations performed well with a median score of 538 and on average better than the 25 nations populated by Europeans (including Australia, Canada, New Zealand, United States, and Uruguay), with a median score of 499. Greece and Serbia in southeast Europe with scores of 445 and 437 perform substantially less well than the remainder of the European peoples on mathematics, as they do on IQ. Turkey scores only a little lower than the two Balkan countries on mathematics (423) and about the same on IQ. Thailand, in the same IQ group between 90–92, scores similarly on mathematics (417). The four countries with the lowest IQs in the 80s—Brazil, Indonesia, Mexico, and Tunisia—obtain the lowest scores on mathematics in the range between 356-385, consistent with their lower IQs.

The correlation between national IQs and scores on mathematics in the 2003 study is 0.871. Once again, the magnitude of the differences in mathematics is broadly comparable to that in IQs. Thus, the difference between the four East Asian nations and the European nations in mathematics is 39 (538–499), the equivalent of $0.39d$ (standard deviation units). The difference between the East Asian nations and the European nations in IQ is identical at 6 IQ points, the equivalent of $0.40d$ (standard deviation units). However, the difference between the four economically developing nations (Brazil, Indonesia, Mexico, and Tunisia) and the European nations in mathematics ($130 = 1.3d$) is almost twice as great as the difference in IQ (11 IQ points $=0.73d$). This suggests that the potential for educational attainment is not being realized in the four economically developing nations.

7. Conclusions

Our critics Susan Barnett and Wendy Williams (2004) have asserted that the national IQs we have calculated and shown to be related to per capita income and economic growth are "virtually meaningless," and similar criticisms have been made by Astrid Ervik (2003, pp. 406–408), Thomas Volken (2003, p. 412), and Thomas Nechyba (2004, pp. 220–221). In answer to these criticisms, we have shown in this chapter that our national IQs are highly correlated with national scores in tests of mathematics and science in ten independent data sets. The correlations range between 0.79 and 0.89. These correlations could not be present if our critics were correct in dismissing national IQs as meaningless. On the contrary, they show that national IQs are meaningful. IQs correlate well with educational achievement across nations just as they do for individuals within nations (see Table 3.4).

A number of economists have spotted that educational attainment is strongly related to national per capita income and have argued that this relationship is causal in so far as educational attainment designated *human capital* promotes economic growth. But they have not understood the reason for this relationship. For instance, Hanushek and Kimko (2000) propose that ability in mathematics enables people to design technologically advanced products, and this contributes to economic growth. This is true but is not the main reason for the association of mathematical ability with economic growth and per capita income. The main reason is that mathematical ability is a measure of intelligence, and intelligence makes a major contribution to the efficiency with which work is performed in all occupations including those for which mathematical ability is not necessary (see Chapter 3). Mathematical ability is a proxy for IQ. Furthermore, IQ is better than mathematical ability as a measure of *human capital* because we have IQs for many more nations (113), while we only have mathematical ability scores for much lower numbers, and these do not include the nations of sub-Saharan Africa which in general have the lowest per capita income.

CHAPTER 5

Measures of Global Inequalities in Human Conditions

1. Measures Used in Previous Studies
2. Measures of Global Inequalities in Human Conditions
3. The Composite Index of the Quality of Human Conditions (QHC)
4. Alternative Measures of Human Conditions
5. Summary

The testing of the hypothesis about the relationship between disparities and inequalities in the quality of human conditions and the average level of mental abilities of a nation presupposes the operationalization of the hypothetical concepts "the quality of human conditions" and "mental abilities." In this relationship, "mental abilities" is assumed to constitute the explanatory factor. "National IQ" as defined in Chapter 4 will be used as the operationalized indicator of "mental abilities." In this chapter we shall introduce, define, and describe indicators intended to measure some aspects of global inequalities in human conditions. It is appropriate to start by reviewing indicators and indices that have previously been used to measure economic and other global inequalities in human conditions.

1. Measures Used in Previous Studies

GNP per capita and GDP per capita have been the most widely used indicators for comparisons of well-being across countries and of economic development. The per capita growth rate is the most common indicator of changes in well-being (see Todaro, 2000, pp. 14, 43; Klasen and Grün, 2003, p. 2). GNP per capita and GDP per capita indicators have been criticized because they are based on the prices of traded goods and therefore they exaggerate inequalities between rich and poor countries. They systematically undervalue the contributions of the non-traded sector in poorer countries. Purchasing power parity (PPP) estimates of GNP and GDP were developed to correct these drawbacks of GNP and GDP (see Nafziger, 1997, pp. 26–28; Todaro, 2000, pp. 43–46; Dowrick and Akmal, 2003, p. 21; Passé-Smith, 2003).

Measures of per capita income indicate global economic disparities satisfactorily, but there are many other aspects of human conditions which they do not take into account. For example, there are significant differences in income distribution within countries. GNP per capita and GDP per capita do not take into account such differences. Therefore, attempts have been made to "combine mean income with some measure of income inequality to arrive at better measures of welfare than average income alone" (Klasen and Grün, 2003, p. 2). The World Bank's *World Development Reports* and *World Development Indicators* (WDI) and UNDP's *Human Development Reports* provide statistical data on the distribution of income or consumption. These data cover more than 100 countries.

Inequalities in human conditions are not limited to economic differences. Human well-being is a multi-dimensional concept, consisting of a number of separate dimensions. Researchers have developed various measures to take into account disparities in objective and subjective well-being (see Gasper, 2003; McGillivray, 2003a, 2003b; Sumner 2003). The problems of measuring the quality of life are discussed extensively in the book *The Quality of Life* (1995), edited by Martha C. Nussbaum and Amartya Sen. The indicators in the Swedish Level of Living Surveys illustrate the multi-dimensionality of the quality of life. The components of these surveys include health and access to health care, employment and working conditions, economic resources, education and skills, family and social integration, housing, security of life and property, recreation and culture, and political resources (Erikson, 1995, p. 68). Erik Allardt stresses that there are both material and non-material basic human needs and that "both types of need have to be considered in indicator systems designed to gauge the actual level of welfare in a society." Having, Loving, and Being are catchwords in his approach to measure human welfare. *Having* refers to material conditions (economic resources, housing conditions, employment, working conditions, health, and education) that are necessary for survival and for avoidance of misery. *Loving* refers to the need to relate to other people and to form social identities. *Being* stands for the need for integration into society and to live in harmony with nature. The indicators of this dimension measure, for instance, participation in decisions and activities influencing life, political activities, opportunities for leisure-time activities and for meaningful work, and opportunities to enjoy nature (Allardt, 1995, pp. 88–91). Dan Brock (1995) discusses various health policy measures of the quality of life.

Of the many variables and indices measuring human well-being and the quality of life, the Human Development Index (HDI) of the United Nations Development Program (UNDP) is the best known. It is a composite index measuring average achievement in three basic dimensions of human development—a long and healthy life, as measured by life expectancy at birth; knowledge, as measured by the adult literacy rate and the combined primary, secondary, and tertiary gross enrollment ratio; and a decent standard of living, as measured by GDP per capita (PPP US$). Besides, UNDP has developed separate indices to measure poverty and gender disparities. Human poverty index (HPI-1) for developing countries and human poverty index (HPI-2) for selected OECD countries are composite indices measuring deprivations in the three basic dimensions captured in the human development index—longevity, knowledge, and standard of living. Gender-related development index (GDI) is a composite index measuring average achievement in the three basic dimensions captured in the human development index, adjusted to account for inequalities between men and women. Gender empowerment measure (GEM) is a composite index measuring gender inequality in three basic dimensions of empowerment—economic participation and decision-making, political participation and decision-making, and power over economic resources (*Human Development Report,* 2002, pp. 264–265; Sumner, 2003). Data on the Human Development Index have been given in *Human Development Reports* since 1990. Frances Stewart (2003) discusses the definition of poverty and the problems of poverty measures. She introduces four approaches to measure poverty and notes that poverty rates seem to differ significantly according to the approach adopted. Foster et al. (2003) draw attention to some drawbacks of HDI, especially to the fact that it is not sensitive to inequality within any of the dimensions considered. They say that "it is possible to have improvements in the HDI while large sectors of society stagnate or even worsen their situation."

Lars Osberg and Andrew Sharpe (2003) have attempted to construct a better index of the economic well-being than GDP per capita and HDI by taking into account four dimensions of economic well-being: current effective per capita consumption flows, net societal accumulation of stocks of productive resources, income distribution, and economic security. Their Index of Economic Well-Being (IEWB) shows that inequality and insecurity matter in international comparisons of well-being.

The Physical Quality of Life Index (PQLI) developed by D. Morris is a function of life expectancy at age one, infant mortality rate, and literacy rate. The Quality of Life Index constructed by Dasgupta and Weale includes per capita income, life expectancy at birth, adult literacy rate, and indices of political rights and civil liberties (see Rahman et al., 2003). Rahman et al. (2003) identified eight important domains of quality of life stressed at different times by different researchers: relationship with family and friends, emotional well-being, health, work and productive activity, material well-being, feeling part of one's local community, personal safety, and quality of environment. On the basis of their empirical analysis, they note that if they "really had to choose one indicator instead of a domain, it would be most appropriate to choose the life expectancy at birth as the indicator of the quality of life" (p. 16).

Susan Harkness (2003) refers to Amartya Sen's thinking on capabilities and its impact on the conceptualizing of human well-being and development. According to Sen, the most essential capabilities include adequate nourishment, leading a long and healthy life, literacy, and shelter. Harkness emphasizes that the ultimate goal in the efforts to improve human well-being is to maximize happiness or satisfaction, and she refers to Easterlin's important observation that happiness varies little across countries, and in the US, had increased little over time.

Andrew Sumner (2003) pays attention to the changes and evolution of poverty and well-being indicators. He notes that "the meaning and measurement of well-being has shifted from purely economic to include non-economic factors" (p. 9). Most commonly used economic well-being measures refer to income per capita, income poverty lines, and income inequality. The GDP per capita, the dollar-a-day poverty measure, and national poverty rates are still the most commonly used poverty indicators. Non-economic measures of well-being refer to education, health and nutrition, environment, and empowerment and participation. Of the composite measures of well-being, Sumner introduces, in addition to UNDP's indices, the World Health Organization (WHO)'s Quality of Life indicators, which cover six quality of life domains: physical, psychological, independence, social relationships, environment, and the spiritual. For the measures of human well-being and the quality of life, see also Dowrick, 2003; Gasper, 2003; Hicks, 2003; McGillivray, 2003a; Mayer-Foulkes, 2003; Silber and Ramos, 2003.

Ruut Veenhoven (2003) makes an interesting distinction between life-chances and life-results. Life-chances are preconditions for a good life; life-results mark a good life itself. Both chances and results can be "external" or "internal." External life-chances comprise environmental conditions required for a good life, especially access to scarce resources. Internal life-chances refer to the individual's capabilities, including appropriate physical and mental abilities, to exploit environmental opportunities. External life-results are the environmental effects of life, including a person's contribution to society. Internal life-results are the outcomes of life for an individual, which are manifested in life-satisfaction. Veenhoven's study is focused on national differences in life-satisfaction, whereas we are principally interested in global disparities in external life-chances.

This review of indicators used to measure disparities in human conditions indicates that no single variable is sufficient for this purpose. The phenomenon is multi-dimensional. Researchers have constructed and used many types of indicators and their combinations to measure differences in living standards, human well-being, quality of life, or human conditions. Some indicators measure disparities or inequalities within societies, and others, differences between nations. We are principally interested in indicators intended to measure global inequalities in the quality of human conditions.

2. Measures of Global Inequalities in Human Conditions

Because the scope of significant global inequalities is extremely large, it would be impossible to take all of them into account. We have to restrict the measurement to some clearly defined aspects of such disparities. We think that our theoretical arguments and the hypothesis based on it can be tested satisfactorily by a limited number of operational variables. The problem is to decide what dimensions of global inequalities are taken into account and to find appropriate indicators to measure differences between countries in the selected dimensions of global inequalities in human conditions.

The above review of previous measures provides material to select appropriate indicators for the purposes of this study. Data on per capita income have been used most frequently to measure differences in the level of economic development and in the wealth of nations. It is reasonable to argue that such differences are highly important. The material standard of living is for most people much higher in rich countries than in poor countries. In rich countries, people do not need to suffer from hunger and from the lack of many other necessities of life as much as in poor countries. Therefore the gap between rich and poor countries represents an important aspect of inequalities in human conditions. However, it alone would be insufficient to measure all the important dimensions of global disparities.

It has been noted that there can be significant differences in the distribution of income and wealth within countries independently of the level of per capita income and the level of economic development. Inequalities in the quality of human conditions are higher in a country in which the gap between the rich and the poor is extremely large than in a country in which income and wealth are more equally distributed among different sections of the population. It can be argued that disparities in human conditions are much more conspicuous in a country in which a small minority lives in prosperity and many others in extreme poverty than in a country in which the differences in living conditions are smaller. Therefore it would be useful to find indicators to measure national differences in income distribution or in the distribution of wealth.

In the contemporary world, differences in the level of education are important. A nation whose population are all literate has probably better chances to succeed in international economic competition than a nation most of whose members, or a significant part of them, are illiterate. The same concerns the relative number of highly educated people. Therefore differences in the level of education indicate global disparities in the quality of human conditions from one important perspective. It would be useful to find indicators to measure global disparities in the level of education.

It can be argued that differences in life expectancy are also important (cf. Rahman et al., 2003). People in countries in which the average life expectancy is high are probably better nourished and healthier than in countries in which the life expectancy is low. A long life provides an opportunity to enjoy more of life than a short life that may end prematurely. Therefore differences in life expectancy are important from the perspective of global disparities in human conditions. We should find some indicators to measure global differences in life expectancy or in the conditions of health and nutrition.

In addition to material conditions and life expectancy, there are also important differences between countries in their economic, social, and political institutions that constitute frameworks for human life. It can be argued that differences in freedoms of life and in the opportunities to pursue one's own economic and social targets and to participate freely in political life and decision-making are also important. Some political and economic systems allow much more extensive freedom for people than some other systems which are dominated by the few and in which resources are principally used to satisfy the needs of the dominating few. We should find indicators to measure global inequalities in human conditions from the perspective of economic and political freedoms.

Finally, five variables were selected to measure global inequalities in the quality of human conditions: (1) PPP-GNI per capita 2002, (2) adult literacy rate 2002, (3) gross tertiary enrollment ratio, (4) life expectancy at birth 2002, and (5) the level of democratization 2002. Certainly these five variables are not the only variables by which it would be possible to measure global disparities in human conditions, but we focus on these five variables because they take into account several important dimensions of human conditions and because empirical data on these variables are available from nearly all the 192 countries of this study. A combination of these variables is assumed to indicate average differences between countries in the quality of human conditions. Unfortunately we had to exclude an indicator of income inequalities for the reason that statistical data on this variable are not available for all countries, but we shall return to this variable and its relation to national IQ in Chapter 8.

2.1. PPP GNI per capita 2002

There are several indicators of per capita income, which differ from each other to some extent: (1) Gross national product per capita (GNP); (2) Gross domestic product per capita (GDP); (3) Gross national income per capita (GNI); (4) GNP per capita measured at purchasing power parity (PPP GNP); (5) GDP per capita measured at purchasing power parity (PPP GDP); and (6) GNI per capita measured at purchasing power parity (PPP GNI).

The basic difference between GNP and GDP is that GDP has been defined as the annual market value of final goods and services produced within the geographical boundaries of a nation, whereas GNP represents the annual market value of all final goods and services produced by the nation both within the country and abroad. With some exceptions, the difference between GDP and GNP is relatively small (see Gardner, 1998, pp. 22-23; Human Development Report, 1999, p. 254; World Development Report, 1999/2000, p. 274). The World Bank replaced GNP by GNI (gross national income) since 2000. GNI, the broadest measure of national income, "is the sum of value added by all resident producers plus any product taxes (less subsidies) not included in the valuation of output plus net receipts of primary income (compensation of employees and property income) from abroad" (World Development Indicators, 2004, p. 17; World Development Report, 2003, p. 265). Data are in current U.S. dollars.

It should be noted that GNP, GDP, and GNI include only the value of goods and services that are produced legally and sold on open markets. They exclude most of the goods and services produced by families for their own consumption because these items are never sold on the market. Non-market activities, such as subsistence agriculture and unpaid work by family members, are relatively more important in poor countries than in rich countries. In order to correct the "traded sector bias" in per capita indicators, the International Comparison Program has generated purchasing power parity estimates of GDP, GNP, and GNI based on international prices (see Gardner, 1998, pp. 26–28; Todaro, 2000, p. 43–46; Klasen and Grün, 2003, p. 4; Dowrick and Akmal, 2003). Purchasing power parity (PPP) converts a country's GDP from its own currency into international dollars "by measuring the country's purchasing power relative to all other countries rather than using the exchange rate" (Nafziger, 1997, p. 26). At the PPP rate, an "international dollar has the same purchasing power over GNI as a U.S. dollar has in the United States" (World Development Indicators, 2004, p. 17). This method reduces the gap between rich and poor countries considerably (Ray, 1998, pp. 12–16; cf. World Development Report, 2003, Table 1; WDI, 2004, Table 1.1). It is reasonable to assume that per capita indicators measured at purchasing power parity (PPP) indicate the differences in per capita income and in the level of economic development more reliably than data on GNP, GDP, and GNI per capita (see Nafziger, 1997, pp. 26–28; Todaro, 2000, pp. 43–46).

All these indicators are based on estimations and, therefore, they include measurement errors. We shall use as our principal measure of per capita income the sixth variable, PPP GNI per capita. In our previous book *IQ and the Wealth of Nations* (2002), the relationships between national IQs and various indicators of per capita income and economic growth rates were analyzed extensively over a long period of time. Data on the PPP GNI per capita variable and other per capita variables are available from many sources. The World Bank's *World Development Report* and *World Development Indicators* (WDI) and UNDP's *Human Development Report* provide the most extensive and probably also the most reliable data on per capita income from nearly all countries of the world. We shall use them as our principal sources of data on per capita income, but because they do not give data from all countries of our study, it is necessary to complement data from other sources and to estimate data in some cases.

In this study we focus on the situation in the most recent years and try to gather empirical data on all measures of global inequalities in human conditions from the period 2000–2002. Data on PPP GNI per capita 2002 for 192 countries are presented and documented in Appendix 2. According to this variable, human conditions are assumed to be the better, the higher the average per capita income.

We can check the contemporary relationship between national IQ and PPP GNI per capita income by historical data on this variable. Angus Maddison's *The World Economy: Historical Statistics* (2003) provides data on per capita GDP (1990 international Geary-Khamis dollars) since 1500 and some estimates since the year 1 (see also Maddison, 1995 and 2001). In this study, contemporary national IQs are correlated with historical data on per capita GDP in 1500, 1600, 1700, 1820, 1913, 1950, 1980, and 2000. Our data for single countries are based partly on Maddison's data for single countries and partly on estimations based on regional averages given in Maddison's book. In many cases, these data and estimations on per capita income cover the geographical areas of present states even before their independence.

2.2. Adult Literacy Rate

Global disparities in the level of education are extremely large and significant. It is obvious that in the modern world differences in education matter much more than during the past centuries when most people were without any formal education. Global inequalities in education have increased since the nineteenth century and may be still increasing. Literacy, which represents the basic level of education, varies significantly in the world, although the relative number of literates has risen in all countries and approaches 100 percent in most countries.

The adult literacy rate is the percentage of people ages 15 and above who can, with understanding, read and write a short, simple statement related to their everyday life (*Human Development Report*, 2002, p. 272). Statistical data on adult literacy are in most cases estimations, which may be based on censuses or school enrollment statistics. The published data on adult literacy certainly include errors. The most extensive statistical data on literacy are available from UNESCO's statistical yearbooks, UNDP's *Human Development Reports,* and the World Bank's *World Development Reports* and *World Development Indicators*. The statistical data used in this study (for 2002) are principally from *Human Development Report 2004*, and they are presented and documented in Appendix 2. Human conditions are assumed to be better in countries in which nearly all people are literate than in countries in which the level of adult literacy is lower.

Historical statistical data on literacy published in *FSDI216 Democratization and Power Resources 1850–2000* (online) make it possible to explore historical trends in the relationship between national IQ and literacy since the 1850s. Contemporary national IQs will be correlated with the adult literacy rate in 1868, 1908, 1948, and 1978.

2.3. Gross Tertiary Enrollment Ratio

Global inequalities in education are even wider at higher levels of education than in adult literacy. Therefore, it is plausible to take into account, in addition to the adult literacy rate, differences at the third level of education. UNESCO's statistical yearbooks and the UNESCO Institute for Statistics have provided data on the number of students at the tertiary level of education (see UNESCO, Statistical Yearbook 1999, Table II.S.1). Such data can be made comparable by calculating the number of students per 100,000 inhabitants (Vanhanen, 2003, pp. 81–82). The World Bank's *World Development Indicators* provide data on the gross enrollment ratio at the tertiary level of education. It is "the ratio of total enrollment, regardless of age, to the population of the age group that officially corresponds to the level of education shown" (WDI, 2004, p. 79). The measures of tertiary education indicate the relative size of the population receiving higher education needed in modern societies.

In this study, we use data on gross enrollment ratios to measure disparities in the extent of higher education. Tertiary education, whether or not leading to an advanced research qualification, normally requires, as a minimum condition of admission, the successful completion of education at the second level. It refers to education at such institutions as universities, teachers' colleges, and higher-level professional schools. However, definitions of tertiary education may differ considerably from country to country, which diminishes the comparability of data (see WDI, 2004, p. 79). Statistical data on the gross enrollment ratio are principally from *World Development Indicators*, 2004, Table 2.11, but because this source does not cover all countries, data have been complemented from other sources, including Unesco's *Statistical Yearbook 1999*, UNDP's *Human Development Report 2002*, and *The Europa World Year Book 2003*. Statistical data are given and documented in Appendix 2. According to this variable, the quality of human conditions is assumed to be the better, the higher the level of the tertiary enrollment ratio.

Historical statistical data on the number of students per 100,000 inhabitants published in *FSD1216 Democratization and Power Resources 1850-2000* (online) make it possible to explore historical trends in the relationship between national IQ and differences at the level of higher education since the 1850s, but such historical data do not cover all countries of this study. Contemporary national IQs will be correlated with the number of students per 100,000 inhabitants in 1868, 1908, 1948, and 1978.

2.4. Life Expectancy at Birth

Various indicators have been used to measure global disparities in health conditions, diseases, nutrition, prevalence of undernourishment, life expectancy, fertility, infant and maternal mortality, and several other health related human conditions (see WDI, 2004, pp. 88–111). The number of available indicators is large, but it seems to us that one indicator, life expectancy at birth, is enough for our purposes to measure global disparities in health and nutrition conditions. Data on this variable are available from nearly all countries of the world.

According to the definition of this indicator, "Life expectancy at birth is the number of years a newborn infant would live if prevailing patterns of mortality at the time of its birth were to stay the same throughout its life" (WDI, 2004, p. 111; Human Development Report, 2002, p. 266). The average life expectancy varies greatly in the world. In some countries, people can expect to live 80 years; in some other countries only 40 years. The disparity in life expectancy is enormous, and it affects many other aspects of human life. People who die young do not have time to achieve and experience as much in life as people who live longer. Differences in life expectancy reflect also inequalities in nutrition, infant mortality, health services, and in several other health related conditions of life. It is reasonable to argue that the higher the expectancy of life, the better human conditions are in a country. Statistical data on life expectancy in 2002 are principally from *Human Development Report 2004*. They are presented and documented in Appendix 2.

Historical statistical data on life expectancy published in the World Bank's *World Development Reports* make it possible to examine, in a limited group of countries, how the relationship between national income and differences in life expectancy has changed over time or remained more or less constant. Contemporary national IQs will be correlated with life expectancy in 1978. Unfortunately these data are not available from earlier periods.

2.5. The Level of Democratization

There are important global inequalities in human conditions not only in material but also in non-material aspects of life. People need not only to eat well and to live long but also to have freedoms in their life; especially economic and political freedoms to pursue their targets, to make choices, to express their opinions, and to participate freely in political decision-making in their society. Unfortunately it is much more difficult to measure the existence and extent of such freedoms than to measure various material aspects of human conditions. In this connection, we focus on measures of democracy because the level of democracy may reflect also the extent of other human freedoms.

The freedom of life has varied and still varies from slavery to extensive civil liberties and political freedoms. Governmental systems vary from despotic autocracies to highly democratic systems. In despotic autocracies people are without any significant political rights and civil liberties and completely dependent on their rulers, whereas in fully developed modern democracies all people and their groups are allowed to compete for the highest political power positions and to select by voting the persons who are entitled to use the highest legislative and executive powers.

The degree of democracy certainly matters and may affect the level of inequalities in other spheres of social life. It is reasonable to assume that when political power is shared by the many, attempts will be made to reduce economic and social inequalities and to further the interests of the many, whereas in despotic autocracies the rulers will primarily further their own and their supporters' interests and discriminate against the interests of the majority of the population. Therefore we shall use indicators of democracy to illustrate and measure global inequalities in political conditions. It is reasonable to argue that the higher the level of democratization, the higher the quality of human conditions in a society.

There are alternative measures of political freedoms and democracy. Freedom House has published since 1977 annual surveys of political rights and civil liberties. Their survey covers all countries of the world (see Freedom House, 2004). The Polity project's democracy and autocracy scales measure democracy since 1800 (see Gurr and Jaggers, 1999). Tatu Vanhanen's Index of Democratization (ID) is a composite index measuring the degree of competition in elections and the level of electoral participation. Statistical data on these measures of democracy cover nearly all countries of the world and extend to the year 1810 (see FSD1289 Measures of Democracy 1810–2002; The Polyarchy Dataset. Vanhanen's Index of Democracy, 2003; Vanhanen, 2003). We shall use in this study Vanhanen's Index of Democratization (ID) to measure global disparities in the extent of democracy and political freedoms. Data on the Index of Democratization and on its two components for 2002 are given and documented in Appendix 3.

Because data on ID extend to the year 1810, it would be possible to explore the relationship between contemporary national IQ and the measures of democracy, in a smaller group of countries, since 1810. In this study, national IQs will be correlated with the Index of Democratization (ID) in 1868, 1908, 1948, and 1978.

3. The Composite Index of the Quality of Human Conditions (QHC)

The five variables defined above can be used separately to measure different dimensions of global disparities in human conditions, but we think that by combining the five variables into a composite index we can get a single measure that indicates relative differences between countries in the quality of some material and non-material human conditions. Then we can see to what extent national IQ is able to explain global variation in average human conditions at the level of nations.

The review of measures used in previous studies indicates that there are several composite indices that are intended to measure disparities in human conditions from different perspectives. The list of such indices includes at least the Human Development Index (HDI), the Human Poverty Index (HPI), the Gender-related development index (GDI), the Gender empowerment measure (GEM), the Index of Economic Well-Being (IEWB), the Physical Quality of Life Index (QOL), and the World Health Organization's Quality of Life indicators. The number of single indicators used in those indices and other measures of economic development, human development, poverty, standard of living, quality of life, and human well-being is large. The variables selected for our study are partly the same as those used in some earlier studies and indices, but our group of indicators differs significantly from the composition of all previous indices, especially for the reason that we use also a measure of democracy to indicate differences in the quality of human conditions.

The five variables are combined into an Index of the Quality of Human Conditions (QHC) in such a way that each single variable has the same weight in the composite index because we do not have any theoretical grounds to weight them differently. For this purpose, it is necessary to standardize the variables into a scale that extends in principle from 0 to 100. Adult literacy rate variable and Gross tertiary enrollment ratio variables are already in such a scale. The values of Adult literacy rate extend from Niger's 17 percent to 99 percent in many countries (99 is the upper limit for this variable). The values of Gross tertiary enrollment ratios vary from zero (Guinea-Bissau) to 85 (Finland).

The original values of PPP GNI per capita in 2002 are given in US dollars. These data on per capita income vary from $500 in Sierra Leone and Somalia to $53,230 in Luxembourg. These data could be standardized to a scale from 0 to 100 by calculating the percentage of per capita income for each country from Luxembourg's $53,230, but because the use of Luxembourg's exceptionally high per capita income as the upper limit (100%) would decrease the variation among other countries significantly, it is reasonable to lower the upper limit of 100% to $35,000. Consequently, the standardized value of PPP GNI variable will be the ratio of a country's per capita income to $35,000. For the countries for which PPP GNI per capita is higher than $35,000 (Bermuda, Luxembourg, Norway, and the United States), the standardized value is 100%. The standardized values of PPP GNI per capita vary from Sierra Leone's and Somalia's 1.4 percent to 100 percent.

It is necessary to standardize the life expectancy at birth (LE) variable, because the original values of this variable do not vary more than from 32.7 (Zambia) to 83.5 (Andorra). The original values are standardized into a scale from zero to 100 first by subtracting 30 years from the original value and then by multiplying the remainder by 2. However, 100 will be used as the upper limit for this variable. The standardized values of LE vary from 5.4 (Zambia) to 100 (Andorra, Japan, and Sweden).

The original values of the Index of Democratization (ID) in 2002 vary from zero (several countries) to 44.2 (Denmark). The values of ID can be standardized to a scale from 0 to 100 by multiplying the original values by 2. After standardization, the values of ID in 2002 vary from zero to 88.4. Now the problem is how to combine the standardized values of the five dependent variables into the composite Index of the

Quality of Human Conditions. All variables are constructed in such a way that the higher the value of a variable, the better human conditions are assumed to be. According to our value judgements, average conditions for human life are better in a rich than in a poor country; human conditions are better in a country in which the adult literacy rate is high than in a country in which it is low; human conditions are better in a country in which the relative number of highly educated people is high than in a country in which it is low; it is better to live a long life than to die young; and democracy provides a better framework for human life than autocratic systems. We also assume that all human beings strive for a good life and use their intelligence to achieve this target by improving their material and non-material living conditions. Therefore, it is reasonable to hypothesize that there should be a positive correlation between national IQ and the five measures of the quality of human conditions and that this relationship should be approximately linear. The same hypothesis concerns the relationship between national IQ and the composite Index of the Quality of Human Conditions.

Because the five variables are assumed to measure equally important dimensions of human conditions and because their values have been standardized to approximately the same scale from zero to 100, they can be combined into an index by calculating their arithmetic mean. In principle, the index values could vary from zero to 100, but because the values of all variables are not equally high or low in all countries, the index values may vary somewhat less than the values of single variables. In fact, the index values vary from 10.7 (Burkina Faso) to 89.0 (Norway). The Index of the Quality of Human Conditions (QHC) will be used as the principal operational measure for the theoretical concept of the "inequalities in human conditions."

4. Alternative Measures of Human Conditions

The hypothesis will be tested principally by empirical data on the five indicators of human conditions and their combined index defined in the previous section, but because we assume that disparities in many aspects of human conditions are causally related to national IQ, we complement our analysis by taking into account some alternative indicators of human conditions. The data on the five basic variables are used for all 192 countries of this study, but in the case of additional indicators, testing will be limited to the number of countries on which data for a dependent variable are available from the original source. Consequently, the number of countries will vary from case to case.

The potential number of variables that could be used to measure disparities in human conditions from different perspectives is large. We cannot take into account all possible variables, and it is not necessary for the purposes of this study. A relatively small sample of alternative variables is enough to test our theory that the relationship between national IQ and differences in the quality of human conditions does not need to be limited to the dimensions of human conditions taken into account in the five components of QHC. The group of alternative variables is intended to measure differences in human conditions from various perspectives. Our hypothesis is that national IQs will be positively correlated with these additional variables as far as they indicate differences in the quality of human conditions caused by human decisions and efforts.

Data on each of the alternative variables are taken only from one original source, although similar data might be available from some other sources, too. The use of only one source makes it relatively easy for interested readers to check our data, although data are not presented in this book. In the following, we introduce and describe the selected sample of alternative measures of human conditions that will be used to test the hypothesis.

4.1. Human Development Index (HDI)

UNDP's Human Development Index (HDI) is the best known and most extensively used measure of human conditions. Three of its components, life expectancy at birth, the adult literacy rate, and GDP per capita (PPP US$), are in principle the same variables as in our QHC index. The two indices differ from each other in two other points. The combined gross enrollment ratio for primary, secondary, and tertiary schools used in HDI is not the same as the gross tertiary enrollment ratio used in our QHC (see Human Development Report, 2004, p. 137–138). Besides, our QHC includes a measure of democracy (ID). Because of some common components, the two indices can be assumed to be highly correlated. Data on HDI for 2002 are from *Human Development Report 2004*, Table 1. They cover 176 countries of this study and vary from 273 (Sierra Leone) to 956 (Norway).

4.2. Gender-related Human Development Index (GDI)

UNDP's Gender-related development index (GDI) is a composite index intended to reflect the inequalities between men and women in the components of HDI. The higher the index value, the smaller the gender inequalities measured by this index (see Human Development Report, 2004, pp. 261–262, 270–271). It is reasonable to argue that the quality of human conditions is higher in a country in which gender inequalities are small than in a country in which they are large. Data on GDI for 2002 are from *Human Development Report 2004*, Table 24. They cover 144 countries of this study and vary from 278 (Niger) to 955 (Norway).

4.3. Economic Growth Rate (EGR)

Long-term differences in economic growth rates over decades and centuries have produced the present disparities in per capita income. Economic growth has improved human conditions from the perspective of economic well-being. Therefore, it is reasonable to argue that a high growth rate implies that economic conditions are improving and a low growth rate that they are stagnating or deteriorating. A major goal of poor countries is economic development through economic growth, because it is assumed that economic growth will diminish poverty and improve human conditions. Michael P. Todaro (2000, p. 114) notes that "Third World development programs are often assessed by the degree to which their national outputs and incomes are growing." The question is to what extent contemporary growth rates are related to national IQ. We test our hypothesis by four datasets on economic growth rates.

The World Bank and UNDP (the United Nations Development Program) publish statistical data on economic growth rates. We use in this study data on gross domestic product (GDP) average annual percentage growth in the period 1990-2002 (WDI, 2004, Table 4.1). The growth rates (EGR 1) given in this source are average annual compound growth rates. These data cover 145 countries of this study and they vary from -7.1 (Ukraine) to 9.7 (China). Similar and different data on growth rates have been published in *World Development Reports* and in *Human Development Reports*.

Two other datasets on economic growth rates are derived from Maddison's (2003) data on per capita GDP (1990 International Geary-Khamis dollars) over the period 1950-2001. His data are available on

134 countries of this study. The average annual growth rate of the period 1950–2001 (EGR 2) is calculated by subtracting from the per capita income in 2001 the per capita income in 1950. Next it is calculated how many percentage points the remainder is from the per capita income in 1950. Finally, the percentage is divided by the number of years (52). For example, in the case of Argentina, per capita GDP was $4,987 in 1950 and $8,137 in 2001. The difference is $3,150. It is 63.16 percent of the per capita income in 1950. When it is divided by the number of years (52), we get the average annual growth rate (1.21%). The average annual growth in dollars over the period 1950–2001 (EGR 3) is calculated by dividing the difference between per capita income in 2001 and 1950 by the number of years (52). For example, in the case of Argentina, we get 60.6 dollars by dividing the difference between 1950 and 2001 ($3,150) by 52. It indicates the average absolute growth in per capita income over the period 1950-2001.

The fourth dataset (EGR 4) is derived from Maddison's (2003) data on per capita GDP over the period 1500–2000. Maddison's data for 1500 cover 23 countries and averages for several regional groups of countries. We increased the sample to 109 countries by using respective regional averages in 86 cases. The average annual growth rate in dollars over the period 1500-2000 is calculated by dividing the difference between per capita income in 2000 and 1500 by the number of years (500). Because the 109 countries of this sample are not indicated in Maddison (2003), we list the countries and give the estimated data on per capita GDP for 1500 as well as Maddison's data for 2000 in Appendix 5.

4.4. Gini Index of Inequality in Income or Consumption (Gini and Gini-WIID)

PPP GNI per capita does not provide information about global disparities in income distribution within nations, because the degree of income distribution within countries is not the same in all countries and not even in the countries at the same level of per capita income. It can be argued that the quality of human conditions is the better, the lower the level of inequality in income distribution.

According to *World Development Indicators* (2002, p. 77), inequality "in the distribution of income is reflected in the percentage shares of either income or consumption accruing to segments of the population ranked by income or consumption levels." Most data on personal or household income or consumption are based on nationally representative household surveys. However, it should be noted that because the underlying household surveys differ in method and in the type of data collected, the distribution indicators are not strictly comparable across countries, and the reliability of data is not high. The sources of non-comparability include differences in surveys (whether they use income or consumption expenditure as the living standard indicator), differences in the definition of income or consumption, differences in the size of households (number of members), and also differences in the extent of income sharing among household members. Besides, there are differences in the years when surveys were made (see also Todaro, 2000, pp. 153–165; Bhalla, 2002, pp. 213–216).

The Gini index provides a summary measure of the degree of inequality. It measures the extent to which the distribution of income "among individuals or households within an economy deviates from a perfectly equal distribution." A Gini index of zero represents perfect equality, while an index of 100 implies perfect inequality. We use two alternative datasets on Gini index in his study: from *World Development Indicators 2004*, Table 2.7 (GINI) and from the UNU/WIDER (United Nations University/World Institute for Development Economics Research) (Gini-WIID) The data from WDI 2004 cover 127 countries of this study. The UNU/WIDER (2004) has collected from different sources a very extensive dataset on income inequality. Their data cover 146 countries of this study. Similar data are available also from Human Development Reports.

4.5. Poverty

Poverty represents one of the most extensively discussed aspects of global inequalities. There are numerous studies on world poverty (see, for example, Allen and Thomas, 2000; Sumner, 2003; Stewart, 2003; Seligson and Passé-Smith, 2003). Researchers have described and measured the variation of poverty in the world, presented various theoretical explanations for poverty, and discussed the means to mitigate or eliminate poverty. Attention in theoretical explanations has nearly always been limited to contemporary or historical social factors and cultural differences, but sometimes explanations have been sought also from geographical factors. The World Bank's *World Development Reports* and UNDP's *Human Development Reports* are principally concerned with the problem of global poverty and with the means to mitigate poverty. Various measures of per capita income and measures of poverty lines have been used to describe the global variation in poverty. The problems of poverty and economic inequalities are quite often discussed in the connection of economic development (see, for example, Fields, 1980; Clague, 1997; Nafziger, 1997; Seligson and Passé-Smith, 1998 and 2003; Barro, 1999; Siebert, 1999; Roberts and Hite, 2000; Todaro, 2000; Bhalla, 2002). Some studies are exclusively focused on the problem of poverty (see, for example, Kothari, 1993; Allen and Thomas, 2000). Andrew M. Kamarck (1976) and Jared Diamond (1998) have sought explanations for economic development and poverty from geographical factors.

The first Millennium Development Goal calls for cutting in half the proportion of people living in extreme poverty, by which is meant those who live on less than $1 a day ($1.08 in 1993 purchasing power parity terms) (WDI, 2004, p. 2). There are different measures of poverty. In this study we limit our attention to statistical data on the percentage of people below the $2 a day international poverty line. It is reasonable to argue that the quality of human conditions tends to be better in countries in which the percentage of people below this poverty line is low than in countries in which it is high. Our statistical data on population below the $2 a day international poverty line are from *World Development Indicators 2004*, Table 2.5. They cover 96 countries of this study and vary from less than 2 percent (several countries) to 90.8 (Nigeria). Data on this variable are not available from economically highly developed countries and from many poor countries.

4.6. Measures of Undernourishment (PUN 1 and PUN 2)

One of the Millennium Development Goals is to reduce hunger and malnutrition to half of its 1990 levels by 2015. *World Development Indicators 2004* (p. 4) argues that the "world produces enough food to feed everyone, but hunger remains a persistent problem." The root cause of hunger is said to be poverty. Certainly poverty and hunger are highly correlated. Both of them are indicators of a low quality of human conditions. We want to see how strongly they are related to national IQ.

We use two variables to measure the prevalence of undernourishment: (1) percentage of undernourished population in 1999-2001 (PUN 1) and

(2) percentage of underweight children under age five in 1999–2002 (PUN 2). The category of undernourished population includes people whose food intake is chronically insufficient to meet their minimum energy requirements. The category of underweight children under five refers to children whose weight for age is more than two standard deviations below the median for the international reference population ages 0-59 months (WDI, 2004, p. 103; Human Development Report, 2004, p. 275). Our data on these two variables are from *World Development Indicators 2004*, Table 2.17. Data on the percentage of undernourished population cover 124 countries of this study and vary from 3% (several countries) to 75% (Democratic Republic of Congo). Data on underweight children cover 101 countries. Similar data on undernourishment are available also from *Human Development Reports*.

4.7. Maternal Mortality Ratio (MMR) and Infant Mortality Rate (IMR)

The quality of human conditions from the perspective of health varies greatly in the world. The Millennium Development Goals calls for reducing child mortality, improving the health of mothers, and combating HIV/AIDS, malaria, and other diseases (WDI, 2004, pp. 7–9). It is justified to assume that the quality of human conditions is better in countries in which people are relatively healthy than in countries in which child mortality is high, the health of mothers is poor, and people are threatened by various serious diseases. In this study, we use data on the maternal mortality ratio and the infant mortality rate to measure disparities in health conditions. According to WDI (2004, pp. 99, 111), the maternal mortality ratio is the number of women who die from pregnancy-related causes during pregnancy and childbirth, per 100,000 live births, and the infant mortality rate is the number of infants dying before reaching age five.

Statistical data on the estimated maternal mortality ratio per 100,000 live births (MMR) are from *World Development Indicators* 2004, Table 2.16. Similar data are published also in *Human Development Reports*. Data on infant mortality rates per 1,000 live births in 2002 (IMR) are from WDI, 2004 (Table 2.19). Data on both variables include 149 countries of this study.

4.8. Corruption Perceptions Index (CPI)

One difference between countries in the quality of human conditions concerns the extent of corruption. It can be argued that the quality of human conditions is better in a country in which the level of corruption is low than in a country in which it is high. The Transparency International Corruption Perceptions Index provides an overview of the state of corruption around the world. Corruption can take place in many fields of social and political life. It is noted in the "Executive summary" of the *Global Corruption Report 2004* (Online) that political "corruption is the abuse of entrusted power by political leaders for private gains." Such gains can be high. For example, "Mohammad Suharto of Indonesia allegedly embezzled up to US $35 billion in a country with a GDP of less than US $700 per capita." Corruption in political finance ranges from vote buying and the use of illicit funds to the sale of appointments and the abuse of state resources. Corruption "may deter foreign investors because it is often associated with a lack of secure property rights as well as bureaucratic red tape and mismanagement." Besides, when "individuals and families have to pay bribes to access food, housing, property, education, jobs, and the right to participate in the cultural life of a community, basic human rights are clearly violated" (Transparency International Corruption Perceptions Index, 2004). George B.N. Ayittey (1999, p. 197) complains that in many African countries today, there is no rule of law: "Public property is brazenly stolen. This culture of bribery and corruption costs Africa dearly" (see also Collier and Gunning, 1999).

We use the Transparency International Corruption Perceptions Index 2003 to illustrate disparities between countries in the extent of corruption. The index scores vary from 1.3 (Bangladesh) to 9.7 (Finland). The higher the index score is, the less corruption there is in the country. Data on this variable cover 132 countries of this study (Transparency International Corruption Perceptions Index 2003, www.transparency.org/cpi/2003/).

4.9. Economic Freedom Ratings (EFR)

Economic freedom constitutes one dimension of the quality of human conditions. It can be argued that a high level of economic freedom in a country provides a better framework for human life than a low level of economic freedom. The Fraser Institute has developed the Economic Freedom of the World index, which ranks countries according to the extent of economic freedom. According to their definition, individuals "have economic freedom when: (a) their property acquired without the use of force, fraud, or theft is protected from physical invasions by others and (b) they are free to use, exchange, or give their property to another as long as their actions do not violate the identical rights of others" (Gwartney and Lawson, 2000, p. 5). Further, economic freedom requires governments to refrain from actions "that interfere with personal choice, voluntary exchange, and the freedom to enter and compete in labor and product markets" (Gwartney and Lawson, 2004, p. 5).

We use the Fraser Institute's economic freedom ratings for 2002. Data are from *Economic Freedom of the World: 2004 Annual Report* (www.freetheworld.com/). In these data, the higher the score, the higher the level of economic freedom. The summary economic freedom ratings cover 123 countries of this study, and the scores vary from 2.5 (Myanmar) to 8.7 (Hong Kong).

4.10. The Index of Economic Freedom (IEF)

The Heritage Foundation and *The Wall Street Journal* have established another index of economic freedom. They are trying to measure the degree of economic freedom in a vast array of countries around the globe. The Index of Economic Freedom is based on ten components of economic freedom. We use their overall scores for 2003. They vary from 1.45 (Hong Kong) to 5.0 (North Korea). The lower the score, the higher the level of economic freedom. Data cover 156 countries of this study (source: www.heritage.org/research/features/index/).

4.11. Population Pyramids (MU-index)

Leonid Andreev and Michael Andreev (2004) have developed the MU (Monaco-Uganda) index based on the population pyramids of 220 countries. The MU index "reflects the degree of uniformity of a population pyramid in comparison to an ideally uniform pyramid pattern where all age groups are represented by equal percentage of the total population." Monaco has a pyramid closest to that model, whereas Uganda has the most dissimilar population pyramid. The population pyramids of all other countries are between those of Monaco and Uganda, which are the extreme opposites. The MU index summarizes some differences in demographic characteristics, which seem to reflect various differences in social conditions. They found that the MU index is correlated with such demographic characteristics as fertility, birth rate, death rate, nation's average IQ, and GDP per capita (Andreev and Andreev, 2004).

The data on the MU index given in their article cover 162 countries of this study. The values of the MU index vary from 0 (Uganda) to 88.7 (Italy). It can be assumed that the quality of human conditions tends to be the higher, the higher the value of the MU index. Consequently, the MU index should be positively correlated with national IQ.

4.12. Human Happiness and Life-satisfaction

The fact that humans are adapted to live in quite different geographical and climatic conditions raises the question of whether people are able to enjoy life and find happiness in the greatly varying circumstances and conditions of life which have been used to measure differences in the quality of human conditions. Is human happiness related to national IQ and our measures of global inequalities in human conditions, or is human happiness more or less independent from human diversity and global inequalities? This is an important question. Ruut Veenhoven (2004) notes that most "people agree that it is better to enjoy life than to suffer, and endorse public policies that aim at creating greater happiness for a greater number of people." He continues that the "aim of creating greater happiness for a greater number requires understanding of happiness." According to his definition, happiness refers to the degree to which an individual judges the overall quality of life-as-a-whole positively. In other words, how well one likes the life one lives. We should grasp the main determinants of happiness and understand not only what makes people happy, but also the reason why. We think that if human happiness is only slightly related to human diversity and global inequalities, there would be better and more realistic opportunities to provide satisfactory life conditions for most people of the world than is the case if human happiness is strongly related to differences in national IQs and measures of global inequalities. In other words, we want to explore whether national IQ is related to human happiness.

The *World Database of Happiness* (2004) established by Ruut Veenhoven and his staff makes it possible to explore these questions and to find out to what extent human happiness and life-satisfaction are related to the variables used in our study. Veenhoven's database brings together findings that are scattered throughout thousands of studies and provides a basis for systematic studies. Empirical data on happiness given in the database are based on survey studies and also on unpublished studies. They present responses to 19 different questions about happiness in nations. In his tables, responses are standardized into national averages, which make possible cross-national comparisons. Unfortunately Veenhoven's database does not cover all countries of our study, and the same questions have not been presented in all countries. The database includes data on some questions from more than 120 nations, but only on two questions are data available from more than 60 nations. We limit our attention to these two questions that measure happiness and life-satisfaction respectively.

The first question (111B) is: Taking all things together, would you say, you are—very happy—quite happy—not very happy—not at all happy. The results are coded in such a way that "very happy" gets 4 points and "not at all happy" 1 point. In the database, results are given by nation on the original range from 4 to 1 and on the standardized range from 10 to 0. Results are given separately for each survey study, but the national averages of all surveys have also been calculated. The number of national surveys concerning this question vary from 1 to 11. The national averages on the original range from 4 to 1 vary from Bulgaria's 2.44 to Venezuela's 3.48. These data are from 66 nations of this study.

The second question (122C) is: All things considered, how satisfied are you with your life as a whole now? 10 satisfied—1 dissatisfied. In these tables, national averages of responses are calculated in the same way as in the case of the first question separately on the original range from 10 to 1 and on the standardized range from 10 to 0. The number of national surveys varies from one to 17, and the national averages vary from Moldova's 3.72 to Colombia's 8.32. These data are from 62 nations. It is interesting to see how strongly these measures of happiness and life-satisfaction are related to our measures of human conditions and national IQ.

5. Summary

The variables introduced and defined in this chapter are intended to measure the quality of human conditions from different perspectives. They are operationally defined measures of the hypothetical concept of "the quality of human conditions." Data on them make it possible to test the research hypothesis by empirical evidence in the next three chapters. In Chapter 6, the research hypothesis is tested by using the five components of QHC as the dependent variables. In Chapter 7, the hypothesis is tested by using the QHC index as the dependent variable. QHC is our principal measure of the quality of human conditions. Finally, in Chapter 8, the hypothesis is tested by using the 12 alternative measures of human conditions as the dependent variables.

National IQ and Five Dimensions of Global Inequalities

The operational definitions of national IQ, which will be used as the explanatory variable, and five measures of global inequalities and their composite index presented in Chapter 5, make it possible to test by empirical evidence the central hypothesis, according to which inequalities in human conditions are causally related to the average level of mental abilities of a nation. Because the hypothetical concepts "the quality of human conditions" and "the average level of mental abilities of a nation" are now operationalized, the original hypothesis can be transformed into a research hypothesis:

The five measures of the quality of human conditions and their composite index (QHC) are positively correlated with national IQ.

In this chapter, we begin the empirical analysis by exploring the relationship between national IQ and each of the five single measures of the global disparities in human conditions. All correlations are expected to be clearly positive because human conditions are assumed to be the better, the higher the value of each indicator. The five variables are intended to measure the quality of human conditions from different perspectives. Thus, each of them measures a different dimension of human conditions, but because all dimensions are assumed to be causally related to national IQ, all variables should be positively correlated with each other, although correlations do not need to be high. In fact, intercorrelations should not be very high because each indicator is intended to measure to some extent a different dimension of human conditions.

1. Intercorrelations of Five Basic Variables and National IQ

The intercorrelations of the five measures of human conditions and national IQ are calculated separately in the group of 113 countries for which we have direct evidence of national IQ, in the group of 79 countries for which national IQs are estimated, and in the total group of 192 countries. In this analysis, we shall focus on the results in the total group of 192 countries. The intercorrelations of these variables in the three groups of countries are presented in Table 6.1.

Table 6.1. Intercorrelations of the five measures of the quality of human conditions and national IQ in the groups of 113, 79, and 192 countries

	PPP GNI per capita	Adult literacy	Tertiary enrollment	Life expectancy	ID-2002	National IQ
Group of 113 countries						
PPP GNI per capita 2002	1.000	0.584	0.769	0.652	0.623	0.684
Adult literacy rate 2002		1.000	0.651	0.710	0.552	0.642
Tertiary enrollment ratio			1.000	0.691	0.696	0.746
Life expectancy (LE) 2002				1.000	0.547	0.773

	PPP GNI per capita	Adult literacy	Tertiary enrollment	Life expectancy	ID-2002	National IQ
Index of Democratization (ID) 2002					1.000	0.568
National IQ						1.000
Group of 79 countries						
PPP GNI per capita 2002	1.000	0.382	0.293	0.491	0.281	0.338
Adult literacy rate 2002		1.000	0.606	0.665	0.405	0.655
Tertiary enrollment ratio			1.000	0.562	0.363	0.699
Life expectancy (LE) 2002				1.000	0.415	0.691
Index of Democratization (ID) 2002					1.000	0.322
National IQ						1.000
Group of 192 countries						
PPP GNI per capita 2002	1.000	0.511	0.680	0.616	0.574	0.601
Adult literacy rate 2002		1.000	0.627	0.700	0.511	0.655
Tertiary enrollment ratio			1.000	0.663	0.657	0.745
Life expectancy (LE) 2002				1.000	0.536	0.754
Index of Democratization (ID) 2002					1.000	0.529
National IQ						1.000

The fact that all intercorrelations of the five measures of human conditions are clearly positive indicates that they are partly overlapping, but only partly overlapping because the co-variation is in most cases less than 50 percent. All the correlations are substantially significant at the 1 percent level of confidence. Because the five variables differ significantly from each other, it is worthwhile to examine separately how each of them is related to national IQ.

Table 6.1 shows that all correlations between national IQ and the five dependent variables are moderately positive. All correlations in the groups of 113 and 192 countries are clearly stronger than in the group of 79 countries, which implies that estimated national IQs have not been biased to support the hypothesis. There are differences in the strength of correlations. Life expectancy and the tertiary enrollment ratio are in all three groups more strongly correlated with national IQ than the three other variables. The explained part of variation varies from 32 (ID) to 60 (LE) percent in the group of 113 countries, from 10 to 49 percent in the group of 79 countries, and from 28 to 57 percent in the total group of 192 countries. These correlations support the research hypothesis and show that several dimensions of human conditions are moderately or strongly related to national IQ.

Table 6.2. Intercorrelations of the five measures of the quality of human conditions and national IQ in the group of 160 countries whose population was more than 500,000 inhabitants in 2000

	PPP GNI per capita	Adult literacy	Tertiary enrollment	Life expectancy	ID-2002	National IQ
Group of 160 countries						
PPP GNI per capita 2002	1.000	0.533	0.730	0.645	0.645	0.642
Adult literacy rate 2002		1.000	0.683	0.714	0.555	0.734
Tertiary enrollment ratio			1.000	0.718	0.706	0.780
Life expectancy (LE) 2002				1.000	0.549	0.822
Index of Democratization (ID) 2002					1.000	0.584
National IQ						1.000

When the smallest countries, whose population was less than 500,000 inhabitants in 2000, are excluded from the group, most correlations rise to some extent in the remaining group of 160 countries (Table 6.2). For some reason, the relationship between national IQ and the measures of human conditions seems to be weaker in the group of small countries than in the total group of 192 countries. It may be that our data on national IQ and on the measures of human conditions are less reliable for small countries than for countries with larger populations.

2. Per Capita Income

The results of our previous study *IQ and the Wealth of Nations* (2002) show that national IQ explains a significant part of the global variation in the level of economic development measured by per capita income and that it has explained it at least since 1820. In the group of 81 countries for which we had direct evidence of national IQs, Pearson correlations between national IQ and various measures of per capita income vary from 0.257 to 0.763 and Spearman rank-order correlations from 0.371 to 0.859 over the period 1820–1998. For 1998 Pearson correlations vary from 0.664 to 0.775 and Spearman rank correlations from 0.816 to 0.839 (Lynn and Vanhanen, 2002, pp. 88–91). In the total group of 185 countries, Pearson correlations vary from 0.273 to 0.730 and Spearman rank correlations from 0.493 to 0.794 over the period 1820–1998. For 1998 Pearson correlations vary from 0.567 to 0.696 and Spearman rank correlations from 0.636 to 0.713 (Lynn and Vanhanen, 2002, pp. 110–112).

The correlations between national IQ and PPP GNI per capita 2002 (Table 6.1) are approximately as strong in the groups of 113 and 192 countries as the abovementioned Pearson correlations for 1998 in the groups of 81 and 185 countries. Spearman rank correlations are somewhat higher than Pearson correlations, 0.768 and 0.633 respectively. In this analysis, we focus on the relationship between national IQ and PPP GNI per capita in the total group of 192 countries. The results of regression analysis, in which national IQ is used as the independent variable and PPP GNI per capita 2002 as the dependent variable, illustrate the dependence of per capita income on national IQ at the level of single countries (Figure 6.1). Residuals of this regression analysis for single countries are given in Appendix 4.

Figure 6.1 shows that the relationship between national IQ and PPP GNI per capita is slightly non-linear. This means that a non-linear model could predict the values of PPP GNI per capita from their national IQs more accurately than the linear model of Figure 6.1. Michael A. McDaniel and Deborah L. Whetzel (2004) and Richard E. Dickerson

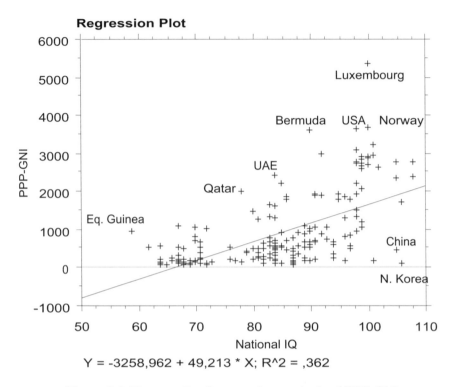

Figure 6.1. The results of regression analysis of PPP GNI per capita 2002 on national IQ in a group of 192 countries

(2004) have observed on the data of our book *IQ and the Wealth of Nations* that non-linear relationships between national IQ and our measures of GDP per capita are significantly stronger than linear relationships. Dickerson's calculations show that, when an exponential correlation is used, the explained part of variation in Real GDP per capita 1998 rises by ten percentage points (from 38 to 48 percent) in the group of 185 countries

We have used exponential and polynomial regressions to measure how much better a non-linear model is able to explain the variation in per capita income. The explained part of variation rises from 36 to 40 percent in the exponential regression in the group of 192 countries and from 47 to 55 percent in the group of 113 countries. In the polynomial regression of PPP GNI per capita on national IQ, the explained part of variation rises from 36 to 43 percent in the group of 192 countries and

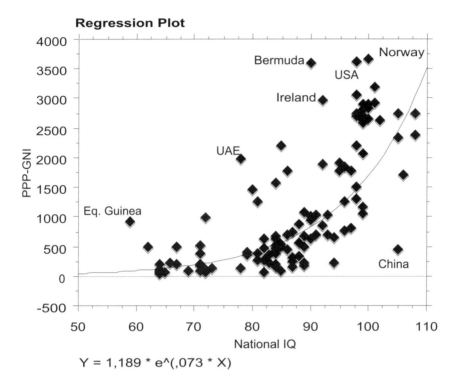

Regression Plot

Y = 1,189 * e^(,073 * X)

Figure 6.2. The results of exponential regression analysis of PPP GNI per capita 2002 on national IQ in a group of 113 countries

from 47 to 55 percent in the group of 113 countries. The significant difference in the strength of correlations between the two samples of countries is partly due to the fact that several highly deviating countries, including the most extremely deviating North Korea, Luxembourg, and Mongolia, are not in the group of 113 countries. Figure 6.2 summarizes the results of the exponential regression in the group of 113 countries. It illustrates the curvilinearity of the relationship between per capita income and national IQ. When national IQ rises above the level of 80–90, per capita income starts to rise more steeply than the linear regression line, but the rise has not until now covered all the countries with national IQ of 90 or higher. It seems to us probable that the scientific and technological revolution or renaissance that began in Europe in the Middle Ages has been behind the emergence of the curvilinear pattern since 1500.

The actual relationship between national IQ and per capita income is slightly curvilinear, but because our hypothesis is linear, we analyze the results on the basis of the linear regression model of Figure 6.1 by assuming that some particular factors have caused the deviations from the linear regression line. Figure 6.1 shows that the relationship between national IQ and per capita income is much stronger at the lowest level of national IQ (below 75) than at the highest level (90 and above). It is obvious that the significance of other factors increases sharply at higher levels of national IQ. We can make assumptions on the nature of those other factors by examining the most deviating countries, but how to define "the most deviating countries"? One standard deviation of residuals provides a suitable criterion to separate the most deviating countries from the less deviating ones. In this case one standard deviation is $7,706. We use this criterion to separate the most deviating countries from the countries that are closer to the regression line.

The group of countries with large positive residuals ($7,706 or higher) includes 30 countries (see Appendix 4): Antigua and Barbuda, Australia, Austria, Bahrain, Barbados, Belgium, Bermuda, Canada, Denmark, Equatorial Guinea, Finland, France, Germany, Iceland, Ireland, Italy, Japan, Kuwait, Luxembourg, the Netherlands, New Caledonia, Norway, Qatar, Saint Kitts and Nevis, the Seychelles, Sweden, Switzerland, the United Arab Emirates, the United Kingdom, and the United States. Positive residuals are larger than two standard deviations only for Bermuda, Ireland, Luxembourg, Norway, and the United States.

Of these 30 countries, 19 are industrially highly developed market economies and democracies for which national IQs are high (90 or above). Bahrain, Equatorial Guinea, Kuwait, Qatar, and the United Arab Emirates are oil-producing countries; Antigua and Barbuda, Barbados, Bermuda, Saint Kitts, and the Seychelles are principally tourist countries. New Caledonia is also partly a tourist country; besides, Europeans constitute nearly 40 percent of its population. These observations imply that technological innovations have helped Western market economies to raise their per capita income considerably higher than expected on the basis of national IQ and that Western technologies and investments have raised per capita income in oil-producing and tourist countries.

The group of countries with large negative residuals (-$7,706 or higher) includes 23 countries: Afghanistan, Armenia, Belarus, Bolivia,

Cambodia, China, Georgia, Iraq, Kazakhstan, Kiribati, North Korea, Kyrgyzstan, Laos, Moldova, Mongolia, Myanmar, Serbia and Montenegro, Tajikistan, Timor-Leste, Ukraine, Uzbekistan, Vietnam, and Yemen. All negative residuals are smaller than two standard deviations.

It is remarkable that 16 of these 23 countries are contemporary or former socialist countries. It is obvious that socialist economic and political systems have hampered economic development in these countries. Most of them rejected socialism in the beginning of the 1990s and have attempted to transform their economic systems into market economies, but these reforms are still unfinished as well as the democratization of their political systems. However, it is reasonable to predict that, as a consequence of economic and political reforms, per capita income will increase significantly in these countries. Civil wars in Afghanistan, Iraq, Myanmar, and Timor-Leste have hampered economic development in these four countries, probably also in Bolivia. Kiribati is a geographically isolated small island state, and Yemen is an Arab country in which oil production started in the 1990s.

According to our hypothesis, the relationship between national IQ and per capita income is expected to be linear in such a way that per capita income increases with national IQs. Figure 6.1 indicates that the real relationship is slightly curvilinear. At the middle level of national IQ, per capita income increases less than the linear regression line presupposes, and at the highest level of national IQ per capita income tends to increase much more than the linear regression line presupposes. Figure 6.2 illustrates the curvilinearity of the relationship. Despite this discrepancy, we keep our hypothesis linear because the same hypothesis is applied to all measures of the quality of human conditions.

Figure 6.1 implies that the enormous gap between rich and poor countries is in most cases principally due to differences in average mental abilities of nations as measured by national IQ, although other factors, especially at the middle and higher levels of national IQ, are also important. The gap between rich and poor countries seems to have existed at least since 1500, although the size of the gap was much smaller in earlier periods when educational and technological differences between civilizations were much smaller than today. The statistical data on the history of the world economy collected by Angus Maddison and published in his book *The World Economy: Historical Statistics* (2003) make it possible to test the hypothesis since the year 1500.

Maddison assumes that two thousand years ago the average level of per capita income was approximately the same in different parts of the world. He traces the origin of the great divergence between the West and the rest of the world to the eleventh century when the technological and institutional ascendancy of the West gradually started in Venice and spread throughout Europe (Maddison, 2001, pp. 17–48; 2003, pp. 241–263). Our data on per capita GDP (1990 international Geary-Khamis dollars) for single countries in 1500, 1600, 1700, 1820, 1913, 1950, 1980, and 2000 are Maddison's data for single countries and regional averages given in his book (Maddison, 2003). It should be noted that these data cover the geographical areas of many present states from the periods before their independence. The correlations between contemporary national IQs and historical data on per capita GDP are given in Table 6.3.

Table 6.3. Correlations between national IQ and per capita GDP in 1500, 1600, 1700, 1820, 1913, 1950, 1980, and 2000 in various groups of countries

Year	N	Pearson correlation	Spearman rank correlation
1500	109	0.755	0.841
1600	109	0.728	0.861
1700	109	0.674	0.905
1820	163	0.620	0.737
1913	164	0.614	0.741
1950	170	0.258	0.523
1980	170	0.534	0.624
2000	189	0.641	0.694

Table 6.3 shows that the hypothesized positive correlation between national IQ and GDP per capita has existed since 1500 and that it has remained approximately at the same level, except for 1950 and 1980. The much lower correlations for 1950 and 1980 are principally due to exceptionally high per capita GDP values for Arab oil-producing countries like Kuwait ($28,874 and $13,271), Qatar ($30,387 and $29,552), and the United Arab Emirates ($15,798 and $27,709). When these three countries are excluded, correlations for 1950 and 1980 rise to 0.522 and 0.636 respectively. Table 6.3 also shows that Spearman rank correlations are considerably stronger than Pearson

correlations.

As a consequence of the technological and institutional development, which had began in the eleventh century, Western Europe seems
to have diverged from the other parts of the world by 1500. The results
of statistical analysis support the research hypothesis and imply that
the positive relationship between national IQ and per capita income
has existed for several centuries, at least since 1500.

3. Literacy

The adult literacy rate measures one important aspect of human
conditions: disparities in the extent of basic education. From this
perspective, human conditions are certainly better in a society in which
the adult literacy rate is high than in a society in which it is low. The
ability to read and write is needed everywhere in modern societies.
According to our hypothesis, differences in national IQs may explain
a significant part of the contemporary global inequalities in literacy,
although it is quite possible that, ultimately, the adult literacy rate will
rise to near 100 percent in all societies. It should be taken into account,
however, that there may be significant differences in the quality of
literacy between countries, although the percentages are the same.

Table 6.1 shows that national IQ explains 41 percent of the
variation in the adult literacy rate 2002 in the group of 113 countries,
43 percent in the group of 79 countries, and 43 percent in the group
of 192 countries. The explained part of variation is approximately
the same as in the case of PPP GNI per capita. In the group of 160
countries, from which small countries are excluded, the explained part
of variation is 54 percent (Table 6.2).

Spearman rank correlations are significantly higher: 0.772 in the
group of 113 countries, 0.737 in the group of 79 countries, and 0.778
in the total group of 192 countries. The explained part of variation
rises to 60 percent in the group of 192 countries.

Because more than half of the variation remains unexplained in the
group of 192 countries (Pearson correlation), many countries deviate
significantly from the average relationship between national IQ and
adult literacy rate. The results of regression analysis in which national
IQ is used as the independent variable and the adult literacy rate as
the dependent variable are presented in Figure 6.3 (for residuals, see

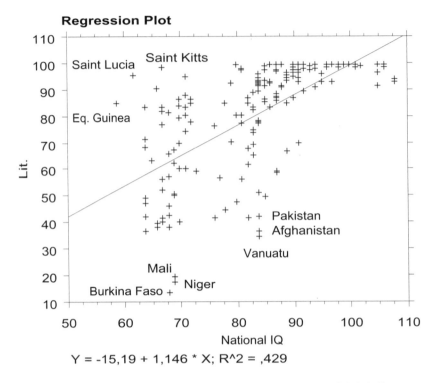

$$Y = -15,19 + 1,146 * X; R^2 = ,429$$

Figure 6.3. The results of regression analysis of Adult literacy rate 2002 on national IQ in the group of 192 coutries

Appendix 4).

Figure 6.3 indicates that the relationship between national IQ and the adult literacy rate 2002 is approximately linear as hypothesized, but many countries deviate from the regression line, especially at lower levels of national IQ. In fact, there does not seem to be any relationship between variables in the category of countries for which national IQ is less than 75. The lack of a positive relationship in this IQ category may be partly due to the unreliability of data on literacy in African countries, but probably even more to religious differences between countries. The examination of the most deviating cases helps us to see whether it is possible to find any common explanations for the most deviating countries. Because one standard deviation of residuals is 15.6 percent, the countries with residuals ±15.6 or higher can be regarded as large outliers.

The group of countries with positive residuals 15.6 or higher includes 20 countries (Appendix 4): Antiqua and Barbuda, Barbados, Congo-Brazzaville, Equatorial Guinea, Grenada, Jamaica, Kenya, Lesotho, the Maldives, Namibia, the Northern Mariana Islands, Saint Kitts and Nevis, Saint Lucia, Saint Vincent and the Grenadines, Sao Tome and Principia, South Africa, Sri Lanka, Swaziland, Trinidad and Tobago, and Zimbabwe. Positive residuals are higher than two standard deviations (31.2) for Equatorial Guinea (31.8), Saint Kitts and Nevis (36.2), and Saint Lucia (39.0). National IQs are very low for these three countries.

All the countries with large positive residuals are developing countries, for which the values of national IQ are relatively low. The group includes nine sub-Saharan African countries, eight Caribbean countries, the Northern Mariana Islands from the Pacific and the Maldives and Sri Lanka from the South Asia. It is characteristic of the sub-Saharan African countries of this group that they are Christian countries. The Caribbean states as well as the Northern Mariana Islands are Christian tourist countries, although Hindus constitute a significant minority in Trinidad and Tobago. The Maldives in the Indian Ocean deviates from this religious pattern. Its people are Sunni Muslims, but this has not prevented the spread of literacy. Sri Lanka is predominantly a Buddhist country.

The group of countries with large negative residuals (-15.6 or higher) includes 30 countries: Afghanistan, Angola, Bangladesh, Benin, Bhutan, Burkina Faso, Cambodia, Chad, the Comoros, Egypt, Ethiopia, Gambia, Guinea, Guinea-Bissau, India, Iraq, Laos, Mali, Mauritania, Morocco, Nepal, Niger, Pakistan, Senegal, Sierra Leone, Singapore, Somalia, Timor-Leste, Vanuatu, and Yemen. Despite the fact that national IQs are relatively low or only moderate for all these countries, the level of literacy is much lower than expected on the basis of national IQ. Negative residuals are larger than two standard deviations for Afghanistan (-45.1), Bangladesh (-37.3), Burkina Faso (-49.9), Mali (-44.9), Niger (-46.8), Pakistan (-39.5), and Vanuatu (-47.0). These seven countries belong to the group of educationally least developed countries. All of them, except Vanuatu, are predominantly Muslim countries.

African countries (17) dominate this group. Muslims or Muslims and followers of indigenous beliefs constitute the majority of the population in nearly all these countries. Angola is the only one of these countries in which Christians constitute a small majority. In this respect

African countries with large positive and negative residuals differ clearly from each other: the predominant religion makes the difference. Literacy seems to have spread more effectively in sub-Saharan Africa by Christian missionaries than what has happened in principally Muslim countries. It is remarkable that the adult literacy rate is 82 for Equatorial Guinea, although its national IQ (59) is lower than for any other country. Assuming that this high rate is valid, this achievement in Equatorial Guinea implies that it might be possible, by adopting appropriate educational policies, to raise the literacy rate to near 100 percent in all countries of the world. Of the other 13 countries of this group, nine are poor South Asian and Southeast Asian countries. The poverty coincides with a relatively low level of literacy in these countries. Iraq and Timor-Leste are countries devastated by wars. Vanuatu is a poor and isolated Pacific island state. Singapore's place in this category is a technical consequence of the regression equation. The predicted level of literacy is over 100 percent for all countries with national IQs of 101 or higher.

Clear positive correlation between national IQ and the adult literacy seems to have continued at least since the 19th century. Our historical data on literacy for the benchmark years 1868, 1908, 1948, and 1978 are from *FSD1216 Democratization and Power Recources 1850–2000* (2003). Correlations between contemporary national IQs and historical literacy rates are given in Table 6.4.

Table 6.4. Correlations between contemporary national IQs and Literacy in 1868, 1908, 1948, and 1978 in various groups of countries

Year	N	Pearson correlation	Spearman rank correlation
1868	39	0.594	0.640
1908	47	0.694	0.715
1948	73	0.623	0.631
1978	116	0.812	0.839

Table 6.4 shows that the relationship between national IQ and Literacy has remained approximately at the same level at least since 1868, which is used as the first benchmark year. It has been easier to extend literacy in countries with high national IQs than in countries with low national IQs. Thus the results of historical analysis support the

central hypothesis that IQ contributes to the quality of life measures.

4. Higher Education

Data on tertiary enrollment ratios measure extremely large global disparities in the extent of higher education and, consequently, in the relative number of people with higher education. We can see from Appendix 2 that variation in tertiary enrollment ratios is much more extensive than variation in the adult literacy rate. Our argument is that human conditions are better in a country in which the rate of tertiary enrollment is high than in a country in which it is low. Tertiary education is needed in modern societies much more than in the past. Economic and social development requires people with various skills provided by higher education. It is reasonable to assume that people with higher education can also improve other aspects of human condititons better than less-educated people. According to our linear hypothesis, national IQ and the tertiary enrollment ratio should be positively correlated in the contemporary world.

Table 6.1 indicates that the correlation between national IQ and the tertiary enrollment ratio is quite high: 0.746 in the group of 113 countries, 0.699 in the group of 79 countries, and 0.745 in the group of 192 countries. The explained part of variation rises to 56 percent in the total group of 192 countries. In the group of 160 large countries, the explained part of variation rises to 61 percent (Table 6.2). Spearman rank correlations are even higher: 0.791 in the group of 113 countries, 0.758 in the group of 79 countries, and 0.797 in the total group of 192 countries. The results of the correlation analysis support the hypothesis. The great global inequalities in the level of higher education seem to be crucially dependent on the level of national IQ. The results of the regression analysis summarized in Figure 6.4 disclose the countries deviating most clearly from the average pattern of relationship (regression line). Residuals for single countries are listed in Appendix 4.

We can see from Figure 6.4 that the pattern of relationship is approximately but not fully linear. The level of tertiary enrollment is very low in all countries for which national IQ is below 75. This observation implies that it has been difficult to extend higher education in the countries with low national IQs, although the extent of adult literacy varies greatly in this category of countries (cf. Figure 6.3).

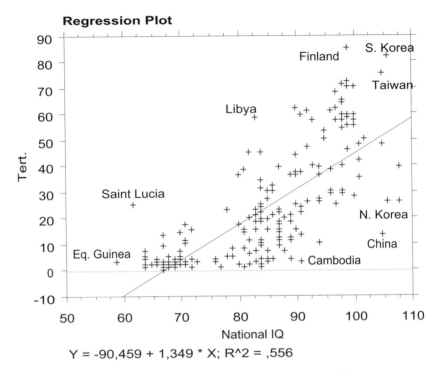

$$Y = -90{,}459 + 1{,}349 * X; R^2 = {,}556$$

Figure 6.4. The results of regression analysis of Tertiary
enrollment ratio on national IQ in the group of 192 countries

One standard deviation of residuals (±14.2) can be used to separate
the most deviating countries from the less deviating ones. Using this
criterion, the group of large positive residuals includes 30 countries
(Appendix 4): Argentina, Australia, Barbados, Belarus, Belgium,
Bermuda, Canada, Denmark, Egypt, Estonia, Finland, Greece, Israel,
South Korea, Latvia, Lebanon, Libya, Lithuania, New Zealand, Norway,
Puerto Rico, Russia, Saint Lucia, Slovenia, Spain, Sweden, Taiwan,
Ukraine, the United Kingdom, and the United States. It is noticeable that
only two of the countries with large positive residuals (Barbados and
Saint Lucia) have large positive residuals also on the basis of literacy.
The low correspondence between the two lists of countries with large
positive residuals indicates that the adult literacy rate and tertiary enrollment ratio variables measure clearly different dimensions of education
and human conditions. Positive residuals are larger than two standard

deviations for Bermuda (31.0), Finland (41.9), South Korea (29.4), Libya (36.5), New Zealand (28,9), Saint Lucia (31.8), and the United States (29.2). It should be noticed that national differences in the definitions of the institutions of higher education may decrease the reliability of data on tertiary enrollment to some extent.

The group of countries with large positive residuals is not homogeneous, but 24 of them are industrially relatively highly developed countries for which national IQ is 90 or higher. Most of them are European countries. Besides, residuals are positive also for nearly all other economically highly developed countries. Belarus, Estonia, Latvia, Lithuania, Russia, Slovenia, and Ukraine are former European socialist countries in which the roots of extensive tertiary enrollment can be traced to the socialist period. Barbados, Puerto Rico, and Saint Lucia are Caribbean countries, and Egypt, Lebanon, and Libya are exceptional Arab countries that have devoted more attention to higher education than most other Arab countries.

The group of countries with large negative residuals includes 32 countries: Afghanistan, Albania, Bangladesh, Bhutan, Bosnia and Herzegovina, Brunei, Cambodia, China, Hong Kong, Kiribati, North Korea, Laos, Luxembourg, Madagascar, the Maldives, Malta, Mauritius, Micronesia, Myanmar, Oman, Papua New Guinea, Samoa, Singapore, the Solomon Islands, Suriname, Timor-Leste, Tonga, Trinidad and Tobago, Uzbekistan, Vanuatu, Vietnam, and Yemen. Only eight of these countries (Afghanistan, Bangladesh, Bhutan, Cambodia, Laos, Timor-Leste, Vanuatu, and Yemen) have large negative residuals also on the basis of adult literacy. Negative residuals are larger than two standard deviations for Cambodia (-29.3), China (-38.2), and Hong Kong (-29.3).

The countries with large negative residuals differ in many respects, especially geographically, from the countries with large positive residuals. Of the 32 countries, 24 are Asian and Pacific countries, and only four of them are European countries (Albania, Bosnia and Herzegovina, Luxembourg, and Malta). Madagascar and Mauritius are the only African countries in this group, and Suriname and Trinidad and Tobago the only Caribbean countries. Half of these countries are relatively small countries in which it is more difficult to organize extensive higher education than in bigger countries. The small size of population is certainly a factor that restricts higher education even in a rich country like Luxembourg. Afghanistan, Bosnia and Herzegovina,

Cambodia, Laos, and Myanmar are poor countries in which civil wars have retarded all types of development. Poverty may have been an obstructing factor also in countries like Bangladesh, Madagascar, and Papua New Guinea. China, North Korea, and Vietnam are authoritarian socialist countries and Uzbekistan a former socialist country. It is possible that higher education has been restricted in these countries for political reasons. Power holders have not wanted to increase the number of highly educated people who might become politically dangerous. Hong Kong and Singapore are more problematic cases. In these economically highly developed countries, tertiary enrollment ratios have remained much lower than expected on the basis of their exceptionally high national IQs.

Global disparities in tertiary enrollment are so strongly connected with the level of national IQ that it is highly questionable whether it is ever possible to equalize the relative extent of higher education in the world. The best chances to extend higher education are in the countries with national IQs higher than 80 and for which residuals are negative. It will be much more difficult to raise the level of higher education in the countries for which national IQs are lower than 80, and even though it would be in principle possible to extend higher education in such countries, the gap between the countries with low and high national IQs will probably remain great. The fact that the relative number of highly educated people in countries with low national IQs is small and will probably remain much smaller than in countries with high national IQs means that the chances to improve human conditions remain unequal.

It is remarkable that most countries with large negative residuals are at the middle level of national IQ, from 80 to 90, and that most countries with large positive residuals are at higher levels of national IQ. Figure 6.4 shows that the relationship between national IQ and tertiary enrollment ratio is slightly curvilinear. In a polynomial regression the explained part of variation in tertiary enrollment ratio rises to 59 percent. However, it is only three percentage points more than in the linear regression of Figure 6.4.

The global inequalities in the extent of higher education have persisted at least since the 19th century. Historical data on the number of students per 100,000 inhabitants published in *FSD1216 Democratization and Power Resources 1850–2000* (2003) make it possible to extend correlation analysis to some benchmark years since the 19th century (Table 6.5).

Table 6.5. Correlations between contemporary national IQ and the number of students per 100,000 inhabitants in 1868, 1908, 1948, and 1978 in various groups of countries

Year	N	Pearson correlation	Spearman rank correlation
1868	39	0.377	0.390
1908	47	0.389	0.528
1948	73	0.448	0.541
1978	116	0.642	0.781

Table 6.5 shows that historical correlations between national IQ and the number of students per 100,000 inhabitants are, until 1948, much weaker than contemporary correlations, and also much weaker than corresponding correlations between national IQ and literacy. The difference may be partly due to the poorer reliability of historical data on higher education. The concept of "higher education" varies greatly from country to country, which has made it difficult to find reliable historical data on the number of students. However, correlations have been positive as hypothesized at least since 1868.

5. Life Expectancy at Birth

Differences in life expectancy at birth measure crucial global disparities in human conditions. According to the data given in Appendix 2, life expectancy at birth varies from 33 years in Zambia and Zimbabwe to 81 years in Japan. The gaps in life expectancy are enormous, although life expectancy has increased in all regions of the world since the 19th century. According to data provided by Maddison (2001, pp. 27–31), life expectancy in the year 1000 was approximately the same (24 years) in all parts of the world. It was no higher in the beginning of our era. In 1820 it had risen to 36 years in the group of Western Europe, Western Offshoots, and Japan (Group A), but it was still 24 years in the other parts of the world (Group B). In 1900 life expectation in Group A had risen to 46 years and in Group B to 26 years. The gap was 20 years. In 1950 it had risen to 66 years in Group A and to 44 years in Group B. The gap was still 22 years. In 1999 the life expectancy had risen to 78 years in Group A and to 64 years in Group B. So the gap has started to decrease, but the average life expectancy conceals great differences within the Group B countries. For African countries, the average life expectancy at birth was not more than 52 years in 1999. An interesting question is whether life expectancy at birth is going to equalize in all countries of the world, or whether the gaps that emerged in the 19th century will persist.

The use of this variable in our analysis is based on the axiomatic assumption that human conditions are better in a country in which people live longer than in a country in which they die younger. A long life provides better chances for people to realize their dreams and to enjoy life than a short life that often ends abruptly. A healthy environment, sufficient nutrition, and adequate health care are needed for a long life. It is reasonable to assume that nations with high national IQs have better capabilities to establish and maintain the frameworks of healthy and good life than nations with low national IQs. Therefore we hypothesize that, in modern societies, there must be a positive correlation between national IQ and life expectancy at birth.

Table 6.1 shows that national IQ correlates with life expectancy (LE) more strongly than with any other measure of the quality of human conditions used in this study. The explained part of variation is 60 percent in the group of 113 countries, 48 percent in the group of 79 countries, and 57 percent in the group of 192 countries. Spearman rank correlations are approximately at the same level: 0.753 in the group of 113 countries, 0.616 in the group of 79 countries, and 0.721 in the group of 192 countries. In the group of 160 countries, the correlation rises to 0.822, and the explained part of variation is 68 percent (Table 6.2). The unexplained part of variation is due to other factors and measurement errors. What are those other explanatory factors? The exploration of most deviating countries may provide some answers to this question. The results of regression analysis are given in Figure 6.5 and residuals for single countries in Appendix 4.

Figure 6.5 indicates that the relationship between variables is linear as hypothesized, but the countries are clustered into two clearly separate groups. Countries below national IQ 75 constitute one group and countries above national IQ 75 another group. Relatively few countries deviate greatly from the regression line. On the other hand, we can see from Figure 6.5 that there is hardly any relationship between variables

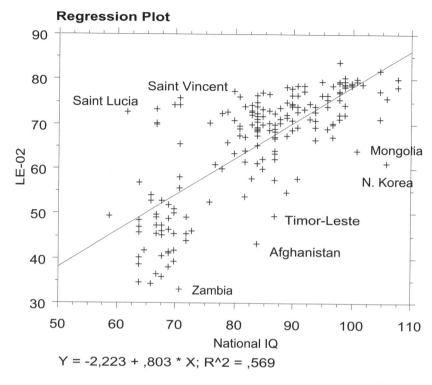

Figure 6.5. The results of regression analysis of Life expectancy at birth 2002 on national IQ in the group of 192 countries

within the category below national IQ 75, whereas they seem to be moderately correlated in the category above national IQ 75.

In this case, one standard deviation of residuals is 8.2 years. We have used this criterion to separate large positive and negative outliers from the countries that are closer to the regression line. The group of large positive outliers constitutes 24 countries (Appendix 4): Antigua and Barbuda, Bahrain, Barbados, Cape Verde, Costa Rica, Cuba, Dominica, El Salvador, Grenada, Jamaica, Kuwait, Lebanon, the Northern Mariana Islands, Panama, Puerto Rico, Qatar, Saint Kitts and Nevis, Saint Lucia, Saint Vincent, Sao Tome and Principe, Sri Lanka, Tunisia, the United Arab Emirates, and Venezuela. Positive residuals are larger than two standard deviations (16.4) for Antigua and Barbuda (19.9), Dominica (21.5), Jamaica (20.8), Saint Kitts and Nevis (18.4), Saint Lucia (24.8), Saint Vincent and the Grenadines (19.2), and Sao Tome and Principe (18.1). All of these extremely deviating countries, except Sao Tome and Principe, are small Caribbean island states.

The group of large positive outliers is dominated by 14 Caribbean and Latin American countries. National IQs are relatively low for them. Bahrain, Kuwait, Qatar, and the United Arab Emirates are oil-producing countries whose wealth has helped them to improve the living conditions of their people. Sri Lanka is a relatively poor South Asian country, in which life expectancy has remained relatively high despite a long ethnic civil war. The same concerns Lebanon. It is a significant achievement. Cape Verde and Sao Tome and Principe are small African island states, which have been able to achieve a higher life expectancy than in other sub-Saharan African countries. In Tunisia, a long period of domestic peace and political stability seems to have raised the level of life expectancy.

The group of countries with large negative residuals includes 28 countries: Afghanistan, Angola, Botswana, Burundi, Cambodia, the Central African Republic, China, Congo-Zaire, Cote d'Ivoire, Kenya, North Korea, Laos, Lesotho, Madagascar, Malawi, Mongolia, Mozambique, Myanmar, Namibia, Russia, Rwanda, Sierra Leone, Swaziland, Tanzania, Timor-Leste, Uganda, Zambia, and Zimbabwe. Negative residuals are larger than two standard deviations for Afghanistan (-22.3), North Korea (-21.9), Swaziland (-16,7), Timor-Leste (-18.4), Zambia (-22.1), and Zimbabwe (-16.9).

The 28 countries with large negative residuals differ from the countries with large positive residuals in some respects. Sub-Saharan African countries (19) dominate this category, whereas most countries with large positive residuals are Caribbean and Latin American countries. It is characteristic for these sub-Saharan African countries that the relative number of people living with HIV/AIDS is high in most of them, especially in south African countries. Residuals are clearly negative also for other sub-Saharan African countries for which the number of people living with HIV/AIDS is high (see UNDP, 2004, Table 8). Afghanistan, Cambodia, Laos, Myanmar, and Timor-Leste are poor Asian and Pacific countries in which long civil wars have damaged social and institutional structures and living conditions. North Korea is an isolated and poor communist country in which hunger may have decreased life expectancy. Mongolia is a former socialist country in which harsh environmental conditions keep life expectancy relatively low. Despite its strong economic growth, life expectancy in China (71 years) is still somewhat lower than expected on the basis of its high national IQ. In Russia, a high level of alcoholism may have lowered life expectancy.

It is characteristic for both categories of large outliers that they do not include any economically highly developed countries and that countries with national IQs above 90 are few among the large outliers. Practically all of these countries are Caribbean, Latin American, African, and Asian developing countries.

The average life expectancy of people has doubled in all parts of the world since the 19th century, but the gap between economically developed and less developed countries is still as wide as in 1820. Because the average life expectancy cannot rise indefinitely, it will be interesting to see whether the gap between rich and poor countries continues to decrease, as it has done since 1950, or whether it persists in the future. It seems reasonable to assume that the average life expectancy will not become equal in all countries for the reason that the high average life expectancy in all economically and educationally developed countries depends crucially on the systems of health care and social security which are too expensive to establish and maintain in poor countries. For that reason it will be difficult for poor countries to raise the average life expectancy to the same level with wealthy countries by improving their health care and social security systems. Because differences in economic and educational development are strongly correlated with differences in national IQs, it is difficult for poor countries with low national IQs to catch up with economically and educationally more developed countries. Therefore, we have to be prepared to live in the world in which many types of inequalities in human conditions persist, although gaps do not need to remain at the present level.

Marina Counter (2004) has explored the relationship between national IQ and life expectancy extensively in her paper "IQ and the Health of Nations." She notes that even "casual observation reveals that more intelligent people tend to do better in most areas of life, including health status, than less intelligent people do." She continues that it is "reasonable to ask if the same observation could be made of nations." She used the national IQ data published in our book *IQ and the Wealth of Nations* and found that the Pearson correlation between national IQ and life expectancy is 0.80. Satoshi Kanazawa (2005) has also demonstrated on 126 nations that income inequality and per capita income have no effect on life expectancy once national IQ is controlled. The results of our analyses are similar.

Historical data on the average life expectancy are fragmentary estimations, which do not make it possible to extend correlation analysis to the 19th century. The World Bank's *World Development Reports* have published data on life expectancy since the 1970s. We use data for 1978 (*World Development Report* 1980, Table 1). The Pearson correlation between national IQ and life expectancy at birth 1978 is 0.807 (N = 122) and Spearman rank correlation 0.817. The strength of the relationship in 1978 was approximately the same as in 2002.

6. Democratization

One important dimension of human conditions concerns the sphere of economic, social, and political freedoms. Humans need not only to eat and live, they need also the freedom of action to pursue their goals in social life. The scope of such freedoms depends crucially on the nature of a country's political system. Our argument is that a democratic political system provides a better framework for human life from the perspective of economic, social, and political freedoms than autocratic systems in which power is concentrated in the hands of the few. We use Vanhanen's Index of Democratization (ID) to measure the level of democratization in contemporary countries. Its values for 2002 vary from zero to 44.2, or from various autocratic systems to highly democratic ones. Because people tend to prefer freedom to subjugation, it is reasonable to assume that from this perspective human conditions are better in democracies than in autocracies. And because humans tend to use their intelligence to improve their living conditions, it is reasonable to hypothesize that there is a positive correlation between national IQ and the level of democratization. This hypothesis can be tested by empirical evidence on the level of democratization (see Appendix 3).

Table 6.1 shows that the correlation between national IQ and ID-2002 is 0.568 in the group of 113 countries, 0.322 in the group of 79 countries, and 0.529 in the group of 192 countries. Thus the explained part of variation is approximately 30 percent. In the group of 160 larger countries, the correlation is 0.584. Spearman rank correlations are at the same level: 0.611 in the group of 113 countries, 0.320 in the group of 79 countries, and 0.535 in the group of 192 countries.

The unexplained part of variation is due to other factors and measurement errors. According to Vanhanen's evolutionary resource distribution theory of democratization, the level of democratization in a society depends crucially on the degree of resource distribution. This theoretical argument is derived from a Darwinian interpretation of politics, according to which politics constitutes one important forum of the general struggle for existence, in which people tend to use all available resources. Consequently, the concentration as well as the distribution of political power depends on the degree of resource distribution. Democratization takes place in conditions in which power resources have become so widely distributed that no group is any longer able to suppress its competitors or to maintain its hegemony. Vanhanen constructed an Index of Power Resources (IPR) to measure differences between countries in the distribution of some important economic and intellectual power resources and then tested his theory by empirical evidence. The results indicate that the correlation between the Index of Power Resources (IPR) and ID-2001 is 0.848 (N = 170). The explained part of variation rises to 72 percent (see Vanhanen 2003).

The degree of resource distribution explains the major part of the variation in the level of democratization, but how to explain the variation in the degree of resource distribution? Differences in national IQs seem to explain a significant part of the variation both in the Index of Democratization (ID) and in the Index of Power Resources (IPR). The correlation between national IQ and IPR (0.692, N = 170) is clearly stronger than the correlation between national IQ and ID-2002 (0.529). The average national intelligence seems to constitute a causal background factor that explains variation in the level of democratization through the degree of resource distribution. It should be noted that national IQ and IPR taken together do not explain more of the variation in ID-2002 (0.840, N = 170) than IPR alone (0.839, N = 170). National IQ's impact on the level of democratization takes place through the Index of Power Resources.

In this connection, we focus our attention on the direct relationship

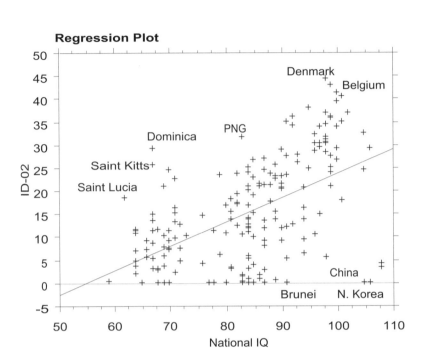

Regression Plot

Y = -29,041 + ,528 * X; R^2 = ,28

Figure 6.6. The results of regression analysis of the Index of Democratization (ID) 2002 on national IQ in the group of 192 countries

between national IQ and the level of democratization and try to examine how well the average relationship between these variables applies to single countries. Figure 6.6 summarizes the results of the regression analysis in which national IQ is used as the independent variable and ID-2002 as the dependent variable. The residuals produced by this regression analysis for single countries are given in Appendix 4.

We can see from Figure 6.6 that the two variables are moderately correlated, although there is considerable dispersion around the regression line especially at higher levels of national IQ. The relationship is approximately linear. One standard deviation of residual ID-2002 is 10.0, which can be used to separate large outliers from the less deviating countries.

The group of countries with positive residuals 10.0 or higher includes 30 countries (Appendix 4): Antigua and Barbuda, Australia, Austria,

Belgium, Brazil, Croatia, Cyprus, Denmark, Dominica, Fiji, Finland, Germany, Greece, Iceland, Ireland, Israel, Italy, Malawi, Malta, the Netherlands, Norway, Papua New Guinea, Saint Kitts and Nevis, Saint Lucia, St. Vincent, Slovakia, Sri Lanka, Sweden, Switzerland, and the United States. Positive residuals are higher than two standard deviations (20.0) only for two countries: Denmark (21.5) and Dominica (22.9).

Economically and educationally highly developed countries (20) characterize the group of countries with large positive residuals. Most of them are European countries. The level of democratization in these 20 countries is even higher than expected on the basis of their relatively high national IQs. Residuals are positive also for nearly all other economically highly developed countries. Ten other countries with large positive residuals deviate from this pattern. Antigua and Barbuda, Dominica, Saint Kitts and Nevis, Saint Lucia, and St. Vincent are Caribbean tourist countries with stable democratic systems. Because of tourism, PPP GNI per capita is also much higher than expected on the basis of national IQ in these countries. Brazil has succeeded in maintaining its highly fragmented multiparty system, which enhances its ID value. In Fiji, Papua New Guinea, and Sri Lanka, the ethnic heterogeneity of their populations has produced multiparty systems and increased their ID values. Despite its extreme poverty, Malawi has successfully maintained a multiparty system since the first free elections in 1994. The party system has become adapted to regional and tribal cleavages. It is remarkable that only a few countries below national IQ 75 deviate significantly from the regression line.

Negative residuals are large (-10.0 or higher) for 35 countries: Afghanistan, Andorra, Bahrain, Bhutan, Brunei, Cambodia, China, the Comoros, Cuba, Egypt, Hong Kong, Iran, Iraq, Jordan, Kazakhstan, North Korea, Kuwait, Laos, Libya, the Maldives, Moldova, Morocco, Myanmar, Oman, Qatar, Saudi Arabia, Singapore, Syria, Tonga, Tunisia, Turkmenistan, the United Arab Emirates, Uzbekistan, Vietnam, and Yemen. Negative residuals are larger than two standard deviations for China (-26.4), Hong Kong (-24.7), North Korea (-26.9), and Singapore (-23.8). Asian countries (26) dominate the group of countries with large negative residuals. Most of them are relatively poor countries, but the group includes also wealthy oil-producing countries as well as Hong Kong and Singapore. Negative residuals are large also for five African, two European, one Latin American, and one Pacific countries.

The group includes five socialist countries (China, Cuba, North Korea, Laos, and Vietnam), in which political power is concentrated in the hands of the hegemonic Communist party, and four former Soviet republics (Kazakhstan, Moldova, Turkmenistan, and Uzbekistan), in which political systems are still less democratized than expected on the basis of the regression model. Bahrain, Brunei, Iran, Iraq, Kuwait, Libya, Oman, Qatar, Saudi Arabia, and the United Arab Emirates are oil-producing countries, in which the economic resources based on the control of oil industries have supported the survival of autocratic governments. Egypt, Jordan, Morocco, Syria, Tunisia, and Yemen are other Arab countries whose political systems have not yet been democratized. In fact, 15 of the 35 large negative outliers are Middle East and Arab countries. The Arab Middle East seems to constitute the core region of autocratic political systems. Afghanistan, Cambodia, the Comoros, and Myanmar are poor Asian and African countries, in which the struggle for power has been violent. Andorra's large negative residual is due to the fact that its chief executive is not democratically elected. Bhutan is still an autocratically ruled traditional monarchy. Democracy in Hong Kong is limited by the dominance of China. the Maldives and Tonga are autocratically ruled small island states. Singapore is an exceptional case. As an economically highly developed country with a high national IQ it should be a democracy. In fact, it has democratic institutional structures, but the hegemony of the ruling party has become so dominant that the country is below the threshold of democracy. It is characteristic for large negative outliers that most of them are socialist or former socialist countries, oil-producing and other Arab countries, or poor countries in which the struggle for power has been violent.

The number of democracies in the world has risen significantly during the last decades. The question is whether it is reasonable to expect that ultimately all countries will cross the threshold of democracy and the big differences in the level of democratization disappear. The number of democracies may still increase, but it is not plausible to expect the disappearance of great differences in the level of democratization for the reason that the level of democracy seems to be moderately related to differences in national IQs. Because differences in national IQs will persist, or they decrease only slowly, we have to predict that global disparities in this dimension of human conditions will most probably persist. All nations are not equally capable of establishing and maintaining democratic institutions and the human freedoms connected with them.

Historical evidence on the level of democratization in the world (see FSD1289 Measures of Democracy 1810–2002, 2003) implies that the positive relationship between national IQ and ID has been present at least since the 1850s. Correlations between national IQ and the Index of Democratization for the benchmark years 1868, 1908, 1948, and 1978 are given in Table 6.6.

Table 6.6. Correlations between contemporary national IQ and the Index of Democratization (ID) in 1868, 1908, 1948, and 1978 in various groups of countries

Year	N	Pearson correlation	Spearman rank correlation
1868	42	0.329	0.552
1908	51	0.457	0.706
1948	77	0.484	0.457
1978	151	0.535	0.491

Table 6.6 shows that the positive relationship between national IQ and ID has continued at least since 1868, although correlations are relatively weak or only moderate. Democratization in the 19th century began in countries for which national IQs were high and started to spread to countries with low national IQs later in the 20th century. Now democracies exist at all levels of national IQ, although they are much more frequent at higher levels of national IQ than at lower levels.

7. Summary of Large Outliers

The use of the five different variables to measure disparities in the quality of human conditions is based on the idea that the concept of "human conditions" is multidimensional and that, therefore, five different variables may cover the concept more satisfactorily than any single variable. Besides, the quality of human conditions may differ from dimension to dimension in single countries. Therefore, the use of several variables intended to measure the same basic phenomenon from different perspectives can be expected to produce a more reliable total picture of the quality of human conditions in a country than any single variable could produce. The intercorrelations of the five variables given in Table 6.1 indicate that variables differ from each other significantly, although all of them are moderately or strongly intercorrelated.

In the previous sections, we have tested the hypothesis on the positive relationship between national IQ and the five measures of the quality of human conditions. Figures 6.1 to 6.6 summarize the results of five regression analyses. One standard deviation was used to separate large outliers from less deviating countries. Now it is interesting to examine to what extent the same countries have large positive or negative residuals on the basis of the five regression equations and in what respects the most frequently deviating countries differ from each other. For this analysis, the 192 countries are classified according to the number of large residuals (Appendix 4) into seven categories: (1) 4-5 large positive residuals, (2) 3 large positive residuals, (3) 2 large positive residuals, (4) one large positive and/or negative residual, (5) 2 large negative residuals, (6) 3 large negative residuals, and (7) 4-5 large negative residuals. The results of this classification are given in Table 6.7. However, the 93 countries of the middle category (one large positive and/or negative residual) are excluded from Table 6.7. It is plausible to assume that the countries for which only one residual is large positive or large negative, or one residual large positive and another residual large negative, do not necessarily deviate systematically from each other. The 38 countries without any large residual are also excluded from Table 6.7. We focus on the most frequently deviating countries.

Table 6.7 includes 36 countries with two or more large positive residuals and 31 countries with two or more large negative residuals. It is easy to see that these two groups of outliers, especially the countries of the two extreme categories, deviate from each other in several respects. The quality of human conditions is much higher than expected on the basis of national IQ in the group of countries with large positive residuals and it is much lower than expected in the group of countries with large negative residuals.

All the four countries with 4-5 large positive residuals are Caribbean tourist countries. St. Vincent in the group of countries with three positive residuals and Dominica, Grenada, Jamaica, and Puerto Rico in the group of 2 large positive residuals belong to the same group of Caribbean countries. It is obvious that successful tourist industries have been beneficial for these countries. Domestic peace prevails, and these countries are stable democracies with market economies. On the other hand, the countries with

Table 6.7. *Countries classified into six categories on the basis of the number of large positive and negative residuals produced by the five regression analyses*

Number of large positive or negative residuals for a country					
Positive 4-5	Positive 3	Positive 2	Negative 2	Negative 3	Negative 4-5
Antigua & B.	Belgium	Australia	Angola	Bhutan	Afghanistan
Barbados	Denmark	Austria	Bangladesh	Egypt	Cambodia
Saint Kitts	Finland	Bahrain	Brunei	Hong Kong	China
Saint Lucia	Norway	Canada	Comoros	Iraq	Laos
		St. Vincent	Dominica	Kazakhstan	Myanmar
		Sri Lanka	Eq. Guinea	Kiribati	North Korea
		Sweden	Germany	Madagascar	Timore-Leste
		USA	Greece	the Maldives	Yemen
			Grenada	Moldova	
			Iceland	Mongolia	
			Ireland	Morocco	
			Israel	Oman	
			Italy	Sierra Leone	
			Jamaica	Singapore	
			Kuwait	Tonga	
			Lebanon	Tunisia	
			Netherlands	Uzbekistan	
			Northern M. Is	Vanuatu	
			Puerto Rico	Vietnam	
			Qatar		
			Sao Tome		
			Swaziland		
			UAE		
			UK		
4	8	24	19	4	8

4–5 large negative residuals are quite different. Afghanistan, Cambodia, Laos, Myanmar, and Timor-Leste are poor Asian countries that have been devastated by civil strife and wars. Yemen is an isolated and poor Arab country. It has been difficult to establish democratic institutions in these countries, and most of them have experimented with socialist economic systems. Two other countries of this category, China and North Korea, are still autocratically ruled socialist countries. It is obvious that civil wars and socialist economic and political systems have hampered the improvement of human conditions in these countries, although national IQs are for them much higher than for Caribbean countries.

Six of the eight countries with 3 large positive residuals are economically highly developed market economies and stable democracies, whereas the four countries with 3 large negative residuals are poor Asian countries. All of them are non-democracies. Vietnam is still a socialist country and Uzbekistan a former Soviet republic. Bhutan is a geographically isolated traditional monarchy. Iraq has suffered from ethnic conflicts, wars, and autocracy. Sri Lanka in the group of large positive residuals is an exceptional case. It has suffered from a long ethnic civil war, but some aspects of human conditions seem to have remained much better than expected on the basis of its national IQ. It is a significant achievement.

There are also significant differences in some characteristics of the countries with 2 large positive residuals and 2 large negative residuals. First, 12 of the 24 countries with large positive residuals are economically highly developed market economies and stable democracies (Australia, Austria, Canada, Germany, Greece, Iceland, Ireland, Israel, Italy, the Netherlands, Switzerland, and the United Kingdom), whereas the group of 19 countries with large negative residuals does not include any such countries. Hong Kong and Singapore are economically highly developed market economies, but they cannot be regarded as stable democracies. Second, the group of large positive residuals includes four Caribbean countries (Dominica, Grenada, Jamaica, and Puerto Rico), whereas the group of large negative residuals does not include any Caribbean country. Third, the group of large positive residuals includes four rich oil-producing countries (Bahrain, Kuwait, Qatar, and the United Arab Emirates), whereas the group of large negative residuals includes only two such countries (Brunei and Oman). This observation implies that oil incomes have been used to improve human conditions in some oil-producing countries. Equatorial Guinea with its two large positive residuals can also be included in the group of oil-producing countries. Equatorial Guinea is an autocracy that has benefited from oil production since the 1990s. Fourth, the group of large negative residuals includes three former socialist countries (Kazakhstan, Moldova, and Mongolia), whereas the group of large positive residuals does not include any former socialist country. Fifth, the rest of the countries with large negative residuals are relatively poor African, Asian, and Pacific developing countries (the Comoros, Egypt, the Maldives, Morocco, Tonga, Tunisia, Angola, Madagascar, Sierra Leone, Bangladesh, Kiribati, and Vanuatu), whereas the group with large positive residuals includes only four such countries (Equatorial Guinea, Lebanon, the Northern Mariana Islands, and Sao Tome and Principe). Lebanon is a somewhat surprising case in this category. Despite its violent past, some indicators of human conditions are relatively good for Lebanon.

Most of the countries with systematic positive residuals are characterized by a high level of socioeconomic development, democracy, and peaceful domestic conditions, or at least some of these features. The group includes countries from all levels of national IQ. The countries with systematic negative residuals are characterized by poverty, domestic conflicts, political instability, the lack of democracy (most of them), and socialist experiments (some of them). This group also includes countries from all levels of national IQ.

8. Summary

In the beginning of this chapter, the research hypothesis on the relationship between national IQ and the measures of the quality of human conditions was formulated on the basis of the operationalized concepts of "average mental abilities of a nation" and "disparities in human conditions." The empirical testing of the hypothesis was started in this chapter by exploring the intercorrelations among the five measures of the quality of human conditions and the strength of correlations between each component of QHC and national IQ.

The results of correlation analysis show (see Table 6.1) that all five components of QHC are moderately or strongly intercorrelated, which is interpreted to support the argument that they measure the quality of human conditions from different perspectives and that their combination may provide a more valid measure for the average quality of human conditions than any of the single variables alone.

There is significant variation in the strength of correlations between national IQ and single variables. In the group of 192 countries, the strongest correlation, 0.754, is between national IQ and life expectancy at birth (LE), followed by the correlation between national IQ and tertiary enrollment ratio (0.745). The correlations between national IQ and PPP GNI per capita (0.601), the adult literacy rate (0.655), and the Index of Democratization 2002 (0.529) are weaker, which means that they leave more room for the impact of other factors. It was found that the sample of countries affects the size of correlations. When the small countries below 500,000 inhabitants are excluded from the group, the strength of all correlations increases (see Table 6.2.). It was also found that Spearman rank correlations are in most cases significantly stronger than Pearson correlations.

Moderate and strong correlations between single measures of human conditions and national IQ support the research hypothesis strongly. The variation in all single measures of the quality of human conditions is significantly dependent on national IQ, although more than half of the variation seems to be due to other factors in the cases of PPP GNI per capita 2002, the adult literacy rate 2002, and ID-2002. According to our interpretation, the positive relationship between national IQ and various measures of the quality of human conditions is causal, because national differences in the average intelligence, as a consequence of evolution, emerged long before the contemporary social conditions reflecting the quality of human conditions.

The application of the average relationship between national IQ and each measure of the quality of human conditions to single countries was illustrated by regression analyses. The results of regression analyses are summarized in Figures 6.1 to 6.6, and the residuals of all these regression analyses are presented in Appendix 4. They give the idea about the pattern of the relationship between variables and indicate the most highly deviating countries, which are listed and discussed in the text. The analysis of the most deviating countries disclosed systematic differences in the characteristics of large positive and negative outliers. Such characteristics refer to other relevant factors that affect the quality of human conditions independently from the level of national IQ. In the next chapter, we shall discuss such factors in greater detail at the level of single countries.

CHAPTER 7

National IQ and the Quality of Human Conditions

In the previous chapter, the research hypothesis was tested by correlating national IQ with various indicators of the quality of human conditions. Each of those indicators is intended to measure a different dimension of the multi-dimensional concept of human conditions. Regression analysis was used to indicate how well national IQ is able to explain the variation in each variable at the level of single countries. In this chapter, we focus on the relationship between national IQ and the composite Index of the Quality of Human Conditions (QHC). As explained earlier, this index combines the five different indicators of human conditions into a composite index, which is intended to measure the average level of human conditions in a country. According to the research hypothesis, the five measures of the quality of human conditions and their composite index (QHC) should correlate positively with national IQ. Because the five components of QHC measure the quality of human conditions from different perspectives, it would be expected that the correlation between national IQ and QHC will be stronger than any correlation between national IQ and single components of QHC.

The construction of the composite index makes it possible to analyze the impact of national IQ on human conditions at the level of single countries and to see in which countries the average human conditions are better and in which countries worse than expected on the basis of the regression equation. Besides, the comparison of these results to the results of previous regression analyses based on single indicators of human conditions allows us to see which dimensions of human conditions are principally responsible for large positive and negative deviations.

1. Correlation Analysis

The correlations between QHC and national IQ as well as correlations between QHC and single measures of the quality of human conditions are given in Table 7.1. It should be noted that the standardized measures of PPP GNI per capita (St. PPP GNI), life expectancy (St. LE), and ID-2002 (St. ID) are used in the construction of the composite index. It was not necessary to standardize the adult literacy rate and tertiary enrollment ratio variables because their original values vary approximately between zero and 100.

Table 7.1 shows that most correlations in the group of 113 countries (in which national IQs are based on intelligence tests) are slightly stronger than in the total group of 192 countries, and that correlations are clearly weaker in the group of 79 countries with estimated national IQs. The composite index QHC is strongly correlated with its five components (St. PPP GNI, literacy, tertiary enrollment, St. LE, and St. ID). Correlations vary from 0.793 to 0.874 in the group of 192 countries (these correlations are not given in Table 7.1). This means that all components of the composite index are important. They measure the same theoretical concept of human conditions from different perspectives. Therefore their composite index can be assumed to be a better measure of the quality of human conditions than any of the single variables separately. Spearman rank correlations are in most cases somewhat stronger than Pearson correlations.

Table 7.1. Pearson product-moment correlations and Spearman rank correlations between national IQ and QHC and its five components in the groups of 113, 79, and 192 countries respectively

	113 countries IQ	79 countries IQ	192 countries IQ
Pearson correlations			
QHC	0.805	0.725	0.791
St. PPP GNI per capita 2002	0.693	0.342	0.616
Adult literacy rate 2002	0.642	0.655	0.655
Tertiary enrollment ratio	0.746	0.699	0.745
St. Life expectancy 2002	0.765	0.690	0.750
St. ID 2002	0.569	0.322	0.530
Spearman rank correlations			
QHC	0.826	0.707	0.797
St. PPP GNI per capita 2003	0.772	0.347	0.635
Adult literacy rate 2002	0.772	0.737	0.778
Tertiary enrollment ratio	0.791	0.758	0.797
St. Life expectancy 2002	0.735	0.616	0.713
St. ID 2002	0.611	0.320	0.535

The most important correlations are between national IQ and QHC. All correlations are strong. The explained part of variation in QHC (Pearson correlations) rises to 63 percent in the group of 192 countries and to 65 percent in the group of 113 countries. The results strongly support our research hypothesis and the theoretical argumentation behind that hypothesis. Differences in the average mental abilities of nations as measured by national IQ seem to explain more than 60 percent of the global inequalities in the quality of human conditions. In the group of 160 countries, from which the smallest countries (population below 500,000 inhabitants in 2000) are excluded, correlations are even stronger (Table 7.2).

Table 7.2. Pearson correlations between national IQ and QHC and its five components in the group of 160 countries (98 with measured IQs and 62 with estimated IQs)

	98 countries IQ	62 countries IQ	160 countries IQ
QHC	0.846	0.800	0.839
St. PPP GNI per capita 2002	0.739	0.266	0.649
Adult literacy rate 2002	0.710	0.746	0.733
Tertiary enrollment ratio	0.778	0.734	0.780
St. Life expectancy 2002	0.833	0.753	0.817
St. ID 2002	0.598	0.408	0.584

In this group of countries, the explained part of variation between national IQ and QHC rises to 70 percent in the total group of 160 countries and to 72 percent in the group of 98 countries with measured national IQs. An explanation for differences between correlations given in Table 7.1 and 7.2 may be in the reliability of our data. It is possible that our data on small countries include more measurement errors than our data on larger countries. In fact, in the group of 32 small countries (population below 500,000 inhabitants), the correlation between national IQ and QHC decreases to 0.566. The explained part of variation is only 32 percent. Many highly deviating countries with large positive (Antigua and Barbuda, Barbados, Bermuda, Iceland, Luxembourg, Saint Kitts and Nevis, and St. Lucia) or negative residuals (Djibouti, Kiribati, the Maldives, Tonga, and Vanuatu) reduce the correlation.

Correlations, of course, do not prove that the relationship between variables is causal and that national IQ is the causal factor, and not vice versa. However, there are other factors which justify the interpretation of a causal relationship. First, differences in average mental abilities of populations measured by national IQs have most probably emerged long before the emergence of contemporary economic, educational, social, and political circumstances measured by our five indicators of human conditions. It is highly improbable that contemporary per capita income, the adult literacy rate, the tertiary enrollment ratio, life expectancy at birth, or the level of democratization have been able to cause national differences in the average mental abilities of people, which differences most probably emerged many thousands of years ago, although it is possible that these factors have some impact on contemporary national IQs. Second, the fact that differences in intelligence are partly based on genetic differences between individuals and populations supports the assumption that differences in average mental abilities of populations emerged many thousands of years ago. The partly genetic basis of differences in national IQs makes these differences persistent, although not unchangeable, because as a consequence of evolution by natural selection and of the transcontinental migration of people, the genetic compositions of populations change continually.

2. Regression of QHC on National IQ

The correlation between national IQ and QHC is very strong, but it is not perfect. More than 30 percent of the variation in QHC remains unexplained in the group of 192 countries. It means that there is room for other explanatory factors, although a part of the unexplained variation may be due to measurement errors both in national IQs and in the measures of the quality of human conditions. We can use the regression analysis of QHC on national IQ to disclose the pattern of relationship between the two variables and to indicate the most deviant cases. It is interesting to see how well the average relationship indicated by the regression equation is able to explain the variation in QHC at the level of single countries and what countries differ most clearly from the regression line. Then we can explore single countries in greater detail, describe common characteristics of deviant cases, and seek possible explanations for large deviations. The results of the regression analysis in the group of 192 countries are summarized in Figure 7.1 and presented for single countries in Table 7.3. For the sake of comparison, the results of the regression analysis of QHC on national IQ in the group of 160 countries are summarized in Figure 7.2. However, because the results of these two regression analysis differ from each other only slightly at the level of single countries, we focus on the results of the regression analyses in the total group of 192 countries.

Both figures show that the relationship between national IQ and QHC is approximately linear as hypothesized, although most countries with national IQs from 75 to 89 are slightly below the regression line and most countries with national IQs above 90 are above the regression line. The QHC index values tend to rise with the values of national

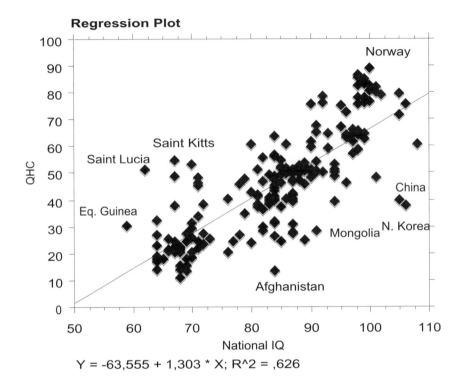

Figure 7.1. The results of regression analysis of QHC on national IQ for single countries in the group of 192 countries

IQ as hypothesized, although several countries clearly differ from the regression lines.

The results of regression analysis in the group of 192 countries are given for single countries in Table 7.3. The values of QHC predicted on the basis of the regression equation are given in the column "Fitted QHC." They are values of QCH at the regression line. Residuals given in the column "Residual QHC" indicate how much the actual value of QHC deviates from the predicted one. A positive residual implies that the quality of human conditions in a country is better than expected on the basis of the average relationship between national IQ and QHC and a negative residual that human conditions are not as good as expected. The larger a residual is, the more the country deviates from the research hypothesis. Small residuals do not matter because they may be due to measurement errors.

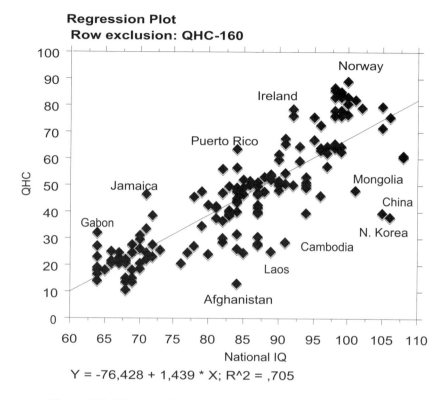

Regression Plot
Row exclusion: QHC-160

$Y = -76,428 + 1,439 * X; R^2 = ,705$

Figure 7.2. The results of regression analysis of QHC on national IQ for single countries in the group of 160 countries

The data given in Table 7.3 make it possible to analyze the characteristics of countries with small and moderate residuals as well as the countries with large residuals, but how to define the criterion to separate the most clearly deviating countries from the less deviating ones? It should be noted that because our operational variables are not perfect measures for the hypothetical concepts and because there are measurement errors in both variables, some variation around the regression line is due to these factors. Consequently, we do not need to pay attention to relatively small deviations, let us say residuals smaller than ±5.0 QHC index points. It is better to focus on more clearly deviating countries. One standard deviation of residual QHC is 11.9 QHC index points in the group of 192 countries. It (±11.9) separates the most deviating countries from the countries that are closer to the regression line. Using these criteria,

Table 7.3. The results of regression analysis of QHC on national IQ for single countries in the group of 192 countries

	Country	National IQ	QHC	Residual QHC	Fitted QHC
1	Afghanistan	84	13.2	-32.7	45.9
2	Albania	90	51.2	-2.5	53.7
3	Algeria	83	39.9	-4.7	44.6
4	Andorra	98	58.7	-5.4	64.1
5	Angola	68	13.7	-11.4	25.1
6	Antigua and Barbuda	70	53.2	25.5	27.7
7	Argentina	93	64.7	7.1	57.6
8	Armenia	94	50.2	-8.7	58.9
9	Australia	98	82.8	18.7	64.1
10	Austria	100	80.7	14.0	66.7
11	Azerbaijan	87	47.2	-2.6	49.8
12	Bahamas	84	56.1	10.2	45.9
13	Bahrain	83	49.3	4.7	44.6
14	Bangladesh	82	29.8	-13.5	43.3
15	Barbados	80	60.9	20.2	40.7
16	Belarus	97	57.2	-5.6	62.8
17	Belgium	99	84.1	18.7	65.4
18	Belize	84	44.2	-1.7	45.9
19	Benin	70	20.5	-7.2	27.7
20	Bermuda	90	75.8	22.1	53.7
21	Bhutan	80	24.1	-16.6	40.7
22	Bolivia	87	49.7	-0.1	49.8
23	Bosnia and Herzegovina	90	51.4	-2.3	53.7
24	Botswana	70	29.4	1.7	27.7
25	Brazil	87	51.1	1.3	49.8
26	Brunei	91	50.8	-4.2	55.0
27	Bulgaria	93	59.1	1.5	57.6
28	Burkina Faso	68	10.7	-14.4	25.1
29	Burundi	69	15.2	-11.2	26.4
30	Cambodia	91	28.6	-26.4	55.0
31	Cameroon	64	23.1	3.3	19.8

	Country	National IQ	QHC	Residual QHC	Fitted QHC
32	Canada	99	77.8	12.4	65.4
33	Cape Verde	76	40.5	5.0	35.5
34	Central African Republic	64	19.1	-0.7	19.8
35	Chad	68	20.4	-4.7	25.1
36	Chile	90	59.5	5.8	53.7
37	China	105	39.7	-33.6	73.3
38	Colombia	84	48.4	2.5	45.9
39	the Comoros	77	24.6	-12.2	36.8
40	Congo-Zaire	65	17.9	-3.2	21.1
41	Congo-Brazzaville	64	26.9	7.1	19.8
42	Cook Islands	89	45.7	-6.7	52.4
43	Costa Rica	89	53.7	1.3	52.4
44	Côte d'Ivoire	69	18.1	-8.3	26.4
45	Croatia	90	61.7	8.0	53.7
46	Cuba	85	46.2	-0.7	47.2
47	Cyprus	91	67.6	12.6	53.0
48	Czech Republic	98	64.5	0.4	64.1
49	Denmark	98	85.4	21.3	64.1
50	Djibouti	68	22.0	-3.1	25.1
51	Dominica	67	48.8	25.1	23.7
52	Dominican Republic	82	46.8	3.5	43.3
53	Ecuador	88	47.4	-3.7	51.1
54	Egypt	81	37.3	-4.7	42.0
55	El Salvador	80	42.6	1.9	40.7
56	Equatorial Guinea	59	30.4	17.1	13.3
57	Eritrea	68	21.4	-3.7	25.1
58	Estonia	99	64.5	-0.9	65.4
59	Ethiopia	64	16.7	-3.1	19.8
60	Fiji	85	51.9	4.7	47.2
61	Finland	99	85.1	19.7	65.4
62	France	98	78.1	14.0	64.1
63	Gabon	64	32.2	12.4	19.8
64	Gambia	66	20.7	-1.7	22.4

	Country	National IQ	QHC	Residual QHC	Fitted QHC
65	Georgia	94	51.2	-7.7	58.9
66	Germany	99	78.0	12.6	65.4
67	Ghana	71	33.7	4.7	29.0
68	Greece	92	76.1	19.8	56.3
69	Grenada	71	45.3	16.3	29.0
70	Guatemala	79	34.6	-4.8	39.4
71	Guinea	67	22.5	-1.2	23.7
72	Guinea-Bissau	67	20.3	-3.4	23.7
73	Guyana	87	46.7	-3.1	49.8
74	Haiti	67	20.4	-3.3	23.7
75	Honduras	81	41.9	-0.1	42.0
76	Hong Kong	108	60.8	-16.4	77.2
77	Hungary	98	64.1	-0.0	64.1
78	Iceland	101	80.0	11.9	68.1
79	India	82	36.3	-7.0	43.3
80	Indonesia	87	40.2	-9.6	49.8
81	Iran	84	40.2	-5.7	45.9
82	Iraq	87	28.1	-21.7	49.8
83	Ireland	92	78.5	22.2	56.3
84	Israel	95	75.3	15.1	60.2
85	Italy	102	78.9	9.5	69.4
86	Jamaica	71	46.5	17.5	29.0
87	Japan	105	71.4	-1.9	73.3
88	Jordan	84	43.4	-2.5	45.9
89	Kazakhstan	94	49.0	-9.9	58.9
90	Kenya	72	27.3	-3.0	30.3
91	Kiribati	85	37.1	-10.1	47.2
92	Korea, North	106	38.0	-36.6	74.6
93	Korea, South	106	75.4	0.8	74.6
94	Kuwait	86	49.9	1.4	48.5
95	Kyrgyzstan	90	48.1	-5.6	53.7
96	Laos	89	24.9	-27.5	52.4
97	Latvia	98	65.5	1.4	64.1
98	Lebanon	82	55.8	12.5	43.3

	Country	National IQ	QHC	Residual QHC	Fitted QHC
99	Lesotho	67	24.3	0.6	23.7
100	Liberia	67	21.2	-2.5	23.7
101	Libya	83	49.3	4.7	44.6
102	Lithuania	91	65.4	10.4	55.0
103	Luxembourg	100	76.4	9.7	66.7
104	Macedonia	91	54.4	-0.6	55.0
105	Madagascar	82	28.6	-14.7	43.3
106	Malawi	69	24.3	-2.1	28.4
107	Malaysia	92	52.1	-6.2	56.3
108	the Maldives	81	38.5	-3.5	42.0
109	Mali	69	13.4	-13.0	26.4
110	Malta	97	66.4	3.6	62.8
111	Marshall Islands	84	44.2	-1.7	45.9
112	Mauritania	76	20.5	-15.0	35.5
113	Mauritius	89	52.2	-0.2	52.4
114	Mexico	88	52.9	1.8	51.1
115	Micronesia	84	39.9	-6.0	45.9
116	Moldova	96	46.2	-15.3	61.5
117	Mongolia	101	48.1	-20.0	68.1
118	Morocco	84	31.7	-14.2	45.9
119	Mozambique	64	18.0	-1.8	19.8
120	Myanmar	87	30.7	-19.1	49.8
121	Namibia	70	31.1	3.4	27.7
122	Nepal	78	26.9	-11.2	38.1
123	Netherlands	100	82.8	16.1	66.7
124	New Caledonia	85	54.9	7.7	47.2
125	New Zealand	99	76.2	10.8	65.4
126	Nicaragua	81	41.3	-0.7	42.0
127	Niger	69	13.5	-12.9	26.4
128	Nigeria	69	27.3	0.9	26.4
129	Northern Mariana Islands	81	51.3	9.3	42.0
130	Norway	100	89.0	22.3	66.7
131	Oman	83	40.6	-4.0	44.6

	Country	National IQ	QHC	Residual QHC	Fitted QHC
132	Pakistan	84	26.2	-19.7	45.9
133	Panama	84	56.6	10.7	45.9
134	Papua New Guinea	83	38.4	-6.2	44.6
135	Paraguay	84	45.2	-0.7	45.9
136	Peru	85	49.2	2.0	47.2
137	Philippines	86	51.6	3.1	48.5
138	Poland	99	62.7	-2.7	65.4
139	Portugal	95	67.0	6.8	60.2
140	Puerto Rico	84	63.6	17.7	45.9
141	Qatar	78	45.6	7.5	38.1
142	Romania	94	53.0	-5.9	58.9
143	Russia	97	64.5	1.7	62.8
144	Rwanda	70	18.5	-9.2	27.7
145	Saint Kitts and Nevis	67	45.5	30.8	23.7
146	Saint Lucia	62	51.1	33.9	17.2
147	St. Vincent and the Grenadines	71	48.4	19.4	29.0
148	Samoa (Western)	88	49.7	-1.4	51.1
149	Sao Tome and Principe	67	37.9	14.2	23.7
150	Saudi Arabia	84	44.1	-1.8	45.9
151	Senegal	66	21.3	-1.1	22.4
152	Serbia and Montenegro	89	53.8	1.4	52.4
153	Seychelles	86	60.6	12.1	48.5
154	Sierra Leone	64	13.8	-6.0	19.8
155	Singapore	108	60.7	-16.5	77.2
156	Slovak Republic	96	63.2	1.7	61.5
157	Slovenia	96	72.4	10.9	61.5
158	Solomon Islands	84	41.5	-4.4	45.9
159	Somalia	68	15.2	-9.9	25.1
160	South Africa	72	38.3	8.0	30.3
161	Spain	98	75.8	11.7	64.1
162	Sri Lanka	79	47.7	8.3	39.4
163	Sudan	71	24.6	-4.4	29.0
164	Suriname	89	50.6	-1.8	52.4

	Country	National IQ	QHC	Residual QHC	Fitted QHC
165	Swaziland	68	22.2	-2.9	25.1
166	Sweden	99	82.9	17.5	65.4
167	Switzerland	101	82.2	14.1	68.1
168	Syria	83	38.9	-5.7	44.6
169	Taiwan	105	79.4	6.1	73.3
170	Tajikistan	87	42.4	-7.4	49.8
171	Tanzania	72	23.2	-7.1	30.3
172	Thailand	91	50.3	-4.7	55.0
173	Timor-Leste	87	27.5	-22.3	49.8
174	Togo	70	26.0	-1.7	27.7
175	Tonga	86	40.5	-8.0	48.5
176	Trinidad and Tobago	85	52.0	4.8	47.2
177	Tunisia	83	40.6	-4.0	44.6
178	Turkey	90	50.2	-3.5	53.7
179	Turkmenistan	87	41.7	-8.1	49.8
180	Uganda	73	25.4	-6.2	31.6
181	Ukraine	97	61.8	-1.0	62.8
182	United Arab Emirates	84	48.8	2.9	45.9
183	United Kingdom	100	76.7	10.0	66.7
184	United States	98	86.6	22.5	64.1
185	Uruguay	96	64.0	2.5	61.5
186	Uzbekistan	87	39.4	-10.4	49.8
187	Vanuatu	84	31.4	-14.5	45.9
188	Venezuela	84	47.4	1.5	45.9
189	Vietnam	94	39.5	-19.4	58.9
190	Yemen	85	24.5	-22.7	47.2
191	Zambia	71	21.8	-7.2	29.0
192	Zimbabwe	66	25.2	2.8	22.4

we can divide the group of 192 countries into five categories on the basis of the direction and size of residuals: (1) countries around the regression line (residuals below ±5.0), (2) moderate positive outliers (from 5.0 to 11.8), (3) moderate negative outliers (from -5.0 to -11.8), (4) large positive deviations (11.9 or higher), and (5) large negative deviations (-11.9 or higher). In the next sections, the relationship between national

IQ and QHC will be analyzed by these five categories.

3. Residuals by Regional Groups

An interesting question concerns the regional distribution of small and large residuals. Are the countries with small and large residuals distributed more or less evenly in different regions of the world, or do some regions deviate clearly from the average world pattern? In other words, does the research hypothesis explain the variation in the QHC index points equally well in all parts of the world?

For the purposes of this analysis, the total group of 192 countries is divided into five regional groups. The group of Europe and European offshoots includes 46 countries. Australia, Canada, New Zealand, and the United States, as well as Armenia, Cyprus, and Georgia belong to this regional group. The group of Latin America and the Caribbean includes 35 countries. The group of the Middle East and North Africa, including Algeria, Egypt, Libya, Morocco, Sudan, and Tunisia from North Africa and Azerbaijan, Kazakhstan, Kyrgyzstan, Tajikistan, Turkmenistan, and Uzbekistan from Central Asia, comprises 26 countries. The group of Asia-Pacific includes the rest of the Asian and Pacific countries (38), and the group of sub-Saharan Africa comprises 47 countries.

The results of the regression analysis given for single countries in Table 7.3 are summarized by these regional groups in Table 7.4. The countries of each regional group are divided into five categories on the basis of residuals: (1) residuals +11.9 and higher, (2) residuals from +5.0 to +11.8, (3) residuals below ±50, (4) residuals form -5.0 to -11.8, and (5) residuals -11.9 and higher.

Table 7.4 shows that there are some clear differences among the five regional groups. Large positive residuals characterize the group of Europe and European offshoot countries. For 26 countries positive residuals are 5.0 or larger (56.6%). This means that the average quality of human conditions measured by QHC is in these countries much higher than expected on the basis of the regression analysis. All of them are economically highly developed countries. Negative residuals are -5.0 or higher for six countries (Andorra, Armenia, Belarus, Georgia, Moldova, and Romania). Five of them are former socialist countries.

Table 7.4. The 192 countries cross-classified by the size of residuals and by regional groups

Regional Group	Number of Countries by Residuals					
	11.9 and above	5.0 to 11.8	Below ± 5.0	-5.0 to -11.8	-11.9 and above	Total
Europe and European offshoots						
Number	17	9	14	5	1	46
%	37.0	19.6	30.4	10.9	2.2	100
Mean	17.1	9.8	0.1	-6.7	-15.3	7.2
Latin America and the Caribbean						
Number	10	4	21	-	-	35
%	28.6	11.4	60.0	-	-	100.0
Mean	22.8	8.5	0.1	-	-	7.6
The Middle East and North Africa						
Number	2	1	13	7	3	26
%	7.7	3.8	50.0	26.9	11.5	100
Mean	13.8	7.5	-1.4	-7.5	-19.5	-3.6
Asia-Pacific						
Number	-	4	10	9	15	38
%	-	10.5	26.3	23.7	39.5	100.0
Mean	-	7.9	-1.3	-7.1	-22.3	-10.2
Sub-Saharan Africa						
Number	4	3	24	10	6	47
%	8.5	6.4	51.1	21.3	12.7	100.0
Mean	13.9	6.7	-0.9	-8.4	-13.7	-2.0
All 192 countries						
Number	33	21	82	31	25	192
%	17.2	10.9	42.7	16.1	13.0	100
Mean	18.2	8.6	-0.5	-7.8	-19.6	0.0

Most of the Latin American and Caribbean countries are around the regression line (60.0%), and positive residuals are 5.0 or higher for the rest of them. Negative residuals are not moderate or large for any country of this group. There is a large difference in residuals between the Caribbean and Latin American countries. Residuals are below ±5.0 for nearly all Latin American countries. Positive residuals are moderate only for Argentina, Chile, and Panama. National IQ seems to explain the variation in QHC exceptionally well in the group of Latin American countries, but not in the group of Caribbean countries. Positive residuals are moderate for the Bahamas and large for ten other Caribbean countries (Antigua and Barbuda, Barbados, Bermuda, Dominica, Grenada, Jamaica, Puerto Rico, Saint Kitts and Nevis, Saint Lucia, and St. Vincent and the Grenadines). Positive residual is around the regression line only for Trinidad and Tobago. It is evident that there are some other factors that have raised the quality of human conditions in the Caribbean countries much higher than expected on the basis of national IQs.

Small residuals characterize the group of the Middle East and North Africa. Residuals are around the regression line for 13 (50.0%) countries. Positive residuals are moderate only for Qatar and large for Israel and Lebanon. Negative residuals are moderate for seven countries (Iran, Kazakhstan, Kyrgyzstan, Syria, Tajikistan, Turkmenistan, and Uzbekistan) and large for Iraq, Morocco, and Yemen. Five of these ten countries are former Soviet republics. All of the countries of this regional group, except Israel, are principally Muslim countries.

Large negative residuals characterize the group of other Asian and Pacific countries. Positive residuals are moderate only for New Caledonia, the Northern Mariana Islands, Sri Lanka, and Taiwan. Negative residuals are moderate or large for 24 countries (63.1%). This means that the level of the quality of human conditions is much lower than expected on the basis of national IQs in most countries of this regional group. The group of countries with moderate and large negative residuals includes poor South Asian countries, contemporary and former socialist countries, small Pacific island states, and economically highly developed East Asian countries (Hong Kong and Singapore). It is obvious that there cannot be any single factor that could explain all these deviations.

For most sub-Saharan African countries (51.1%), residuals are around the regression line, which means that national IQ explains the variation in QHC satisfactorily for these countries, but there are also some highly deviating cases. Positive residuals are large for Equatorial Guinea, Gabon, Sao Tome and Principe, and the Seychelles. Equatorial

Guinea and Gabon are oil-producing countries, and the Seychelles is a successful tourist country just like the Caribbean countries. Negative residuals are large for Burkina Faso, the Comoros, Madagascar, Mali, Mauritania, and Niger. All of them are extremely poor countries.

It can justifiably be concluded that the average quality of human conditions is highly dependent on the level of national IQ in all regions of the world, but the regional means of residuals disclose significant regional differences in the direction and size of residuals. The mean of residuals is strongly positive for the group of Europe and European offshoots (7.2) as well as for the group of Latin American and Caribbean countries (7.6), whereas the means are negative for the three other regional groups. The negative residuals are relatively small for the groups of the Middle East and North Africa (-3.6) and sub-Saharan Africa (-2.0), but it is strongly negative for the group of other Asian and Pacific countries (-10.2). The discrepancy between the predicted level of QHC and the actual level is greatest in Asia. On the other hand, large negative residuals imply that there is a lot of unused human potential to improve the quality of human conditions in most of the Asian and Pacific countries.

4. Countries Around the Regression Line

Table 7.4 shows that residuals are around the regression line for 82 countries. Their actual values of QHC differ only a little from the predicted values (regression line), and because of measurement errors, we cannot always be sure about the real direction of deviations. This category includes the following countries (Table 7.3): Albania, Algeria, Azerbaijan, Bahrain, Belize, Bolivia, Bosnia and Herzegovina, Botswana, Brazil, Brunei, Bulgaria, Cameroon, Central African Republic, Chad, Colombia, Congo-Zaire, Costa Rica, Cuba, the Czech Republic, Djibouti, Dominican Republic, Ecuador, Egypt, El Salvador, Eritrea, Estonia, Ethiopia, Fiji, Gambia, Ghana, Guatemala, Guinea, Guinea-Bissau, Guyana, Haiti, Honduras, Hungary, Japan, Jordan, Kenya, South Korea, Kuwait, Latvia, Lesotho, Liberia, Libya, Macedonia, Malawi, the Maldives, Malta, the Marshall Islands, Mauritius, Mexico, Mozambique, Namibia, Nicaragua, Nigeria, Oman, Paraguay, Peru, the Philippines, Poland, Russia, Samoa, Saudi Arabia, Senegal, Serbia and Montenegro, Slovakia, Solomon Islands, Sudan, Suriname, Swaziland,

Thailand, Togo, Trinidad and Tobago, Tunisia, Turkey, Ukraine, the United Arab Emirates, Uruguay, Venezuela, and Zimbabwe.

In these countries, the average level of the quality of human conditions seems to be more or less consistent with the level predicted on the basis of the regression equation. They comprise 43 percent of the total number of countries. Table 7.4 shows that these countries are well represented in all regional groups, but they are relatively most frequent in the groups of Latin America, the Middle East and North Africa, and sub-Saharan Africa. From Appendix 4, we can see how well different dimensions of human conditions are consistent with each other in these countries. Most residuals produced by the regression analyses of the five measures of human conditions on national IQ and presented in Appendix 4 are relatively small, slightly positive or slightly negative, for these 82 countries, but in several cases some dimensions differ significantly in a positive or negative direction. Let us see in which of these 82 countries there are clear discrepancies between the five dimensions of human conditions. It is reasonable to use one standard deviation as the criterion in each case to separate large residuals from smaller ones (GNI PPP per capita ±$7,060, literacy ±15.6 percent, tertiary ±14.2 percent, life expectancy 8.2 years, and ID 10.0 index points).

All residuals are smaller than one standard deviation for 30 of these 82 countries, but there are some clear discrepancies in residuals in the other 52 cases. Discrepancies are evenly distributed across the five variables. The number of large residuals varies from 13 in the case of PPP GNI per capita and 14 in the case of literacy to 17 in the cases of the tertiary enrollment ratio, life expectancy, and ID. In each case, there are some clear differences between the countries with large positive and large negative residuals.

In the case of PPP GNI per capita 2002, positive residuals are higher than 7,060 for Bahrain, Japan, Kuwait, Trinidad and Tobago, and the United Arab Emirates, and negative residuals are higher than -$7,060 for Azerbaijan, Bolivia, Ecuador, the Marshall Islands, Russia, Serbia and Montenegro, Solomon Islands, and Ukraine. Of the five countries with large positive residuals, Japan is an economically highly developed country, and the other four are oil-producing countries. Of the eight countries with large negative residuals, four are former socialist economies, Bolivia and Ecuador are Latin American countries, and the Marshall Islands and the Solomon Islands are remote Pacific island states.

The level of adult literacy is much higher (residual 15.6 or above) than expected in Kenya, Lesotho, the Maldives, Namibia, Swaziland, Trinidad and Tobago, and Zimbabwe, and much lower (residual -15.6 or above) than expected in Chad, Egypt, Ethiopia, Gambia, Guinea, Guinea-Bissau, and Senegal. There are not many clear differences in the characteristics of these countries. Nearly all of them are poor African countries. Large positive and negative residuals may be partly due to measurement errors, but there is also one systematic factor. Countries with large positive residuals, except the Maldives, are principally Christian countries, whereas all countries with large negative residuals are Muslim countries. The Maldives is an exception. It is a Muslim country with a high level of literacy.

In the case of the tertiary enrollment ratio, positive residuals are large (14.2 or above) for Egypt, Estonia, South Korea, Latvia, Libya, Russia, Trinidad and Tobago, and Ukraine, and negative residuals are large (-14.2 or above) for Bosnia and Herzegovina, Brunei, the Maldives, Malta, Mauritius, Oman, Samoa, the Solomon Islands, and Suriname. The countries with large positive residuals are economically more highly developed than most countries with large negative residuals. Seven of the countries with large negative residuals are small island states or other small countries, in which it is more difficult to organize institutions of higher education than in larger countries. Bosnia and Herzegovina still suffers from the devastations of the civil war in the 1990s. Egypt has traditionally been the center of higher education in the Arab world.

In the case of life expectancy at birth, positive residuals are large (8.2 or higher) for Bahrain, Costa Rica, Cuba, El Salvador, Kuwait, the United Arab Emirates, and Venezuela, and negative residuals are large for Botswana, the Central African Republic, Congo-Zaire, Kenya, Lesotho, Mozambique, Namibia, Russia, Swaziland, and Zimbabwe. There are some clear differences between these two groups of countries. Four of the countries with large positive residuals are relatively stabilized Latin American countries and three others are rich oil-producing countries. Nine of the countries with large negative residuals are sub-Saharan African countries, especially countries of southern Africa, in which HIV/AIDS has decreased life expectancy significantly. In Russia, alcoholism may be the principal reason for the decline of life expectancy.

The level of democratization (ID) in 2002 was much higher than expected (residual 10.0 or above) in Brazil, Fiji, Malawi, Malta, and Slovakia, and much lower than expected in Bahrain, Brunei, Cuba, Egypt, Jordan, Kuwait, Libya, the Maldives, Oman, Saudi Arabia, Tunisia, and the United Arab Emirates. In some characteristics, the two groups differ clearly from each other. Intensive multiparty competition has increased the degree of democratization in the five countries with large positive residuals. Nine of the 12 countries with large negative residuals are more or less autocratically ruled Arab countries, Brunei is a traditional monarchy supported by oil resources, Cuba is a socialist country, and the Maldives a small island state dominated by an autocratic president.

There are discrepancies between the five components of QHC in these 52 countries. Large positive residuals in some dimensions of human conditions are balanced by significant negative residuals in some other dimensions, and vice versa. For example, in the group of oil-producing countries (Bahrain, Brunei, Kuwait, Oman, Saudi Arabia, and the United Arab Emirates), moderate or large positive residuals in the case of PPP GNI per capita are balanced by large negative residuals for ID. The discrepancies are relatively small in the group of 32 countries for which only one residual is larger than one standard deviation. It is greater in the group of 14 countries for which two residuals are large, and it is greatest in the group of six countries (Egypt, Kuwait, the Maldives, Russia, Trinidad and Tobago, and the United Arab Emirates) for which three residuals are large. In Egypt, tertiary enrollment is much higher than expected, whereas literacy and the level of democratization are much lower. In Kuwait, per capita income and life expectancy are much higher than expected, whereas the level of democratization is low. In the Maldives, positive residual is high for literacy, whereas negative residuals are high for tertiary enrollment and ID. In Russia, tertiary enrollment is considerably higher and per capita income and life expectancy much lower than expected. In Trinidad and Tobago, per capita income and literacy have high positive residuals, whereas the residual of tertiary enrollment is much lower than expected. Finally, in the United Arab Emirates, per capita income and life expectancy are much higher and the level of democratization much lower than expected on the basis of national IQ. The patterns of discrepancies vary from country to country. Therefore, small residuals based on the regression equation of QHC on national IQ do not always mean that all dimensions of human conditions are consistent with national IQ. Consistency is best in the group of 30 countries for which all residuals based on single variables are smaller than one standard deviation.

5. Moderate Positive Outliers

For 21 countries (see Table 7.3) positive residuals are moderate (5.0 to 11.8): Argentina, the Bahamas, Cape Verde, Chile, Congo-Brazzaville, Croatia, Italy, Lithuania, Luxembourg, New Caledonia, New Zealand, the Northern Mariana Islands, Panama, Portugal, Qatar, Slovenia, South Africa, Spain, Sri Lanka, Taiwan, and the United Kingdom. What factors could explain their significant positive deviations? Appendix 4 shows that at least 3, in most cases 4 or 5, residuals produced by regressions of the five components of IQHC on national IQ are positive, but the size and composition of positive residuals varies so much among these 21 countries that it is difficult to find any common pattern. The group includes countries from all regional groups and also from all levels of national IQ, but European countries are relatively more frequent than the countries of the Middle East and North Africa and sub-Saharan Africa.

The group includes eight economically highly developed countries (Italy, Luxembourg, New Zealand, Portugal, Slovenia, Spain, Taiwan, and the United Kingdom). Most aspects of human conditions measured by the five indicators of the quality of human conditions are in these countries somewhat better than expected on the basis of national IQs. In all of them, per capita income is higher than expected, and all of them are democracies. Further, it is characteristic for them, except for Luxembourg, that tertiary enrollment ratios are much higher than expected. In Croatia and Lithuania, per capita income is still lower than expected, but the levels of tertiary enrollment and democratization are much higher than expected (see Appendix 4).

Bahrain and Qatar are rich oil-producing countries for which the level of per capita income is much higher than expected, whereas residuals for ID are highly negative. In these countries, oil money has been used to further education and social services, and, consequently, residuals of life expectancy are highly positive (see Appendix 4).

Argentina, Chile, and Panama are Latin American countries in which per capita income is lower but the levels of education, life expectancy, and democratization higher than expected on the basis of respective regression analyses (see Appendix 4). Consequently, the average human conditions seem to be considerably better than expected on the basis of the average relationship between national IQ and QHC.

Cape Verde, Congo-Brazzaville, and South Africa are the three sub-Saharan African countries in this category. They are quite different countries, but the level of literacy is higher than expected in all of them. Cape Verde's moderately positive residual based on QHC seems to be due to higher than expected level of literacy and life expectancy; Congo-Brazzaville's primarily to much higher than expected level of literacy; and South Africa's to higher than expected levels of per capita income and literacy.

The Bahamas, New Caledonia, the Northern Mariana Islands, and Sri Lanka are separate cases. Much higher than expected levels of per capita income have made their residuals moderately positive. The Bahamas' wealth is based on flourishing tourism industries; New Caledonia's, principally to the contributions of its significant European population. The Northern Mariana Islands' position in this category of countries is due to much higher than expected levels of literacy and life expectancy, and also to a higher than expected level of per capita income. Sri Lanka is an exceptional country. Despite its long ethnic civil war, it has been able to maintain other aspects of human conditions satisfactorily. Positive residuals for literacy, life expectancy, and ID are large. The long tradition of democracy may have helped Sri Lanka to improve human conditions (cf. Freedom in the World 2004, pp. 528–532).

One common characteristic for these countries is that nearly all of them are democracies. Only Congo-Brazzaville and Qatar were clearly non-democracies in 2002. This common characteristic implies that different aspects of human conditions tend to be better in democracies than in autocracies. A moderate or high level of economic development and per capita income is also common for most of them.

6. Moderate Negative Outliers

The category of moderate negative residuals (-5.0 to -11.8) includes 31 countries (see Table 7.3): Andorra, Angola, Armenia, Belarus, Benin, Burundi, the Cook Islands, Côte d'Ivoire, Georgia, India, Indonesia, Iran, Kazakhstan, Kiribati, Kyrgyzstan, Malaysia, Micronesia, Nepal, Papua New Guinea, Romania, Rwanda, Sierra Leone, Somalia, Syria,

Tajikistan, Tanzania, Tonga, Turkmenistan, Uganda, Uzbekistan, and Zambia. The group does not include any Latin American country, but the other regional groups are well represented, and national IQs vary from high to low

In some respects, the 31 countries of this category differ clearly from the countries with moderate positive residuals. This category includes only one economically highly developed European country (Andorra). The group is dominated by former socialist countries (9), sub-Saharan African countries (10), and small Pacific island states (5). It is characteristic for these countries that, except in the cases of Andorra and Sierra Leone, three or more of the five residuals reported in Appendix 4 are negative. They indicate that in most dimensions human conditions are worse than expected on the basis of national IQs. Per capita income is lower than expected in 27, the level of democratization in 26, tertiary enrollment in 24, and life expectancy in 23 of the 31 countries, whereas literacy is better than expected in 19 countries.

It is common for the nine former socialist countries that residuals of per capita income are negative for all of them and more than one standard deviation for eight of them. The level of democratization is lower than expected in all of them, but negative residual is large only for Kazakhstan, Turkmenistan, and Uzbekistan. The level of literacy is higher than expected in all of them, whereas the level of tertiary enrollment is lower than expected in six countries and higher than expected in Belarus, Kazakhstan, and Kyrgyzstan. Life expectancy does not differ much from the predicted level. Moderate negative residuals of QHC seem to be principally due to a low levels of per capita income and democracy in the former socialist countries.

The values of various components of QHC are lower than expected for the sub-Saharan African countries of this category. For most of these poor countries, residuals of PPP GNI per capita and ID are slightly negative, but the largest negative residuals concern Life expectancy. In eight cases these negative residuals are more than one standard deviation. HIV/AIDS disease worsens human conditions in many sub-Saharan African countries. The level of literacy is lower than expected in seven countries, and the level of tertiary enrollment in six countries. Moderate negative residuals of QHC seem to be principally due to much lower than expected life expectancy in these sub-Saharan African countries.

In the group of five Pacific island states, moderate negative residuals of QHC are principally due to much lower than expected levels of the tertiary enrollment ratio. For four countries, negative residuals are more than one standard deviation. As noted above, it is much more difficult to provide higher education in very small countries than in bigger countries. Other aspects of human conditions are more consistent with national IQs, although per capita income is much lower than expected in Kiribati, and the level of democratization in Tonga. For Papua New Guinea, the level of ID is exceptionally high (cf. Freedom in the World 2004, pp. 439–441).

The other seven countries of this category are more or less special cases. Andorra's position in this category seems to be due to its much lower than expected level of ID. However, its ID may be artificially low (see Appendix 3) for the reason that although France and Spain formally control the government, it does not need to restrict the liberty of people (cf. Freedom in the World 2004, pp. 26–28). India's much lower than expected level of literacy has lowered its negative residual of QHC to -7.0. Other aspects of human conditions are more consistent with the country's national IQ, although its per capita income is also much lower than expected. Nepal is a similar case. Indonesia's place in this category is principally due to significant negative residuals of PPP GNI per capita, the tertiary enrollment ratio, and ID. The same combination of negative residuals explains Malaysia's place in this category. Iran's negative residual (-5.7) is due to its low level of democratization. Syria is a similar case.

Compared to the countries with moderate positive residuals, nearly all of the 31 countries of this category are much poorer and less democratic. For most of them, the level of per capita income is much lower than expected on the basis of national IQs. Only 12 of the 31 countries were clearly above the threshold of democracy in 2002 (see Appendix 3): Armenia, Benin, the Cook Islands, Georgia, India, Indonesia, Kiribati, Malaysia, Nepal, Papua New Guinea, Romania, and Uganda. The other 19 countries were more or less below the minimum threshold of democracy.

Moderate or large negative residuals of PPP GNI per capita and ID for the former socialist countries imply that the nature of a country's economic and political systems matters. Socialist economic and political systems seem to have hampered economic development and the improvement of human conditions. In the case of sub-Saharan African countries, HIV/AIDS seems to be a significant factor which has impaired the quality of human conditions. The geographical isolation and small populations of Pacific island states have impeded especially the development of higher education and industrialization.

7. Countries with Large Positive Residuals

The group of countries with large positive residuals (11.9 or higher) includes the following 33 countries: Antigua and Barbuda, Australia, Austria, Barbados, Belgium, Bermuda, Canada, Cyprus, Denmark, Dominica, Equatorial Guinea, Finland, France, Gabon, Germany, Greece, Grenada, Iceland, Ireland, Israel, Jamaica, Lebanon, the Netherlands, Norway, Puerto Rico, Saint Kitts and Nevis, Saint Lucia, St. Vincent and the Grenadines, Sao Tome and Principe, the Seychelles, Sweden, Switzerland, and the United States. Most of these countries are European and Caribbean countries. The group does not include any country from the regional group of other Asian and Pacific countries. Nearly all residuals produced by regressions of the five components of QHC on national IQ are positive for these countries (see Appendix 4).

The 33 countries of this category deviate from the research hypothesis because the quality of human conditions in these countries is much higher than expected on the basis of the regression of QHC on national IQ. It should be noted, however, that the relative significance of a deviation of 11.9 or more QHC index points from the regression line is not the same at the national IQ level of 100 as at the level of national IQ of 70. The fitted QHC is 66.7 at the level of national IQ 100, whereas it is only 27.6 at the level of national IQ 70 (see Figure 7.1). This means that large positive residuals of the same size are relatively much more significant for countries with a national IQ of 70 than for countries with a national IQ of 100. In the following, each country will be discussed separately in order to find out what factors might explain its outlying position. However, because the European and European offshoots countries of this category can be assumed to have many common characteristics, they will be discussed first. The same concerns the Caribbean countries of this category. They will be discussed in the next subgroup. Finally, the other six countries are discussed.

7.1. European and European offshoots countries

Australia. The country's highly deviating position is principally based on large positive residuals of per capita income, tertiary enrollment, and democratization (see Appendix 4). The levels of literacy and life expectancy do not differ much from the regression line. High levels of economic development, higher education, and democratization have helped Australia to raise the quality of human conditions much higher than expected on the basis of the average relationship between national IQ and QHC. Technological innovations, market economy systems, and political freedoms seem to be behind these exceptional achievements (cf. Gwartney and Lawson, 2000, p. 23; Freedom in the World 2004, pp. 43–45).

Austria. The pattern of sectional residuals is the same as in Australia. Positive residuals are large for PPP GNI per capita, the tertiary enrollment ratio, and ID components of QHC and near zero in the cases of the adult literacy rate and life expectancy at birth variables.

Belgium. The pattern is exactly the same as in Australia and Austria.

Canada. The pattern is the same as in Australia with one small exception. The Index of Democratization (ID) is only slightly higher than expected.

Cyprus. The pattern differs from that of Australia in one significant point. The level of tertiary enrollment is clearly lower than expected (residual -10.3). The small size of Cyprus makes it understandable that the country cannot provide extensive programs of higher education such as those of bigger countries. Successful tourism industries have furthered economic development and the improvement of human conditions in Cyprus.

Denmark. The pattern is the same as in Australia and Austria.

Finland. The pattern is again the same as in Australia and Austria.

France. The pattern is the same as in Australia and Austria with two small differences. The positive residuals of tertiary enrollment and democratization are slightly smaller than one standard deviation.

Germany. The pattern is the same as in Australia and Austria with one exception. The level of tertiary enrollment seems to be only slightly higher than expected on the basis of national IQ. Differences in the definitions of tertiary education may explain this difference.

Greece. The pattern is the same as in Australia and Austria, but because of its lower national IQ, the levels of literacy and life expectancy are clearly higher than expected.

Iceland. The pattern is the same as in Australia and Austria with one exception. The residual of tertiary enrollment is only slightly positive. This difference is due to Iceland's small population just as in the case of Cyprus.

Ireland. The pattern is the same as in Australia and Austria, but because of its relatively low national IQ, the residuals of literacy and life expectancy are clearly positive, as in the case of Greece.

The Netherlands. The pattern is the same as in Australia and Austria, although the residual of tertiary enrollment is slightly smaller than one standard deviation.

Norway. The pattern is exactly the same as in Australia and Austria.

Sweden. The pattern is exactly the same as in Australia and Austria.

Switzerland. The pattern of residuals differs from Australia and Austria in one point. The residual of tertiary enrollment is slightly negative. It may be that a stricter definition of higher education has reduced the number of students in the institutions of higher education.

The United States. The pattern is again the same as in Australia and Austria.

In these 17 European and European offshoot countries, the patterns of the components of QHC are nearly the same. Their outlying positions are based in nearly all cases on exceptionally high levels of per capita income, tertiary enrollment, and democratization. All these countries are democracies and market economies. The level of life expectancy does not differ much from the predicted level. National IQs of these countries vary from 92 (Greece and Ireland) to 101 (Iceland and Switzerland).

7.2. Caribbean countries

Antigua and Barbuda. Its exceptionally large positive residual of QHC (25.5) is due to large residuals of PPP GNI per capita, adult literacy rate, life expectancy, and ID. Despite its low level of national IQ (70), Antigua and Barbuda has been able to establish much better than expected human conditions for its population. Tourism industries introduced by western investors and enterprises have furthered economic development, the market economy, and the improvement of human conditions. The political system has been democratic since independence in 1981.

Barbados. The pattern of large positive residuals is the same as in Antigua and Barbuda, although the residual of ID is only slightly positive. The success of these two countries implies that the transfer of people, technologies, enterprises, and managerial skills from countries of higher national IQs can help economic development and the improvement of human conditions in countries with low national IQs (cf. Gwartney and Lawson, 2000, p. 26).

Bermuda. The basic pattern is the same as in Antigua and Barbuda, but there are some clear differences. The level of PPP GNI per capita differs more than three standard deviations from the expected level. Bermuda has achieved an exceptionally high level of per capita income by providing financial services for international firms and luxury tourism facilities for hundreds of thousands of visitors principally from the United States. Its geographical location is excellent for these purposes (see *The World Factbook* 2000, p. 55). Besides, whites constitute nearly 40 percent of its population. The level of tertiary enrollment is much higher than expected, whereas the level of democratization is lower than expected. Bermuda is an overseas territory of the UK.

Dominica. The pattern of residuals is nearly the same as in Antigua and Barbuda, although the level of per capita income is only moderately higher than expected. Economic and political institutions are similar.

Grenada. The basic pattern is the same as in Antigua and Barbuda.

Jamaica. The pattern of residuals differs somewhat from the pattern of Antigua & Barbuda in two points. The level of per capita income is only slightly higher than expected. Because of its larger population, Jamaica has not been economically as successful as smaller Caribbean countries. Tourism is not as important as in smaller island states. The large positive residual of QHC is principally due to the much higher than expected levels of literacy and life expectancy, and to a lesser degree to the clearly higher than expected level of democratization.

Puerto Rico. The pattern is nearly the same as in Antigua and Barbuda, but the level of democratization is only moderately higher than expected. Puerto Rico's association with the United States has facilitated economic and educational development as well as the stabilization of democratic institutions. Tourism is also important for Puerto Rico.

Saint Kitts and Nevis. The pattern is exactly the same as in Antigua and Barbuda. All residuals of the five components of QHC are positive and large.

Saint Lucia. The pattern of residuals is again the same as in Antigua and Barbuda.

St. Vincent and the Grenadines. The pattern is the same as in Antigua and Barbuda, but the level of per capita income is only slightly higher than expected on the basis of national IQ. Tourism has not yet become as successful as in some other Caribbean countries.

It is common for these Caribbean countries that the levels of per capita income, education, life expectancy, and democracy are much higher than expected on the basis of national IQs. As a consequence, residuals of QHC are highly positive, and these countries deviate from our hypothesis. We believe that their outlying position is principally due to the transfers of technologies, investments, managerial skills, and also people from the countries of higher national IQs. Their geographical position near the great world markets has made such transfers profitable. Tourism from economically highly developed countries has become the crucial industry in the Caribbean countries.

7.3. Other positive outliers

Equatorial Guinea. The country's high positive residual of QHC is partly due to its exceptionally low value of national IQ (59). Of the five components of QHC, the highest positive residuals are for PPP GNI per capita and adult literacy rate (see Appendix 4). The discovery of an oil and gas field north of Bioko Island has increased per capita income dramatically. Equatorial Guinea's PPP GNI per capita of $9,110 in 2002 is among the three highest in sub-Saharan Africa. This exceptional achievement is completely due to oil production carried out by foreign companies and technologies (cf. Esterhuysen, 1998, pp. 158–161). Because of the high level of adult literacy (83%), the positive residual of adult literacy (31.8) is among the highest in the world. Dramatically increased oil production provides an explanation for Equatorial Guinea's outlying position.

Gabon. Just as in the case of Equatorial Guinea, oil production has raised the level of per capita income much higher than expected, although there are also other important natural resources (see Esterhuysen, 1998, pp. 174–178). The residuals of the adult literacy rate, the tertiary enrollment ratio, and life expectancy are also clearly positive. It is reasonable to argue that the introduction of western oil technologies and managerial skills have helped to raise the average level of human conditions in

Equatorial Guinea and Gabon much higher than expected on the basis of their national IQs.

Israel. The average human conditions measured by QHC are much better than expected on the basis of its national IQ. The pattern of positive residuals of the five measures of human conditions is principally the same as in Australia and in other economically highly developed countries. In the case of Israel, the highest positive residuals are for the tertiary enrollment ratio and ID.

Lebanon. Despite its long civil war and conflict with Israel, human conditions have remained in Lebanon much better than expected on the basis of its national IQ. The five components of QHC are relatively well balanced. The residual of PPP GNI per capita is negative, but the other four residuals are clearly positive. Its large positive residual of QHC is primarily due to the exceptionally high level of tertiary enrollment.

Sao Tome and Principe. The country's outlying position is primarily due to its much higher than expected levels of literacy and life expectancy. For the other three components of QHC residuals are only slightly positive. The country's high level of literacy (83%) is a heritage from its population's Afro-European origin. Cocoa is the country's only significant export crop. Since 1987 the cocoa plantations have been under foreign management (see Esterhuysen, 1998, p. 291; Freedom in the World 2004, pp. 483–485),

The Seychelles. This small island state is comparable to the Caribbean tourist countries. Its large positive residual of QHC is a consequence of the much higher than expected level of per capita income. Economic development and growth has been led by the tourist sector, which employs about 30 percent of the labor force and provides more than 70 percent of hard currency earnings (see *The World Factbook*, 2000, p. 431). "Income from tourism has helped to make the Seychelles a comparatively affluent state, with the highest per capita GNP of all African countries" (Esterhuysen, 1998, pp. 301–303). The Seychelles is an example of a poor country which has benefited from foreign investments and technologies

The review of these 33 countries has disclosed some common characteristics of the countries in which human conditions as measured by QHC are much better than expected on the basis of the regression of QHC on national IQ. Of these 33 countries, 17 are economically highly developed European and European offshoot democracies. It is common for these countries that in nearly all cases the levels of per capita income, tertiary enrollment, and democratization are much higher than expected on the basis of national IQs and that the actual values of literacy and life expectancy do not differ much from the predicted ones. Thus it can be concluded that in this group of 17 countries large positive residuals of QHC are in nearly all cases due to three components of QHC, whereas the other two components are consistent with the average relationships between these components and national IQ.

In the ten Caribbean countries of this category, the emergence of large positive residuals of QHC has been a consequence of extensive investments, especially in tourist industries and transfers of technologies and skills from economically highly developed countries. The geographical location of Caribbean countries has made such investments profitable. In this respect, the Seychelles is comparable to the Caribbean countries. Western investments in oil industries and transfers of technologies and, to a limited extent, also of people, provide an explanation for exceptional economic growth in Equatorial Guinea and Gabon. In Israel the pattern of residuals is exactly the same as in the group of economically highly developed European countries.

Nearly all of these 33 countries are democracies. Only Equatorial Guinea differs clearly from this common democratic pattern (cf. Freedom in the World 2004, pp. 192-194). The same democratic pattern was evident already in the previous group of 21 countries with moderate positive residuals.

8. Countries with Large Negative Residuals

The group of countries with large negative residuals (-11.9 or higher) includes the following 25 countries: Afghanistan, Bangladesh, Bhutan, Burkina Faso, Cambodia, China, the Comoros, Hong Kong, Iraq, North Korea, Laos, Madagascar, Mali, Mauritania, Moldova, Mongolia, Morocco, Myanmar, Niger, Pakistan, Singapore, Timor-Leste, Vanuatu, Vietnam, and Yemen.

These 25 countries deviate from the research hypothesis. The quality of human conditions seems to be much worse than expected on the basis of the regression of QHC on national IQ. The countries of this category differ from the countries with large positive residuals in many respects. There are no economically highly developed European democracies in this group and no country from Latin America. The category is dominated by Asian countries. In the following, each country will be discussed separately. The purpose is to examine what measures of human conditions are responsible for large negative residuals and what additional factors might explain these deviations. It is possible to separate three sub-regional groups from these 25 countries: East Asian countries (6), South and Southeast Asian countries (7), and sub-Saharan African countries (6). Each sub-regional group may have some common characteristics.

8.1. East Asian countries

China. China's negative residual is extremely large (-33.6), and it is one of the most highly deviating countries in the world. The reasons can be traced to history. China suffered from serious civil wars since the 19th century and from the Japanese attack and occupation during the first half of the 20th century, but since the 1950s the new Communist government has maintained domestic peace. Economic development has been rapid in China during the last two decades, but the residuals of all components of QHC are still highly negative, which indicates that various aspects of human conditions are much worse than expected on the basis of China's high national IQ. The socialist system has not been able to improve human conditions as effectively as market economies in South Korea and Taiwan (cf. Gwartney and Lawson, 2000, p. 35). The highest negative residuals are in the cases of tertiary enrollment and democratization. It is possible that China's extremely large population makes it difficult to improve human conditions.

It should be noted that China has not always been less developed than expected on the basis of its high national IQ. According to Angus Maddison's (1999) historical analysis, China's per capita income was approximately at the same level as in Europe in the year 50; in the period 1000-1500 it was higher than in Europe, but from the sixteenth century Europe started to outperform China, which had isolated itself from new scientific and technological developments in Europe.

Hong Kong. The level of per capita income in Hong Kong is much higher than expected on the basis of its extremely high national IQ (cf. Gwartney and Lawson, 2000, p. 49), but the residuals of the four other components of QHC are negative. The residuals of tertiary enrollment and ID are larger than two standard deviations. Because of its status as a part of China, full democratization of its political system is hardly possible. Therefore, Hong Kong's position in this category is partly a technical consequence of its status as a Special Administrative Region of China.

North Korea. The extremely harsh and peculiar Communist government, which has ruled the country since 1948, can be regarded as responsible for the poverty and misery in North Korea. The negative residual of QHC for North Korea (-36.6) is higher than for any other country in the world (see Figure 7.1). It indicates that the quality of human conditions in relation to national IQ is very poor. The residuals of all five components of QHC are highly negative, and three of them are larger than two standard deviations (PPP GNI per capita, life expectancy, and ID). The improvement of human conditions in North Korea is hardly possible without a change of its economic and governmental system (cf. Freedom in the World 2004, pp. 419–422).

Mongolia. Mongolia is a former socialist country, which has not yet been able to establish an effective market economy. The country's isolated geographical position constitutes an additional factor which has hampered economic development. The large negative residual of QHC is primarily due to Mongolia's extremely low per capita income and to a lesser degree to negative residuals of tertiary enrollment and life expectancy. Literacy is already as high as expected on the basis of its national IQ. Mongolia has had a democratic system since the 1990s (cf. Freedom in the World 2004, pp. 386–389). A problem is to what extent its harsh geographical conditions can permanently retard socioeconomic development.

Singapore. Despite its higher than expected level of per capita income, the residual of QHC is highly negative for Singapore. Life expectancy differs only slightly from the expected level, but the levels of the other three components of QHC are clearly lower than expected on the basis of Singapore's high national IQ. Singapore and Hong Kong are the only economically highly developed and wealthy countries in this category of the largest negative outliers. Just as in Hong Kong, large negative residuals of tertiary enrollment and ID have made Singapore a negative outlier (cf. Freedom in the World 2004, pp. 502–506).

Vietnam. Vietnam's large negative residual of QHC is primarily due to the much lower than expected levels of per capita income, tertiary enrollment, and democratization. The pattern is the same as in China. The long civil war and the war with the United States damaged the country badly and caused poverty, but after the war the socialist economic system and the lack of democracy have retarded economic recovery and the improvement of human conditions. It should be noted that negative residuals of QHC are considerably smaller for Indonesia, Malaysia, and Thailand than for socialist and former socialist Cambodia, Laos, and Vietnam.

Because of their high national IQs, East Asian countries should achieve a higher level of the quality of human conditions (QHC) than most other countries of the world. These six negative outliers are still far away from the target level, but the examples of Japan, South Korea, and Taiwan show that it is not impossible for East Asian countries to improve all aspects of human conditions. Socialist experiments have probably hampered development in China, North Korea, Mongolia, and Vietnam. Also, Mongolia's geographical conditions and isolation may damper economic development. In China, the enormous size of its population may constitute an additional restrictive factor. It will be difficult to extend the benefits of economic development to all sections of the country's population.

8.2. South and Southeast Asian countries

Afghanistan. Long civil wars and ethnic conflicts have devastated Afghanistan badly. Its negative residual of QHC is extremely high (-32.7). The negative residuals of all components of QHC are large, especially for literacy and life expectancy. It is reasonable to argue that the country's geographical isolation and violent conflicts have been primarily responsible for the poor quality of human conditions in the country (cf. Freedom in the World 2004, pp. 15–19).

Bangladesh. Large negative residuals of per capita income, literacy, and tertiary enrollment have raised Bangladesh' residual of QHC to being highly negative. The negative residual of literacy is larger than two standard deviations. The level of life expectancy and democratization are consistent with its national IQ. The extremely high density of population may be an additional factor that maintains poverty and low level of education in Bangladesh.

Bhutan. With one exception, the pattern of negative residuals is similar to that of Bangladesh. The residual of ID is also highly negative for Bhutan (cf. Freedom in the World 2004, pp. 77–80). The country's geographic isolation and difficult mountainous nature may be additional factors that maintain poverty and hamper development in the country.

Cambodia. Just as in the case of Afghanistan, long civil wars ruined Cambodia's economy and increased poverty and misery. The residuals of all components of QHC are highly negative. A significant difference from Afghanistan is that Cambodia is not geographically isolated and that it has a relatively stable government, which has been able to restore domestic peace (cf. Freedom in the World 2004, pp. 109–112). Therefore, Cambodia may have better chances than Afghanistan to improve human conditions.

Laos. Laos has also suffered from long civil wars and other domestic conflicts but also from its autocratic socialist economic and political systems. The negative residual of QHC is extremely large (-27.5). The residuals of all components of QHC are highly negative. The pattern is the same as in Afghanistan and Cambodia. The country's isolated geographical position constitutes an additional factor that has hampered economic development. The example of neighboring Thailand indicates that a different economic and political system would help to improve human conditions.

Myanmar. The country has suffered from ethnic civil wars and autocratic military rule since the 1960s. The military government's socialist experiments and isolationalist policies have retarded economic development. The negative residuals of all components of QHC, except literacy, are large. The pattern is principally the same as in Afghanistan, Cambodia, and Laos. The improvement of human conditions in Myanmar presupposes the replacement of the military government by a more democratic system and the restoring of domestic peace (cf. Freedom in the World 2004, pp. 101–105).

Pakistan. The pattern of residuals is approximately the same as in Bangladesh. The largest negative residual is in the case of literacy. Contrary to Bangladesh, the residual of ID is also negative. The lack of a stable democratic system may have hampered the improvement of human conditions in Pakistan (cf. Freedom in the World 2004, pp. 428–434).

All of these South and Southeast Asian negative outliers are poor countries. Most of them have suffered from civil wars and ethnic conflicts as well as from the lack of stable political systems and democracy.

8.3. Sub-Saharan African countries

Burkina Faso. The country's large negative residual of QHC is entirely due to its exceptionally low level of literacy. The size of its negative residual of literacy (-49.9) is three standard deviations. It reflects the country's low level of socioeconomic development. Besides, Burkina Faso is a relatively isolated landlocked land (see Easterhuysen, 1998, pp. 95–98).

The Comoros. Four residuals of the components of QHC are negative, and residuals of literacy and ID are large. Only life expectancy is consistent with national IQ. As an island state, the Comoros is not geographically isolated, but the lack of a stable political system has impeded socioeconomic development. Besides, the country's natural resources are limited (see Esterhuysen, 1998, pp. 125–129; Freedom in the World 2004, pp. 140–142).

Madagascar. Madagascar is an island state. All residuals of the components of QHC are negative, but only the residuals of tertiary enrollment and life expectancy are larger than one standard deviation. The country has suffered from the lack of a stable political system and democracy like the Comoros, and now the HIV/AIDS disease constitutes a new factor that impedes socioeconomic development (see Esterhuysen, 1998, pp. 221–225; Freedom in the World 2004, pp. 347–350).

Mali. The pattern of residuals is the same as in Burkina Faso. The country's extremely low level of literacy is responsible for Mali's position in this group of large negative outliers. The residuals of the four other components of QHC are small. Mali is also a landlocked country like Burkina Faso.

Mauritania. The pattern of Burkina Faso and Mali is repeated in Mauritania. The negative residual of literacy is nearly two standard deviations large. Mauritania is not a landlocked country, but the ethnic heterogeneity of its population has made it difficult to maintain domestic peace and to establish a democratic system (cf. Freedom in the World 2004, pp. 369–371).

Niger. The pattern is exactly the same as in Burkina Faso. Niger is also a landlocked country.

Poverty and a low level of education are common for all these sub-Saharan African countries. Most of them have suffered from political instability and also from ethnic conflicts. Three of them are neighboring landlocked countries, which has probably impeded economic development.

8.4. Other countries with large negative residuals

Iraq. Violent domestic and external conflicts and the lack of democracy have hampered socioeconomic development and kept Iraq poor despite its large oil reserves. The residuals of all components of QHC are negative, and residuals of per capita income, literacy, and ID are larger than one standard deviation. The destruction of Saddam Hussein's autocratic government by foreign intervention in 2003 may have opened a way to establish a better governmental system, to establish domestic peace, and to improve human conditions (cf. Freedom in the World 2004, pp. 272–275).

Moldova. The poverty of Moldova can be traced to its socialist inheritance. The new governments of independent Moldova have not yet been able to establish effective institutions of a market economy. The residuals of per capita income and ID are highly negative. The stabilization of the democratic system and economic reforms might help to improve the quality of human conditions in Moldova, especially to raise its extremely low per capita income (cf. Karaynycky et al., 2001, pp. 272–282).

Morocco. Morocco is a traditional Arab monarchy without oil resources. Its large negative residual of QHC is primarily due to the large negative residual of literacy and to a lesser degree to negative residuals of per capita income, tertiary enrollment, and ID. Too many people are still illiterate, and too few of its young people receive higher education.

Timor-Leste. The long independence war against Indonesia devastated the country. All residuals of the five components of QHC are negative, and four of them are larger than one standard deviation. It will take time to improve human conditions in Timor-Leste, but the establishment of a democratic political system provides a favorable starting point for socioeconomic development (cf. Freedom in the World 2004, pp. 178–180).

Vanuatu. The exceptionally large negative residual of literacy (-47.0) is responsible for Vanuatu's dropping to the category of large negative outliers. In principle, it should be relatively easy to raise the level of literacy to the same level as in the other Pacific island states. The small size of Vanuatu's population explains the large negative residual of tertiary enrollment. Life expectancy and the level of democratization are already in balance with its national IQ (cf. Freedom in the World, 2004, pp. 620–622).

Yemen. All residuals of the five components of QHC are negative, and they are especially large for literacy and tertiary enrollment. The pattern is approximately the same as in Morocco. The country's traditionally isolated position has retarded economic and educational development. It is one of the poorest Arab countries.

Most countries with large positive residuals of QHC are characterized by much higher than expected levels of per capita income, tertiary enrollment, and democratization. The opposite is true for the countries with large negative residuals. In most of them, the levels of per capita income, tertiary enrollment, and democratization are much lower than expected on the basis of national IQs. Also, negative residuals of literacy are even larger than of tertiary enrollment for most of these countries. Further, it is characteristic for these countries that most of them have suffered from civil wars and ethnic conflicts and that nearly all of them are non-democracies (cf. Vanhanen, 1999). Only Bangladesh, Mongolia, and Vanuatu were clearly above the threshold of democracy in 2002. In addition, six of them are present or former socialist countries. Poverty, civil wars, ethnic conflicts, socialist experiments, and the lack of democracy have characterized the countries in which the average level of human conditions is much lower than expected on the basis of national IQs. Several of them are geographically isolated and landlocked countries. These factors may explain a considerable part of the difference between the countries with large positive and large negative residuals of QHC.

9. The Impact of Latitude and Annual Mean Temperature

According to our research hypothesis, national differences in the quality of human conditions as measured by QHC are assumed to be causally related to national IQs. We have argued that national differences in the average intelligence of nations emerged as a consequence of evolution when human populations that migrated out of Africa became adapted to greatly differing geographical and climatic conditions in other parts of the world. Therefore, it is reasonable to ask to what extent geographical and climatic differences are related to contemporary national IQs and to the measures of human conditions and to what extent they can explain variation in the measures of human conditions independently from national IQ. In other words, could they increase the explained part of variation in QHC? In the 18th century Montesquieu emphasized the significance of climate and other geographical factors, and Philip Parker (2000, p. viii) claims that latitude explains some seventy percent of the variances in income per capita.

Our argument is that human—economic, social, and political—conditions are principally under human control and that, therefore, differences in the average national intelligence may have a crucial impact on the nature of these conditions, but we do not want to deny the possibility that differences in geographical and climatic conditions may have some impact on human conditions independently from national IQ. It is possible that some geographical and climatic conditions, for example in tropical Africa, in deserts, or in the Arctic regions, are so inhospitable for human activities that it becomes impossible to establish conditions for human life similar to those in more hospitable environmental circumstances. Our hypothesis is that the impact of geographical and climatic conditions on the quality of human conditions takes place through evolved differences in national IQs, but it would be interesting to find out to what extent differences in geographical and climatic conditions explain the variation in the measures of human conditions directly and independently from national IQs. Furthermore, indicators of geographical and climatic conditions can be regarded as the most independent variables in their relation to contemporary human conditions.

This argument leads us to complement the causal analysis by taking into account two indicators of geographical and climatic conditions: latitude and annual mean temperature. Latitude measures distance on a meridian north or south of the equator, expressed in degrees and minutes. Data on this variable are derived from John L. Allen's *Student Atlas of World Geography* (2003, Part IX: Geographic Index). In some cases, data have been complemented from *The World Factbook 2000*.

Data on annual mean temperature are derived from the data-set on annual mean temperature (TYN CY 1.0) produced by the Climatic Research Unit, Tyndall Centre for Climatic Change Research, University of East Anglia (Mitchell et al., 2001, 2003). In this data-set, the annual mean temperatures are averages of the period 1961-1990. Mean temperature is given in degrees Celcius and tenths. Their data are primarily based on the observations gathered by the World Meteorological Organization (WMO) from nearly 4,000 stations around the world (see WMO, Climatological Normals [CLINO] for the period 1961–1999, WMO No. 847). In the TYN CY 1.0 data-set, the observations from meteorological stations are assimilated onto a 0.5 latitude by 0.5 latitude grid covering the land surface of the earth. The grid data are transformed into country averages by allowing each 0.5 grid box to a single country. Our data on latitude and annual mean temperature are presented and documented in Appendix 3. We now examine how these ultimate independent variables are related to national IQ and to QHC and its five components. Correlations are given in Table 7.5. National IQ's correlations with QHC and its five components are presented in Table 7.1.

Table 7.5. Latitude (LAT) and annual mean temperature (MT) correlated with national IQ, QHC, and its five components in the group of 192 countries

Variable	Latitude	Annual mean temperature
Degrees latitude	1.000	-0.885
Annual mean temperature	-0.885	1.000
National IQ	0.677	-0.632
PPP GNI per capita 2002	0.528	-0.407
Adult literacy rate 2002	0.482	-0.467
Tertiary enrollment ratio	0.718	-0.649
Life expectancy at birth 2002	0.505	-0.379
Index of Democratization 2002	0.512	-0.460
QHC	0.659	-0.562

Table 7.5 shows that latitude (LAT) and annual mean temperature (MT) are moderately or strongly correlated with national IQ as well as with QHC and its five components. The values of national IQ and the measures of human conditions tend to be the higher, the greater a country's distance from the equator. In the case of MT, all correlations are negative. LAT and MT are negatively correlated with each other (-0.885) because MT tends to decrease when the distance from the equator increases.

The fact that national IQ is moderately or strongly correlated with

LAT and MT supports our theoretical argument about the emergence of differences in the average intelligence of nations as a consequence of adaptation to greatly varying geographical and climatic conditions during the evolutionary history of the human species. Latitude explains 46 percent of the contemporary variation in national IQs and MT 40 percent.

LAT explains from 23 to 52 percent of the variation in the five components of QHC and 43 percent of the variation in QHC. MT explains 32 percent of the variation in QHC and from 14 to 42 percent of the variation in the five components of QHC. Both of them are good explanatory variables, but they explain significantly less of the variation in the measures of the quality of human conditions than national IQ. As Table 7.1 shows, national IQ explains 63 percent of the variation in QHC in the group of 192 countries. It is 20 percentage points more than in the case of LAT and 31 percentage points more than in the case of MT.

However, because LAT and MT explain directly a significant part of the variation in QHC, an interesting question is how much the explained part of variation rises when national IQ, latitude, and annual mean temperature are used together as independent variables. Multiple correlation analysis provides an answer to this question. When LAT, MT, and national IQ are taken together to explain the variation in QHC, the multiple correlation rises to 0.814 and the explained part of variation to 66 percent. It is only 3 percentage points more than national IQ explains alone. This result indicates that the impact of latitude and annual mean temperature on QHC takes place nearly completely through national IQ. This result can be checked by a multiple regression analysis, in which national IQ, LAT, and MT are used to explain variation in QHC (Table 7.6).

Multiple regression analysis shows the impact of each explanatory variable on the dependent variable when the impact of the other explanatory variables is controlled. Table 7.6 shows that national IQ is the best explanatory variable (standardized coefficient 0.649). The explanatory power of latitude is also statistically highly significant, whereas annual mean temperature explains only a little of the variation in QHC independently from the other two variables. Thus the results of multiple correlation and multiple regression analyses show that the impact of LAT and MT on QHC is quite small independently from national IQ.

Table 7.6. The results of multiple regression analysis in which national IQ, latitude (LAT), and annual mean temperature (MT) are used to explain variation in the Index of the Quality of Human Conditions (QHC) in the group of 192 countries

Variable	Coefficient	Std. Error	Std. Coeff.	t-Value	P-Value
Intercept	-63.703	9.972	-63.703	-6.388	<.0001
National IQ	1.069	0.095	0.649	11.222	<.0001
Latitude	0.450	0.111	0.390	4.046	<.0001
Mean temperature	0.454	0.216	0.193	2.106	.0365
R = 0.814					
R squared = 0.662					

The explained part of variation does not increase more than 3 percentage points. However, both of them, as background factors of national IQ, are moderately correlated with QHC and its components. This observation supports our argument that the causal roots of differences in per capita income and other measures of human conditions can be traced, to a significant extent, to national IQ and further to geographical and climatic conditions that are background factors of the variation in national IQ.

Because LAT explains 43 percent of the variation in QHC and because the co-variation between LAT and national IQ is not more than 46 percent, it is interesting to examine whether there are important differences between the results of regression analysis of QHC on latitude and of QHC on national IQ at the level of single countries. The results of regression of QHC on national IQ in the group of 192 countries are given in Figure 7.1 and in Table 7.3. The results based on latitude are summarized in Figure 7.3.

Figure 7.3 shows that the relationship between latitude and QHC is linear, but the dispersion around the regression line is extensive, and there are many extreme outliers. Now the question is whether the most deviating countries are more or less the same as in the regression of QHC on national IQ (Figure 7.1 and Table 7.3) or whether they are different countries. For the purposes of this analysis, it is necessary to separate countries with large positive and negative residuals from the countries that are closer to the regression line and to compare them to large positive and negative outliers of the regression of QHC on

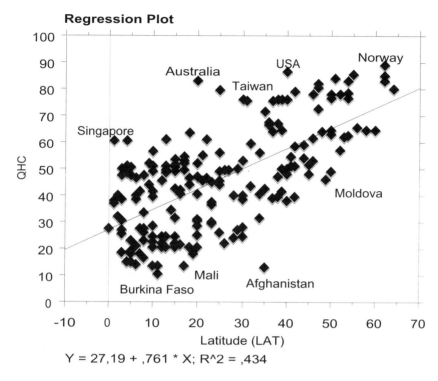

Figure 7.3. The results of regression analysis of QHC on latitude for single countries in the group of 192 countries

national IQ (Table 7.3). One standard deviation of residuals of QHC (±14.6) can be used as the criterion of large deviations. The comparison is made in Tables 7.7 and 7.8.

In the countries with large positive residuals, the level of QHC is much higher than expected on the basis of latitude, and in the countries with large negative residuals it is much lower. All countries with large positive residuals (except the Seychelles) are European, Latin American, East Asian, and Pacific countries, whereas nearly all of the 36 countries with large negative residuals are poor Asian (13) and African (20) countries.

Table 7.7 shows that the correspondence between the results of the two regression analyses is relatively good. Of the 33 countries with large positive residuals, 14 have large and 5 moderate positive residuals on the basis of the regression of QHC on national IQ (see Table 7.3). For 11 other countries residuals based on national IQ are around the

Table 7.7. The countries with large positive residuals (14.6 or higher) based on the regression of QHC on latitude compared to the results of the regression analysis of QHC on national IQ in the group of 192 countries

		Residuals in the regression of QHC on national IQ			
	Residual	11.9 and above	5.0 to 11.8	Below ±5.0	Larger than ±5.0
Australia	40.4	*	-	-	-
Austria	17.7	*	-	-	-
Barbados	23.8	*	-	-	-
Belgium	18.1	*	-	-	-
Bermuda	25.8	*	-	-	-
Brazil	16.3	-	-	*	-
Brunei	20.6	-	-	*	-
Colombia	18.2	-	-	*	-
Costa Rica	15.1	-	-	*	-
Denmark	16.4	*	-	-	-
Ecuador	17.9	-	-	*	-
France	15.9	*	-	-	-
Greece	19.2	*	-	-	-
Guyana	14.9	-	-	*	-
Hong Kong	16.9	-	-	-	-16.4
Israel	24.5	*	-	-	-
Italy	19.7	-	*	-	-
Japan	17.6	-	-	*	-
Korea, South	20.1	-	-	*	-
Malaysia	20.6	-	-	-	-6.2
New Zealand	18.6	-	*	-	-
Norway	14.6	*	-	-	-
Panama	21.8	-	*	-	-
Puerto Rico	22.7	*	-	-	-
Seychelles	30.4	*	-	-	-
Singapore	32.7	-	-	-	-16.5
Spain	19.7	-	*	-	-
Suriname	19.6	-	-	*	-
Switzerland	19.2	*	-	-	-
Taiwan	33.2	-	*	-	-
Trinidad & Tobago	18.0	-	-	*	-
United States	29.0	*	-	-	-
Venezuela	16.4	-	-	*	-

Table 7.8. The countries with large negative residuals (-14.6 or higher) based on the regression of QHC on latitude compared to the results of the regression analysis of QHC on national IQ in the group of 192 countries

		Residuals in the regression of QHC on national IQ			
	Residual	-11.9 and above	-5.0 to -11.8	Below ±5.0	Larger than +5.0
Afghanistan	-40.6	*	-	-	-
Angola	-21.9	-	*	-	-
Bangladesh	-14.9	*	-	-	-
Bhutan	-24.4	*	-	-	-
Botswana	-15.3	-	-	*	-
Burkina Faso	-24.9	*	-	-	-
Burundi	-15.0	-	*	-	-
Chad	-18.2	-	-	*	-
China	-16.4	*	-	-	-
Eritrea	-18.0	-	-	*	-
Ethiopia	-16.6	-	-	*	-
Gambia	-16.4	-	-	*	-
Guinea-Bissau	-16.0	-	-	*	-
Haiti	-20.5	-	-	*	-
Iraq	-21.9	*	-	-	-
Kazakhstan	-16.2	-	*	-	-
Korea, North	-19.6	*	-	-	-
Laos	-17.5	*	-	-	-
Lesotho	-25.7	-	-	*	-
Mali	-26.7	*	-	-	-
Mauritani	-21.9	*	-	-	-
Moldova	-18.3	*	-	-	-
Morocco	-21.4	*	-	-	-
Mozambique	-23.6	-	-	*	-
Nepal	-22.4	-	*	-	-
Niger	-21.3	*	-	-	-
Pakistan	-20.0	*	-	-	-
Senegal	-17.3	-	-	*	-
Sierra Leone	-18.0	-	*	-	-
Somalia	-15.8	-	*	-	-
Swaziland	-24.8	-	-	*	-
Syria	-16.4	-	*	-	-
Turkmenistan	-15.2	-	*	-	-
Uzbekistan	-19.8	-	*	-	-
Zambia	-16.8	-	*	-	-
Zimbabwe	-17.2	-	-	*	-

regression line. It means that in these cases the results differ from each other significantly. These 11 countries (except Japan and South Korea) are tropical countries in which the quality of human conditions (QHC) is much higher than expected on the basis of latitude, but in which it is more or less consistent with national IQs. Hong Kong, Malaysia, and Singapore are the most extreme deviating countries. On the basis of latitude, the level of QHC is much higher than expected in these tropical countries, but on the basis of national IQ, it is much lower than expected. In this category, predictions based on national IQ are in 16 cases more accurate than predictions based on latitude, and in 14 cases predictions are approximately similar (large positive residuals in both regressions).

There are 19 other countries for which positive residuals based on national IQ are large (Antigua and Barbuda, Canada, Cyprus, Dominica, Equatorial Guinea, Finland, Gabon, Germany, Grenada, Iceland, Ireland, Jamaica, Lebanon, the Netherlands, Saint Kitts and Nevis, Saint Lucia, Saint Vincent and the Grenadines, Sao Tome and Principe, and Sweden). For these countries, positive residuals based on latitude are moderate (15) or around the regression line (4). Most of these countries are economically highly developed countries in the north or Caribbean tourist countries. In these cases, predictions based on latitude have been more accurate than predictions based on national IQ.

Of the 36 countries with large negative residuals, 14 have large and 10 moderate negative residuals on the basis of national IQs. For 12 other countries residuals based on national IQ are around the regression line. They are tropical or near tropical poor African countries in which the quality of human conditions as measured by QHC is much lower than expected on the basis of latitude, but in which it is approximately consistent with national IQs. In this category, predictions based on national IQ are in 22 cases more accurate than predictions based on latitude. There are five other countries for which negative residuals based on national IQ are large (the Comoros, Madagascar, Mongolia, Myanmar, and Timor-Leste). For these countries negative residuals based on latitude are only moderate or small, which means that predictions based on latitude are more accurate.

The comparison of the results of the two regression analyses discloses that the correspondence in the results is relatively good, but the predictions based on national IQ are in most cases more accurate than predictions based on latitude. This is a natural consequence of the fact that national IQ explains 63 percent of the variation in QHC but latitude only 43 percent. According to our interpretation, the impact of latitude and annual mean temperature on the quality of human conditions takes place principally through national IQ, which is the intervening variable in the relationship between geographical and climatic factors and the quality of human conditions.

10. Summary

In this chapter, the research hypothesis on the positive relationship between national IQ and the composite index of the quality of human conditions (QHC) was tested by empirical evidence covering 192 contemporary countries. The results show that correlations between national IQ and QHC are quite strong: 0.805 in the group of 113 countries, 0.725 in the group of 79 countries, and 0.791 in the total group of 192 countries. The correlation is even stronger (0.839) in the group of 160 countries whose population was more than 500,000 inhabitants in 2000. The explained part of variation in QHC is so high that we can justifiably conclude that large global differences in the quality of human conditions depend crucially on the differences in national IQ. The countries with higher national IQs have been able to create better human conditions for their people than countries with lower national IQs.

However, this relationship is not perfect. The unexplained part of variation indicates that there are some other factors that affect the hypothesized linear relationship between national IQ and QHC and cause some countries to differ significantly from the regression line. Regression analysis of QHC on national IQ in the group of 192 countries was used to disclose how well the average relationship between variables applies to single countries and which countries deviate most clearly from the average relationship.

It was found that some patterns of residuals of the five components of QHC are common for particular groups of countries and that there are significant differences in these patterns between groups of countries. For example, in most countries with large positive residuals of QHC, the levels of per capita income, tertiary enrollment, and democratization are much higher than expected on the basis of national IQs, whereas the levels of literacy and life expectancy do not differ much from the expected levels. In the opposite group of countries with large negative residuals of QHC, the levels of per capita income, tertiary enrollment, and democratization tend to be much lower than expected on the basis of national IQs, whereas the residuals of the two other components of QHC tend to vary from country to country.

Further, it was possible to find some clear differences between the two opposite groups of the most deviating countries and to get hints of the factors that are related to large deviations. First, there are some clear regional differences between the two opposite groups. Most countries with moderate and large positive residuals of QHC are clustered in the regional group of Europe and European offshoot countries and in the group of Caribbean countries, whereas countries with moderate and large negative residuals of QHC are most frequent in the regional group of Asian and Pacific countries. Second, there are clear differences in the nature of economic systems. Market economies dominate in the group of countries with moderate and large positive residuals of QHC, whereas many of the countries with moderate or large negative residuals have or had socialist economic systems. Third, there are clear differences in the nature of political systems from the perspective of democracy. Nearly all countries with moderate or large positive residuals are democracies or near democracies, whereas various types of autocratic systems dominate in the group of countries with moderate and large negative residuals of QHC. Fourth, domestic peace seems to be a highly relevant factor. Most of the countries with large negative residuals of QHC have experienced devastating domestic conflicts and wars, whereas violent domestic conflicts and civil wars have been rare in the group of countries with moderate or large positive residuals.

The results were checked by analyzing the impact of two other independent variables—latitude and annual mean temperature—on global inequalities as measured by QHC. Because these two variables are background factors of national IQ, their impact was assumed to take place through national IQ. In fact, both of them are moderately correlated with QHC and its five components, but when added to national IQ, they increase the explained part of variation in QHC only slightly. Consequently, national IQ remains as the most important explanatory factor for the quality of human conditions.

CHAPTER 8

Other Measures of Global Inequalities in Human Conditions

1. Human Development Index (HDI)
2. Gender-Related Human Development Index (GDI)
3. Economic Growth Rate (EGR)
4. Gini Index of Inequality (Gini)
5. Poverty
6. Measures of Undernourishment (PUN 1 and PUN 2)
7. Maternal Mortality Ratio (MMR) and Infant Mortality Rate (IMR)
8. Corruption Perceptions Index (CPI)
9. Economic Freedom Ratings (EFR)
10. The Index of Economic Freedom (IEF)
11. Population Pyramids (MU-index)
12. Human Happiness and Life-Satisfaction
13. Summary

In the previous chapters, we tested the research hypothesis on the positive relationship between national IQ and the quality of human conditions by five single measures of global inequalities in human conditions (Chapter 6) and by their composite index QHC (Chapter 7) in the group of 192 countries. The results of correlation and regression analyses support the hypothesis strongly. The higher the national IQ of a country, the better various aspects of human conditions tend to be. However, we assume that this relationship is not limited to some particular measures of human conditions. Our hypothesis is universal. It presupposes that all measurable aspects of human conditions that are under conscious human control tend to be better in countries with high national IQs than in countries with low national IQs. In this chapter, we test the hypothesis by using some alternative indicators to measure various aspects of human conditions. Twelve such indicators were introduced and defined in Chapter 5. Now our intention is to test the hypothesis by these alternative variables. The results of these analyses will check the results achieved in the two previous chapters.

The following 12 additional variables (see Chapter 5) were selected to test the hypothesis: (1) Human Development Index (HDI), (2) Gender-related human development index (GDI); (3) Economic growth rate (EGR); (4) Gini index of inequality in income or consumption (Gini); (5) Population below $2 a day international poverty line (Poverty); (6) Measures of undernourishment (PUN); (7) Maternal mortality ratio (MMR) and infant mortality rate (IMR); (8) Corruption Perceptions Index (CPI); (9) Economic freedom ratings (EFR); (10) the Index of Economic Freedom (IEF); (11) Population pyramids (MU-index); and (12) Human happiness and life-satisfaction. All of these variables are to some extent related to the five components of QHC, but, on the other hand, because they represent different aspects of human conditions, they help to check the application of the research hypothesis to other measurable human conditions.

As explained in Chapter 5, all data on each variable are taken from one particular source. Data are not complemented from other possible sources. This makes it easier for interested readers to check our data and to make reanalyses. Unfortunately data on these variables are not available from all 192 countries. In each case, analysis is limited to a sample of the 192 countries from which data are available. Because the sample of countries varies from case to case, it is not possible to calculate the intercorrelations of these variables, but in each sample, the respective alternative measure is intercorrelated with our basic variables analysed in chapters 6 and 7.

In the next sections, we describe and analyze the relationship between national IQ and each variable separately on the basis of the results of correlation and regression analyses. To some extent, analyses are extended to the level of single countries. It is interesting to see what types of countries deviate most from the regression lines and what factors might explain those deviations. It is also interesting to see whether the deviating countries are more or less the same in all cases or whether they vary from variable to variable.

1. Human Development Index (HDI)

We use UNDP's Human Development Index 2002 as the first alternative measure of the quality of human conditions because it is the most frequently used measure of human development and well-being (cf. Rahman et al., 2003; McGillivray, 2003; Foster et al., 2003). According to UNDP's definition, human development is about people, about expanding their choices to lead lives they want. The Human Development Index is a composite index "measuring average achievement in three basic dimensions of human development – a long and healthy life, knowledge, and a decent standard of living" (UNDP, 2002, pp. 13, 265). The intercorrelations of HDI with national IQ, QHC, and its five components are given in Table 8.1.

Table 8.1. Intercorrelations of HDI 2002, national IQ, QHC, and its five components in a group of 176 countries

Variable	HDI 2002	National IQ	QHC	PPP GNI 2002	Literacy 2002	Tertiary enroll.	Life expect.	ID 2002
HDI 2002	1.000	0.776	0.940	0.748	0.853	0.761	0.918	0.616
National IQ		1.000	0.811	0.626	0.659	0.757	0.769	0.555
QHC			1.000	0.822	0.794	0.874	0.847	0.803
PPP GNI per capita 2002				1.000	0.514	0.675	0.610	0.597
Adult literacy rate 2002					1.000	0.633	0.686	0.512
Tertiary enrollment ratio						1.000	0.664	0.664
Life expectancy at birth 2002							1.000	0.538
ID 2002								1.000

Because of the extremely strong correlation between HDI and QHC (0.940), the pattern of correlations is approximately the same as in Figure 7.1. However, it is interesting to note that the correlation between national IQ and QHC is in this sample of 176 countries clearly stronger than between national IQ and HDI. The difference in the explained part of variation is six percentage points. Our composite index QHC, which includes also a measure of democracy, may measure the average quality of human conditions a little better than HDI.

The regression analysis of HDI-2002 on national IQ discloses how

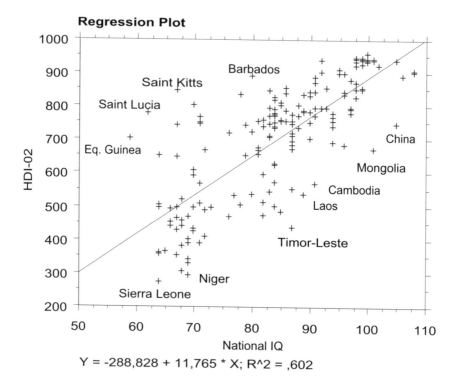

Regression Plot

$Y = -288,828 + 11,765 * X; R^2 = ,602$

Figure 8.1. The results of regression analysis of the Human Development Index (HDI) 2002 on national IQ in a group of 176 countries

well the average relationship between national IQ and HDI applies to single countries. The results of this regression analysis are summarized in Figure 8.1.

Figure 8.1 shows that the pattern of relationship between national IQ and HDI 2002 is in most points similar to the pattern of relationship between national IQ and QHC (Figure 7.1), although residuals differ from each other in some cases. Let us focus on the most extremely deviating countries, using as the criterion one standard deviation (±113.7). Using this criterion, the category of large positive outliers includes 18 countries: Antigua and Barbuda, the Bahamas, Bahrain, Barbados, Dominica, Equatorial Guinea, Gabon, Grenada, Ireland, Jamaica, Kuwait, Qatar, Saint Kitts and Nevis, Saint Lucia, Saint Vincent and the Grenadines, Sao Tome and Principe, the Seychelles, and United

Arab Emirates. Caribbean and other tourist countries (10) and oil-producing countries (6) dominate this category of large positive outliers. Of these 18 countries, positive residuals based on QHC are large for 13 countries, which means that both regressions produce in most cases similar results for single countries.

The category of large negative outliers (-113.7 or higher) includes 30 countries: Angola, Bangladesh, Benin, Bhutan, Burkina Faso, Burundi, Cambodia, Chad, China, Côte d'Ivoire, Guinea-Bissau, Laos, Madagascar, Malawi, Mali, Mauritania, Moldova, Mongolia, Myanmar, Nepal, Niger, Pakistan, Papua New Guinea, Sierra Leone, Tanzania, Timor-Leste, Vanuatu, Vietnam, Yemen, and Zambia. This group is dominated by poor sub-Saharan African (15), South Asian (7), and Pacific (3) countries, but it includes also China, Moldova, Mongolia, Vietnam, and Yemen. Of these 30 countries, 19 have large negative residuals also on the basis of the regression of QHC on national IQ.

Clear differences in the characteristics of large positive and negative outliers refer to factors that may explain their deviations from the regression line. The countries with large positive residuals are more prosperous than the countries with large negative residuals. National IQ is below 90 for nearly all of the large positive outliers, but these countries have benefited from their close contacts with economically highly developed countries, which have made investments and transferred technologies to profitable industries. Countries with large negative residuals have not yet been able to attract foreign investments, people, and technologies to the same extent as the countries with large positive residuals. Besides, many of the large negative outliers suffer from the lack of domestic peace.

2. Gender-Related Human Development Index (GDI)

UNDP's Gender-related human development index (GDI) measures inequalities between men and women in the components of HDI. Our hypothesis is that the equality between men and women (GDI) correlates positively with national IQ. Data on GDI 2002 are for 144 countries. The intercorrelations of our eight variables are given in Table 8.2.

In this sample of 144 countries, GDI is very strongly correlated with national IQ, but correlation between national IQ and QHC is even

Table 8.2. Intercorrelations of GDI 2002, national IQ, QHC, and its five components in a group of 144 countries

Variable	GDI 2002	National IQ	QHC	PPP GNI 2002	Literacy 2002	Tertiary enroll.	Life expect.	ID 2002
GDI 2002	1.000	0.849	0.951	0.765	0.864	0.812	0.915	0.689
National IQ		1.000	0.860	0.671	0.717	0.791	0.844	0.635
QHC			1.000	0.842	0.804	0.900	0.856	0.841
PPP GNI per capita 2002				1.000	0.548	0.706	0.638	0.665
Adult literacy rate 2002					1.000	0.675	0.681	0.574
Tertiary enrollment ratio						1.000	0.713	0.731
Life expectancy at birth 2002							1.000	0.589
ID 2002								1.000

higher. It is justified to conclude that national IQ explains 72 percent of the variation in gender equality and inequality (GDI). Because the correlation between HDI and GDI is 0.999 in this sample of 144 countries, the results for single countries are practically the same as in the case of HDI. Therefore it is not necessary to examine the results for single countries on the basis of the regression analysis of GDI on national IQ.

3. Economic Growth Rate (EGR)

It is evident that contemporary gaps in per capita income and in the level of economic development are due to long-term differences in economic growth rates. Therefore, it it reasonable to assume that high growth rates are preferable to low growth rates from the perspective of the quality of human conditions. Our hypothesis presupposes a clear positive correlation between national IQ and the rate of economic growth. However, this hypothesis is assumed to apply better to long-term differences in economic growth rates than to short-term differences. Because of considerable short-term fluctuations in economic growth rates, clear positive correlation does not need to appear if the period of comparison is short. Besides, because of the enormous differences in the level of per capita income, a growth rate of one percent does not mean the same at the level of per capita income $20,000 as at the level of per capita income $1,000.

This hypothesis will be tested by four datasets on growth rates, EGR 1, EGR 2, EGR 3, and ERG 4 introduced and defined in Chapter 5. EGR 1 covers the period 1990-2002 (WDI, 2004, Table 4), EGR 2 and EGR 3 the period 1950-2001 (Maddison, 2003), and ERG 4 the period 1500-2000 (Maddison, 2003). The correlation between EGR 1 and national IQ is near zero (-0.060) in a group of 145 countries. It is clear that national IQ does not provide any explanation for short-term variations in economic growth rates. However, the fact that the average annual growth rate has been approximately the same in rich and poor countries means that, for example, an average one percent absolute annual growth in per capita income has been $200 in a country for which per capita income is $20,000, but only $10 in a country for which per capita income is $1,000. In other words, per capita income in dollars has grown 20 times more in a rich country than in a poor country, although the growth rate calculated in percentages has been the same.

When the period of comparison becomes longer, correlations between national IQ and average annual growth rates turn clearly positive. Our datasets EGR 2 and EGR 3 (N = 132) cover the period of 52 years from 1950 to 2001. Intercorrelations are presented in Table 8.3. Kuwait and Qatar are excluded from this analysis because they are extremely exceptional cases. Kuwait's per capita income was $28,878 in 1950 and only $10,210 in 2001; Qatar's per capita income was $30,387 in 1950 and only $8,268 in 2001.

Our dataset EGR 4 (N = 109) covers the period of 1500-2000. It should be noted that in this dataset most data for 1500 are regional averages for countries which did not exist at that time but were later established within these regions (see Appendix 5). Countries in which the racial composition of the population has changed significantly since 1500 are excluded from this sample. For that reason all North and South American and the Caribbean countries (except Mexico) as well as Australia, New Zealand, and Singapore are excluded from this sample of 109 countries. The contemporary countries of the former USSR and Yugoslavia are also excluded. Russia represents the whole area of the former USSR and Serbia and Montenegro represents the area of the former Yugoslavia. Small Pacific island states are also excluded, as well as several other contemporary countries of our total sample of 192 countries.

Table 8.3. Intercorrelations of EGR 2 and EGR 3, national IQ, QHC, and its five components over the period 1950-2001 in a group of 132 countries

Variable	EGR 2 1950-2001	EGR 3 1950-2001	National IQ	QHC	PPP GNI 2002	Literacy 2002	Tertiary enroll.	Life expect.	ID 2002
EGR 2	1.000	0.580	0.388	0.378	0.419	0.359	0.371	0.302	0.194
EGR 3		1.000	0.747	0.840	0.936	0.603	0.767	0.641	0.673
National IQ			1.000	0.885	0.754	0.715	0.826	0.856	0.665
QHC				1.000	0.879	0.825	0.918	0.861	0.840
PPP GNI per capita 2002					1.000	0.621	0.796	0.669	0.697
Adult literacy rate 2002						1.000	0.689	0.702	0.602
Tertiary enrollment ratio							1.000	0.740	0.756
Life expectancy at birth 2002								1.000	0.587
ID 2002									1.000

In the sample of 132 countries, all correlations between EGR 2 (average annual percentage growth rate of per capita GDP over the period 1950-2001) and other variables are clearly positive, although they are weak. National IQ explains 15 percent of the variation in EGR 2. The results based on percentage growth rates support the hypothesis, but when growth rates are calculated on the basis of absolute growth in dollars (EGR 3), the relationship becomes much stronger. The correlation between national IQ and EGR 3 is 0.747, and the explained part of variation in EGR 3 rises to 56 percent. This illustrates the significant

Table 8.4. Intercorrelations of EGR 4, national IQ, QHC, and its five components over the period 1500-2000 in a group of 109 countries

Variable	EGR 4 1500– 2000	National IQ	QHC	PPP GNI 2002	Literacy 2002	Tertiary enroll.	Life expect.	ID 2002
EGR 4	1.000	0.709	0.871	0.983	0.627	0.743	0.701	0.725
National IQ		1.000	0.858	0.700	0.720	0.803	0.848	0.649
QHC			1.000	0.876	0.825	0.907	0.868	0.854
PPP GNI per capita 2002				1.000	0.633	0.740	0.701	0.728
Adult literacy rate 2002					1.000	0.693	0.689	0.614
Tertiary enrollment ratio						1.000	0.751	0.754
Life expectancy at birth 2002							1.000	0.593
ID 2002								1.000

difference between percentage growth rates and absolute growth rates. The correlation between EGR 2 and EGR 3 is not higher than 0.580. The correlation between national IQ and QHC is extremely strong (0.885) in this sample of 132 countries. Correspondingly, most correlations between national IQ and the components of QHC are considerably stronger in this sample than in the total group of 192 countries. The clearly higher correlations in this sample of 132 countries than in the total sample of 192 countries (see Table 6.1 and Table 7.1) are completely due to differences in the composition of the samples.

The growth rate in dollars over the period 1500–2000 (ERG 4) correlates with national IQ nearly as strongly (0.709) as ERG 3 (0.747). Because differences between countries in per capita income in 1500 were relatively small in dollars, the growth rate over the period 1500–2000 correlates extremely strongly with per capita GDP in 2000 (0.998, N = 109) and also with PPP GNI per capita in 2002 (0.983, N = 109). Figures 8.2 and 8.3 summarize the results of regressions of EGR 3 on national IQ and EGR 4 on national IQ.

Figure 8.2 illustrates the strong relationship between national IQ and EGR 3 and the nature of the most clearly deviating countries. Positive residuals are higher than one standard deviation (74.9) for 20 countries: Australia, Austria, Belgium, Botswana, Canada, Denmark, Equatorial Guinea, Finland, France, Germany, Hong Kong, Ireland, Italy, Japan, the Netherlands, Norway, Puerto Rico, Singapore, Trinidad

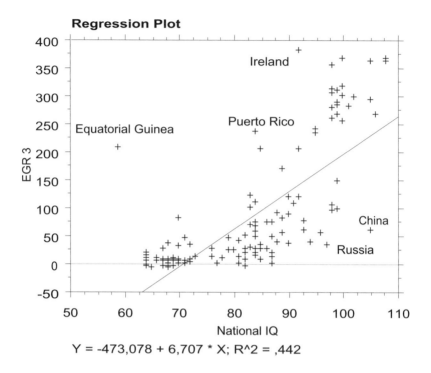

Figure 8.2. The results of regression analysis of EGR 3 (average annual growth in dollars per capita GDP 1950-2001) on national IQ in a group of 132 countries

and Tobago, and the United States. The group is dominated by economically highly developed European and European offshoot countries (13). It reflects the fact that most scientific and technological innovations were made in Europe and European offshoot countries. These countries are market economies and democracies.

In Botswana, economic growth since the 1960s has been based on the mining sector, especially on diamond mining. Foreign investments, people, and technologies made this exceptional growth possible. Equatorial Guinea's extremely outlying position in Figure 8.2 is completely due to the impact of oil production carried out by foreign companies and technologies since the 1990s. Puerto Rico has benefited from its association with the United States. Trinidad and Tobago is an oil-producing and also a tourist country, which has been able to attract

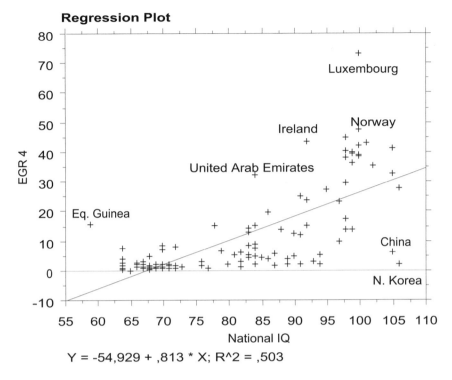

Figure 8.3. The results of regression analysis of EGR 4 (average annual growth in dollars per capita 1500-2000) on national IQ in a group of 109 countries

technologies and investments from the countries of higher national IQs. Hong Kong, Japan, and Singapore are East Asian countries with the highest national IQs. Economic growth in these countries has been even stronger than expected on the basis of their high national IQs. Of course, foreign investments have also been important for East Asian countries, but it is reasonable to argue that their high national IQs provide the best theoretical explanation for their exceptional growth rates since the 1950s. Economic growth in these countries has been principally based on the mobilization of the previously unused human capital, not on any special natural resources as in oil-producing countries.

Negative residuals are larger than one standard deviation (-74.9) for 22 countries: Albania, Argentina, Bangladesh, Bolivia, Bulgaria, China, Cuba, Ecuador, Hungary, Iraq, Madagascar, Myanmar, Nicaragua,

Peru, Philippines, Poland, Romania, Russia (USSR), Serbia and Montenegro (Yugoslavia), the United Arab Emirates, Uruguay, and Venezuela. This group is dominated by former and present socialist countries (9) and Latin American countries (8). This implies that the socialist command economy has not been as successful as the market economy in the countries with large positive residuals. Economic growth in Latin America has been relatively slow. A reason may be that in their market economies economic resources are too highly concentrated in the hands of small groups. Bangladesh, Madagascar, and Myanmar are poor South Asian and African countries. Residuals are negative also for most other countries of these regions. Iraq has been devastated by wars. For some reasons economic development has been slower in the Philippines than in some other Southeast Asian countries. The large negative residual of the United Arab Emirates is due to its high starting point in 1950 ($15,798). For the same reason, negative residuals for Kuwait and Qatar, which are excluded from this analysis, would be extremely large.

Because of the nearly complete correlation between EGR 4 and PPP GNI per capita 2002 (0.983), the results of regression analysis of EGR 4 on national IQ (Figure 8.3) are similar to the results of the regression of PPP GNI per capita 2002 on national IQ (Figure 6.1).

Positive residuals are larger than one standard deviation (10.8) for 16 countries: Andorra, Austria, Belgium, Denmark, Equatorial Guinea, Finland, France, Iceland, Ireland, Luxembourg, the Netherlands, Norway, Sweden, Switzerland, the United Arab Emirates, and the United Kingdom. Nearly all of them are economically highly developed market economies and democracies, just as in the regressions of PPP GNI per capita 2002 (Figure 6.1) and of EGR 3 on national IQ (Figure 8.2). This is a consequence of the fact that the scientific and technological inventions that created the modern world started in Europe in the 15th century. Equatorial Guinea is in this group for the reason that the oil production which started in the 1990s has increased the country's per capita income phenomenally. In the United Arab Emirates oil production started in the 1950s. It should be noted the Caribbean tourist countries are excluded from this sample of 109 countries. Positive residuals would be large for several of them just as in Figure 6.1.

Negative residuals are larger than one standard deviation (-10.8) for 16 countries: Afghanistan, Albania, Bulgaria, Cambodia, China, Hungary,

Iraq, North Korea, Laos, Madagascar, the Philippines, Poland, Romania, Russia (USSR), Serbia and Montenegro, and Vietnam. The nature of these outliers is similar to the regression of PPP GNI per capita 2002 (Figure 6.1). Eleven of these countries are present or former socialist countries, which highlights the significance of economic and political systems. Afghanistan, Cambodia, and Iraq are countries devastated by wars and civil wars. Madagascar's position among large negative outliers is principally due to its national IQ (82), which is more than 10 points higher than for other sub-Saharan African countries. The Philippines is a more problematic case. A reason may be in the fact that there are discrepancies in data on per capita income. According to Maddison (2003), per capita GDP for the Philippines in 2000 was $2,385, whereas according to WDI 2004 (see Appendix 2), PPP GNI per capita 2002 was $4,450 for the Philippines. In the case of Indonesia, the corresponding figures were $3,203 and $3,070. This comparison of two neighboring countries implies that some fluctuation in residuals may be due to errors in data on per capita income.

The evidence presented in this section shows that differences in the average national intelligence explain a significant part of the differences in economic growth rates. Economic growth has tended to correlate with national IQ quite strongly since 1500, especially so when economic growth is measured by average annual growth in dollars per capita GDP. Differences in economic systems and also in geographical conditions of countries seem to have been principal factors that have caused countries to deviate from the regression line.

4. Gini Index of Inequality (Gini)

The Gini index of inequality in income or consumption (Gini) is intended to measure relative differences between countries in the distribution of income or consumption. It is assumed, from this perspective, that human conditions are the better, the lower the index values are (see Chapter 5). Consequently, correlations between Gini index values and national IQ are expected to be negative. The correlation between national IQ and Gini (WDI, 2004), which covers 127 countries, is -0.511, and between national IQ and Gini (WIID), which covers 146 countries, -0.538. Because the Gini (WIID) dataset includes more countries, we limit correlation and regression analyses to this dataset (Table 8.5).

Table 8.5. Intercorrelations of Gini (WIID2BE2, 2004), national IQ, QHC, and its five components in a group of 146 countries

Variable	Gini WIID 2BE2	National IQ	QHC	PPP GNI 2002	Literacy 2002	Tertiary enroll.	Life expect.	ID 2002
Gini WIID2BE2	1.000	-0.538	-0.464	-0.420	-0.340	-0.422	-0.454	-0.464
National IQ		1.000	0.850	0.656	0.729	0.783	0.843	0.608
QHC			1.000	0.838	0.800	0.898	0.864	0.846
PPP GNI per capita 2002				1.000	0.518	0.708	0.619	0.700
Adult literacy rate 2002					1.000	0.665	0.711	0.559
Tertiary enrollment ratio						1.000	0.724	0.718
Life expectancy at birth 2002							1.000	0.609
ID 2002								1.000

The Gini values in Table 8.5 are derived from the UNU/WIDER World Income Inequality Database, Version 2.0 beta, 3 December 2004. The Gini index values of our dataset are arithmetic means of the five (or fewer than five if not five) most recent Gini values given in the UNU/ WIDER database. Table 8.5 shows that Gini is moderately correlated with national IQ and also with the other measures of human conditions, although national IQ does not explain more than 29 percent of the variation in the Gini index. A part of the unexplained variation is probably due to a low reliability of data on income distribution, but the high share of unexplained variation shows also the significance of other explanatory factors. The regression analysis of the Gini WIID on national IQ is used to disclose the application of the average relationship to single countries (Figure 8.4).

We can see from Figure 8.4 that the negative relationship between national IQ and Gini WIID is linear but only moderate. Many countries at all levels of IQ deviate significantly from the regression line. One standard deviation of residual Gini (±8.4) can be used to separate large outliers from smaller ones. The group of countries with large positive residuals (8.4 or higher) includes 26 countries: Argentina, Armenia, Bolivia, Brazil, Chile, Colombia, Ecuador, El Salvador, Gambia, Georgia, Guatemala, Honduras, Hong Kong, Iraq, Lebanon, Lesotho, Mali, Mexico, Nicaragua, Panama, Paraguay, Russia, Singapore, South Africa,

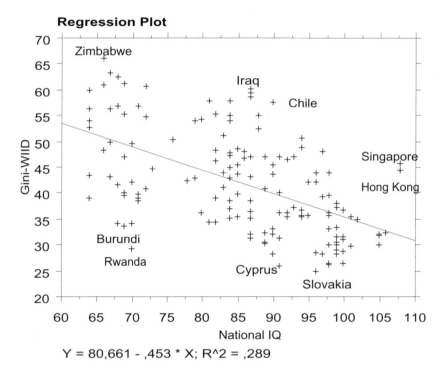

Figure 8.4. The results of regression analysis of Gini-WIID on national IQ in a group of 146 countries

Swaziland, and Zimbabwe. Income inequality in all these countries is much higher than expected on the basis of the regression equation. The group is dominated by Latin American countries (13), but it includes also several countries of sub-Saharan Africa (6). Economically highly developed countries are few (Hong Kong and Singapore) among large positive outliers.

The group of countries with large negative residuals includes 28 countries: Albania, Barbados, Belarus, Burundi, Chad, Congo-Brazzaville, Côte d'Ivoire, Cyprus, the Czech Republic, Djibouti, Egypt, Ethiopia, Ghana, India, Indonesia, Jamaica, Laos, Luxembourg, Macedonia, Niger, Rwanda, Slovakia, Slovenia, Spain, Sudan, Suriname, Togo, and Turkmenistan. In these countries, income inequality is much lower than expected. It is remarkable that the group does not include any Latin American country. It is dominated by former socialist (7) and poor sub-Saharan African countries (11). The other ten countries are scattered around the world.

The results of regression analysis imply that income inequality is most conspicuous in Latin American countries. It characterizes Latin American economic systems and social structures. The frequency of sub-Saharan African countries among both large positive and large negative outliers may be partly due to the unreliability of data on income distribution. National IQ seems to explain quite well the relatively low level of income inequality in nearly all economically highly developed market economies and democracies.

5. Poverty

The World Bank's President James D. Wolfensohn (2001, p. V) notes in his Foreword to World Development Report 2000/2001 that "Poverty amid plenty is the world's greatest challenge." Of the world's 6 billion people, 2.8 billion live on less than $2 a day, and 1.2 billion live on less than $1 a day (World Development Report 2000/2001, p. 3). According to the UN Millennium Declaration, the first Millennium Development Goal is to halve, between 1990 and 2015, the proportion of people whose income is less than $1 a day. Poverty affects human conditions in many ways. Poverty does not mean only low income and consumption but also low achievement in education, health, nutrition, and other areas of human development (see UNDP, 2003, p. 1; World Development Report 2000/2001, p. V). Therefore it can be justifiably argued that human conditions are better in a country in which the level of poverty is relatively low than in a country in which the level of poverty is high.

Various indicators have been used to measure global inequalities in poverty, but, as is emphasized in WDI, 2003 (p. 61), international comparisons of poverty data entail both conceptual and practical problems. Because different countries have different definitions of poverty, it is difficult to make consistent comparisons between countries, especially between rich and poor countries. Therefore we exclude data based on national poverty criteria and focus on data based on an international poverty criterion, which attempts to hold the real value of the poverty line constant across countries. There are data based on two international poverty lines: population below $1 a day and population below $2 a day. We use in this study data on population below $2 a day

(WDI, 2004, Table 2.5). These data are the percentages of the population living on less than $2 a day at 1993 international prices. The poverty rates are intended to be comparable across countries, but they certainly include various estimate errors. Besides, the data are available from only 96 countries. The missing countries include practically all economically highly developed countries and also many developing countries. Similar data on poverty are published in UNDP's Human Development Reports (see UNDP, 2003, pp. 198-202, 245-247).

Because economic conditions in a country depend to a significant extent on human choices and policies, we assume that a nation whose national IQ is high is better able to eradicate extreme poverty than a nation whose national IQ is low. Consequently, it is justified to hypothesize that the percentage of population below the poverty line tends to be the higher, the lower the national IQ. Thus the hypothesized correlation between national IQ and Poverty should be negative (Table 8.6).

Table 8.6. Intercorrelations of poverty, national IQ, QHC, and its five components in a group of 96 countries

Variable	Poverty	National IQ	QHC	PPP GNI 2002	Literacy 2002	Tertiary enroll.	Life expect.	ID 2002
Poverty	1.000	-0.653	-0.799	-0.702	-0.642	-0.701	-0.706	-0.530
National IQ		1.000	0.844	0.576	0.699	0.761	0.810	0.536
QHC			1.000	0.780	0.829	0.862	0.838	0.777
PPP GNI per capita 2002				1.000	0.532	0.671	0.571	0.608
Adult literacy rate 2002					1.000	0.623	0.627	0.533
Tertiary enrollment ratio						1.000	0.631	0.641
Life expectancy at birth 2002							1.000	0.478
ID 2002								1.000

The correlation between national IQ and the poverty variable is moderately strong and negative as hypothesized. In this sample of 96 countries, national IQ explains 43 percent of the variation in poverty. It means that poverty is concentrated in countries with low national IQs. If there were more countries with high national IQs in the sample, the relationship would probably become even stronger. Figure 8.5 on the results of the

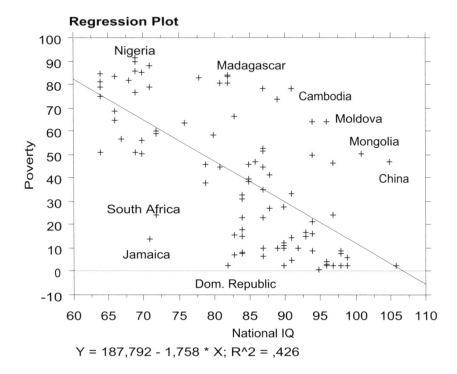

Regression Plot

$Y = 187{,}792 - 1{,}758 * X;\ R^2 = {,}426$

Figure 8.5. The results of regression analysis of the population below $2 a day international poverty line on national IQ in a group of 96 countries

regression analysis of poverty on national IQ illustrates the relationship between the two variables at the level of single countries and discloses the most deviating countries.

Figure 8.5 shows that the relationship between the two variables is approximately linear as hypothesized, but many outlying countries weaken the relationship. It also shows that the sample of 96 countries includes relatively few countries with national IQs 95 or higher. Positive residuals indicate that the level of poverty is higher than expected on the basis of the regression equation and negative residuals that the level of poverty is lower than expected.

One standard deviation of residual poverty (±22.3) can be used to separate large outliers from the less deviating countries. Positive residuals are large for 19 countries: Armenia, Bangladesh, Burundi, Cambodia,

China, India, Laos, Madagascar, Mali, Moldova, Mongolia, Nepal, Nicaragua, Nigeria, Oman, Ukraine, Uzbekistan, Vietnam, and Zambia. Asian (10) and sub-Saharan African (5) countries dominate this group. Surjit S. Bhalla (2002) and Glenn Firebaugh (2003) emphasize that the number of extremely poor people has decreased dramatically in China, but their percentage is still much higher than expected on the basis of China's high national IQ. The group includes three former European socialist countries and Nicaragua from Latin America. It should be noted that the data on poverty may include significant measurement errors, especially in the case of African countries.

Negative residuals are large for 14 countries: Algeria, Azerbaijan, Cameroon, Croatia, the Dominican Republic, Guyana, Iran, Jamaica, Jordan, Macedonia, Morocco, Pakistan, South Africa, and Tunisia. These countries are regionally more widely distributed than the countries with large positive residuals. The group includes four North African countries, three former socialist countries, two sub-Saharan African countries, three Latin American and Caribbean countries, and Iran and Pakistan from Asia.

Poverty is strongly correlated with PPP GNI per capita (-0.701), but not all poor countries have large positive residuals. In several relatively poor countries the number of extremely poor people is much smaller than expected on the basis of national IQ. However, when national IQ and PPP GNI per capita taken together are used to explain variation in poverty, the multiple correlation rises to 0.765 and the explained part of variation to 58 percent. It is 15 percentage points more than what national IQ explains alone.

Empirical evidence supports strongly the research hypothesis about the impact of national IQ on the percentage of population below the poverty line. National IQ seems to be the most important ultimate explanatory factor, but PPP GNI per capita provides an equally good proximate explanation. A significant part of the variation in poverty remains unexplained. It is due to various other factors. It is stated in the UNDP's Human Development Report 2003 (p. 1) that addressing poverty requires understanding its causes. This is true, but the report does not address this causal question, although it makes several reasonable recommendations on policies and reforms needed to eradicate extreme poverty. The same is true for the World Bank's World Development Report 2000/2001, in which various strategies for poverty reduction are discussed and recommended (see also WDI, 2003, and 2004). In *Poverty and Development into the 21st Century*, edited by Tim Allen and Alan Thomas (2000), the problem of poverty is explored from many perspectives, but the book does not try to explain ultimate causes of great global differences in poverty, and there is no discussion about the significance of intelligence. The results of our study imply that it is impossible to understand ultimate causes of poverty without taking into account the fact that the average intelligence of nations varies greatly and that this variation is strongly correlated with the relative extent of extreme poverty.

6. Measures of Undernourishment (PUN 1 and PUN 2)

Opportunity to get sufficient nourishment can be regarded as one of the basic needs of all human beings. Human conditions are certainly better in a country in which people get sufficient nourishment than in a country in which people or some significant sections of the population are undernourished. We measure undernourishment by two variables, PUN 1 (percentage of undernourished population in 1999-2001) and PUN 2 (percentage of underweight children under age five in 1999-2002) (see Chapter 5). Our data on these variables are from The World Bank's World Development Indicators 2004, Table 2.17. It is noted in this source that the proportion of children who are underweight is the most common indicator of malnutrition. Consequences of child malnutrition are serious. It increases the risk of death and inhibits cognitive development in children (WDI, 2004, p. 103). The samples of countries are to some extent biased. Developing countries are better represented in these samples than developed countries. In fact, data are available only from few economically highly developed countries, in which the prevalence of undernourishment is near zero.

The use of these indicators is based on the assumption that the prevalence of undernourishment and malnutrition depends partly on national IQ and partly on policies adopted by governments. Nations whose national IQ is high are assumed to be better able to take care of the nutrition of their people, including children, than nations whose national IQ is low. Consequently, we expect that national IQ correlates negatively with these measures of malnutrition. The intercorrelations of PUN 1 with the other variables are given in Table 8.7.

Table 8.7. Intercorrelations of PUN 1, national IQ, QHC and its five components in a group of 124 countries

Variable	PUN 1	National IQ	QHC	PPP GNI 2002	Literacy 2002	Tertiary enroll.	Life expect.	ID 2002
PUN 1	1.000	-0.500	-0.648	-0.567	-0.465	-0.533	-0.653	-0.363
National IQ		1.000	0.822	0.545	0.703	0.729	0.791	0.457
QHC			1.000	0.701	0.840	0.849	0.867	0.707
PPP GNI per capita 2002				1.000	0.481	0.534	0.585	0.353
Adult literacy rate 2002					1.000	0.648	0.668	0.477
Tertiary enrollment ratio						1.000	0.661	0.554
Life expectancy at birth 2002							1.000	0.443
ID 2002								1.000

Table 8.7 shows that the negative correlation between national IQ and PUN 1 is moderate (-0.50), but the explained part of variation is not more than 25 percent. This means that some other factors are clearly more important than national IQ, although 25 percent represents a significant part of the variation. In the case of PUN 2 (percentage of underweight children under age five in 1999-2002), the correlation is only -0.421 (N = 101) and the explained part of variation 18 percent. Other factors are more important, but the clearly negative correlation implies that national IQ may constitute an important factor. Regression analysis is limited to the relationship between national IQ and PUN 1 (Figure 8.6).

Figure 8.6 shows that the relationship between national IQ and PUN 1 is linear as hypothesized, but many highly deviating countries weaken the correlation between them. The relationship is also weakened by the fact that only few economically highly developed countries with national IQs over 95 are represented in this sample of 124 countries. Positive residuals mean that the percentage of undernourished population is higher than expected on the basis of the regression equation and negative residuals mean that it is lower than expected. One standard deviation of residual PUN 1 (±15.3) can be used to separate large outliers from less deviating countries.

Positive residuals are large (15.3 or higher) for 16 countries: Afghanistan, Angola, Armenia, Burundi, Cambodia, Congo-Zaire,

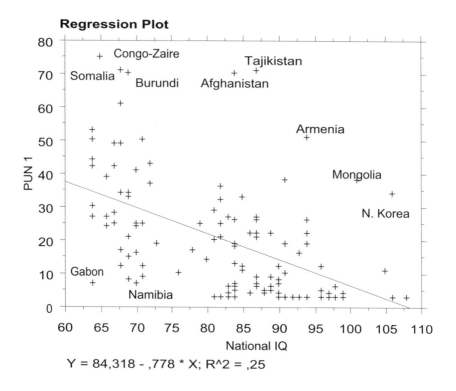

Regression Plot

$Y = 84,318 - ,778 * X; R^2 = ,25$

Figure 8.6. The results of regression analysis of PUN 1 (percentage of undernourished population) on national IQ in a group of 124 countries

Eritrea, Haiti, North Korea, Madagascar, Mongolia, Mozambique, Sierra Leone, Somalia, Tajikistan, and Zambia. Relative poverty characterizes all these countries, but poverty alone does not provide a satisfactory explanation for the high level of undernourishment in these countries, because there are many other poor countries in which the level of undernourishment deviates less from the regression line. It is possible to find an additional explanatory factor from wars and civil wars which have more or less devastated nearly all of these countries. Mongolia has escaped civil war, but its harsh environmental conditions may explain the country's poverty and undernourishment. The extremely autocratic and peculiar governmental system of North Korea is responsible for undernourishment and hunger in that country.

Negative residuals are large (-15.3 or higher) for 14 countries: Côte d'Ivoire, Egypt, Gabon, Ghana, Jamaica, Lesotho, Libya, Namibia, Nigeria, Saudi Arabia, Swaziland, Syria, Tunisia, and the United Arab Emirates. It is not possible to find any common explanation for large negative outliers. The level of undernourishment is clearly lower than expected on the basis of national IQ in all these countries, but, for most of them, negative residuals are only slightly above the criterion of one standard deviation. In Gabon, Libya, Nigeria, Saudi Arabia, and the UAE, oil incomes may have helped to improve human conditions and nourishment, and in Egypt, Jamaica, and Tunisia tourism may have done the same.

Empirical evidence based on the prevalence of undernourishment (PUN 1) and the prevalence of child malnutrition (PUN 2) supports the hypothesis on the dependence of the quality of human conditions on national IQ, although in this case most of the variation in dependent variables is clearly due to other factors which have increased or decreased undernourishment independently from the level of national IQ. The lack of domestic peace seems to have been one detrimental factor.

7. Maternal Mortality Ratio (MMR) and Infant Mortality Rate (IMR)

Health conditions vary greatly from country to country. It is reasonable to argue that human conditions are better in a country in which people are in good health than in a country in which they are in poor health. Many indicators have been used to measure global disparities in health conditions. We focus on indicators measuring reproductive health and the infant mortality rate. According to WDI, 2004 (p. 99), "Means of achieving reproductive health include education and services during pregnancy and childbirth, provision of safe and effective contraception, and prevention and treatment of sexually transmitted diseases." These services depend crucially on governmental policies and decisions. We assume that nations with high national IQs tend to be able to provide better health conditions than nations with low national IQs.

Of the various available indicators of health conditions, we selected the maternal mortality rate per 100,000 live births to measure reproductive health and the infant mortality rate per 1,000 live births to measure child mortality and, indirectly, differences in general health conditions. It should be noted that there are certainly defects in the reliability of these data. It is noted in WDI 2004 that even "in high-income countries with vital statistics registration systems, misclassification of maternal deaths has been found to lead to serious underestimation" (p. 99). Data on many developing countries are based on estimates.

Our data on maternal mortality rates in 2000 (MMR) are taken from WDI, 2004 (Table 2.16). They are national estimates based on national surveys, vital statistics registration, or surveillance, or are derived from community and hospital records. They cannot be assumed to provide an accurate estimate of maternal mortality in any of the countries, but they are sufficient for our purposes to indicate relative differences between countries. Our data on infant mortality rate in 2002 (IMR) are from WDI, 2004 (Table 2.19). These two variables are expected to correlate negatively with national IQ. Correlations are given in Table 8.8

Table 8.8. Intercorrelations of MMR, IMR, national IQ, QHC, and its five components in a group of 149 countries

Variable	MMR 2000	IMR 2002	National IQ	QHC	PPP GNI 2002	Literacy 2002	Tertiary enroll.	Life expect.	ID 2002
MMR 2000	1.000	0.886	-0.730	-0.759	-0.510	-0.781	-0.631	-0.855	-0.456
IMR 2002		1.000	-0.771	-0.861	-0.638	-0.796	-0.719	-0.908	-0.596
National IQ			1.000	0.847	0.640	0.744	0.791	0.835	0.601
QHC				1.000	0.848	0.809	0.906	0.861	0.833
PPP GNI per capita 2002					1.000	0.526	0.742	0.631	0.695
Adult literacy rate 2002						1.000	0.687	0.715	0.556
Tertiary enrollment ratio							1.000	0.730	0.717
Life expectancy at birth 2002								1.000	0.573
ID 2002									1.000

The hypothesized negative correlation between national IQ and MMR is relatively strong (-0.73). The explained part of variation in MMR rises to 53 percent. It represents a high level of explanation. MMR is correlated very strongly with life expectancy (-0.855). It indicates that in the countries in which life expectancy is high, the maternal mortality rate tends to be low. Maternal mortality rates seems to depend on national IQ more than on any other factor, but there are also other

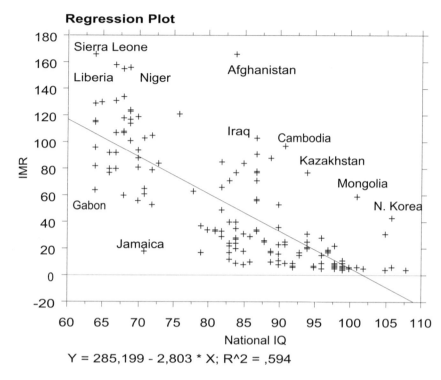

Figure 8.7. The results of regression analysis of IMR (infant mortality rate) on national IQ in a group of 149 countries

important factors because 47 percent of the variation in MMR remains unexplained. The correlation between national IQ and IMR is even stronger, and the explained part of variation in IMR rises to 59 percent. The infant mortality rate seems to depend on national IQ more than on any other explanatory factor, although it is strongly correlated with several other variables, especially with Life expectancy (-0.908).

Because MMR and IMR are strongly correlated with each other (0.855) and because IMR is more strongly correlated with national IQ than MMR, regression analysis is limited to the regression of IMR on national IQ (Figure 8.7). Positive residuals indicate that the infant mortality rate is higher than expected on the basis of the regression equation, and negative ones that it is lower than expected.

Figure 8.7 shows that the relationship between national IQ and

IMR is linear as hypothesized, but several outliers, especially above the regression line, weaken the relationship. Positive residuals indicate that the infant mortality rate is higher than expected on the basis of the regression equation, and negative residuals indicate that it is lower than expected. One standard deviation of residuals of IMR (±27.9) can be used to separate the most deviating countries from the less deviating ones.

Positive residuals are large (27.9 or higher) for 24 countries: Afghanistan, Angola, Azerbaijan, Burundi, Cambodia, China, Guinea-Bissau, Iraq, Kazakhstan, North Korea, Laos, Liberia, Madagascar, Mali, Mauritania, Mongolia, Myanmar, Niger, Rwanda, Sierra Leone, Somalia, Tajikistan, Turkmenistan, and Yemen. Most of these countries have experienced civil wars and ethnic conflicts, which have certainly deteriorated health services. Afghanistan is the most extremely deviating country. Azerbaijan, China, Kazakhstan, North Korea, Laos, Mongolia, Tajikistan, and Turkmenistan are present or former socialist countries.

Negative residuals are large (-27.9 or higher) for 17 countries: Colombia, Cuba, El Salvador, Eritrea, Gabon, Jamaica, Kuwait, Libya, Namibia, Oman, Panama, South Africa, Sri Lanka, Trinidad and Tobago, Tunisia, the United Arab Emirates, and Venezuela. Do these countries differ systematically from the countries with large positive residuals? Contrary to the countries with large positive residuals, it is characteristic for these countries (except Colombia, Eritrea, and Sri Lanka) that they have been able to maintain domestic peace. However, domestic peace alone does not explain their much lower than expected infant mortality rates. There are some other favorable factors. Cuba is a socialist country in which the state has taken care of health services. Gabon, Kuwait, Libya, Oman, the United Arab Emirates, and Venezuela are oil-producing countries that have benefited from the wealth generated by oil production. Tourism is important for Jamaica, Trinidad and Tobago, and Tunisia. Namibia's relatively good position depends crucially on mining industries based on foreign investments. Panama has benefited from the control of the Panama Canal. It is common for most of these countries that they have benefited from economic investments and personal contributions from the countries of higher national IQs much more than the countries with large positive residuals. Colombia, Eritrea, and Sri Lanka are exceptional cases. Despite their long civil wars, some aspects of human conditions have remained significantly better than expected on the basis of national IQ.

Empirical evidence supports strongly the research hypothesis on the negative relationship between national IQ and IMR. There are clear differences between the countries with large positive and negative residuals. First, most countries of the first group are characterized by civil wars and the lack of domestic peace, whereas domestic peace is characteristic of most countries of the second group. Second, several countries with large negative residuals seem to have benefited from Western technologies, investments, and personal contributions more than the countries of the first category.

8. Corruption Perceptions Index (CPI)

The Transparency International Corruption Perceptions Index (CPI) measures the perceived extent of corruption in various countries. It is reasonable to argue that human conditions are better in a country in which the level of corruption is low than in a country in which it is high. We assume that there is a causal relationship between national IQ and the extent of corruption. The nations with high national IQs have better chances to root out corruption than the nations with low national IQs. Because the values of CPI are the higher the less corruption there is in a country, the correlation between national IQ and CPI should be positive. Correlations are given in Table 8.9.

Positive correlation between national IQ and CPI is moderately strong. The explained part of variation in CPI rises to 35 percent, which means that 65 percent of the variation remains unexplained. CPI is extremely strongly correlated with PPP GNI per capita (0.893). In fact, the multiple correlation in which PPP GNI per capita and national IQ are used together to explain variation in CPI is the same 0.893. National IQ does not seem to explain anything of the variation in CPI independently from the level of per capita income, but it should be noted that national IQ explains 43 percent of the variation in PPP GNI per capita in this sample of 132 countries. Therefore it is a significant factor. The results of regression analysis of CPI on national IQ are summarized in Figure 8.8.

Figure 8.8 shows that the relationship between national IQ and CPI is slightly curvilinear, just like the relationship between national IQ and PPP GNI per capita (cf. Figure 6.1). Most of the economically highly

Table 8.9. Intercorrelations of CPI, national IQ, QHC, and its five components in a group of 132 countries

Variable	CPI 2003	National IQ	QHC	PPP GPI 2002	Literacy 2002	Tertiary enroll.	Life expect.	ID 2002
CPI 2003	1.000	0.591	0.762	0.893	0.450	0.618	0.559	0.551
National IQ		1.000	0.858	0.652	0.730	0.773	0.826	0.599
QHC			1.000	0.824	0.788	0.880	0.825	0.816
PPP GPI per capita 2002				1.000	0.494	0.650	0.599	0.612
Adult literacy rate 2002					1.000	0.648	0.688	0.550
Tertiary enrollment ratio						1.000	0.665	0.681
Life expectancy ar birth 2002							1.000	0.493
ID 2002								1.000

developed countries are outliers above the regression line, and most of the countries with national IQs from 78 to 90 are below the regression line. Let us see the groups of the most deviating countries. One standard deviation of residuals of CPI is ±1.8.

Positive residuals are large (1.8 or higher) for 26 countries: Australia, Austria, Bahrain, Belgium, Botswana, Canada, Chile, Denmark, Finland, Germany, Iceland, Ireland, Israel, Luxembourg, Namibia, the Netherlands, New Zealand, Norway, Oman, Qatar, Singapore, South Africa, Sweden, Switzerland, the United Kingdom, and the United States. Of these countries, 19 are economically highly developed countries, and Bahrain, Oman, and Qatar are oil-producing countries. Botswana, Namibia, and South Africa are exceptional sub-Saharan countries, and Chile the only Latin American country in this group.

Negative residuals are large (-1.8 or higher) for 27 countries: Albania, Argentina, Armenia, Azerbaijan, Bangladesh, Bolivia, China, Ecuador, Georgia, Indonesia, Iraq, Kazakhstan, South Korea, Kyrgyzstan, Latvia, Macedonia, Moldova, Myanmar, Paraguay, Poland, Romania, Russia, Serbia and Montenegro, Tajikistan, Ukraine, Uzbekistan, and Vietnam. Former and present socialist countries (18) and Latin American countries (4) dominate this group of countries with much larger than expected negative residuals. Bangladesh, Indonesia, Iraq, South Korea, and Myanmar are special cases. There are some clear differences in the characteristics of large positive and negative outliers.

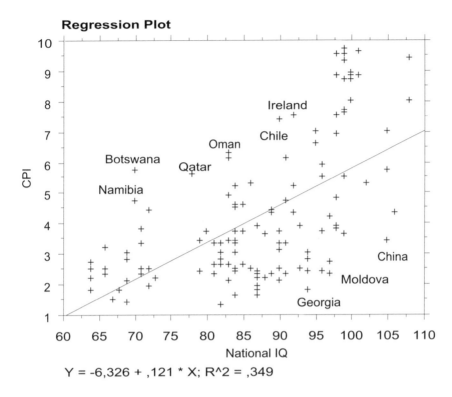

Figure 8.8. The results of regression analysis of CPI (Corruption Perceptions Index) on national IQ in a group of 132 countries

Economically highly developed countries are less corrupted than less developed countries. It should be remembered, however, that there are certainly defects in the reliability of these data on corruption.

9. Economic Freedom Ratings (EFR)

The quality of human conditions can be regarded as better in the countries in which human freedoms—economic and political in particular—are extensive than in the countries in which human freedoms are seriously restricted or suppressed. A measure of political freedom, the Index of Democratization (ID), constitutes a component of our composite Index of the Quality of Human Conditions (QHC). Now we want to explore to what extent economic freedom in the world is related to differences in national IQ. But what is "economic freedom"?

According to James Gwartney and Robert Lawson (2004, p. 5), economic freedom consists of personal choice, voluntary exchange, freedom to compete, and protection of the person and property. The existence of these freedoms requires the rule of law, property rights, limited government intervention, freedom to trade, and sound money.

Gwartney and Lawson have measured and estimated the degree of economic freedom in economies in their annual reports Economic Freedom of the World since 1996. The results are given in the Economic Freedom of the World (EFR) index. It measures the degree of economic freedom in five major areas: (1) size of government: expenditures, taxes, and enterprises; (2) legal structure and security of property rights; (3) sound money; (4) freedom to trade with foreigners; and (5) regulation of credit, labor, and business. Within the five major areas, various components are used to measure the extent of economic freedom. Each component and sub-component is placed on a scale from 0 to 10, and the component ratings are averaged to derive ratings for each of the five areas. The summary rating is the average of the five area ratings, and it can vary from 0 to 10 (Gwartney and Lawson, 2004, 5-20). They say that the index "captures most of the important elements and provides a reasonably good measure of differences among countries in economic freedom," but they add that because economic freedom is difficult to measure with precision, small differences between countries should not

Table 8.10. Intercorrelations of EFR, national IQ, QHC, and its five components in a group of 123 countries

Variable	EFR 2002	National IQ	QHC	PPP GNI 2002	Literacy 2002	Tertiary enroll.	Life expect.	ID 2002
EFR 2002	1.000	0.606	0.674	0.708	0.490	0.555	0.604	0.461
National IQ		1.000	0.889	0.727	0.735	0.811	0.853	0.661
QHC			1.000	0.850	0.820	0.897	0.859	0.830
PPP GNI per capita 2002				1.000	0.583	0.707	0.664	0.635
Adult literacy rate 2002					1.000	0.681	0.708	0.598
Tertiary enrollment ratio						1.000	0.704	0.729
Life expectancy at birth 2002							1.000	0.571
ID 2002								1.000

Regression Plot

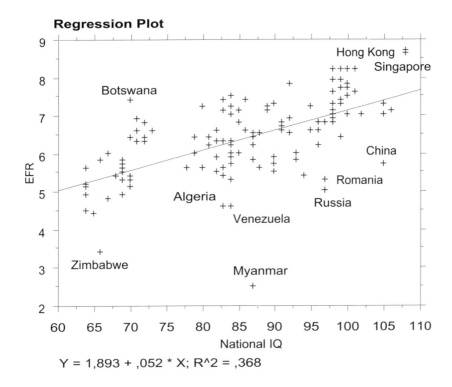

Y = 1,893 + ,052 * X; R^2 = ,368

Figure 8.9. The results of regression analysis of EFR (economic freedom ratings) on national IQ in a group of 123 countries

be taken seriously (p. 20).

The data on the EFR index used in this study are taken from the Economic Freedom of the World: 2004 Annual Report, and they are for the year 2002. The data cover 123 countries of our study. Because the institutions of economic freedom depend on human choices and decisions, it is reasonable to argue that nations with high national IQs are better able to create and maintain conditions of economic freedom than nations with low national IQs. Consequently, the correlation between national IQ and the EFR index should be clearly positive (Table 8.10).

Economic freedom ratings (EFR) are moderately correlated with national IQ (0.606). The explained part of variation in EFR rises to 37 percent. This result shows that economic freedom tends to rise with national IQ, although the relationship is not strong. The major part of the variation in EFR remains unexplained. Regression analysis of EFR on national IQ discloses how well this relationship applies to single countries and which countries deviate most from the regression line (Figure 8.9).

Figure 8.9 shows that the relationship between national IQ and EFR is approximately linear as hypothesized, but many widely deviating countries weaken the relationship significantly. One standard deviation of residual EFR (±0.8] can be used to separate large outliers from the countries which are closer to the regression line.

Positive residuals are large (0.8 or higher) for 21 countries: Australia, Bahrain, Botswana, Canada, El Salvador, Hong Kong, Ireland, Jamaica, Kuwait, Namibia, New Zealand, Oman, Panama, Singapore, South Africa, Switzerland, Uganda, the United Arab Emirates, the United Kingdom, the United States, and Zambia. What is characteristic for them? There are large outliers at all levels of national IQ. The group includes nine high-income industrial economies, four oil-producing countries, three Latin American and Caribbean countries, and five sub-Saharan African countries. It is difficult to find any common characteristics for them.

Negative residuals are large (-0.8 or higher) for 18 countries: Albania, Algeria, Argentina, Bulgaria, the Central African Republic, China, Colombia, Democratic Congo-Zaire, Ecuador, Myanmar, Romania, Russia, Syria, Turkey, Ukraine, Venezuela, and Zimbabwe. This group of countries differs from the first group on at least one point. Six of these countries are present or former socialist countries in which the transition to institutions of the market economy is still unfinished. Economic systems differentiate them from the nine high-income industrial economies with large positive residuals, although they are approximately at the same level of national IQ. Three other countries, Algeria, Myanmar, and Syria, have also experimented with socialist economic systems. Domestic peace seems to have been more fragile in many of these countries than in the countries of the first group. This concerns, in particular, Algeria, Argentina, the Central African Republic, Colombia, Democratic Congo-Zaire, Myanmar, Russia, Turkey, Venezuela, and Zimbabwe.

Empirical evidence supports the hypothesis about positive relationship between national IQ and economic freedom ratings (EFR), although many highly deviating cases contradict the hypothesis. The average level of EFR for the countries with high national IQs is clearly higher than for the countries with low national IQs. Differences in economic systems and domestic politics seem to explain a part of the variation in EFR.

10. The Index of Economic Freedom (IEF)

The Index of Economic Freedom (IEF), established by the Heritage Foundation and *The Wall Street Journal*, is another measure of economic freedom. We use in this study their overall scores for 2003 as a measure of economic freedom. According to original scores, the lower the score, the higher the level of economic freedom (see Chapter 5). For this calculation, we reversed the scores in such a way that the higher the score, the higher the level of economic freedom. Human conditions are assumed to be the better, the higher the level of economic freedom. Consequently, national IQ is expected to correlate positively with the reversed IEF scores. The reversed IEF scores vary from North Korea's 0 to Hong Kong's 3.55. Correlations are given in Table 8.11.

Table 8.11. Intercorrelations of IEF, national IQ, QHC, and its five components in a group of 156 countries

Variable	IEF 2003	National IQ	QHC	PPP GNI 2002	Literacy 2002	Tertiary enroll.	Life expect.	ID 2002
IEF 2003	1.000	0.418	0.620	0.740	0.306	0.485	0.458	0.532
National IQ		1.000	0.840	0.618	0.717	0.771	0.820	0.584
QHC			1.000	0.823	0.786	0.887	0.850	0.815
PPP GNI per capita 2002				1.000	0.495	0.666	0.611	0.628
Adult literacy rate 2002					1.000	0.648	0.685	0.516
Tertiary enrollment ratio						1.000	0.695	0.691
Life expectancy at birth 2002							1.000	0.540
ID 2002								1.000

Table 8.11 shows that the correlation between national IQ and IEF is positive as hypothesized. The relationship is statistically highly significant but only moderate (0.418). The explained part of variation in IEF is not more than 17 percent. IEF is strongly correlated with PPP GNI per capita just like EFR (see Table 8.10). Because IEF and EFR are strongly correlated (0.855, N = 120) and because the relationship between national IQ and IEF is weak, it is not necessary to present and

analyse the results of the regression analysis of IEF on national IQ. The Index of Economic Freedom (IEF) may be a poorer measure of economic freedom than EFR discussed in the previous section.

11. Population Pyramids (MU-index)

The Monaco-Uganda index (MU-index), developed by Leonid Andreev and Michael Andreev and based on population pyramids, is a kind of summary measure of human conditions. Population pyramids vary from a uniform pyramid pattern (Monaco) in which all age groups are represented by equal percentage of the total population to the most dissimilar population pyramid (Uganda). The index values vary from Uganda's 0 to Monaco's 100 (see Chapter 5). It can be assumed that the quality of human conditions tends to be the better, the closer a country's population pyramid reflects the uniform Monaco pattern. They found that their MU-index correlates strongly with many social variables, including our national IQ (see Andreev and Andreev, 2004). Consequently, the correlation between national IQ and the MU-index should be clearly positive. We test their MU-index's ability to measure the quality of human conditions by correlating it with our measures of human conditions (Table 8.12).

Table 8.12 shows that positive correlation between national IQ and the MU-index is very strong (0.806). Their co-variation rises to 65 percent. The MU-index has an even stronger correlation with QHC (0.901) and strong correlations with all its components, which indicates that in some way it reflects differences in the quality of human conditions. The MU-index is correlated strongly also with UNDP's Human Development Index (0.822, N = 155). An interesting question is to what extent the MU-index could increase the explained part of variation in QHC independently from national IQ. The results of a multiple regression analysis in which national IQ and the MU-index are used as independent variables and QHC as the dependent variable indicate that the explained part of variation in QHC rises to 84 percent (R = 0.915). It is 18 percentage points more than what national IQ explains alone, but only 3 percentage points more than what the MU-index explains alone. However, it should be noted that it is not justified to regard the MU-index as a really independent variable in its relation to QHC because it reflects the same differences in human conditions as our index of human conditions

Table 8.12. Intercorrelations of MU-index, national IQ, QHC, and its five components in a group of 162 countries

Variable	MU Index	National IQ	QHC	PPP GPI 2002	Literacy 2002	Tertiary enroll.	Life expect..	ID 2002
MU-index	1.000	0.806	0.902	0.718	0.723	0.831	0.752	0.774
National IQ		1.000	0.816	0.619	0.705	0.771	0.789	0.558
QHC			1.000	0.826	0.808	0.887	0.857	0.819
PPP GPI per capita 2002				1.000	0.529	0.670	0.630	0.624
Adult literacy rate 2002					1.000	0.670	0.713	0.544
Tertiary enrollment ratio						1.000	0.695	0.700
Life expectancy at birth 2002							1.000	0.553
ID 2002								1.000

(QHC). Regression analysis of the MU-index on national IQ is used to disclose how well the average relationship between these variables applies to single countries (Figure 8.10).

We can see from the regression plot (Figure 8.10) that the relationship between national IQ and the MU-index is approximately linear as hypothesized. The pattern is more or less similar as in the case of QHC (Figure 7.1). Let us see to what extent the most deviating countries are the same in both regression analyses. One standard deviation of residual MU-index (±15.0 or higher) can be used to separate large outliers.

Positive residuals are large for 24 countries: Antigua and Barbuda, Barbados, Belgium, Bulgaria, Croatia, Cuba, Cyprus, Denmark, Dominica, Equatorial Guinea, France, Germany, Greece, Italy, Jamaica, Lithuania, Portugal, Puerto Rico, Romania, Slovenia, South Africa, Spain, Sri Lanka, and Sweden. Of these countries, 13 are the same as in the regression of QHC on national IQ (Figure 7.1) and 11 others are different. However, for eight of these 11 countries, positive residuals are moderate also on the basis of the regression of QHC on national IQ. The results are clearly different only in three cases. For Bulgaria and Cuba, residuals based on regression of QHC on national IQ are near zero, and for Romania moderately negative (-5.9).

Negative residuals are large for 32 countries: Afghanistan, Belize, Bolivia, Brunei, Cambodia, China, Ecuador, Honduras, Iraq, Jordan, North

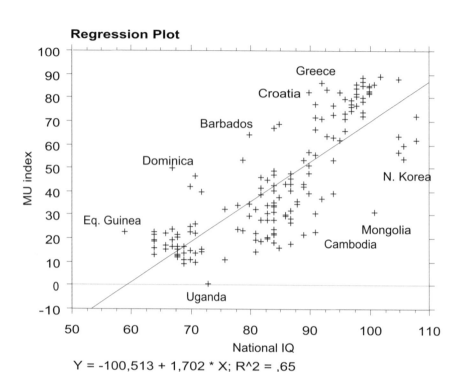

Regression Plot

Y = -100,513 + 1,702 * X; R^2 = ,65

Figure 8.10. The results of regression analysis of the MU-index on national IQ in a group of 162 countries

Korea, South Korea, Kuwait, Laos, Madagascar, Malaysia, the Maldives, Mauritania, Mongolia, Nicaragua, Oman, Pakistan, the Philippines, Saudi Arabia, Singapore, Syria, Taiwan, Tajikistan, Turkmenistan, Uganda, Vietnam, and Yemen. Of these 32 countries, 13 are the same as in the regression of QHC on national IQ. Negative residuals are moderate for five other countries and small for ten countries. Thus in 28 cases residuals are negative in both regression analyses. Positive residuals are near zero for South Korea, Kuwait, and the Philippines and moderate for Taiwan (61).

Because the results of this regression analysis at the level of single countries do not differ much from the results of the regression of QHC on national IQ, it is not necessary to discuss outlying countries in greater detail. Most of the largest outliers are the same in both cases: Barbados and Dominica with extremely large positive residuals and Afghanistan, Cambodia, Iraq, North Korea, Mongolia, and Yemen with extremely large negative residuals.

Table 8.13. Intercorrelations of Question 111B on human happiness, national IQ, QHC, and its five components in a group of 66 countries

Variable	Question 111B	National IQ	QHC	PPP GNI 2002	Literacy 2002	Tertiary enroll.	Life expect.	ID 2002
Question 111B	1.000	0.029	0.315	0.535	-0.040	0.050	0.317	0.223
National IQ		1.000	0.769	0.598	0.644	0.710	0.809	0.557
QHC			1.000	0.868	0.690	0.834	0.842	0.882
PPP GNI per capita 2002				1.000	0.424	0.568	0.682	0.745
Adult literacy rate 2002					1.000	0.604	0.671	0.477
Tertiary enrollment ratio						1.000	0.622	0.647
Life expectancy at birth 2002							1.000	0.666
ID 2002								1.000

Table 8.14. Intercorrelations of Question 122C on life satisfaction, national IQ, QHC, and its five components in a group of 62 countries

Variable	Question 122c	National IQ	QHC	PPP GNI 2002	Literacy 2002	Tertiary enroll.	Life expect.	ID 2002
Question 122C	1.000	0.033	0.396	0.605	-0.065	0.067	0.298	0.403
National IQ		1.000	0.765	0.585	0.678	0.703	0.805	0.547
QHC			1.000	0.864	0.675	0.836	0.827	0.877
PPP GNI per capita 2002				1.000	0.426	0.563	0.669	0.738
Adult literacy rate 2002					1.000	0.609	0.673	0.438
Tertiary enrollment ratio						1.000	0.602	0.655
Life expectancy at birth 2002							1.000	0.638
ID 2002								1.000

12. Human Happiness and Life-Satisfaction

In Chapter 5, we introduced two measures of human happiness (111B) and life-satisfaction (122C). These measures are from Ruut Veenhoven and his staff's database (The World Database of Happiness). We correlate them with national IQ and QHC and its five components in order to see to what extent human happiness is related to national IQ and our measures of global inequalities (Table 8.13 and Table 8.14).

The zero correlations between national IQ and the two measures of human happiness and life-satisfaction (0.029 and 0.033) show that human happiness and life-satisfaction do not depend on the level of national IQ. They are also independent of the level of literacy and tertiary enrollment, whereas both measures have a moderate positive correlation with per capita income and weak positive correlations with life expectancy and the level of democratization. These results imply that people tend to be somewhat happier and more satisfied with their lives in rich countries than in poor countries, in countries with long life expectancy than in countries with short life expectancy, and in democracies than in non-democracies. However, because correlations are weak, human happiness and life-satisfaction seem to depend more on other factors than on the level of per capita income, life expectancy, and democracy. The results imply that human happiness and life-satisfaction are not strongly dependent on material conditions of life. The regression of Question 111B (human happiness) on national IQ illustrates the observation that these variables are independent of each other (Figure 8.11).

We can see from Figure 8.11 that there is no relationship between national IQ and Question 111B on happiness. It also shows that countries with low national IQ are underrepresented in the sample. The examination of the most deviating countries may provide hints about other factors that are related to the average level of happiness. One standard deviation of residual 111B (±0.3) separates large positive and large negative outliers from the countries that are closer to the regression line.

Positive residuals are large for 14 countries: Australia, Belgium, Canada, Colombia, Denmark, Iceland, Ireland, Luxembourg, Netherlands, Sweden, Switzerland, the United Kingdom, the United States, and Venezuela. It is remarkable that all large positive outliers, except Colombia and Venezuela, are economically highly developed countries. This means that the level of socioeconomic development matters from the perspective of happiness. They are also democracies. These observations are in harmony with the fact that the correlation between Question 111B and PPP GNI per capita is 0.535 and between Question 111B and ID 0.315 (see Table 8.13).

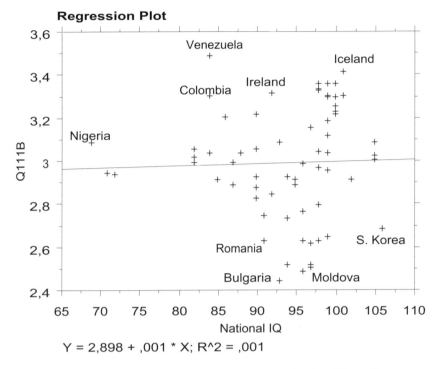

Figure 8.11. The results of regression analysis of Question
111B (human happiness) on national IQ in a group of 66 countries

Negative residuals are large for 12 countries: Armenia, Belarus, Bulgaria, Estonia, South Korea, Latvia, Lithuania, Moldova, Romania, Russia, Slovakia, and Ukraine. All these countries, except South Korea, are former socialist countries. The contrast between large positive and negative outliers is dramatic. People tend to be somewhat happier in economically more developed countries than in less developed countries as well as in long-term democracies and market economies, but these relationships are relatively weak. For China and India, for example, residuals are zero.

It is encouraging to note that human happiness and life-satisfaction do not depend on national IQ. A high level of national IQ does not guarantee happiness for a nation, and a low level of national IQ does not prevent people from finding satisfaction in life. This is consoling from the perspective of nations with low national IQs, and it is significant also from the perspective of global development policies. It may be possible to provide satisfactory conditions for relatively happy human life in all countries of the world despite the existence and persistence of many global inequalities in human conditions.

13. Summary

The results of correlation and regression analyses based on alternative measures of global inequalities support our central hypothesis about the relationship between national IQ and global inequalities in the quality of human conditions. It is obvious that the research hypothesis applies to many types of global inequalities measured by our alternative indicators of the quality of human conditions. Nearly all correlations are positive or negative as hypothesized, and the strength of the correlations is moderate or strong. Nations whose average intelligence is high seem to be able to organize all dimensions of human conditions better than nations whose average intelligence is low, but the fact that the unexplained part of variation in dependent variables is in some cases much more than half indicates that national IQ is not the only relevant factor, although it seems to be the major factor or at least an important factor behind many types of global disparities in human conditions. However, human happiness seems to be nearly independent of the level of national IQ.

The 14 tables of this chapter also indicate that differences in the samples of countries affect the strength of correlations between national IQ and QHC and its five components The samples of countries vary from 62 (Table 8.14, Question 122C) to 176 (Table 8.1, HDI). The correlation between national IQ and QHC is 0.791 in the total sample of 192 countries (Table 7.1). In these samples the same correlation varies from 0.765 (Table 8.14) to 0.889 (Table 8.10) and the explained part of variation in QHC from 58 to 79 percent. The mean of the 14 correlations is 0.837. There is similar variation in the strength of correlations between national IQ and the five components of QHC.

The unexplained part of variation indicates that there are other significant factors affecting the relationship between a measure of the quality of human conditions and national IQ. We have focused in this study on exploring the explanatory power of national IQ, but we used the results of regression analyses for single countries to provide hints about the nature of other factors that may have caused some countries to deviate greatly from the regression lines. Several assumptions about the nature of such factors were made in connection of single variables.

CHAPTER 9

Genetic and Environmental Determinants of National Differences in IQ and Wealth

We have established that there are differences in average IQs between nations and that these are significantly related to per capita incomes and rates of economic growth. We will now consider the reasons for the differences in national IQs. We believe that both genetic and environmental factors are likely to be involved. We doubt whether we shall encounter any opposition to the proposal that environmental factors contribute to the national differences in intelligence. The populations of many poor nations have inadequate nutrition and a high prevalence of disease, both of which can impair intelligence. Many of them also have less-well-developed educational systems and this may well have an adverse effect on the intelligence of the population. We anticipate that our proposal that genetic factors also contribute to the national differences in IQs is likely to be more controversial. We will therefore begin this chapter by arguing that genetic differences are likely to be an important determinant of national differences in intelligence. We begin by showing that genetic factors are important determinants of differences in intelligence and of income within national populations. We show next that genetic factors are also important determinants of differences in educational attainment and socioeconomic status within national populations. Our argument is that because genetic factors are important determinants of differences in intelligence, income, educational attainment, and socioeconomic status within national populations, it is likely that genetic differences are also partly responsible for these differences between nations.

1. Heritability of Intelligence

By the last two decades of the 20th century a consensus had emerged that genetic factors are a significant determinant of intelligence. In the statement drawn up by Gottfredson and endorsed by 52 experts it is stated that "Heritability estimates range from .4 to .8, most indicating that genetics plays a bigger role than environment in creating IQ differences among individuals" (Gottfredson, 1997, p. 14). The genetic contribution to the variation of a trait in a population is known in genetics as heritability. The heritability of a trait is therefore the proportion of the variation of a trait that is attributable to genetic differences between individuals in the population. Heritabilities are expressed as coefficients (h^2) that can range from zero to 1.0, and are also expressed as percentages. A heritability of zero means that genetic factors make no contribution to variation in a trait, while a heritability of 1.0 means that genetic factors are solely responsible for variation in a trait. A heritability of 0.5 means that genetic factors contribute to half of the variation in a trait, while environmental factors determine the other half.

Studies of the heritability of intelligence have been made in the United States and Britain since the 1930s, and have been made in a number of other countries from around 1970. Three methods for calculating the heritability of intelligence have been devised. The first of these consists of examining the correlation of the IQs of identical (monozygotic) twins reared apart. Because these pairs of twins are genetically identical and are not reared in the same environment, the magnitude of the correlation is a direct measure of the heritability. Identical twins who have been separated soon after birth and reared in different families are quite rare. Nevertheless, there have been six studies of them, one of which by Burt is now generally disregarded because of inconsistencies in the data which make the results suspect. The results of the remaining five studies are summarized in Table 9.1.

Table 9.1. Correlations between the IQs of pairs of identical twins reared apart

Country	N	r	Reference
USA	19	0.71	Newman et al., 1937
Britain	38	0.75	Shields, 1962
Denmark	12	0.69	Juel-Nielson, 1980
USA	48	0.75	Bouchard et al., 1990
Sweden	45	0.78	Pederson et al., 2002

It will be seen that the correlations range between 0.69 and 0.78 and are consistently high in the five studies carried out in the four countries. Bouchard (1998) has calculated the weighted average of the correlations between the twin pairs as 0.75. This figure needs to be corrected for the unreliability of test measurement. Assuming the tests have a reliability of approximately 0.85 as concluded by Bouchard (1993), the corrected correlation between the twin pairs is 0.88. This correlation is a direct measure of heritability, and therefore indicates that the heritability is 0.88 or 88 percent.

The second method for quantifying the heritability of intelligence consists of comparing the degree of similarity between identical twins and same-sex fraternal (non-identical) twins brought up in the same families. Identical twins are genetically identical whereas fraternal twins have only half their genes in common, so the operation of genetic factors should make identical twins more alike than fraternals. The simplest method for quantifying the genetic effect was proposed by Falconer (1960) and consists of doubling the difference between the correlations of identical and same-sex fraternal twins. Studies of the correlations obtained in a number of countries between the IQs of identical and same-sex fraternal twins are summarized in Table 9.2. The studies are listed by date of publication. It will be seen that the heritabilities are consistently appreciable over the period of 73 years and in a number of different countries. Some of the inconsistencies are attributable to the ages at which the IQs were measured. As shown by Bouchard (1993) in his compilation of studies, heritabilities increase steadily from 0.40 among 4–6-year-olds to 0.76 among adults.

Table 9.2. Studies of the heritability of intelligence: correlations of Mz and Dz twins

Country	Age	Mz N	r	Dz N	r	h^2	Reference
United States	-	50	0.90	47	0.62	0.56	Holzinger, 1929
England	8–14	65	0.86	99	0.48	0.76	Herman & Hogben, 1932
Sweden	18	215	0.90	416	0.70	0.40	Husen, 1951
Australia	16	27	-	19	-	0.79	Martin, 1975
Norway	18	757	0.83	1,093	0.51	0.64	Sundet et al., 1988
Norway	18	507	-	575	-	0.80	Tambs et al., 1989
Japan	12	543	0.78	134	0.49	0.58	Lynn & Hattori, 1990
United States	4–6	124	0.78	213	0.58	0.40	Bouchard, 1993
United States	6–12	1,564	0.84	2,495	0.58	0.52	Bouchard, 1993
United States	12–16	3,435	0.86	-	0.59	0.54	Bouchard, 1993
United States	Adults	127	0.78	99	0.51	0.76	Bouchard, 1993
India	Adults	-	-	-	-	0.90	Nathawat & Puri, 1995
India	Adults	30	-	30	-	0.81	Pal et al., 1997
Ireland	6	33	0.84	35	0.64	0.40	Lynn et al., 1997
England	6–7	66	0.70	60	0.32	0.76	Hohnen & Stevenson, 1999
Belgium	8–14	270	-	181	-	0.83	Jacobs et al., 2001
Netherlands	10–12	80	0.83	77	0.56	0.52	Bartels et al., 2002

Bouchard's heritability of 0.76 among adults needs to be corrected for the imperfect reliability of the tests. The reliability of IQs is approximately 0.85 (i.e., IQs measured on one occasion are correlated at about 0.85 with IQs measured on another occasion: Bouchard, 1993). Using this reliability coefficient, the corrected heritability coefficient becomes 0.89. This is virtually identical to the heritability of 0.88 derived from the studies of identical twins reared apart. This is why many experts have estimated the heritability of intelligence among adults as approximately 0.80 or 80% (Eysenck, 1998, p. 40; Jensen, 1998, p. 78). The reason that this estimate is lower than 0.88 is that they have not corrected the correlations for test reliability.

The third method for estimating the heritability of intelligence is to examine the correlation between the IQs of unrelated children adopted and reared in the same families. The magnitude of the environmental effect is expressed by the correlation between the pairs. The summary of the research literature by Bouchard (1998) concludes that among children the correlation is 0.28. This is a measure of the environmental contribution, indicating a heritability of 0.72. Among adults the correlation is 0.04, indicating a heritability of 0.96. These results corroborate those derived from the studies of twins in regard both to the very high heritability of intelligence among adults and the somewhat lower although appreciable high heritability of intelligence among children.

The high heritability of intelligence for individuals makes it probable that there is also an appreciable heritability of intelligence between nations. It shows that differences in intelligence between the individuals within countries are largely determined genetically. It has sometimes been suggested that the heritability of intelligence is likely to be lower in economically developing nations where there are greater environmental inequalities. The two studies of the heritability of intelligence in India (0.81 and 0.90) given in Table 9.2 show that this is incorrect. Because numerous studies in a wide range of countries have shown that intelligence has a high heritability, the probability that differences in intelligence between the populations of nations are entirely determined environmentally is very remote.

2. Heritability of Income

Income also has some heritability within national populations. The major reason for this is that intelligence has a high heritability (0.88) and is a determinant of income in national populations at a correlation of approximately 0.35 (see Chapter 3, Table 3.1). Studies to ascertain whether income has any heritability have been carried out by examining the correlations between the incomes of identical and same-sex fraternal twins, and the correlations between siblings and half-siblings. These studies have been largely carried out on samples in the United States but there is also a study from Australia. The results are summarized in Table 9.3.

Row 1 gives the figure of 0.14 calculated by Christopher Jencks (1972), who was the first person to analyze this issue in his book *Inequality*. His

Table 9.3. Studies of the heritability of income: correlations of Mz and Dz twins

	Country	Age	Mz N	r	Dz N	r	h²	Referencer
1	United States	-	-	-	-	-	0.14	Jencks, 1972
2	United States	-	-	-	-	-	0.34	Rowe, 1994
3	United States	-	1,019	0.54	907	0.30	0.48	Taubman, 1976
4	United States	-	-	-	-	-	0.42	Rowe et al., 1998
5	United States	51	942	0.56	840	0.32	0.48	Lynn, 2005
6	United States	42	582	0.50	454	0.33	0.34	Lynn, 2005
7	Australia	36	1,204	0.68	1,136	0.32	0.72	Miller et al., 1995

figure for the heritability of income is quite low. He was unable to explain most of the variation in income and concluded that incomes are largely a matter of luck. This seems improbable. The more likely explanation is that he was unable to identify and quantify accurately the relevant determinants. His method of analysis seriously underestimated the heritability of income because he assumed a causal chain in which genes determine IQ (0.71), IQ determines education (0.58), and education determines income (0.35). He multiplied these three correlations to give a correlation of 0.14 between genes and income. The flaw in his analysis is that intelligence affects income only partly through education but also independently of education. Thus two people with the same education can and often do have very different incomes that are partly attributable to their differences in IQ. Row 2 gives David Rowe's (1994, pp. 138–139) recalculation of the heritability of income at 0.34 using Jencks's own data and allowing for an effect of IQ on income independent of education. Row 3 gives the estimate of 0.48 for the heritability of income made by the American economist Paul Taubman. He examined the correlations for income of 1,019 identical and 907 fraternal twin pairs and found that this was 0.54 for Mz and 0.30 for Dz pairs. Doubling the difference gives a heritability of 0.48 (the age at which incomes were obtained is not given). Row 4 gives the estimate of 0.42 for the heritability of income calculated by Rowe, Vesterdal, and Rodgers (1998) from the correlations between pairs of siblings and half siblings in the National Longitudinal Study of Youth data set.

Rows 5 and 6 give two further estimates of the heritability of income of 0.49 and 0.34. The first of these uses the United States' National Academy of Science National Research Council's twin sample of white male veterans born between 1917–1927. There were 942 pairs of Mz twins and 840 pairs of Dz for whom annual incomes were obtained at a mean age of 51. The correlations for income were 0.56 for Mz and 0.32 for Dz pairs. Doubling the difference gives a heritability of 0.48. Row 6 uses the Minnesota Twin Registry sample of male twins born in Minnesota between 1936–1955. There were 582 pairs of Mz twins and 454 pairs of Dz for whom annual incomes were obtained at a mean age of 42. The correlations for income were 0.50 for Mz and 0.33 for Dz pairs. Doubling the difference gives a heritability of 0.34. Row 7 gives a much higher estimate of 0.72 for the heritability of income obtained from a large Australian twin sample.

Apart from the first figure of 0.14 given by Jencks, which is now recognized as an underestimate, the remaining six figures lie in the range between 0.34 and 0.72 and show that income has a moderate to high heritability. The median of the six studies is 0.45 and is the best estimate of the heritability of income. It should be noted that all these studies underestimate the heritability of income because they do not correct the correlations for reliability. IQs have a reliability of around 0.85. The reliability of incomes is not known, but obviously income in a particular year is not a wholly reliable measure of average lifetime income. A person may earn a modest income in one year and the next year secure a new job with a much higher income. Alternatively, a person may have a high income in one year and then be laid off and have to take a job with a much lower income the next year. The reliability of incomes is probably about the same as that of socioeconomic status that is given by Teasdale and Owen (1984) as 0.75. If we adopt this estimate, the true correlation between IQ and income increases from 0.45 (the median figure) to 0.56.

Income has a moderately high heritability, partly because intelligence is a determinant of income at a magnitude of around 0.35, and partly because income is also determined by the personality quality of conscientiousness at a magnitude of 0.41 (Judge, Higgins, Thoresen, and Barrick, 1999). Both intelligence and conscientiousness have moderate to high heritabilities. The heritability of conscientiousness is 0.72 according to the study of 660 Mz and 304 Dz twins reported by Reitman, Angleitner, and Strelau (1997). Other personality characteristics that also have some effect on earnings also have a moderately high heritability including the extent to which people value achievement, which has a heritability of 0.68, and the valuation of status, which has a heritability of 0.63 (Keller, Bouchard, Arvey, Segal, and Dawis, 1992). Because all the determinants of income (intelligence, conscientiousness, valuation of achievement and status) have moderate to high heritabilities, incomes also have the moderate to high heritabilities that have been found empirically, as shown in Table 9.3. Because differences in income between individuals within countries are significantly determined genetically, it is probable that differences in income between nations also have some heritability. As with intelligence, the probability that differences in incomes between the populations of nations are entirely determined environmentally must be very remote.

3. Heritability of Educational Attainment

There have been a number of studies of the heritability of educational attainment and these have shown that educational attainment also has a high heritability. Studies of the heritability of educational attainment listed by country are summarized in Table 9.4. Educational attainment is measured either by marks in examinations or tests, or by level or years of education. All of the eighteen studies show a moderate to high heritability of educational attainment, with coefficients ranging between 0.32 and 0.81, with a median of 0.56. These results are relevant for our argument because the national differences in educational attainment are closely similar to the national differences in intelligence (see Chapter 4, Sections 3 and 4) and also to national differences in per capita income. Thus genes are a partial determinant of educational attainment and through this of incomes. Once again it seems probable that because educational attainment has a moderate to high heritability in a number of countries, it is likely that differences in educational attainment between nations are also to some degree genetically determined.

4. Heritability of Socioeconomic Status

Socioeconomic status is a measure of the status people attach to various occupations. People normally attach high status to the major

Table 9.4. *Heritability of educational attainment*

Country	Age	Sex	N	Subject	h²	Reference
Australia	16	MF	79	Mathematics	0.81	Martin, 1975
Australia	16	MF	130	English	0.79	Martin, 1975
Australia	36	MF	2340	Level	0.58	Miller et al., 1995
Australia	Adults	M	310	Level	0.63	Baker et al., 1996
Australia	Adults	F	819	Level	0.48	Naker et al., 1996
England	6/7	M/F	252	Reading	0.67	Hohnen & Stevenson, 1999
Finland	Adults	M	7766	Level	0.47	Silventoinen et al., 2000
Finland	Adults	F	6498	Level	0.47	Silventoinen et al., 2000
Norway	Adults	M	1082	Level	0.60	Tambs et al., 1989
Norway	Adults	M	1370	Level	0.70	Heath et al., 1985
Norway	Adults	F	1836	Level	0.42	Heath et al., 1985
Sweden	18	M	314	Reasing	0.54	Husen, 1951
Sweden	18	M	315	Arithmetic	0.70	Husen, 1951
Sweden	59	M	150	Level	0.32	Lichtenstein et al., 1992
Sweden	59	F	219	Level	0.54	Lichtenstein et al., 1992
United States	27	M	3571	Level	0.81	Behrman & Taubman, 1989
United States	7	M/F	412	Reading	0.44	Wadsworth et al., 2001
United States	12	M/F	390	Reading	0.38	Wadsworth et al., 2001
United States	16	M/F	220	Reading	0.57	Wadsworth et al., 2001

professional and senior managerial occupations such as physicians, lawyers, and presidents and directors of large corporations, while they attach low status to unskilled work. Socioeconomic status is highly associated with income. It is therefore interesting to inquire whether socioeconomic status has any heritability. Studies of the heritability of socioeconomic status are summarized in Table 9.5. Row 1 gives a summary of earlier studies up to 1975 that concluded that the heritability of socioeconomic status lies between 0.28 and 0.46. Subsequent studies have broadly confirmed this conclusion. Rows 2 and 3 give heritabilities obtained in Denmark of 0.30 for adopted men and 0.12 for adopted women derived as the correlations between the socioeconomic status of the biological parents and that of the children. Because the biological parents can have had no environmental effect on the socioeconomic status of their children, the positive and significant correlations must be caused by genetic transmission and probably largely by the transmission of intelligence. Rows 4 and 5 give heritabilities of 0.20 for adopted men and 0.12 for adopted women obtained in another study in Denmark of the correlations between the socioeconomic status of the biological fathers and of the children. The correlation for men is lower than in row 2 because it is based on the biological fathers, while that in row 4 is based on the average of fathers and mothers. Row 6 gives a further estimate from Denmark consisting of the correlation of 0.23 for the heritability of socioeconomic status based on a study of 292 adopted men. The correlation is between the socioeconomic status of the biological fathers and that of the men at the ages of 35–38. The correlation of 0.23 is a measure of the heritability. The true heritability will be higher because of measurement error, which can be estimated at 0.75 for socioeconomic status because this is the reported correlation between the socioeconomic status of the men at the age of 25–28 and 35–38. Correction for measurement error gives a true heritability of socioeconomic status of 0.31. Row 7 gives a heritability of socioeconomic status of 0.41 for Norway derived from the difference in the correlations of identical and fraternal twins.

Rows 8 and 9 give heritabilities of socioeconomic status in Sweden of 0.88 for men obtained by comparing the correlations for SES of 38 MZ and 26 DZ twins (0.82 and 0.38, respectively). The heritability of socioeconomic status of women in the same study was rather lower at 0.44 obtained by comparing the correlations for SES of 36 MZ and 39 DZ twins (0.58 and 0.36, respectively).

Rows 10 and 11 give further estimates of the heritability of socioeconomic status in Sweden derived from the correlations for SES for men of 42 MZ and 50 DZ twins (0.84 and 0.36, respectively, giving a heritability of 0.96). The heritability of the socioeconomic status of women in the same study was much lower at 0.18 obtained by comparing the correlations for SES of 36 MZ and 40 DZ twins (0.56 and 0.47, respectively). Row 12 gives the results of an American study showing a heritability of socioeconomic status of 0.46 for men obtained by comparing the correlations for SES of 38 MZ and 26 DZ twins (0.43 and 0.20, respectively).

Notice that in all the studies that give heritabilities of socioeconomic status for men and women the heritability is greater for men than for women. The median of the seven studies of men is 0.41, while for the four

Table 9.5. Studies of the heritability of socioeconomic status

	Country	N	Sex	h²	Reference
1	United States	-	M/F	0.28-0.46	Fulker, 1978
2	Denmark	388	M	0.30	Teasdale, 1979
3	Denmark	242	F	0.12	Teasdale, 1979
4	Denmark	789	M	0.20	Teasdale & Sorensen, 1983
5	Denmark	628	F	0.12	Teasdale & Sorensen, 1983
6	Denmark	292	M	0.23	Teasdale & Owen, 1984
7	Norway	1,082	M	0.41	Tambs et al., 1989
8	Sweden	74	M	0.88	Lichtenstein et al., 1992
9	Sweden	75	F	0.44	Lichtenstein et al., 1992
10	Sweden	92	M	0.96	Lichtenstein et al., 1992
11	Sweden	76	F	0.22	Lichtenstein et al., 1992
12	United States	64	M	0.46	Behrman et al., 1977
13	Median		M	0.41	
14	Median		F	0.17	

studies of women the median is 0.17. Evidently women do not realize their genetic potential to achieve high socioeconomic status so effectively as men. The main reason for this is that many women interrupt their careers to have children and either do not resume their careers or resume them in positions of modest socioeconomic status.

Further evidence of a different kind showing a heritability of socioeconomic status comes from a study by Teasdale and Owen (1984) of 255 pairs of biologically unrelated adopted children reared by the same adoptive parents. Their socioeconomic status was recorded at the average age of 39, and the correlation between the SES of the pairs was 0.133. This is just statistically significant but very low and shows that common family environment has virtually no effect on the socioeconomic status that the children achieve when they are adults. The inference is that genetic factors are likely to be operating.

5. Heritability of Intelligence and Incomes between Nations

We have seen that intelligence, earnings, educational attainment, and socioeconomic status all have moderate to high heritabilities within nations. This makes it probable that intelligence and earnings have at least a moderate heritability between nations. The peoples of different nations are likely to differ genetically in their intelligence and in their capacities to achieve high earnings, just as do the peoples within nations. It has sometimes been argued that the existence of a high heritability of intelligence among individuals does not imply that there must be any heritability between populations. The example is given of plants in different soils. The height of plants has a high heritability, but a plant with a genetic disposition for height will not grow tall in an impoverished soil. This analogy does not hold well for humans. Plants are placed in good or poor soils, but humans are able to make their own environments. This distinction has been understood for some twenty years following the formulation of the concept of genotype-environment correlation by Plomin, Loehlin, and DeFries (1985). The essence of this concept is that individuals with the genes for high intelligence are able to build favorable environments for themselves and their children and they do this partly by providing higher incomes for their families. This process brings the genotype and the environment into positive correlation.

It was recognized by Fisher (1929) that the principle genotype-environment correlation holds for socioeconomic classes within national populations. The higher social classes have genotypes for higher intelligence because over the course of generations those with higher IQs have tended to rise in the socioeconomic status hierarchy while those with lower IQs have tended to fall. This has been shown for the twentieth century by Waller (1971) in the United States and by Saunders (1995) and Nettle (2003) in Britain.

The same principle of genotype-environment correlation applies to national populations. Here too populations with the genotypes for high intelligence have been able to build favorable environments, one of the important components of which is high per capita income. The favorable environments consisting of better nutrition, health care, and possibly education enhance the genotypes of the more intelligent peoples, producing populations whose phenotypic intelligence is a product of favorable genes and favorable environments.

6. Racial Basis of National IQs

The genetic basis for national differences in intelligence lies in the racial identity of the populations. This becomes apparent when nations are categorized by race. We show this in Table 9.6 for the nations that are largely racially homogeneous and for which we have the measured IQs given in Chapter 4 (the racially mixed populations of Latin America and the Caribbean are not included here but are considered separately in Section 7 below). The nations are grouped into the races of classical anthropology (e.g., Coon, Garn, and Birdsell, 1950) and consist of the East Asians (Mongoloids), the Europeans (European Caucasoids), the South Asians and North Africans (South Asian and North African Caucasoids), Southeast Asians (Malays), the Pacific Islanders, and the sub-Saharan Africans (Negroids). The existence of these genetic races has been confirmed by Cavalli-Sforza, Menozzi, and Piazza (1994), although they prefer to call them "genetic clusters."

A race can be defined as a breeding population that is to some degree genetically different from other populations as a result of geographical isolation, cultural factors, and endogamy, and which is shown in a number of inter-correlated genetically determined characteristics, such as the color of hair, skin, and eyes, body shape, blood groups, etc., as compared with other breeding populations. Geographical proximity between races generally produces a zone containing racial hybrids who show intermediate values of gene frequencies from the more central distributions of the two races. These hybrid and mixed race populations are known as *clines*. One of these is present in Table 9.6. This is the European-South Asian group that is found in the zone between Europe and Asia, embracing the Balkan states of South East Europe and Turkey in West Asia.

Table 9.6 gives first the median IQ for each race and then the IQs of the nations in that racial category. It will readily be seen that when nations are categorized by race they have similar IQs. The East Asians are shown first with a median IQ of 105. The six nations of this race have closely similar IQs in the range between 105 and 108. Shown next are the Europeans with a median IQ of 99. The IQs of the 29 European nations range between 91 in Lithuania and 102 in Italy. Shown next is the European-South Asian cline or hybrid population with a median IQ of 92 and a range between 89 in Serbia and 94 in Romania and 95 in Israel. Israel is included in this group because approximately 20 per cent of the population are Arabs, whose IQ of 86 is virtually the same as that of other South Asians in the Near East. Approximately 40 per cent of the population are European Jews (mainly Ashkenazim from Russia and Eastern Europe), whose IQ is 103, and approximately 40 per cent are Oriental Jews from Asia and North Africa (Yaish, 2001) whose IQ is 91. The IQ of 95 for Israel is the weighted mean of the IQs of the Arabs, Ashkenazim Jews, and Oriental Jews. A more detailed account of the IQs of the different ethnic groups in Israel is given in Lynn (2005a).

Shown next are the six nations of the Southeast Asians with a median IQ of 90 and a range between 86 in the Philippines and 94 in Vietnam. After these come the eight nations of the Pacific Islanders whose median IQ is 85 and whose IQs lie in the range between 81 in the Mariana Islands and 89 in the Cook Islands. Shown next are the fifteen nations of the South Asians and North Africans with a median IQ of 84 and whose IQs lie in the range between 78 in Nepal and Qatar and 89 in Mauritius. The high IQ in Mauritius is a little higher than that of the other nations in this group due to the presence of 6 per cent of Europeans and Chinese in the island.

Finally, there are the nineteen nations of sub-Saharan Africa with a median IQ of 67 and whose IQs lie in the range between 59 in Equatorial Guinea and 73 in Uganda. The IQ of 72 in South Africa is close to the top of the range because this is derived from the Africans and also from the European, Indian, and Colored minorities whose IQs are higher and are given in Appendix 1. Madagascar with its IQ of 82 has been omitted from the sub-Saharan Africans category because the population has a substantial South East Asian element whose ancestors migrated to the island. The precise proportion of South East Asian admixture is unknown, but the effect of the admixture is to produce an IQ of 82 that is intermediate between that of the South East Asians (90) and the sub-Saharan Africans (67).

Table 9.6. The intelligence of nations categorized by race

Nations	IQ	Nations	IQ	Nations	IQ
East Asian	105	Switzerland	101	Iran	84
China	105	United Kingdom	100	Iraq	87
Hong Kong	108	United States	98	Jordan	84
Japan	105			Kuwait	86
Singapore	108	**European South-Asian**	92	Lebanon	82
South Korea	106	Bulgaria	93	Mauritius	89

Nations	IQ	Nations	IQ	Nations	IQ
Taiwan	105	Croatia	90	Morocco	84
		Greece	92	Nepal	78
European	99	Israel	95	Pakistan	84
Australia	98	Turkey	90	Qatar	78
Austria	100	Romania	94	Sri Lanka	79
Belgium	99	Serbia	89	Syria	83
Canada	99			Yemen	85
Czech Republic	98	**Southeast Asian**	90		
Denmark	98	Indonesia	87	**S-Saharan African**	67
Estonia	99	Laos	88	Cameroon	64
Finland	99	Malaysia	92	Cent. African Republic	64
France	98	Philippines	86	Congo-Brazzaville	64
Germany	99	Thailand	91	Congo-Zaire	65
Hungary	98	Vietnam	94	Equatorial Guinea	59
Iceland	98			Ethiopia	64
Ireland	92	**Pacific Islanders**	85	Ghana	71
Italy	102	Cook Islands	89	Guinea	67
Lithuania	91	Fiji	85	Kenya	72
Malta	97	Mariana Islands	81	Mozambique	64
Netherlands	100	Marshall Islands	84	Nigeria	69
New Zealand	99	New Caledonia	85	Sierra Leone	64
Norway	100	Papua New Guinea	83	South Africa	72
Poland	99	Tonga	86	Sudan	71
Portugal	95	Western Samoa	88	Swaziland	72
Russia	97			Tanzania	72
Slovakia	96			Uganda	73
Slovenia	96	**South Asia/N. Africa**	84	Zambia	71
Spain	98	Egypt	81	Zimbabwe	66
Sweden	99	India	82		

7. Racial Basis of National IQs in Latin America and the Caribbean

We now consider the mixed race nations of Latin America and the Caribbean. All of these have varying proportions of Europeans, Native

Amerindians, mestizos (mixed European and Native Amerindian), sub-Saharan Africans, and mulattos (mixed European and sub-Saharan African). We examine how far the IQs of these nations can be predicted from the racial mix of the populations. To carry out this exercise, it is assumed that the IQ of the Europeans is 99 and the IQ of the sub-Saharan Africans is 67 (as given in Table 9.6). The IQ of Native Americans is assumed to be 83 as found in Mexico (Lynn, Backhoff, and Contreras, 2005). The IQ of mestizos (mixed European and Native Amerindian) is assumed to be 91 (the mean of the two parent races), and the IQ of mulattos (mixed European and sub-Saharan African) is assumed to be 83 (the mean of the two parent races). With these assumptions, we can calculate the expected IQ of the populations of the nations of Latin America and the Caribbean by weighting the IQs of the racial groups by their proportions in the population. The results are given in Table 9.7, which shows the measured IQs, the predicted IQs, and the proportions of the racial groups in the population given in Philip's (1996), in the CIA's *World Factbook* (Central Intelligence Agency, 2000); Kurian (1987), and *World Directory of Minorities* (1997). As an example of the calculations, for Argentina Philip's gives 85 per cent of the population as European, who have been assigned the European IQ of 99, and 15 percent of the population as Amerindian and mestizo. These have been assigned an IQ of 87, the average of the two groups. Weighting by the proportions in the population gives a predicted IQ of 97.

The correlation between the measured IQs and the IQs predicted from the racial composition of the population is 0.814. This confirms the data set out in Table 9.6 showing that the intelligence of nations is principally determined by the racial composition of their populations.

8. Further Evidence for Racial Differences in Intelligence

The conclusion that race differences in intelligence are the major determinant of national differences in intelligence is substantiated by a number of different lines of evidence. These have been set out in detail in *Race Differences in Intelligence: An Evolutionary Analysis* (Lynn, 2006) and will only be briefly summarized here. First, races are sub-populations of the human species, and it is a basic principle of evolutionary biology that when sub-populations become geographically isolated in different environments, they become genetically differentiated for all

Table 9.7. National IQs in Latin America and the Caribbean predicted from racial composition of the populations

Nations	Measured IQ	Predicted IQ	Racial Composition
Argentina	93	97	85% European, 15% Amerindian & Mestizo
Barbados	80	71	80% African, 16% Mulatto, 4% European
Bermuda	90	85	61% African & Mulatto, 37% European
Bolivia	87	88	42% Amerindian, 31% Mestizo, 15% European
Brazil	87	90	53% European, 3% Amerindian, 12% Mestizo, 11% African, 22% Mulatto
Chile	90	92	92% Mestizo & European, 7% Amerindian
Colombia	84	89	1% Amerindian, 58% Mestizo, 20% European, 4% African, 14% Mulatto, 3% African-Amerindian
Cuba	85	92	12% African, 22% Mulatto, 66% European
Dominica	67	68	90% African, 6% Mulatto, 4% Amerindian
Dominican Republic	82	84	11% African, 73% Mulatto, 16% European
Ecuador	88	87	40% Amerindian, 40% Mestizo, 5% European, 5% African
Guatemala	79	85	55% Amerindian, 42% Mestizo, 3% European
Honduras	81	90	90% Mestizo, 7% Amerindian
Jamaica	71	71	76% African, 15% Mulatto, 3% European, 3% East Indian
Mexico	88	88	30% Amerindian, 60% Mestizo, 9% European
Paraguay	84	91	3% Amerindian, 90% Mestizo, 7% European
Puerto Rico	84	93	76% European, 24% African & Mulatto
St. Lucia	62	75	90% African, 6% Mulatto, 3% East Indian
St. Vincent	71	73	65% African, 23% mixed and other, 6% East Indian, 2% Amerindian, 4% European
Suriname	89	83	10% African, 35% Mulatto, 3% Amerindian, 33% East Indian, 16% SE Asian
Uruguay	96	96	8% Mestizo, 86% European, 6% African
Venezuela	84	85	67% Mestizo, 21% European, 10% African, 2% Amerindian

characteristics for which there is genetic variation. Thus, Dawkins (1988, pp. 238–9) has written that when two populations become isolated from one another they become so unlike each other that, after a while, naturalists would see them as belonging to different races; the theory of speciation resulting from initial geographical separation has long been a cornerstone of mainstream, orthodox neo-Darwinism. The racial differences that have evolved include body shape, the color of skin, hair, and eyes, the prevalence of genetic diseases, and blood groups. It is inconceivable that intelligence would be the sole exception to these genetic differences between the races. Some racial differences in intelligence must inevitably have evolved as a matter of general biological principle.

Second, the consistency of the IQs of the races in a wide range of geographical locations can only be explained by some genetic determination. For instance, in the 57 studies of general population samples of Africans in 17 African countries all the IQs lie in the range between 59 and 89, and in the 59 studies of indigenous East Asians in 6 countries all the IQs lie in the range between 100 and 120 (see Appendix 1). Only a genetic factor can explain the consistency of these race differences in so many different environments. It is noteworthy that those who support the environmentalist theory of race differences in intelligence such as Neisser (1996), Mackintosh (1998), Jencks and Phillips (1998), Nisbett (1998), Fish (2002), and Brody (2003), fail to make any mention of the consistency of the racial differences in so many different environments and nations.

Third, the races differ consistently in IQ when they live in the same environments. Thus, Africans in the United States, Britain, the Netherlands, and Brazil have consistently lower IQs than Europeans. The same is true of South Asians and North Africans in Britain, Continental Europe, Africa, Fiji, Malaysia, and Mauritius; of Native Americans living with Europeans in the United States, Canada, and Mexico; and of Pacific Islanders living with Europeans in New Zealand and Hawaii. (For detailed data for this conclusion, see Lynn, 2005a). All these differences are consistent and add to the credibility of the genetic theory, while they cannot be explained by environmental theory.

Fourth, when babies from other races are adopted by Europeans in Europe and the United States, they retain the IQs characteristic of their race. This has been shown for Africans in the United States, where black infants adopted by white middle class parents have the same IQ as blacks reared in their own communities (Lynn, 1994c); and for East Asians in the United States and Europe, where Korean infants adopted by Europeans have IQs in the range between 102-110 (Winnick, Meyer, and Harris, 1975; Frydman and Lynn, 1989).

Fifth, mixed race individuals have IQs intermediate between those of the two parent races. Thus, in Weinberg, Scarr, and Waldman's (1992) study of children adopted by white middle-class families, at the age of 17 years blacks had an IQ of 89, those of mixed black-white parentage an IQ of 98, and whites an IQ of 106 (Lynn, 1994c). When the amount of European ancestry in American blacks is assessed by skin color, dark skinned blacks have an IQ of 85 and light skinned blacks have an IQ of 92 (Lynn, 2002), and there is a statistically significant association between light skin and intelligence.

Sixth, there are race differences in brain size that are associated with differences in intelligence. These are shown in Table 9.8. The IQs are taken from Table 9.6 and the mean brain sizes of the races from the data assembled by the American anthropologists Smith and Beals (1990) consisting of approximately 20,000 crania of 91 populations world wide. It will be seen that there is a perfect linear relation between the average intelligence and the average brain size of the six races.

Table 9.8. Race differences in brain size (cc) and intelligence

Race	IQ	Brain Size (cc)
East Asians	106	1416
Europeans	99	1369
Southeast Asians	90	1332
Pacific Islanders	85	1317
South Asians	84	1293
Africans	67	1282

The significance of this association is that there is a positive association between brain size and intelligence. This has been shown in numerous studies carried out from the first decade of the twentieth century. The research has been reviewed by Vernon, Wickett, Bazana, and Stelmack (2000) who report 54 studies that used an external measure of head size. All of the studies showed a positive relationship and the overall correlation was 0.18. They also report 11 studies of normal populations that measured brain size by CT (computerized axial tomography) and MRI (magnetic resonance imaging) which give a more accurate measure of brain size, and for which there was an overall correlation of 0.40. A further study published subsequent to this review found a correlation for 40 subjects between brain size measured by MRI and intelligence of 0.44 (Thompson, Cannon, Narr et al., 2001). Vernon et al. conclude that the most reasonable interpretation of the correlation is that brain size is a determinant of intelligence. Larger brains have more neurons and this gives them greater processing capacity.

9. Environmental Determinants of National Differences in Intelligence

While we believe it is impossible to avoid the conclusion that genetic factors are partly responsible for the race differences in intelligence that underlie national differences, we also believe that environmental factors contribute to the national differences in intelligence. Widespread sub-optimal nutrition and poor health undoubtedly impair the intelligence of populations of the poor nations. We have shown in detail that improvements in nutrition are the principal factor responsible for the increases in intelligence that have occurred in economically developed countries during the twentieth century (Lynn, 1990). We do not doubt that improvements in nutrition would increase intelligence in economically developing countries.

It may also be that intelligence in economically developing countries is impaired by poor education. There is some evidence that education can increase intelligence, and it has been estimated that in the United States the effect of one year of schooling increases the IQ by about 1 IQ point (Herrnstein and Murray, 1994) or even 2-4 IQ points (Winship and Korenman, 1997; Hansen, Heckman, and Mullen, 2004). However, it has generally been found that the effect of education wears off after a few years. Moreover, virtually all our national samples comprise children at school, many of whom have had the same amount of schooling as the British or American comparison samples. Second, even if some of our samples had a little less schooling than the British or American comparison samples (say, by starting school at the age of 7 rather than 5 or 6) the IQ difference amounting to approximately 30 IQ points in the case of sub-Saharan Africans is much too large to be explicable by minimal schooling differences.

10. Genotype-environment Co-variation

The problem of the relative contributions of environmental and genetic factors to national and racial differences in intelligence is made more difficult by the principle of genotype-environment co-variation. This states that the genes for high intelligence tend to be associated with favorable environments for the optimum development of intelligence (Plomin, 1994). Intelligent parents normally provide their children with good quality nutrition because they understand the general principles of what constitutes a healthy diet, and a healthy diet is a determinant of intelligence. Intelligent parents are also more likely to give their children cognitive stimulation, which is widely believed (not necessarily correctly) to promote the development of the intelligence of their children. The same principle operates for national populations. Those with high intelligence provide their children with the double advantage of transmitting favorable genes to their children and providing them with a favorable environment with good nutrition, health care, and education that possibly enhances the development of their children's intelligence. Conversely, the children of the less intelligent nations tend to transmit the double disadvantage of poor quality genes and a poor quality environment. Thus it is problematical whether the poor nutrition and health that impair the intelligence of many third world peoples should be regarded as a purely environmental effect or as to some degree a genetic effect arising from the low intelligence of the populations that makes them unable to provide good nutrition and health for their children. The principle of genotype-environment co-variation implies that differences in intelligence between nations for which the immediate cause is environmental are also attributable to genetic factors that contribute to the environmental handicaps.

The extent to which national and racial differences in intelligence are determined genetically must be expected to vary according to which pairs of nations or races are compared. The magnitude of the heritability depends on the variability in the environmental determinants of intelligence in the population and, in the case of two populations, the differences in the environmental determinants between the two. In the comparison between Africans in Africa and Europeans the environmental differences between the two populations, consisting of the quality of nutrition and health, are quite large. Consequently they will have a significant impact and possibly explain about 50 percent of the differences in intelligence between the two populations. This estimate is derived from the IQs of Africans in the United States and Europe, which are approximately 85 (for a comprehensive review, see Lynn 2005a). Thus, when Africans are reared in approximately the same environment as Europeans, the IQ difference is approximately half that of Africans in Africa (approximately 15 IQ points as compared with approximately 30 IQ points). Note, however, that Africans in the United States have on average approximately 25 percent European ancestry (Reed, 1971; Chakraborty, Kamboh, Nwamko, and Ferrell, 1992) and this increases their genotypic IQs as compared with Africans in Africa by about 25 per cent. Taking all these factors into consideration, we estimate that genetic factors explain about half of the IQ difference between Europeans and Africans. This means that if Africans could be provided with the same environment (i.e., the same nutrition, health care, and education) as Europeans, their IQs would be expected to increase from an average of around 67 to around 80, i.e., about the same as that of pure and nearly pure Africans in the southeastern United States, which, in a substantial sample of 1,800, has been found to be 80.7 (Kennedy, Van der Reit, and White, 1963). When the national IQs of populations that have about the same standards of living, nutrition, health, and education are compared, the environmental effect is much smaller and the heritability correspondingly greater. This applies in particular to comparison between East Asian and European nations. The environmental conditions in which they live are closely similar insofar as they enjoy approximately the same standards of living, nutrition, health care, and education, so the slightly higher IQ of the East Asians is probably largely determined genetically.

CHAPTER 10

The Causal Nexus

Hitherto we have presented the relationships between national IQs and a variety of measures of the quality of human conditions as a set of correlations. We are well aware that correlations are not the same as causes. Hence in this chapter we set out what we believe are the most reasonable causal relationships between national IQs and the economic and demographic variables. We begin by showing these in Figure 10.1 as a path diagram. We will concede immediately that the reality is more complex than the model shown in the figure and remind readers that all theories in the natural and social sciences are simplified versions of the real world.

In the model given in Figure 10.1 the proposed causal sequences flow from left to right and the strength of the relationships between the variables is indicated by correlation coefficients for 192 nations where these are available, or for lesser numbers where the data are incomplete. At the left of the model are the genetic and environmental determinants

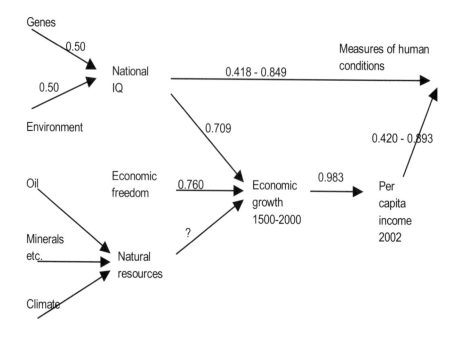

Figure 10.1. Path diagram of determinants of economic growth, per capita income, and measures of the quality of human conditions

of national IQs, each of which has been assigned a value of 0.50. In the next column are IQ, economic freedom, and natural resources, each of which is conceptualised as contributing independently to economic growth over the period 1500–2001. We theorize that these three factors have been the major determinants of national differences in economic growth during the last five centuries. The correlation (0.709) between national IQ and economic growth 1500–2000 (EGR 4) is based on a sample of 109 nations. The correlation (0.760) between economic freedom (EFR) and economic growth 1500–2000 (EGR 4) is based on a sample of 77 nations. These correlations suggest that national IQ and economic freedom contributed about equally to economic growth during the period 1500–2000, although correlations are not directly comparable with each other because they are based on different samples of countries. The results of multiple regression analysis confirm that their independent contributions have been approximately equal. Together national IQ and EFR explain 69 percent of the variation in EGR 4 (multiple correlation 0.832). Because we do not have variables to quantify natural resources, we have not been able to measure the impact of natural resources on economic growth over the period 1500–2000.

The next stage in the causal path is from economic growth over the period 1500–2000 to per capita income in 2002 ($r = 0.983$). This almost perfect correlation indicates that national differences in rates of economic growth over the last five centuries have determined national differences in per capita income in 2002. This is a natural consequence of the fact that differences in per capita income were quite small in 1500. The final stage of the model shows IQ and per capita income as joint determinants of various measures of the quality of human conditions analyzed in chapters 6 through 8. The correlations, 0.418 to –0.849 in the case of national IQ and 0.720 to 0.893 in the case of PPP GNI 2002, are based on various samples of countries, which vary from 96 (poverty) to the total sample of 192 countries (see Table 10.1). It is clear that national IQ and PPP GNI 2002 cannot be regarded as equally independent explanatory variables because PPP GNI 2002 is partly determined by national IQ ($r = 0.601$, $N = 192$). We now look more closely at these proposed causal sequences.

1. Genetic and Environmental Determinants of National IQs

The values of 0.50 for the genetic and environmental determinants of national IQs are rough estimates. Within national populations the heritability of IQ among adults is approximately 0.8 and the environmental contribution approximately 0.2 (as documented in Chapter 9, Section 1). It may be that the heritability of national IQs is somewhat lower than that of individual IQs. In Chapter 9, Section 9, we discussed the genetic and environmental contributions to the IQ difference between Europeans and sub-Saharan Africans and concluded that they each contributed approximately 0.50. This means that if sub-Saharan Africans were reared in the same environments as Europeans, the IQ difference would be reduced to approximately 0.50 of its present size, i.e., from about 32 IQ points (99–67) to around 16

IQ points (about the same as the IQ difference in the United States and Britain, where Europeans and Africans do live in approximately the same environments). We have assumed that the heritability of IQ between Europeans and sub-Saharan Africans can be generalized to all national differences. Notice however that the precise or even approximate value of the heritability of national IQs is not crucial for our general theory that there is a significant genetic contribution to national IQs.

The problem of the relative contributions of environmental and genetic factors to national differences in intelligence is complicated by the principle of genotype-environment co-variation, as discussed in Chapter 9, Section 10. This states that the genes for high intelligence tend to be associated with favorable environments for the optimum development of intelligence. Intelligent parents typically provide their children with a healthy diet and this improves their children's intelligence. Thus, intelligent parents provide their children with the double advantage of transmitting favorable genes to their children and providing them with a favorable environment. Less intelligent parents transmit less favorable genes to their children and provide them with a less favorable environment. This brings the genes and the environment into correlation and hence the concept of genotype-environment co-variation. It can be argued that the ultimate cause of environmental factors affecting intelligence is genetic, because parents with genes for high intelligence provide their children with favorable environments.

The ultimate cause of national differences in intelligence is also genetic because it lies in the racial identity of the population, as shown in Chapter 9. IQs in poor nations are undoubtedly impaired by environmental disadvantages of poor nutrition and health, but these environmental disadvantages are themselves genetic. Nevertheless, in the model we present genetic and environmental factors as independent determinants of per capita income.

2. Relation between IQ and Economic Freedom

IQ and economic freedom are considered as joint determinants of national per capita income. The fact that differences in economic systems were found to be related to many large deviations in the regression of

PPP GNI per capita 2002 on national IQ (Chapter 6, Section 2) supports this assumption. In the year 2002 the national IQ and economic freedom (EFR) variables were themselves correlated at 0.606 (N = 123). We propose a positive feedback loop to explain this association, such that each tends to augment the other. We suggest two principal processes. First, nations with high IQs will tend to have intelligent political leaders who understand that economic freedom is likely to promote economic growth and will introduce measures to free their economies. Nations with low IQs will tend to have less intelligent political leaders who fail to understand this and believe that their economies can be strengthened by controls, permits, the creation of state monopolies, and so on. Second, economic freedom leads to high per capita income (r = 0.708, N = 123) (see Table 8.10), and this enhances IQ environmentally because nations with high per capita income provide their populations with good nutrition and health care that increase IQs.

3. Determinants of Economic Growth and Per Capita Income

Our model gives three determinants of economic growth from 1500 to 2000. These are IQ (r = 0.709, N = 109)), economic freedom (r = 0.760, N = 77), and natural resources, which we have not been able to measure. We believe that the theoretical explanations are as follows. IQ is a determinant of economic growth and per capita income because the intelligence of the population determines the efficiency with which work is performed throughout the economy. A considerable number of studies within nations have shown that more intelligent individuals secure higher incomes (Chapter 3, Section 1), and the same principle must hold between nations, which are aggregates of individuals. Among nations, however, we propose a positive feedback loop between IQ and per capita income, such that each tends to augment the other. High national IQ will increase economic growth and produce high per capita income, while high per capita income will raise IQ environmentally.

In the period 1500-2000 IQ is correlated with economic growth at 0.709 (see Table 8.4) and in the period 1950–2001 at 0.747 (Table 8.3) (this is for absolute growth in $US). The principal reason for the positive effect of national IQ on economic growth is that nations with highly intelligent populations can make and market complex technological goods like computers, aircraft, televisions, automobiles, etc. that sell well in world markets, and this produces rapid economic growth. Conversely, nations with less intelligent populations are unable to make and market these complex technological goods and largely sell raw materials (if they have any), less cognitively demanding goods such as clothing, and agricultural products for which there is a world surplus, and hence command only low prices in world markets. The results are that nations with less intelligent populations are able to achieve only low economic growth rates, or even growth rates that are negative. There is a positive relation between national per capita income (GDP per capita) in 1500 and economic growth 1500–2000 (0.726, N = 109). However, there is no relationship between per capita GDP 1950 and economic growth 1950–2001 (-0.122) when extremely exceptional Kuwait and Qatar are in the sample (N = 134). When Kuwait and Qatar are removed from the sample, the correlation rises to 0.512 (N = 132). We believe that a major reason for this is that nations with high per capita income in 1500 and 1950 had high IQs and these made a major contribution to economic growth from 1500 to 2000 and from 1950 to 2001. It is doubtful whether high per capita income in 1500 or 1950 had any direct causal effect on subsequent economic growth 1500–2000 and 1950–2001 respectively. On the contrary, the economic theory of convergence tells us that a high per capita income is a disadvantage for economic growth because countries with low per capita income have a competitive advantage from their low wage costs and this should enable them to produce faster economic growth. The main reason for the failure of convergence theory is that it does not recognize that nations with high IQs can increase their already high per capita income because their IQ advantage outweighs their disadvantage of high labor costs.

Economic freedom is a determinant of per capita income because a free market economy promotes economic growth and therefore higher per capita income. This has become widely recognized, but there are still large national differences in economic freedom and many countries in which economic freedom is limited, or even, in the cases of North Korea and Cuba, virtually non-existent. The main reasons for this are that the leaders of authoritarian governments do not understand that economic freedom promotes economic growth, or because they maintain their power by economic controls and monopolies.

The possession of natural resources (such as oil, valuable minerals and metals such as diamonds, gold, uranium, etc., and a favorable climate for tourism such as that in the Caribbean) contributes to per capita income, but we are not able to quantify these because their nature varies qualitatively from country to country. Differences in geographical conditions such as navigable rivers, good natural harbors, etc. can be regarded as additional natural resources that may also affect per capita income.

4. Determinants of the Quality of Human Conditions

In the final stage of the model, IQ and per capita income are shown as joint determinants of measures of human conditions. The strength of correlations is similar (see Figure 10.1), which indicates that these two variables may contribute equally to measures of the quality of human conditions.

The contributions of IQ and per capita income to measures of human conditions are analyzed in chapters 6 through 8 and are summarized in Table 10.1 The measures of economic growth rates, MU index, and the measures of human happiness and life-satisfaction are excluded from this table. In the next sections, some of these relationships are analyzed in greater detail.

Table 10.1. Correlations of measures of human conditions with IQ and per capita income

Variable	N	National IQ	PPP GNI per capita 2002
Life expectancy (LE) 2002	192	0.754	0.616
Adult literacy rate 2002	192	0.655	0.511
Tertiary enrollment ratio	192	0.745	0.680
Level of Democratization (ID) 2002	192	0.529	0.574
Human Development Index (HDI) 2002	176	0.776	0.748
Gender-related Human Development Report 2002	144	0.849	0.765
Gini Index of Inequality (Gini WIID)	146	-0.538	-0.420
Poverty ($2 a day poverty line)	96	-0.653	-0.702
Percentage of undernourished population (PUN 1)	124	-0.500	-0.567
Maternal mortality ratio (MMR) 2000	149	-0.730	-0.510
Infant mortality rate (IMR)	149	-0.771	-0.638
Corruption Perceptions Index (CPI)	132	0.591	0.893
Economic freedom ratings (EFR) 2002	132	0.606	0.708
Index of economic freedom (IEF) 2003	156	0.418	0.740

5. Determinants of Life Expectancy

Our model gives IQ and per capita income as the two determinants of life expectancy with correlations of 0.754 and 0.616 respectively. A number of economists have noted the positive relationship between per capita income and life expectancy. The research has been reviewed by Bloom, Canning, and Sevilla (2004). There should be no difficulty in understanding why national per capita income is a determinant of life expectancy. Nations with high per capita income can afford to provide better nutrition and health care for their populations and so their populations live longer.

Economists have not, however, understood that intelligence is a determinant of life expectancy and that much of the relationship between life expectancy and per capita income is attributable to the effects of national IQ on both. Notice that national IQ correlates more highly than per capita income with life expectancy. The results of multiple regression analysis illustrate the combined explanatory power of national IQ and per capita income as well as their relative significance (Table 10.2).

Table 10.2. The results of multiple regression analysis in which national IQ and PPP GNI per capita 2002 are used to explain variation in Life expectancy 2002 in the group of 192 countries

Variable	Coefficient	Std. Error	Std. Coeff.	t-Value	P-Value
Intercept	8.587	4.766	8.587	1.802	.0732
National IQ	0.640	0.061	0.601	10.587	<.0001
PPP GNI per capita	0.003	0.001	0.255	4.484	<.0001
R = 0.781					
R squared = 0.610					

Table 10.2 shows that both variables are statistically highly significant explanatory variables independently from each other, but national IQ explains much more (standardized coefficient 0.601) of the variation in life expectancy independently from per capita income than vice versa. The combined explanation (61%) is only five percentage points more than national IQ explains alone. This conclusion has also been reached by Kanazawa (2005).

Substantial evidence that IQ is a determinant of life expectancy has been reviewed by Gottfredson (2004). The relation of intelligence to life expectancy at the group level seems to have been first shown by Maller (1933) who found that across the districts of New York the average IQ of the school children was correlated at -0.43 with the death rate and at -0.51 with the infant mortality rate. The relation of intelligence to life expectancy at the individual level seems to have been first shown in Australia by O'Toole and Stankov (1992) in a study of 2,309 National Servicemen. These were conscripted between 1965 and 1971 at the age of 18 into the military, and their intelligence was tested. They were followed up in 1982, when they were aged between 22 and 40, and it was found that 523 had died. These had an IQ 4 points lower than those who remained alive, a statistically highly significant difference. By far the largest cause of death was accidents of various kinds (389), of which motor vehicle accidents (217) were the most frequent. It seems probable that the explanation for this association is that those with lower IQs make more misjudgements. Some of these misjudgements result in accidents, and some of these are fatal.

A second study confirming the association between intelligence and life expectancy has been published by Whalley and Deary (2001). Their initial sample was 2,230 babies born in Aberdeen (Scotland) in 1921, whose intelligence was measured when they were 11 years old. They were traced in 1997, and it was found that the IQ of those who had died was 4.3 IQ points lower than those who had survived. The difference was greater for women, among whom the survivors had an IQ 4.9 points higher than those who had died, than for men, among whom it was 3.6 IQ points higher. The reason for this sex difference was largely that the men who died in World War II had higher than average IQs.

There are four principal reasons why intelligence contributes to life expectancy. First, individuals with high intelligence have fewer accidents because they can foresee potentially dangerous situations and avoid them; for example, they are more likely to wear seat belts, drive carefully, and keep their automobiles in good operating conditions. Second, intelligent individuals look after themselves more effectively and take more care of their health by not smoking or using drugs, avoiding excessive alcohol consumption and unhealthy diets, not allowing themselves to become overweight, and so forth, because they have more knowledge that these either promote or are injurious to health. Third, intelligent individuals have greater knowledge of potentially dangerous symptoms and are more likely to consult their physicians about these. Fourth, intelligent individuals take their medication more efficiently: it has been estimated that about 40 percent of prescriptions in the United States are ineffective because patients do not use them properly, and these are predominantly those with the least education and the lowest IQs (Gottfredson, 2004).

Linda Gottfredson (2004) argues convincingly that differences in intelligence are the main reason for the social class gradient for life expectancy, which is such that life expectancy is greater in the higher socioeconomic classes. This has been found in a number of countries for several decades, and has frequently been attributed to socioeconomic differences in income that enable the higher socioeconomic classes to buy more health care. But Gottfredson points out that in Britain, where health care has been free for more than half a century, the socioeconomic differences in longevity are as strong as in the United States.

Low infant mortality contributes to longevity. There are several lines of evidence showing that the intelligence of mothers is related to the infant mortality of their babies. This is not surprising, because mothers have to take care of the health of their infants, and this is a cognitive task that, like all cognitive tasks, requires intelligence. Mothers have to anticipate possible accidents and take steps to prevent them happening, judge whether illnesses are sufficiently serious to justify seeing a physician, and give medications that are prescribed. It would therefore be expected that mothers with low intelligence would have a greater prevalence of infant mortality. Direct evidence for this has been produced by Savage (1946) and by Herrnstein and Murray (1994, p. 218), who showed that the mothers of infants who had died in their first year had an average IQ of 94, compared with 100 of the mothers of infants who had not died in their first year. Ecological correlations between IQs and infant mortality have been shown for the regions of the British Isles ($r = 0.78$), of France ($r = 0.30$), and of Spain ($r = 0.54$) (Lynn, 1979, 1980, 1981). There have also been several studies showing that the educational level of mothers is related to the infant mortality of their babies. For instance, it was reported by Cramer (1987) that in all births to white mothers in California in 1978, infant deaths per 1,000 numbered 12.2 for those with fewer than twelve years of education, 8.3 for those with twelve years of education, and 6.3 for those with thirteen years of education. In view of the high association between years of education and intelligence (documented in Chapter 3) these differences will reflect the IQs of the mothers. Further studies of an association between the educational level of mothers and the greater prevalence of infant mortality in their children have been reported by Bross and Shapiro (1982) and Keller and Fetterly (1978). We therefore predict that the same relationship will be present across nations such that there will be a negative relation between national IQs and the prevalence of infant mortality.

We envision a positive feedback loop between longevity, IQ, and per capita income. Longevity is a proxy for good health, and healthy workers work more efficiently than unhealthy workers. Hence good health (indexed by longevity) promotes high per capita income and IQ, while high per capita income and IQ promote good health and longevity.

6. Determinants of Adult Literacy

Our model gives IQ and per capita income as the two determinants of adult literacy, with correlations of 0.655 and 0.511, respectively. The principal reason for these positive relationships is that nations with high IQs have higher per capita income and can afford to provide more and possibly better education in which greater proportions of their populations are taught to read. The results of multiple regression analysis illustrate the relative significance of national IQ and per capita income as explanatory variables (Table 10.3).

We can see from Table 10.3 that national IQ explains much more of the variation in Adult literacy (standardized coefficient 0.545) independently from per capita income than vice versa and that the combined explanation (45%) is only two percentage points more than national IQ explains alone (43%). There may be a positive feedback loop between IQ, per capita income, and adult literacy such that high levels of literacy promote economic growth, high per capita income, and higher IQs.

7. Determinants of Tertiary Education

Our model gives IQ and per capita income as the two determinants of the percentage of the population enrolled in tertiary education with correlations of 0.745 and 0.680, respectively. The results of multiple regression analysis presented in Table 10.4 indicate that the independent explanatory power of per capita income is somewhat smaller

Table 10.3. The results of multiple regression analysis in which national IQ and PPP GNI per capita 2002 are used to explain variation in the adult literacy rate 2002 in the group of 192 countries

Variable	Coefficient	Std. Error	Std. Coeff.	t-Value	P-Value
Intercept	-2.417	9.303	-2.417	-0.260	.7953
National IQ	0.953	0.118	0.545	8.066	<.0001
PPP GNI per capita	0.004	0.001	0.183	2.715	<.0072
R = 0.671					
R squared = 0.450					

(standardized coefficient 0.362) than that of national IQs (standardized coefficient 0.528). The combined explanation (64%) is nine percentage points higher than the explanation provided by national IQ alone (55%).

Here again, we propose the possible operation of a positive feedback loop between IQ, per capita income, and enrollment in tertiary education. Nations with high IQs have high per capita incomes which enable them to afford more tertiary education for their populations. It may be that more tertiary education raises per capita income in a positive feedback loop, but despite much debate among economists over several decades, there is no consensus that greater expenditures on tertiary education promote economic growth and hence higher per capita income. The alternative explanation for the greater proportions with tertiary education in rich nations is that this is a consumption good and has no beneficial effect on their economies.

8. Determinants of Democratization

Our model gives IQ and per capita income as the determinants of national differences in democratization, with correlations of 0.529 and 0.574 respectively. The results of multiple regression analysis (Table 10.5) show that in this case the independent explanatory power of per capita income is somewhat greater than that of national IQ. Taken together they explain nine percentage points more of the variation in the level of democratization than national IQ alone.

Table 10.4. The results of multiple regression analysis in which national IQ and PPP GNI per capita 2002 are used to explain variation in the tertiary enrollment ratio in the group of 192 countries

Variable	Coefficient	St. Error	Std. Coeff.	t-Value	P-Value
Intercept	-64.347	7.792	-64.347	-8.258	<.0001
National IQ	0.955	0.099	0.528	9.651	<.0001
PPP GNI per capita	0.008	0.001	0.362	6.625	<.0001
R = 0.800					
R squared = 0.639					

Table 10.5. The results of multiple regression analysis in which national IQ and PPP GNI per capita 2002 are used to explain variation in the level of democratization (ID) 2002 in the group of 192 countries

Variable	Coefficient	Std. Error	Std. Coeff.	t-Value	P-Value
Intercept	-13.133	5.615	-13.133	-2.339	.0204
National IQ	0.287	0.071	0.288	4.031	<.0001
PPP GNI per capita	0.005	0.001	0.401	5.601	<.0001
R = 0.619					
R squared = 0.383					

We propose that the causal processes are that populations with high IQs and high per capita income are less willing to tolerate authoritarian regimes and more prone to demand democracy. The association between national IQ and democratization is, however, only moderate, and there are notable exceptions. India is the world's largest democracy but has an average IQ of only 82. China, with a much higher IQ of 105, has been an autocracy for most of the twentieth century. To some degree it seems to be a matter of historical accident whether a country is a democracy or an autocracy. If Lenin had lost the civil war of 1920–22 in Russia, the country would probably have evolved into a democracy. Democracy is associated with economic freedom (EFR 2002) (r = 0.461, N = 132). The explanation is probably largely that in democracies people will use their voting power to demand economic freedom. Once again, we propose the operation of a positive feedback loop between IQ, per capita income, and democratization, such that democracies tend to have economic freedom, this increases their per capita income, and this in turn raises the IQs of the population.

Table 10.6. The results of multiple regression analysis in which national IQ and PPP GNI per capita 2002 are used to explain variation in PUN 1 (the percentage of undernourished population 1999-2001) in the group of 192 countries

Variable	Coefficient	Std. Error	Std. Coeff.	t-Value	P-Value
Intercept	62.559	10.311	62.559	6.067	<.0001
National IQ	-0.423	0.133	-0.272	-3.170	<.0019
PPP GNI per capita	-0.016	0.003	-0.419	-4.884	<.0001
R = 0.611					
R squared = 0.374					

9. Determinants of Malnutrition

Our model gives IQ and per capita income as the two negative determinants of the percentage of the population suffering from malnutrition (PUN 1) and the percentage of underweight children under age five (PUN 2) with correlations of -0.500 and -0.421, respectively. Table 10.6 giving the results of multiple regression analysis discloses the relative significance of national IQ and per capita income as explanatory variables. It is interesting to note that PPP GNI per capita 2002 seems to be a more significant explanatory variable than national IQ (see standardized coefficients). In this connection, it should be remembered that the variation in per capita income is moderately related to national IQ. Taken together, national IQ and per capita income explain 37 percent of the variation in PUN 1, which is 12 percentage points more than national IQ explains (25%).

We propose that the causal processes are that populations with high IQs are able to secure high per capita income and use this to give adequate nutrition to their children. A high per capita income contributes directly to adequate nutrition. We envision the operation of a positive feedback loop between IQ, per capita income, and nutrition, in which nations with high IQs secure high per capita income, which enables them to afford better nutrition, and this in turn raises the IQs of the population. Considerable evidence that malnutrition impairs intelligence is given in Lynn (1990, 2005a).

CHAPTER 11

Criticisms and Rejoinders

1. Reliability of the National IQs
2. Validity of National IQs
3. The Direction of Causation
4. Genetic Basis of National IQs
5. Other Determinants of Economic Development

O ur analysis of the contribution of national differences in IQs to national per capita wealth and economic growth presented in our book *IQ and the Wealth of Nations* was subjected to a number of criticisms by Astrid Ervik (2003), Thomas Volken (2003), Thomas Nechyba (2004), and Susan Barnett and Wendy Williams (2004). We anticipate that similar criticisms are likely to be made of the present book, and we therefore devote this chapter to discussing and answering them. The major criticisms that are made by most of the reviewers concern the reliability and validity of the national IQs, the direction of causation from national IQs to national differences in wealth, our conclusion that differences in national IQs have some genetic basis, and our alleged neglect of other determinants of economic development.

1. Reliability of the National IQs

Several of our critics have criticised our work on the grounds that the national IQs have low reliability (the reliability of a psychometric test is the degree to which its result is replicable). Thus, Astrid Ervik

(2003, p. 406) writes: "the authors fail to establish the reliability of intelligence (IQ) test scores" and that the results of the national IQs "differ considerably and result in large disparities in test scores for the same country." Thomas Volken (2003, p. 411–2) also seems to criticise our IQ measures on the grounds of their reliability when he writes that "IQ samples differ greatly in size." We are unable to understand the point of this criticism. The sample sizes are given in Appendix 1. It is true that the samples do differ in sample size. Some samples consist of several thousands, some of several hundreds, while some are below a hundred. As a matter of general principle a large sample size is likely to give a more reliable result than a small sample size, but the most important criterion for a good sample is the degree to which it is representative of the population rather than its size. Even very small samples can give highly reliable results. For instance, Herrnstein and Murray (1994, p. 275) give an IQ of 112.6 for the IQ of American Jews based on a sample size of only 98, but this IQ is closely similar to that obtained in a number of other studies reviewed in Lynn (2004). They give an IQ of 103 for East Asians based on a sample size of only 42 (p. 273), but again this IQ is closely similar to that obtained in a number of other studies reviewed in Lynn (2005a).

Volken goes on to assert that the samples differ in "the point of time the IQ test was performed"; this does not matter because we adjusted for this as explained (page 197); and "the IQ samples can hardly be considered to be representative at the national level. One may be particularly concerned about the sampling in remote rural areas of Africa during the 1960s" (if the samples are not representative, the results will not be reliable).

Barnett and Williams also criticise the reliability of the IQs. They write that the samples "are, in many cases, not representative of the countries from which they are derived" (if the samples are not representative, the results will not be reliable). They point out, for example, that the IQ of Indonesia is based on data for school children in the city of Bandung, while one of the studies of the IQ in Japan was obtained from a study of school children in the city of Sendai. Maybe, they say, these children of these cities are not representative of their respective countries.

We do not know whether school children in the city of Bandung are representative of Indonesia, although we think this is a reasonable assumption. However, in the case of Japan, we presented ten studies and showed that all ten give closely similar IQs, showing that the measures have high reliability. However, rather than criticising individual studies, there is a well-established procedure for determining whether a test is reliable. This is to make two measurements of a trait and examine the extent to which they give the same results. The reliability of the measure is expressed by the correlation between the two scores, which shows the degree to which they are consistent. The correlation between the two measures is called the *reliability coefficient*. Some measuring instruments used in psychology have quite low reliability. One of these is the Rorschach Ink Blot test, devised in the 1920s by the Swiss psychiatrist Herman Rorschach. The test consists of inkblots on cards that people are asked to look at and describe what they mean. Their descriptions are interpreted for revelations about their preoccupations and concerns. It has been found that different psychologists and psychiatrists interpret the descriptions differently—"the judges often disagree in interpreting the same test responses and many inaccurate predictions are made with the instrument," so it has been described as "a fairly weak measuring instrument" with very low reliability (Baron, Byrne, and Kantowitz, 1980, p. 50; Gordon, 1976). Thus, our critics Ervik, Volken, and Barnett and Williams, who have asserted that the national IQs we presented have low reliability are saying that they are like the Rorschach Ink Blot. One measure gives one result while another measure of what purports to be the same phenomenon shows something quite different. Such a test is worthless. This conclusion has led Barnett and Williams (2004) to assert that our cross-country comparisons are "virtually meaningless."

We anticipated this objection in our *IQ and the Wealth of Nations* and answered it in a section headed *Reliability of National IQs* (p. 64). We handled the problem of the reliability of the measures by examining 45 countries in which the intelligence of the population has been measured in two or more independent investigations. This is the same procedure that is used to examine the reliability of tests given to sets of individuals. We reported that the correlation between two measures of national IQs is 0.94, showing that the measures give highly consistent results and have high reliability. This reliability coefficient is a little higher than that of tests of the intelligence of individuals, which are typically around 0.85 and 0.90 (Bouchard, 1993; Mackintosh, 1998, p. 56). In view of this, it is difficult to understand how Astrid Ervik, Thomas Volken, and Susan Barnett and Wendy Williams can have asserted that the national IQs we presented have low reliability. The only possible explanations seem to be either that they did not read the section where we demonstrated the high reliability of the IQs or that they do not understand the meaning of the concept of reliability. We discuss the reliability of the national IQs in the present study in Chapter 4, Section 2. We now have 65 countries for which there are two or more scores. The correlation between the two scores, excluding the two extreme scores and using the next lowest and highest scores of countries for which we have five or more IQ scores is 0.95. This figure establishes beyond dispute that the national IQs have high reliability.

The problem of the reliability of the national IQs has also been addressed by McDaniel and Whetzel (2004). They suggested that perhaps the IQs in sub-Saharan Africa are too low at an average of around 70. So they say let it be assumed that the IQs in these countries have an average of 90. They calculated that on this assumption the correlation between national IQ and per capita real gross domestic product increases from 0.62 to 0.68. Thus "our truncated analysis suggests that any mean IQ less than 90, on average, is a detriment to GDP per capita regardless of its specific value" (p. 32). Second, they say let it be assumed that all the national IQs have low reliability and all we can do is divide the nations into three categories of those whose populations have an IQ below 90, those with an IQ between 90–99, and those whose populations have an IQ of 100 and above. On this assumption the correlation between national IQ and per capita real gross domestic product increases from 0.62 to 0.66. They conclude that "this analysis shows that even very approximate estimates of IQ are excellent predictors of real gross domestic product per capita" (p. 32).

2. Validity of National IQs

Several critics have raised the problem of the validity of the national IQs (the validity of a psychometric test is the degree to which it provides an accurate estimate of the construct it is intended to measure). Thus, Astrid Ervik (2003, p. 406) writes: "the authors fail to establish the reliability and cross-cultural comparability of intelligence (IQ) test scores" (if the scores are not comparable, the test will not be valid). Barnett and Williams (2004) assert that our cross-country comparisons are "virtually meaningless," implying that they are not valid. Volken also impugns the validity of the tests when he writes of the "highly deficient data on the national levels of IQ."

There are certain circumstances in which intelligence tests have poor validity in the sense that they do not provide a valid or fair measure of an individual's intelligence. For instance, a verbal test administered in a foreign language will not give a valid IQ for a person who does not speak that language. A test of general knowledge will provide a valid measure of intelligence for people in a particular culture who have equal chances of acquiring that knowledge, but will not give a valid IQ for those in another culture that does not possess this general knowledge. This problem was recognized in the 1930s and to overcome it Raymond Cattell in 1940 constructed what he called the Culture Free intelligence test (Cattell, 1971) consisting of problems in the format of designs and pictures. However, it has not been universally accepted that such tests are genuinely culture-free or fair for all cultures.

Some critics have argued that the national IQs in our study are not valid because the populations tested lack experience of the kinds of problems presented in the tests. According to this view, the peoples of sub-Saharan Africa, whose IQs average around 67, are just as intelligent as the peoples of Europe, whose IQs average around 99, and the peoples of East Asia, whose IQs average around 105.

This criticism of the validity of the national IQs is made by Barnett and Williams, who write that the general knowledge questions that occur in some intelligence tests cannot be valid measures of the intelligence of peoples who have not had an opportunity to acquire these items of information. They give a number of examples such as "what is an umbrella?" and they say that this cannot be a fair or valid test of the intelligence of peoples who have little or no experience of umbrellas. This criticism is misplaced because virtually all of the tests used in our study are non-verbal and of the kind that Cattell designated *culture-fair and -free*. Most of the data have been obtained from the Raven's Progressive Matrices Test. This is a non-verbal reasoning test that presents a series of designs (three in the easier to eight in the more difficult) that progress in a logical sequence. The problem is to work out the principle governing the sequence and then deduce the next design from a number of options. Another non-verbal test used to measure a number of national IQs is the Cattell Culture Fair Test, which presents problems in both design and picture format. Barnett and Williams criticize the use of these tests as well, on the grounds that children in western cultures have more experience of the shapes and colors of the designs and of the scenes depicted in the pictures than children in economically underdeveloped countries. They fail to note that virtually all the samples are of children at school or adults who have been to school, where they would have had experience of shapes and colors similar to those of as western children.

However, this criticism of the validity of the tests is just a conjecture about whether tests in design and picture format are biased against the populations of economically underdeveloped countries. Perhaps they are, but perhaps they are not. What is needed is some objective method of determining whether the intelligence tests are valid measures. The problem of the validity of intelligence tests has long been recognized and has been addressed by examining whether IQs predict educational attainment. There are numerous studies, summarized in Chapter 3 (Table 3.4) showing that they predict earnings (Tables 3.1, 3.2, and 3.3) and socioeconomic status (Table 3.4).

In *IQ and the Wealth of Nations* we anticipated the objection that the IQ tests are not valid for many nations and we devoted a page and a half to answering it in a section headed *Validity of National IQs* (pp. 64–65). We adopted the same method as has been long employed for examining the validity of the tests among individuals, i.e., by examining whether they are correlated with educational attainment. We showed that there are substantial positive correlations between national IQs and educational attainment in mathematics and science obtained in the International Studies of Educational Achievement. The correlations between national IQs and achievement in mathematics and science of 10- and 14-year-olds in 1994 are 0.84 and 0.70. In the present study we have again examined this issue with data for the IQs of a larger number of nations. We show in Chapter 4 (Table 4.2) that national scores on mathematics and science obtained for 53 countries in the International Studies of Achievement in Mathematics and Science are correlated at between 0.78 and 0.89 with national IQs. We also show that there are equally high correlations between national IQs and achievement in mathematics and science obtained in other studies. These results show that the different cognitive abilities of national populations found in intelligence tests are confirmed in tests of mathematics and science and establish that the national IQs are valid measures of cognitive ability.

The validity of the national IQs is further confirmed by their high correlations with national per capita income and other measures of global inequality shown in Chapters 6 through 8. If, as Barnett and Williams (2004) assert, our cross-country comparisons are "virtually meaningless," they would not be highly correlated with national attainment in per capita income and other indices of global inequality between nations.

3. The Direction of Causation

The problem of the direction of causation in the association between national IQs and national per capita income has been raised by Ervik, Barnett and Williams and by Nechyba. Ervik reminds us that "correlation need not imply causation"; Barnett and Williams write critically that we "argue that the direction of causality is from IQ to income and not vice versa," while Nechyba (2004) writes that "the causation behind the correlations identified in this book is likely to run in exactly the opposite direction from what is asserted by the authors: economic development leads to changes in environments that cause increases in measured IQs." Once again, we wonder whether these critics have read our book with any attention. We did not and do not advance a one-way causal relationship from IQ to income. We proposed and continue to propose a reciprocal interaction relationship between IQ and national wealth such that national IQs are a determinant of wealth, while national wealth is a determinant of intelligence. In *IQ and the Wealth of Nations* we devoted much of Chapter 10 to a discussion of environmental determinants of national IQs and the ways in which poverty in developing nations impairs the intelligence of the populations, particularly by poor nutrition and health. We recommended that rich countries should direct some of their aid programs to improving the nutrition and health of pregnant women and young children because this would be the most promising way of raising their intelligence. Nechyba and Barnett and Williams suggest that the direction of causal relationship between national IQ and national incomes could be entirely one way from national incomes to IQs. There are two reasons why this is implausible. First, there is an extensive research literature showing that within countries the IQs of children are a significant determinant of their future incomes (reviewed in Chapter 3, Sections 1 and 2), indicating a causal effect from IQ to income. In view of this, the suggestion that between countries the causal relationship is wholly in the opposite direction, from income to IQ, seems exceedingly improbable. Second, national differences in IQs almost certainly have some genetic basis, and if this is so they cannot be wholly caused by national differences in per capita income.

4. Genetic Basis of National IQs

This brings us to the question of the probable genetic basis of national IQs. Ervik, Nechyba, and Barnett and Williams all question our contention that national differences in IQs are likely to have some genetic basis. Ervik questions our contention that intelligence has a high heritability. In support of this position we summarized the studies of the similarity of identical twins separated shortly after birth and reared in different families, the higher correlation between the IQs of identical than of non-identical twins reared together, and the low correlations between adopted children and their adoptive parents. Ervik complains that we do not quote sample sizes or give other statistical information. For these we referred readers to the literature. There is in fact a universal consensus among behavior geneticists that intelligence has a moderate to high heritability (see e.g., Plomin, DeFries, and McClearn, 1990). The high heritability of intelligence and the effect of this on earnings is discussed by economists, and papers on this and its implications for economics are published from time to time in economic journals. For instance Zak, (2002) in a recent paper in the *Journal of Evolutionary Economics* cites a range of heritability estimates of IQ between 48% and 75%. The high heritability of intelligence is well known to a number of economists, but apparently Susan Ervik is not among them.

Some of our critics have argued that the high heritability of intelligence in national populations does not necessarily imply that there is any heritability of intelligence between nations. Thus, Barnett and Williams write that "the variance within a group does not predict the variance between that group and another, as the differences in genes and environments within a group do not say anything about the differences in genes and environments between groups; if national IQ differences are not necessarily genetically driven, then they might well be caused by rich countries simply spending more on education, nutrition, health care, and related factors." The same point is made by Nechyba, who reiterates the well worn fertilizer analogy which reminds us that the height of plants can be increased by the application of fertilizer. The height of plants has a high heritability, but a plant with a genetic disposition for height will not grow tall in an impoverished soil. He writes that the same may be true of nations: "developed countries may simply be like plants that received fertilizer earlier for reasons having nothing to do with IQ." However, this analogy does not hold well for humans, as indicated in Chapter 9, Section 5.

We do, however, accept that the heritability of 80 to 90 per cent of intelligence for adults within national and mainly Western populations does not necessarily imply that the same magnitude of heritability exists between nations. Nevertheless, we continue to assert that with such a high heritability of intelligence in the United States (in both blacks and whites: see Lynn, 2005a), in several European nations, in Japan, and in India (see Chapter 9), the likelihood that there could be a zero heritability of intelligence between nations is very low. Consider these parallels. Height has a high heritability within economically developed nations, but it is also influenced by environmental factors, and average height increased in many countries during the twentieth century. There is a large difference in height between Europeans and the pygmies of the West African rain forests. The high heritability of height does not prove that the difference in height between Europeans and the pygmies has any genetic basis. It is theoretically possible that the causes of the difference could be entirely environmental. But the high heritability of height makes it probable that the low stature of pygmies has a genetic basis. It is now known that this is the case and the low stature of pygmies is caused by a low level of the insulinlike growth factor I (Cavalli-Sforza, Menozzi and Piazza (1994, p. 177). Another example is skin color. This also has genetic and environmental determinants. There are national and racial differences in skin color, and it is theoretically possible that these might be solely environmentally determined. But this is very unlikely.

Because of the reluctance of some of our reviewers and no doubt others to accept the probability of some genetic basis of national differences in intelligence IQs, we have devoted Chapter 9 to restating and elaborating the arguments that genetic factors are involved. We do not, however, dispute that environmental factors contribute to national differences in IQs. The determination of national IQs is likely to be similar to that of individual IQs in that both genetic and environmental factors are involved. This probability is enhanced by studies showing that black and Oriental infants adopted and reared by Europeans have the intelligence typical of their own race rather than the race of the adoptive family (see Chapter 9, Section 8).

5. Other Determinants of Economic Development

Both Volken and Ervik criticize our study by asserting that we consider only intelligence as a determinant of national differences in economic development and fail to discuss other factors. Volken writes that we "fail to adequately use multivariate techniques and only simple correlations are presented"; and Ervik criticises that "the book's strong conclusions rest on simple bivariate correlations between IQ scores and income *per capita* levels. The empirical estimates fail to control for alternative explanations of income differences across countries." Contrary to these assertions, we devoted a chapter to the discussion of alternative explanations of economic development. In Chapter 9, entitled "Intelligence and Markets as Determinants of Economic Development," we presented a multiple correlation of national IQ and economic freedom as joint predictors of per capita income, and show that the two measures give a multiple correlation of 0.799 with per capita income at PPP (purchasing power parity) (page 155). This is higher than the correlation between IQ and per capita income and shows that economic freedom makes an independent contribution to national per capita income over and above IQ. We demonstrated that the results of the multiple correlation analysis showed that economic freedom ratings (the extent to which countries have a market economy) explain approximately ten percentage points of the variation in the measures of per capita income independently from national IQs. We provided an extensive discussion of other determinants of economic growth and per capita income, including the contribution of democratic political structures, the possession of valuable raw materials such as oil and minerals, climate, health, nutrition, and culture, all of which are identified in the index. We also examined the contribution of democratic political structures, quantified as the index of democratization, to economic development, and found that the independent contribution of the level of democratization (ID) is negligible, consisting of only one or two percentage points independently from national IQs. Yet again it appears that these critics cannot have read our book with any attention.

We give credit to Barnett and Williams for having read and noted that we provided a discussion of a number of determinants of economic growth and per capita income, but they disparage these by writing that "these discussions appear, in many cases, to be somewhat arbitrary (post-hoc rationalizations can be used to 'explain' many things if there is no control over the number of factors that can be invoked and the selectiveness with which they are applied)." We wonder whether they really believe that our attribution of the high per capita income of the Gulf States to the possession of oil and of Botswana to the possession of diamonds can be reasonably described as "arbitrary."

Volken advances a further criticism that "motivational and structural factors should have been adequately discussed and modelled." Contrary to this criticism, we provided a quite extensive discussion of the possible contributions of the work ethic, achievement motivation, and cultural values to economic development (pages 6–9). We do not deny that these motivational factors may be significant, but we do not believe they have as yet been adequately measured. It cannot be reasonably expected that our book, which proposed and quantified intelligence as a major new determinant of economic development, would also provide evidence for a number of motivational factors that might also be involved but that no one has yet succeeded in quantifying.

Ervik also criticises our use of mean IQs of the population as our explanatory variable: "choosing the mean of IQ scores seems arbitrary and without clear theoretical base. One could make a case that the smartest people drive economic development of a country." Contrary to this criticism, the mean IQ of the population does have a sound theoretical base, because intelligence is a determinant of efficient work at all levels of society (see Chapter 3), all of which contribute to the efficiency of production. For this reason the average IQ is the best index of the intelligence level of national populations to examine in relation to their per capita income. However, the adoption of Ervik's proposal to use the proportion of individuals with high IQs would come to the same thing, because the variance of intelligence is approximately the same in all populations, and hence a population with a high mean has greater numbers of the highly intelligent individuals at the top end of the distribution.

Moreover, we made Ervik's point about the contribution of highly intelligent people to national per capita income in a discussion of the various ways in which a high average IQ contributes to economic development (pp. 159–164), where we wrote that "nations whose populations possess high IQs have a large scientific elite who are able to produce economically valuable goods and services and can provide other non-scientific but complex and cognitively demanding goods and services that command high prices in international markets" (p. 160). However, we explain that this is not the only reason why nations whose populations have high IQs have high per capita incomes. A population with a high mean IQ has more competent people at all levels of society, including those in middle management and those carrying out skilled and unskilled manual work. Ervik concludes her review by asking "Are people in rich countries smarter than those in poorer countries?" and writes that "the authors fail to present convincing evidence." Contrary to this conclusion, we presented measured national intelligence for 81 nations in our *IQ and the Wealth of Nations* and showed that these are correlated with per capita income at approximately 0.7. In the present study we have confirmed this association with data on the IQs of a further 32 countries, making a total of 113 (see Chapter 4). We do not think that any reasonable person could dispute the existence of an association between national IQ and per capita income. Nor could any reasonable person doubt that there is some causal effect of national IQ on national income, and that national IQs are to some degree determined genetically. The answer to Ervik's question *Are people in rich countries smarter than those in poorer countries?* is Yes.

CHAPTER 12

Conclusions

1. National IQ as a Measure of Human Diversity
2. Global Inequalities Explained by National IQ
3. Hypothesis Tested by Alternative Measures of Human Conditions
4. Genetic Versus Environmental Determinants of IQ
5. The Causal Nexus
6. Policy Implications

The results of our study show that great global inequalities in human conditions persist despite all efforts to mitigate disparities and to help economic and social development in poor countries. According to our interpretation, the major cause of global inequalities can be traced to the diversity of human aptitudes and especially to significant differences in the mental abilities of nations measured by national IQs. Because differences in the average intelligence of nations and of racial groups are partly based on small genetic differences between populations, it has been and will be extremely difficult to equalize human conditions. We are bound to live in the world of great inequalities. The problem is how to organize the co-existence of human societies in such a world. After summarizing some major results of our study, we shall discuss the problem of adaptation and policy implications in this chapter.

1. National IQ as a Measure of Human Diversity

Our basic theme is that global inequalities in human conditions are causally related to evolved human diversity, especially to differences in the average intelligence of nations. According to our hypothesis, the quality of human conditions is expected to be the higher, the higher the average level of mental abilities (intelligence) of a nation. This hypothesis differentiates our study from many other theories and studies, reviewed and discussed in Chapter 1, that have attempted to explain the differences between rich and poor countries in economic development and growth and other global inequalities in human conditions. The 192 contemporary countries that have been used as the units of empirical analysis in this study were introduced at the end of Chapter 1.

The concept of intelligence was defined and discussed in Chapter 2. We emphasize that a wide degree of consensus had emerged on the nature and measurement of intelligence by the end of the twentieth century, and that it is possible to measure differences in general intelligence (g) by intelligent tests.

In Chapter 3 it is shown that intelligence is a significant determinant of earnings, and also of educational attainment and socioeconomic status among individuals. Many studies indicate consistently that people with high IQs tend to earn more than people with low IQs. The correlation between IQ, educational attainment, and socioeconomic status was found to be even stronger. This evidence on the relationship between IQ and earnings, educational attainment, socioeconomic status, and other measures of human attainments among individuals makes it reasonable to expect that similar relationships would appear also at the level of nations.

Chapter 4 deals with the calculation of national IQs. National IQs of 113 nations are derived from the administration of intelligence tests. The details of these studies are documented in Appendix 1. For the other 79 nations, national IQs were estimated on the basis of neighboring or otherwise comparable countries. The reliability of the measured national IQs was checked by examining the extent to which two or more measurements give the same results. The reliability was found to be strong. The correlation between the two extreme measurements is 0.92 (N= 71). The correlation rises even higher when the second lowest and highest scores are taken into account (0.95). Our conclusion is that the reliability of intelligence tests is sound. The validity of national IQs was checked by examining their relation to average national scores based on international studies of achievement in mathematics and science carried out in schools in a number of countries. Tables 4.4 to 4.6 show that correlations between national IQs, and ten measures of national scores in mathematics and science, vary from 0.785 to 0.894, indicating that national IQs and scores in mathematics and science are consistent. These high correlations attest to the validity of our national IQs.

2. Global Inequalities Explained by National IQ

It was noted in Chapter 1 that social scientists and historians have not reached any consensus or found any complete explanation for the existence and persistence of the great gaps in per capita income and other global inequalities in human conditions. Our argument is that differences in the average mental abilities of populations measured by national IQ provides the most powerful, although not complete, theoretical and empirical explanation for many types of inequalities in human conditions.

The indicators of human conditions used in this study were introduced and defined in Chapter 5. In Chapter 6, the hypothesis was tested by empirical evidence on global inequalities in per capita income, adult literacy rate, tertiary enrollment ratio, life expectancy at birth, and the level of democratization. These variables, which are used as the components of the combined Index of the Quality of Human Conditions (QHC), measure global inequalities in human conditions from different perspectives. The results of statistical analyses show that national IQ explains 28-57 percent of the variation in these five components of QHC. Regression analysis was used to consider the results at the level of single countries. It was found that human conditions tend to be much better than expected on the basis of regression equations in certain types of countries and much worse than expected in some other types of countries. These findings provide starting points to explore institutional, economic, social, and geographical factors that affect human conditions independently from the level of national IQ. Most of the countries with much higher than expected level of human conditions are economically highly developed democracies or countries which have benefited from investments and technologies transferred from countries with higher national IQs. Many of the countries with much lower than expected level of human conditions have suffered from civil wars, or they suffer from tropical climates or unfavorable geographical conditions, which do not attract people and investments from highly developed countries.

In Chapter 7, the relationship between national IQ and the Index of the Quality of Human Conditions (QHC) was explored. It was found that national IQ explains 63 percent of the variation in QHC in the total group of 192 countries and 70 percent in the group of 160 countries, from which small countries (with populations below 500,000 inhabitants) are excluded. Our conclusion is that differences in national IQs explain better than any other independent factor the average differences in the quality of human conditions. This can be regarded as the major result of our study. We have shown that the enormous global inequalities in human conditions are principally due to significant differences in national IQs.

The strong relationship between national IQ and global inequalities in human conditions helps to explain significant regional differences and their changes in human conditions. This can be done by comparing the regional averages of national IQs to the regional averages of various measures of human conditions and their changes. The regions of this analysis are the same as in Chapter 7 with one exception. The eight East Asian countries (China, Hong Kong, Japan, North Korea, South Korea, Mongolia, Singapore, and Taiwan) have been separated from the category of the other Asian and Pacific countries. They constitute their own regional group (Table 12.1).

Table 12.1. Regional averages of national IQ, QHC, and its five components in the group of 192 countries

Region	N	IQ	QHC	PPP GNI	Literates 2002	Tertiary enroll.	LE 2002	ID 2002
Europe and European offshoots	46	96.7	69.4	18,507	98.2	48.0	75.7	29.0
Latin America and the Caribbean	35	81.6	50.3	7,591	88.8	22.5	71.0	18.2
Middle East and North Africa	26	84.8	43.3	7,558	80.4	23.5	69.9	6.0
East Asia	8	105.5	52.2	15,774	95.8	43.0	73.4	13.9
Other Asia and Pacific	30	85.4	38.8	4,550	76.8	10.7	64.9	12.0
Sub-Saharan Africa	47	69.4	24.5	2,644	60.1	3.7	47.8	7.7

It is easy to see that there are clear differences in the regional averages of national IQs as well as in the regional means of the other variables and that there are correspondences between the regional means of national IQs and the other six variables. The results of correlation analysis illustrate the strength of regional relationships between national IQ and the measures of human conditions (Table 12.2).

Table 12.2. Regional intercorrelations of national IQ, QHC, and its five components in a group of six regions

Variable	IQ	QHC	PPP GNI	Literates 2002	Tertiary enroll.	LE 2002	ID 2002
National IQ	1.000	0.850	0.875	0.872	0.888	0.813	0.478
QHC		1.000	0.951	0.978	0.965	0.905	0.811
PPP GNI per capita 2002			1.000	0.895	0.990	0.773	0.740
Adult literacy rate 2002				1.000	0.930	0.953	0.725
Tertiary enrollment ratio					1.000	0.837	0.696
Life expectancy at birth 2002						1.000	0.586
ID 2002							1.000

We can see from Table 12.2 that most correlations are stronger than in the total group of 192 countries (cf. Table 7.1). This difference is principally due to the small number of regions. Table 12.2 shows that national IQ explains quite well regional differences in the measures of the quality of human conditions. Less than 30 percent of the regional variation in QHC seems to be due to other factors; in the cases of PPP GNI per capita and literacy, only 24 percent, and in the case of tertiary enrollment, not more than 21 percent. In the case of the level of democratization (ID), national IQ does not explain more than 23 percent of the regional variation in ID.

Figure 12.1 shows the results of regression analysis of regional means of QHC on regional means of national IQ and illustrates the application of the average relationship to various regions. It shows that in the groups of European and European offshoot countries and the Latin American and Caribbean countries average human conditions are clearly better than expected on the basis of the regression equation,

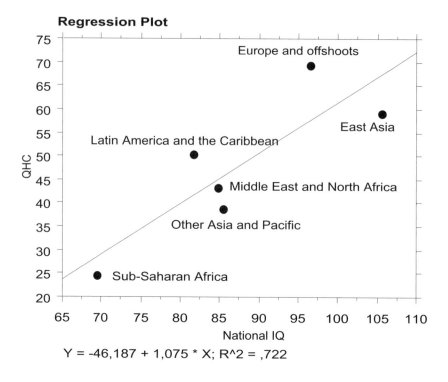

Regression Plot

Y = -46,187 + 1,075 * X; R^2 = ,722

Figure 12.1. The results of regression analysis of QHC (regional averages) on national IQ in a group of 6 regions

whereas in the groups of East Asian and other Asian and Pacific countries they are somewhat worse than expected. In sub-Saharan Africa and in the Middle East and North Africa the average levels of human conditions do not seem to differ much from the expected levels.

The results of regional analyses presented in Tables 12.1 and 12.2 and in Figure 12.1 show that national IQ explains a significant part of regional differences both in the composite index of human conditions (QHC) and in its five components. In the next sections, we summarize our conclusions concerning the five components of QHC.

2.1. PPP GNI per capita

In the case of PPP GNI per capita, national IQ explains why East Asian countries are achieving the same level of technological development and per capita income as Europe and European offshoots and why per capita income in other regions, and especially in sub-Saharan Africa, is much lower. Intellectual human potential for economic growth is in East Asia as great as in Europe, whereas it is significantly lower in other parts of Asia and in Latin America and lowest in sub-Saharan Africa. Because the relationship between national IQ and regional means of PPP GNI per capita is very strong, it would be unreasonable to expect the disappearance of great regional gaps in the level of per capita income. The gap between rich and poor countries can be expected to persist as far as it corresponds to differences in national IQs. Regional differences in per capita income have persisted since 1500 (cf. Table 6.3).

Furthermore, it was found that the correspondence between national IQ and per capita income is relatively poor at the highest level of national IQ. Several countries with the largest negative residuals are the present and former socialist countries, which indicates that socialist economic and political systems have hampered their economic development. This finding implies that economic and political reforms might help such countries to further their economic development. In fact, most of these countries in Eastern Europe replaced the socialist political system by democratic institutions at the beginning of the 1990s and started to transform their economic systems into market economies. Similar economic reforms carried out in China since 1978 have produced a high economic growth rate. It was also found that the contribution of foreign technologies and management is substantial in all tourist and oil-producing countries with large positive residuals. This finding implies that technologies and people from the countries of higher national IQs can help to raise the level of per capita income significantly higher than expected on the basis of national IQ. However, many poor countries with low national IQs do not have natural resources which could attract human and technological investments from countries of higher national IQs.

2.2. Adult literacy rate

Regional differences in the adult literacy rate are diminishing, but there are still significant regional gaps that are approximately consistent with regional averages of national IQ. National IQ explains why the level of literacy has risen most steeply in East Asia and why the level of literacy in Africa is lower than in any other region of the world. In fact, a moderate or strong correlation between national IQ and the adult literacy rate has persisted at least since the middle of the 19th century (see Table 6.4).

In the latter half of the 20th century, global inequalities in the level of literacy decreased dramatically. In nearly all countries of Europe, the level of literacy approached 100 percent. East Asia was only slightly behind Europe, Latin America approached 90 percent, and other parts of Asia approached 80 percent. In Africa, the average level of literacy jumped to 60 percent. So it is evident that global inequalities are decreasing in this dimension of human conditions. It is quite possible that literacy will rise to 90 percent or over in nearly all countries of the world, including African countries, but it is reasonable to expect that significant gaps in the level of "functional literacy" will persist.

The appearance of many large positive and negative residuals indicates the impact of other explanatory factors. Data show, in particular, that educational development in sub-Saharan Africa has been uneven. Some of these countries have large positive residuals and some others high negative residuals. This finding implies that by appropriate educational policies it is possible to raise the adult literacy rate in all sub-Saharan countries. Now the countries with exceptionally large positive residuals are Christian countries and the countries with large negative residuals are principally Muslim countries. It is remarkable that most countries with large positive residuals also in other parts of the world are Christian countries and most countries with large negative residuals are Muslim countries.

2.3. Tertiary enrollment ratio

The regional differences in tertiary enrollment ratio are strongly correlated with regional means of national IQ. This relationship was much weaker in the 19th century (see Table 6.5). In Asia, the number of students per 100,000 inhabitants remained near zero until 1900. National IQ explains the rapid expansion of higher education in East Asia that has taken place since 1900, and it explains why the expansion of higher education has been slow in Africa. Regional differences in the provision of higher education are much greater than in literacy, and it is justifiable to predict that great global disparities both in the quality and extent of higher education will continue.

The relative number of students has continually been highest in the group of Europe and European offshoots and lowest in Africa. Latin

American countries had the second place until the 1950s, but since then the relative number of students has risen more rapidly in East Asia than in Latin America. The expansion of higher education has been uneven in other parts of Asia. In the latter half of the 20th century, universities and other institutions of higher education were established in all sub-Saharan African countries, but there is still a great gap between the provision of tertiary education in North African Arab countries and those in sub-Saharan Africa.

The rise in the number of students in East Asia has been so rapid that the East Asian countries will likely soon reach the average level of Europe and European offshoots, whereas it is quite probable that great gaps will separate other regional groups from Europe and East Asia in the future.

The correlation between national IQ and the tertiary enrollment ratio is strong, but several highly deviating countries imply the impact of other explanatory factors. It was found that most of the countries with large positive residuals are economically highly developed countries, whereas most of the countries with large negative residuals are poor Asian and Pacific countries. In some of them (for example, in Afghanistan, Laos, and Cambodia), civil wars have retarded all types of development. Because of the strong relationship between national IQ and tertiary enrollment ratio, it does not seem possible to reduce global gaps significantly in the extent of higher education. The best chances to increase tertiary education seem to be in countries with national IQs higher than 80 and for which residuals are highly negative.

2.4. Life expectancy at birth

The correspondence between national IQ and average life expectancy is now stronger than it was in 1820 (see Maddison, 2001, p. 30), but average life expectancy was already in 1820 much higher in Europe and Japan than in the other regions of the world. Since 1950 life expectancy has risen more steeply in Asia than in Africa. Regional gaps in average life expectancy seem now to be decreasing, but because national IQ still explains 66 percent of the regional variation in life expectancy, it is reasonable to expect that significant regional gaps will persist. The rise in life expectancy accelerated in the latter half of the 20th century, but average life expectancy in many countries of Asia is still about ten years lower than in Europe, Latin America, and East Asia and more than 20 years lower in sub-Saharan Africa. Average life expectancy can be expected to remain significantly lower in sub-Saharan Africa than in the other regions of the world.

The strong positive correlation between life expectancy and national IQ does not leave much room for other explanatory factors. However, the appearance of several large positive and negative residuals shows the impact of other factors in some countries. It is evident that HIV/AIDS has already decreased life expectancy in several sub-Saharan African countries. In some Asian countries, extreme poverty seems to keep life expectancy lower than expected on the basis of national IQ.

2.5. Level of democratization

In 1850 there were hardly any regional differences in the level of democratization because the process of democratization had just started in Western Europe and North America. The United States and France were the only countries above the minimum threshold of democracy in 1850. Regional gaps in the level of democratization remained small until 1900, but the process of democratization accelerated in Western Europe. In 1950, nearly all countries of Western Europe as well as western offshoots and Japan were above the threshold of democracy, but in Asia and Latin America democracies were rare, and Africa was still without any democracy. Regional gaps in the level of democratization were great. In the latter half of the 20th century, democratization reached all parts of the world, but as Table 12.1 shows, regional differences were still extensive.

The present regional differences in democratization are not strongly related to national IQ. The average level of democratization in Asia is much lower than expected on the basis of national IQs. Consequently, the results imply that we could expect further democratization in many Asian countries. Factors that are independent of national IQ seem to affect democratization more than several other aspects of human conditions. Nearly all countries with large positive residuals are economically and educationally highly developed countries with high national IQs, whereas most countries with large negative residuals are socialist or former socialist countries and oil-producing or other Arab countries. The number of democracies is increasing, but it is reasonable to assume that significant regional gaps will persist.

Our general conclusion is that because of the strong relationship between national IQ and the measures of human conditions, it is not reasonable to expect the disappearance of regional gaps in the quality of human conditions. Some gaps may diminish over time, but some others may grow. The contemporary gap between the countries with the highest and the lowest values of the components of QHC is wide in all dimensions of human conditions, as Table 12.3 shows (see appendices 2 and 3).

Table 12.3. The countries with the highest and the lowest values of the five variables measuring the quality of human conditions in the group of 192 countries

Variable	Highest value		Lowest value	
PPP GNI per capita 2002	53,230	Luxembourg	500	Sierra Leone, Somalia
Adult literacy rate 2002	99	Austria, etc.	12.8	Burkina Faso
Tertiary enrollment ratio	85	Finland	0	Guinea-Bissau
Life expectancy at birth 2002	83.5	Andorra	32.7	Zambia
Index of Democratization 2002	44.2	Denmark	0	Afghanistan, Angola, etc.

It is remarkable that the countries with the highest values are European and East Asian and the countries with the lowest values are in most cases sub-Saharan African countries. The contrast between Europe and East Asia and sub-Saharan Africa illustrates the greatest global gap in the quality of human conditions. Similarly, the greatest gap in national IQs is between Europe/East Asia and sub-Saharan Africa.

The results of our analyses indicate that national IQ is the best single factor that explains global inequalities in the dimensions of human conditions taken into account in our study, but we do not try to deny or undervalue the significance of other explanatory factors. The results of regression analysis disclosed some of the factors that have caused many countries to deviate from the regression line significantly, but most of such additional factors remain unknown. We are focused on exploring the explanatory power of national IQ. Because changes in average national intelligence are slow, it is justifiable to conclude that global inequalities in human conditions based on differences in national IQs will most probably persist. However, because this relationship is not complete, the present inequalities are not fixed; by appropriate policies it is possible to reduce or increase global disparities in human conditions. It was noted that most countries with large positive residuals are characterized by much higher than expected levels of per capita income, tertiary enrollment ratio, and democratization, whereas the opposite is true for most countries with large negative residuals. Also, several of the countries with large negative residuals have suffered from domestic violence and civil wars. Such differences in social conditions are in many cases independent of national IQs, which means that in principle it would be possible to improve the quality of human conditions by economic, social, and political reforms.

The unexplained part of variation in the measures of human conditions is due to other explanatory factors, of which only some have been identified, and probably also to errors of measurement. Because of the impact of other factors, global inequalities are not fixed for individual countries, but the impact of national IQ is so strong that we have to expect the persistence of great global inequalities despite all efforts to equalize human conditions.

In Chapter 7, the causal relationship between national IQ and the measures of human conditions was traced to two ultimate independent factors, latitude and annual mean temperature. According to our theoretical argument, differences in national IQs emerged as a consequence of human adaptation to different climatic and geographical conditions outside Africa. Consequently, differences in latitude and annual mean temperature can be assumed to be still correlated with differences in national IQ, and through it, with various measures of human conditions. Correlation analysis showed that both latitude and mean temperature are moderately correlated with national IQ and also with QHC and its five components, but they do not increase the explained part of variation in QHC more than 3 percentage points independently of national IQ. This means that the impact of latitude and mean temperature on human conditions takes place principally through national IQ.

3. Hypothesis Tested by Alternative Measures of Human Conditions

In Chapter 8, the results of empirical analyses were checked by correlating national IQ with various alternative measures of human conditions. The purpose was to show that the relationship between national IQ and global inequalities in the quality of human conditions is not limited to the dimensions of human conditions taken into account in the Index of the Quality of Human Conditions (QHC). The results indicate that various other aspects of global inequalities are indeed moderately or strongly correlated with national IQ. However, the results of statistical analyses carried out in Chapter 8 are not fully comparable to the results achieved in Chapters 6 and 7 because the data on alternative measures do not cover all 192 countries of this study. In each case, the sample of countries is to some extent different. The differences in the samples affect also the correlations between national IQ and QHC and its five components. In most cases, these correlations are stronger than in the total sample of 192 countries.

UNDP's Human Development Index (HDI) was used as the first alternative measure of global inequalities in human conditions. It is nearly as strongly correlated with national IQ (0.776) as our QHC (0.811) in the sample of 176 countries. This result is a natural consequence of the fact that HDI and QHC are extremely strongly intercorrelated (0.940). This means that the replacement of QHC by HDI would not significantly change the central results of this study. Human development as measured by UNDP is strongly correlated with national IQ.

UNDP's Gender-related Human Development Index (GDI) was used as the second alternative measure. Because it is extremely highly correlated with HDI (0.999), the results were the same as in the case of HDI. However, in this smaller sample of countries (144), correlations became even stronger than in the case of HDI. The results show that women's conditions tend to be better at higher levels of national IQ.

Four different measures of economic growth were used to measure the relationship between national IQ and economic growth rate. It was found that absolute per capita growth measured in dollars is much more strongly correlated with national IQ than percentage growth rates. In a sample of 132 countries, the correlation between national IQ and the average annual percentage growth rate of per capita GDP over the period 1950-2001 is 0.388, but in the case of absolute growth in dollars the correlation rises to 0.747. In the same sample of 132 countries, the correlation between national IQ and QHC is extremely strong (0.885). It is evident that absolute per capita growth rates measured in dollars are strongly correlated with national IQ. This means that nations with high national IQs have better chances to accelerate economic growth than nations with low national IQs. The contrast between East Asian and African growth rates illustrates this relationship.

The Gini index of inequality based on the UNU/WIDER World Income Inequality Database is moderately correlated with national IQ (-0.538) in a sample of 146 countries. The level of income inequality tends to decrease when the level of national IQ rises. This result implies that global differences in income inequality will most probably continue. The countries with low national IQs are characterized not only by poverty but also by higher level of income inequality.

The relationship between poverty and national IQ was measured by data on the percentage of the population below the $2 a day international poverty line in a sample of 96 countries. The moderate negative correlation (-0.653) indicates that extreme poverty is much more common in countries with low national IQs than in countries with high national IQs, although many countries deviate from this relationship. As in the cases of other variables, regression analysis was used to disclose the most clearly outlying countries.

Not only poverty but also undernourishment of people is related to national IQ. The negative correlation between national IQ and the percentage of undernourished population is -0.500 in a group of 124 countries. The result was similar when undernourishment was measured by the percentage of under-weight children under age five (-0.421). These correlations are not strong, but they indicate that various forms of poverty and global inequalities tend to accumulate and correlate with national IQ.

This line of analysis was complemented by correlating national IQ with maternal mortality ratio (-0.730) and infant mortality rate (-0.771) in a sample of 149 countries. These correlations are much stronger than the correlations in the three previous cases. They support strongly our argument about the relationship between national IQ and the quality of human conditions.

Corruption Perceptions Index (CPI) measures global disparities in human conditions from a quite different perspective. The correlation of 0.591 between national IQ and CPI shows that corruption tends to be much more significant in countries with low national IQs than in countries with high national IQs. However, as the results of regression analysis indicate, many countries deviate from the average relationship, which means that national IQ is not the only important factor connected with the level of corruption.

Economic freedom can be regarded as representing an important dimension of human conditions. We used two indicators - Gwartney and Lawson's economic freedom ratings (EFR) and the Heritage Foundations's Index of Economic Freedom (IEF) - to measure the extent of economic freedom and found that the correlation between national IQ and EFR is 0.606 in a sample of 132 countries and that the correlation between national IQ and IEF is -0.416 in a sample of 156 countries. Economic freedom seems to be moderately correlated with national IQ, but many deviating countries indicate the impact of other explanatory factors, especially in the case of IEF. Because more than half of the variation in the measures of economic freedom is due to other factors, it means that there is room to improve economic freedom in all countries by appropriate policies independently of national IQ.

Leonid and Michael Andreev's MU-index based on population pyramids is an interesting indirect measure of human conditions. Because their MU-index is very strongly correlated with our QHC (0.902), its correlation with national IQ is also strong (0.806). Their invention shows that various variables can be used to measure global inequalities in human conditions.

Finally, we wanted to explore whether human happiness and life satisfaction are related to national IQ and to our measures of human conditions, or is human happiness more or less independent of material conditions of life. Our measures of human happiness were derived from Ruut Veenhoven and his staff's World Database of Happiness. The results of statistical analyses show that human happiness seems to be completely independent of national IQ and that it is only slightly related to most measures of human conditions. Correlations between PPP GNI per capita and human happiness (0.535) and life satisfaction (0.605) are moderate. The correlation between life satisfaction and the level of democratization (ID) is also moderate (0.403). These results show that human happiness and life satisfaction depend on some material conditions of life to some extent, although a major part of variation in these measures of human happiness seems to be due to other factors. Because these results are based on relatively small samples of countries (66 and 62 respectively), it is questionable to what extent the results can be generalized to all countries of the world. Nevertheless, from the perspective of poor countries of the world, it is encouraging to note that human happiness seems to be independent of national IQ and that it is relatively slightly related to various material conditions of life.

4. Genetic versus Environmental Determinants of IQ

Our argument about the contribution of genetic factors to differences in national IQs and wealth is controversial and will no doubt be difficult for many to accept. Therefore, in Chapter 9 we presented further evidence on the heritability of intelligence, income, educational attainment, and socioeconomic status among individuals. The evidence based on many studies of other researchers shows that intelligence, earnings, educational attainment, and socioeconomic status have moderate to high heritabilities within nations. Consequently, it is justifiable to assume that the heritability of intelligence and earnings extends to the level of nations, too. Our argument, which has been tested in this study by empirical evidence, is that the peoples of different nations are likely to differ genetically in their intelligence and in their capacities to achieve higher earnings and to build favorable environments for themselves and their children, just as do the people within nations.

This argument leads to the much debated questions of the racial basis of national IQs and racial differences in intelligence. We support our argument by showing (Table 9.6) that all measured national IQs of racially homogeneous nations tend to be around the average of the respective racial group. This concerns equally well East Asian, European, European/South-Asian, South East Asian, South Asia/North African, and sub-Saharan African nations as well as Pacific islanders. How can we explain the closely similar national IQs of the same racial group and clear differences between racial groups? We think that these facts imply the impact of genetic factors. There is further evidence for racial differences in intelligence in race differences in brain size, which is known to be associated with intelligence.

Our conclusion is that genetic factors are partly responsible for the race differences in intelligence, but we emphasize also the contribution of environmental factors. Such factors are likely to include the impact of nutrition, education, and social environment. It is not possible to determine the relative contributions of environmental and genetic factors, but it is clear that there is genotype-environment co-variation. Environmental differences may explain about 50 percent of the differences in intelligence between some populations. However, if the populations have about the same standards of living, nutrition, health, and education, the impact of environmental factors is certainly smaller and the heritability correspondingly greater.

It should be noted that in this study we have been focused on exploring the extent to which various global inequalities in human conditions can be traced to differences in national IQs. From this perspective, it is not necessary to know exactly the relative contributions of genetic and environmental factors. For our purposes, it is enough to know that differences in national IQs are partly based on genetic factors.

5. The Causal Nexus

In this book we have explored to what extent national IQ is able to explain global differences in the quality of human conditions. According to our theoretical argumentation and research hypothesis, the quality of human conditions is expected to be the higher, the higher the average level of mental abilities (intelligence) of a nation. The results of empirical analyses indicate that national IQ explains a significant part of the variation in various measures of human conditions, although a part of the variation has remained unexplained. Our theory does not presuppose that national IQ should provide a complete explanation for global inequalities in human conditions.

In Chapter 10, we focus on exploring the causal relationships between variables by taking into account other possible factors that can be assumed to affect human conditions. Figure 10.1 illustrates our argument about the impact of some other factors on the quality of human conditions. The diagram refers to the combined effects of genes, environment, various natural resources, and climate, although we have not been able to measure the effects of all factors. National IQ, economic freedom, and national resources are assumed to have affected economic growth since 1500 and to have produced the great contemporary gaps in per capita income. Finally, the diagram refers to the combined impact of national IQ and per capita income on various measures of human conditions.

The relationships indicated in the diagram are analyzed in greater detail in Chapter 10. We come to the conclusion that the ultimate cause of national differences in intelligence is more genetic than environmental.

We explain why national IQ, economic freedom, and natural resources can be assumed to further economic growth. In the sections dealing with life expectancy, adult literacy, tertiary enrollment, democratization, and malnutrition we explore the combined effects of national IQ and per capita income on these measures of human conditions. The results show that in the cases of life expectancy, adult literacy, and tertiary enrollment, national IQ is a more important explanatory variable than per capita income, whereas in the cases of democratization and malnutrition, per capita income is a somewhat better explanatory variable than national IQ.

Finally, in Chapter 11, we replied to arguments presented in several critical reviews of our previous book *IQ and the Wealth of Nations*. Our counter-arguments are that it is possible to check by empirical evidence the reliability and validity of national IQs, that the direction of causation is principally from national IQs to human conditions, and that we have presented evidence for a substantial genetic basis of national IQs. Besides, we have not argued that intelligence is the only determinant of differences in per capita income. On the contrary, we referred in our book to several other explanatory factors, including the impact of economic freedom and the nature of political and economic institutions.

6. Policy Implications

Our study has two major policy implications. First, economists and political leaders believe—or pretend to believe—that all peoples of the world have the same intelligence. If this were so, closing the gap between rich and poor nations should be relatively easy. All that is required is for rich nations to give poor nations more money so that they can improve education and this will increase their human capital up to the level at which they can produce goods and services that are competitive with those of rich nations. As a condition of this aid, the donor nations should require the recipient nations to introduce free market economies. Our study has shown that the belief that all peoples of the world have the same average intelligence is incorrect. On the contrary, there are large differences in the intelligence of nations and these are the most important cause of the differences in wealth and poverty. These intelligence differences will be hard to change because they are partly determined by genetic differences and the environmental factors contributing to them will be difficult to modify. It will therefore be much more difficult to alleviate world poverty than is generally believed.

Second, in so far as intelligence is determined environmentally, there is a growing consensus that the major environmental factor affecting intelligence is the quality of nutrition. Inadequate nutrition stunts the growth of the body and also of the brain, and this impairs the development of intelligence. The most promising way of increasing the intelligence of the populations of poor countries would therefore be to direct some of the aid programs to the improvement of the quality of nutrition for pregnant women and infants. While we believe that this would increase the intelligence of the populations of poor countries and this would lead to a reduction in world poverty, it cannot be anticipated that it would eradicate the intelligence differences between nations and the consequent differences in per capita incomes. The persistence of differences in intelligence between nations is inevitable, and so too will be the consequence: the persistence of national differences in wealth. Or, as St. John put it two thousand years ago: *The poor you have always with you.*

Appendix 1

The Calculation of National IQs

Studies of the IQs of nations are set out in the Table below. All IQs have been calculated in relation to a British mean of 100 and standard deviation of 15. All IQs have been adjusted for *Flynn effects,* i.e., secular increases in IQ. Flynn effect adjustments are 3 IQ points per decade (Flynn, 1987) for all tests except the Progressive Matrices, for which they are 2 IQ points per decade reported for Britain by Lynn and Hampson (1986). When data for more than one study in a country have been reported, the mean of two studies is given, while for three or more studies, median IQs have been used. These are given in italics and represent the best estimates of the IQs of the nations. Decimal points are rounded to the nearest whole number. IQs of multi–racial societies are obtained by weighting the IQs of the races by their proportion in the population given in Philips (1996). Descriptions of many of the studies are given in Lynn (2005). Further details of the studies are calculations given at the bottom of this table (countries marked by *).

Country	Age	N	Test	IQ	Reference
Argentina	9–15	1,680	SPM	93	Rimoldi, 1948
Argentina	5–11	420	CPM	98	Raven et al., 1998
Argentina	10	4,000	V-R	93	UNESCO, 1998
Argentina				*93*	
Australia	9–13	35,000	Otis	97	McIntyre, 1938
Australia	18	6,700	SPM	100	Craig, 1974
Australia	5–10	700	CPM	98	Raven et al., 1995
Australia				*98*	
Austria	14	67	SPM	98	Moyles & Wolins, 1971
Austria	Adults	187	CF	101	Buj, 1981
Austria				*100*	
Barbados	9–15	207	WISC-R	*80*	Galler et al., 1986
Belgium	7–13	944	CPM	99	Goosens, 1952a
Belgium	10–16	920	CF	103	Goosens, 1952b
Belgium	Adults	247	CF	99	Buj, 1981
Belgium				*99*	
Bermuda	7–11	161	WISC-R	88	Sandoval et al., 1983
Bermuda	4	125	SB	92	Scarr & McCartney, 1988
Bermuda*				*90*	
Bolivia	10	4,000	V-R	*87*	UNESCO, 1998
Brazil	14	160	SPM	88	Natalicio, 1968
Brazil	7–11	505	CPM	84	Angelini et al., 1988
Brazil	5–11	1,131	CPM	90	Angelini et al., 1988
Brazil	5–11	1,547	CPM	85	Angelini et al., 1988
Brazil	10	4,000	V-R	92	UNESCO, 1998
Brazil-Europeans	9–10	735	SPM	95	Fernandez, 2001
Brazil-Coloreds	9–10	718	SPM	81	Fernandez, 2001

Country	Age	N	Test	IQ	Reference
Brazil-Africans	9	100	DAM	70	Paine et al., 1992
Brazil-Africans	Adults	88	SPM	64	Paine et al., 1992
Brazil-Africans	9–10	223	SPM	71	Fernandez, 2001
Brazil*				*87*	
Bulgaria	Adults	215	CF	94	Buj, 1981
Bulgaria	11–17	1,456	CF	91	Lynn et al., 1998
Bulgaria				*93*	
Cameroon	Adults	80	CPM	64	Berlioz, 1955
Canada	7–12	313	SPM	97	Raven et al., 1998
Canada	6–16	2,200	WISC-3	100	Prifitera et al., 1998
Canada				*99*	
Central African Republic	Adults	1,149	SPM	64	Latouche & Dormeau, 1956
Chile	5–11	2,210	CPM	88	Marincovich et al., 2000
Chile	11–18	2,003	SPM	90	Marincovich et al., 2000
Chile	10	4,000	V-R	92	UNESCO, 1998
Chile				*90*	
China	6–16	660	WISC-R	107	Dan et al., 1990
China	6–15	5,108	SPM	101	Lynn, 1991c
China	14–15	297	Various	103	Li et al., 1996
China	6–12	269	SPM	104	Geary et al., 1997
China	4	60	Arith.	109	Ginsburg et al., 1997
China	6–13	463	DAM	103	Cox et al., 1998
China	6–8	160	SPM	107	Cox et al., 1998
China	17	218	SPM	103	Geary et al., 1999
China	19	218	SPM	113	Geary et al., 1999
China	6–8	300	NTBC-R	107	Zhou & Boehm, 2001
China				*105*	

Country	Age	N	Test	IQ	Reference
Colombia	4	120	QR	84	Ginsburg et al., 1997
Colombia	10	4,000	V-R	83	UNESCO, 1998
*Colombia**				84	
Congo-Brazzaville	Adults	1,596	SPM	64	Latouche & Dormeau, 1956
Congo-Brazzaville	17–29	320	SPM	64	Ombredane et al., 1952
Congo-Brazzaville	8	73	SPM	73	Nkaya et al., 1994
Congo-Brazzaville				64	
Congo-Zaire	Adult	67	SPM	64	Verhagen, 1956
Congo-Zaire	10–15	222	SPM	68	Laroche, 1959
Congo-Zaire	8	47	KABC	62	Boivin & Giodani, 1993
Congo-Zaire	7–12	95	LABC	68	Boivin et al., 1995
Congo-Zaire	7–9	130	KABC	65	Giordani et al., 1996
Congo-Zaire				65	
Cook Islands	4–6	110	PIPS	89	St George, 1974
Croatia	13–16	299	SPM	90	Sorokin, 1954
Cuba	12–18	1,144	SOM	85	Alonso, 1974
Czech Republic	Adults	363	CF	98	Buj, 1981
Czech Republic	5–11	832	CPM	96	Raven et al., 1995
Czech Republic	11	64	SPM	100	Persaud, 1972
Czech Republic				98	
Denmark	5–11	628	SPM	97	Vejlevskov, H., 1968
Denmark	Adults	122	CF	99	Buj, 1981
Denmark				98	
Dominica	3	64	PPVT	67	Wein & Stevenson, 1972
Dominican Republic	10	4,000	V-R	82	UNESCO, 1998

Country	Age	N	Test	IQ	Reference
Ecuador	6–7	48	DAM	89	Dodge, 1969
Ecuador	17	120	WISC-R	88	Fierro–Benitez et al., 1989
Ecuador	5–17	104	MAT	82	Proctor et al., 2000
Ecuador				88	
Egypt	6–10	206	DAM	77	Dennis, 1957
Egypt	12–15	111	CCF	81	Sadek, 1972
Egypt	6–12	129	SPM	83	Ahmed, 1989
Egypt				81	
Equatorial Guinea	10–14	48	WISC-R	59	Fernandez–Ballesteros, 1997
Estonia	12–18	2,689	SPM	100	Lynn et al., 2002
Estonia	7–11	1,835	SPM	98	Lynn et al., 2003a
Estonia				99	
Ethiopia	15	250	SPM	65	Lynn, 1994b
Ethiopia	14–16	–	SPM	63	Kazulin, 1998
*Ethiopia****				64	
Fiji	8–13	216	QT	85	Chandra, 1975
Finland	7	755	CPM	98	Kyöstio, 1972
Finland	Adults	122	CF	99	Buj, 1981
Finland				99	
France	6–9	618	CPM	97	Bourdier, 1964
France	6–11	328	CMM	102	Dague et al., 1964
France	Adults	1,320	CF	94	Buj, 1981
France	6–16	1,120	WISC-3	98	Georgas et al., 2003
France				98	
Germany	7–11	454	SPM	90	Kurth, 1969

Country	Age	N	Test	IQ	Reference
Germany	5–7	563	CPM	99	Winkelman, 1972
Germany	11–15	2,068	SPM	105	Raven, 1981
Germany	11–15	1,000	SPM	99	Raven, 1981
Germany	Adults	1,320	CF	107	Buj, 1981
Germany	7	200	CPM	97	Guthke & Al–Zoubi, 1987
Germany	6–10	3,607	CPM	101	Raven et al., 1995
Germany	5–10	980	CPM	97	Raven et al., 1995
Germany	6–16	990	WISC-3	99	Georgas et al., 2003
Germany				99	
Ghana	Adults	225	CF	80	Buj, 1981
Ghana	15	1,693	CPM	62	Glewwe & Jaccoby, 1992
Ghana				71	
Greece	9–14	400	WISC	88	Fatouros, 1972
Greece	6–12	227	DAM	97	Georgas & Georgas, 1972
Greece	Adults	220	CF	95	Buj, 1981
Greece	6–17	731	MAT	89	Petrogiannis et al., 1999
Greece	6–16	990	WISC-3	92	Georgas et al., 2003
Greece				92	
Guatemala	6–12	256	DAM	79	Johnson et al., 1967
Guinea	5–14	50	AAB	63	Nissen et al., 1935
Guinea	Adults	1,144	SPM	70	Faverge & Falmagne, 1962
Guinea				67	
Honduras	10	4,000	V-R	*81*	UNESCO, 1998
Hong Kong	9–11	1,007	CCT	105	Godman, 1964
Hong Kong	16	5,209	AH4	106	Vernon, 1982
Hong Kong	10	1,000	SPM	109	Chan & Vernon, 1988
Hong Kong	6–13	13,822	SPM	103	Lynn, Pagliari, & Chan, 1988

Country	Age	N	Test	IQ	Reference
Hong Kong	6–15	4,500	SPM	110	Lynn, Pagliari, & Chan, 1988
Hong Kong	10	197	SPM	108	Lynn, Pagliari, & Chan, 1988
Hong Kong	9	376	CCF	104	Lynn, Hampson, & Lee, 1988
Hong Kong	9	479	SPM	122	Chan et al., 1991
Hong Kong	15	341	APM	120	Lynn & Chan, 2003
Hong Kong				*108*	
Hungary	Adults	260	CF	98	Buj, 1981
Iceland	6–16	665	SPM	*101*	Pind et al., 2003
India	5–11	1,339	CPM	88	Gupta & Gupta, 1966
India	14–17	1,359	SPM	87	Chopra, 1966
India	12–14	5,607	CPM	81	Sinha, 1968
India	5–10	1,050	CPM	82	Rao & Reddy, 1968
India	15	3,536	SPM	84	Majumdar & Nundi, 1971
India	10–16	180	SPM	79	Mohanty & Babu, 1983
India	13	100	SPM	78	Agrawal et al., 1984
India	9–12	748	WISC-R	79	Afzal, 1988
India	5–12	500	CPM	86	Bhogle & Prakash, 1992
India	11–15	569	SPM	82	Raven et al., 1996
India	7–15	8,040	SPM	88	Raven, 2000
India	11–15	569	SPM	81	Raven et al., 2000
India				82	
Indonesia	5–12	1,149	DAM	86	Thomas & Shah, 1961
Indonesia	5–20	163	CPM	87	Bleichrodt et al., 1980
Indonesia	4	139	PPVT	87	Soewondo et al., 1989
Indonesia	6–8	483	CPM	87	Hadidjaja et al., 1998
Indonesia				87	
Iran	15	627	SPM	84	Valentine, 1959
Iran	14	250	AH4	83	Mehryer et al., 1972
Iran	6–11	1,600	BG	89	Yousefi et al., 1992

Country	Age	N	Test	IQ	Reference
Iran	6–10	1,195	DAM	80	Mehryer et al., 1987
Iran				*84*	
Iraq	14–17	204	SPM	87	Abul–Hubb, 1972
Iraq	18–35	1,185	SPM	87	Abul–Hubb, 1972
Iraq				*87*	
Ireland	6–13	3,088	SPM	87	Gill & Byrt, 1973
Ireland	Adults	75	CF	97	Buj, 1981
Ireland	6–12	1,361	SPM	93	Carr, 1993
Ireland	9–12	2,029	SPM	91	Carr, 1993
Ireland				*92*	
Israel	13–14	200	WISC	95	Ortar, 1952
Israel	11–15	267	SPM	95	Moyles & Wolins, 1973
Israel	10–12	180	LT	97	Miron, 1977
Israel	10–12	268	SPM	95	Globerson, 1983
Israel	11	2,781	SPM	89	Lancer & Rim, 1984
Israel	5	52	CPM	96	Tzuriel & Caspi, 1992
Israel	9–15	1,740	SPM	90	Lynn, 1994
Israel	13	–	SPM	96	Kazulin, 1998
*Israel**				*95*	
Italy	11–16	2,432	SPM	103	Tesi & Young, 1962
Italy	Adults	1,380	CF	102	Buj, 1981
Italy				*102*	
Jamaica	11	1,730	MH	72	Manley, 1963
Jamaica	11	50	V, M, KB	75	Vernon, 1969
Jamaica	5–12	71	WISC	60	Hertzig et al., 1972
Jamaica	10	128	CEFT	75	Bagley et al., 1983
Jamaica	15	31	WISC-R	67	Gratham–McGregor et al., 1994
Jamaica	25	54	PPVT	60	Gratham–McGregor et al., 1994

Country	Age	N	Test	IQ	Reference
Jamaica	9–10	30	PPVT	71	Simeon & Gratham–McGregor, 1989
Jamaica				*71*	
Japan	5–15	1,070	WISC	102	Lynn, 1977a
Japan	35	316	WAIS	102	Lynn, 1977a
Japan	5–10	760	MFFT	107	Salkind et al., 1978
Japan	10	212	Kyoto	106	Lynn & Dziobon, 1980
Japan	8–11	97	WRAT	108	Tarnopol & Tarnopol, 1980
Japan	9	223	CEFT	112	Bagley et al., 1983
Japan	49	347	CMMS	107	Misawa et al., 1984
Japan	6–11	480	Various	105	Stevenson et al., 1985
Japan	6–16	1,100	WISC-R	103	Lynn & Hampson, 1986
Japan	4–6	600	WPPSI	105	Lynn & Hampson, 1987
Japan	14	2,100	Kyoto	104	Lynn et al., 1987a
Japan	13–15	178	DAT	104	Lynn et al., 1987b
Japan	2–8	548	McCarth	103	Ishikuma et al., 1988
Japan	6–12	142	KABC	101	Kaufman et al., 1989
Japan	16	175	A,MR, M	113	Mann et al., 1990
Japan	9	444	SPM	110	Shigehisa & Lynn, 1991
Japan	5–7	454	CCAT	109	Takeuchi & Scott, 1992
Japan	14–15	239	Various	103	Li et al., 1996
Japan	6–17	93	Gen Info	100	Chen et al., 1996
Japan	19	72	GMRT	102	Flaherty, 1997
Japan	7–11	60	DAM	102	Cox et al., 2001
Japan	17	1,119	Gen Info	105	Evans et al., 2002
Japan				*105*	
Jordan	6–12	210	KABC	*84*	El–Mneizel, 1987
Kenya	Adults	205	CPM	69	Boissiere et al., 1985
Kenya	6–10	1,222	CPM	75	Costenbader & Ngari, 2000
Kenya	12–15	85	CPM-MH	69	Sternberg et al., 2001
Kenya	7	118	CPM	76	Daley et al., 2003

Country	Age	N	Test	IQ	Reference
Kenya	7	537	CPM	89	Daley et al., 2003
Kenya	6	184	KABC	63	Holding et al., 2004
Kenya				*72*	
Kuwait	6–15	6,529	SPM	86	Abdel–Khalek & Lynn, 2005
Laos	8	22	KABC	90	Boivin et al., 1996
Laos	8	22	KABC	88	Boivin et al., 1996
Laos*				*89*	
Lebanon	5–10	502	DAM	82	Dennis, 1957
Lithuania	8–12	259	CPM	90	Lynn & Kuzlauskaite, 2002
Lithuania	6–16	381	WISC-3	92	Georgas et al., 2003
Lithuania				*91*	
Madagascar	Adults	147	CPM	82	Raveau et al., 1976
Malaysia	7–12	5,412	SPM	92	Chaim, 1994
Malta	5	134	CPM	97	Martinelli & Lynn, 2005
Mariana Islands	5–16	200	Arthur	*81*	Joseph & Murray, 1951
Marshall Islands	12–18	407	CF	84	Jordheim & Olsen, 1963
Mauritius*	11	1,385	WISC	89	Liu et al., 2003
Mexico	6–13	520	DAM	87	Modiano, 1962
Mexico	7–10	155	SPM	88	Lynn et al., 2005
Mexico	10	4,000	V-R	88	UNESCO, 1998
Mexico*				*88*	

Country	Age	N	Test	IQ	Reference
Morocco	Children	177	RAKIT	75	Resing et al., 1986
Morocco	Children	76	RAKIT	79	Resing et al., 1986
Morocco	11	720	CITO	84	Pieke, 1988
Morocco	5–8	94	LPTP	85	Hamers et al., 1966
Morocco	Adult	167	GATB	84	Te Nijenhuis, 1997
Morocco				*84*	
Mozambique	20	149	CPM	64	Kendall, 1976
Netherlands	Adults	333	CF	107	Buj, 1981
Netherlands	5–10	1,920	CPM	99	Raven et al., 1995
Netherlands	6–12	4,032	SPM	101	Raven et al., 1996
Netherlands	6–16	1,100	WISC-3	99	Georgas et al., 2003
Netherlands				*100*	
Nepal	4–16	807	DAM	78	Sundberg & Ballinger, 1968
New Caledonia	5–10	–	–	85	Cottereau–Reiss & Lehalle, 1988
New Zealand-whites	9–15	26,000	OTIS	99	Redmond & Davis, 1940
New Zealand-whites	9–17	3,108	SPM	101	Reid & Gilmore, 1989
New Zealand-whites	8–9	1,692	WISC-R	102	Ferguson & Horwood, 1997
New Zealand-Maoris	–	–	–	90	Lynn, 2005
*New Zealand**				99	
Nigeria	Children	480	Leone	70	Farron, 1966
Nigeria	Adults	86	SPM	64	Wober, 1969
Nigeria	6–13	375	CPM	69	Fahrmeier, 1975
Nigeria				*69*	
Norway	Adults	100	CF	*100*	Buj, 1981
Pakistan	15	349	GEFT	84	Alvi et al., 1986

Country	Age	N	Test	IQ	Reference
Pakistan	6–8	140	SPM	84	Rahman et al., 2002
Pakistan				*84*	
Papua New Guinea	17–18	152	SOP	82	Waldron & Gallimore, 1973
Papua New Guinea	7–10	241	BG	83	Robin & Shea, 1983
Papua New Guinea				*83*	
Paraguay	10	4,000	V-R	*84*	UNESCO, 1998
Peru	10	4,000	V-R	83	UNESCO, 1998
Peru–Amerinds	8–11	4,382	CPM	87	Raven et al., 1995
Peru–Amerinds	6–7	300	WISC	85	Llanos, 1974
*Peru**				*85*	
Philippines	12–13	203	SPM	86	Flores & Evans, 1972
Poland	Adults	835	CF	106	Buj, 1981
Poland	6–15	4,006	SPM	92	Jaworowska & Szustrowa, 1991
Poland				*99*	
Portugal	Adults	242	CF	101	Buj, 1981
Portugal	6–12	807	CPM	88	Simoes, 1989
Portugal				*95*	
Puerto Rico	5–11	2,400	CPM	83	Raven et al., 1995
Puerto Rico	8–15	2,911	SPM	84	Raven & Court, 1989
Puerto Rico				*84*	
Qatar	10–13	273	SPM	78	Bart et al., 1987
Romania	6–10	300	CPM	94	Zahirnic et al., 1974
Russia	14–15	432	SPM	97	Lynn, 2001

Country	Age	N	Test	IQ	Reference
Russia	27–55	745	CF	96	Grigorenko & Sternberg, 2001
Russia				97	
Serbia	15	76	SPM	89	Moyles & Wolins, 1971
Sierra Leone	Adult	122	CPM	64	Berry, 1966
Sierra Leone	Adult	33	CPM	64	Binnie–Dawson, 1984
Sierra Leone				64	
Singapore	13	337	SPM	103	Lynn, 1977b
Singapore	15	459	APM	114	Lim, 1994
*Singapore**				108	
Slovakia	5–11	823	CPM	96	Raven et al., 1995
Slovenia	8–18	1,556	SPM	96	Raven et al., 2000
Slovenia	6–16	1,080	WISC-3	95	Georgas et al., 2003
Slovenia				96	
South Africa-whites	15	1,056	SPM	94	Owen, 1992
South Africa-blacks	9	350	SPM	63	Lynn & Holmshaw, 1990
South Africa-blacks	10–12	293	AAB	65	Fick, 1929
South Africa-blacks	8–16	1,008	SPM	75	Notcutt, 1950
South Africa-blacks	Adults	703	SPM	64	Notcutt, 1950
South Africa-blacks	15	1,093	SPM	74	Owen, 1992
South Africa-colored	10–12	6,196	AAB	83	Fick, 1929
South Africa-colored	13	815	GSAT	86	Claassen, 1990
South Africa-colored	15	778	SPM	80	Owen, 1992
South Africa-Indians	10–12	762	AAB	77	Fick, 1929
South Africa-Indians	18	284	GFT	88	Taylor & Radford, 1986
South Africa-Indians	6–8	600	JSAIS	86	Landman, 1988
South Africa-Indians	15	1,063	SPM	91	Owen, 1992
South Africa-Indians	15	1,063	JAT	83	Lynn & Owen, 1994

Country	Age	N	Test	IQ	Reference
*South Africa**				72	
South Korea	2–12	440	KABC	113	Moon, 1988
South Korea	9	107	SPM	109	Lynn & Song, 1994
South Korea	4	56	Arith	103	Ginsburg et al., 1997
South Korea	6–16	2,231	WISC-3	100	Georgas et al., 2003
South Korea				*106*	
Spain	Adults	848	CF	98	Buj, 1981
Spain	6–9	854	CPM	97	Raven et al., 1995
Spain	11–18	3,271	APM	102	Albade, Paz, & Monoz, 1993
Spain				*98*	
Sri Lanka	8	46	CTMM	79	Strauss, 1954
St. Lucia	4	60	PPI-T	62	Murray, 1983
St. Vincent	8–11	174	CPM	71	Durbrow et al., 2002
Suriname	30	535	GATB	89	Te Nijenhuis & van der Frier, 1997
Sudan	7–16	291	Various	69	Fahmy, 1964
Sudan	6	80	DAM	64	Badri, 1965a
Sudan	9	293	DAM	74	Badri, 1965b
Sudan	8–12	148	SPM	72	Ahmed, 1989
Sudan				*71*	
Sweden	6–14	1,106	WISC	97	Scandinaviska, 1970
Sweden	Adults	205	CF	104	Buj, 1981
Sweden	6–16	2,231	WISC-3	99	Georgas et al., 2003
Sweden				*99*	
Switzerland	Adults	163	CF	101	Buj, 1981

Country	Age	N	Test	IQ	Reference
Switzerland	6–10	200	CPM	101	Raven et al., 1995
Switzerland	9–15	246	SPM	104	Spicher, 1993
Switzerland				*101*	
Syria	7	241	CPM	83	Guthke & Al–Zoubi, 1987
Taiwan	16	1,290	CCF	102	Rodd, 1959
Taiwan	6–8	1,865	CPM	102	Hsu, 1971
Taiwan	9–10	1,384	SPM	110	Hsu et al., 1973
Taiwan	6–7	43,825	CPM	105	Hsu, 1976
Taiwan	8–11	193	WRAT-A	107	Tarnopol & Tarnopol, 1980
Taiwan	6–11	480	Various	104	Stevenson et al., 1985
Taiwan	6–8	764	CPM	105	Rabinowitz et al., 1991
Taiwan	6–11	169	Gen Info	100	Chen et al., 1996
Taiwan	9–12	2,476	CPM	105	Lynn, 1997
Taiwan	6–15	118	SPM	105	Lai et al., 2001
Taiwan	17	1,469	Gen Info	107	Evans et al., 2002
Taiwan				*105*	
Tanzania	13–17	2,959	SPM	78	Klingelhofer, 1967
Tanzania	Adults	179	CPM	65	Boissiere et al., 1985
Tanzania	11–13	458	WCST	72	Sternberg et al., 2002
Tanzania				*72*	
Thailand	8–10	2,268	SPM	91	Pollitt et al., 1989
Tonga	8–9	80	PAT	86	Beck & St. George, 1983
Turkey	11–12	92	D 48	84	Kagitcibasi, 1972
Turkey	6–15	2,272	SPM	90	Sahin & Duzen, 1994
Turkey	7–9	180	DAM	96	Ucman, P., 1972
Turkey				*90*	
Uganda	–	–	–	73	Heynman & Jamison, 1980

Country	Age	N	Test	IQ	Reference
United Kingdom	Adults	1,405	CF	100	Buj, 1981
United Kingdom	6–15	3,250	SPM	100	Raven et al., 1998
United Kingdom				*100*	
United States	11	1,000	SB	100	Scottish Council, 1932
United States	11	1,215	TM	97	Scottish Council, 1949
United States	14–18	10,000	DAT	98	Lynn et al., 1987b
United States	18–70	625	SPM	98	Raven et al., 1996
*United States**				*98*	
Uruguay	–	–	–	96	Risso, 1961
Venezuela	10	4,000	V-R	84	UNESCO, 1998
*Vietnam**	12–16	391	SPM	94	Flynn, 1991
Western Samoa	5–7	80	Verbal	90	Clay, 1971
Western Samoa	8–9	80	PAT	86	Beck & St. George, 1983
Western Samoa	9–17	65	SPM	88	Reid & Gilmore, 1989
Western Samoa				*88*	
Yemen	6–11	1,000	CPM	*85*	Al–Heeti et al., 1997
Zambia	13	759	SPM	77	MacArthur et al., 1964
Zambia	Adults	152	SPM	64	Pons, 1974
Zambia				*71*	
Zimbabwe	12–14	204	WISC-R	61	Zindi, 1994
Zimbabwe	12–14	204	SPM	70	Zindi, 1994
Zimbabwe				*66*	

Notes on data

Brazil. The four studies of the population give IQs of 88, 84, 90, and 92. The IQ of the Europeans is 95 (53% of the population), the coloreds (mulattos and mestizos: 34% of the population) is 81, and the IQ of the Africans (11% of the population) is 68. Weighting by percentages in the population gives an IQ of 86. The median of the six studies is an IQ of 87.

Bermuda. A study by Sandoval, Zimmerman, and Woo–Sam (1983) reported an IQ of 88 for a sample of 161 7–11-year-old children in Bermuda tested with the WISC–R. Scarr and McCartney (1988) have reported a study of 125 4-year-olds given the Stanford Binet. The sample was approximately representative of the racial mix, consisting of 61 percent Africans and 37 percent Europeans (Phillips', 1996). The IQ of the sample was 92. The average of the two studies gives an IQ of 90 for Bermuda.

Colombia. In *IQ and the Wealth of Nations* the IQ was estimated at 89 on the basis of a European IQ of 95 reported by Ardila, Pineda, and Poselli (2000) for a sample of 50 13–16-year-olds and estimates of 89 for the IQs of the Native Americans and 72 for blacks. A more satisfactory estimate is given in the table consisting of the results of a study by Ginsburg et al. (1997, p.172) in which a test of quantitative reasoning was given to a sample of 120 4-year-olds described as "approximately equally divided among SES groups." These were compared with 156 American children described as representative of the United States. In relation to an American mean of 100, the Columbian children obtained an IQ of 86, and therefore in relation to a British mean of 100 the Colombian children obtained an IQ of 84. This result is preferred to our earlier estimate and has been entered in the table.

Cyprus. The samples are of Cypriot immigrants in Britain.

Ethiopia. The samples are of Ethiopian immigrants in Israel.

Israel. The eight studies of the IQ in Israel lie in the range between 89–97 and have a median of 95. In our *IQ and the Wealth of Nations* we estimated the IQ in Israel at 94 on the basis of two studies. This result has been criticised by a number of people on the grounds that Jews in the United States and Britain have IQs well above those of European gentiles and the same would be expected for Israel. These critics have failed to understand that the Jews in the United States and Britain are Ashkenazim (European), who comprise only approximately

40 percent of the population of Israel (Yaish, 2001). The Ashkenazim Jews of relatively recent European origin in Israel have an IQ of 103; a further 40 percent are Oriental Jews (Mizrahim) from Asia and North Africa who have an IQ of 91; approximately 20 percent of the population are Arabs, who have an IQ of 86 (Lieblich & Kugelmass, 1981), virtually exactly the same as that of other South Asians in the Near East. The IQ of 95 for Israel is the weighted mean of the three groups. A more extensive account of the IQ in Israel is given in Lynn (2005).

Laos. A study by Boivin, Giordani, Crist et al. (1996, p. 590) gives an IQ of 90 for Lao children living in a village "not from families living in abject poverty."

Mauritius. A study of 11-year-olds in Mauritius described as "a community sample" obtained an IQ of 89 on the WISC (Raine, Reynolds, Venables, and Mednick, 2002). Sixty-nine percent of the sample were Indians, 29 percent Creoles of mixed European and sub–Saharan African descent whose IQ is 2.5 points lower than that of Indians, and 6 percent Other (French, English, Chinese, and unidentified). These percentages closely match those in the population.

Mexico. The populations consists of 9 percent Europeans, IQ 98; 30 percent mestizos, IQ 94; and 60 percent Native Americans, IQ 83 (Lynn, Backhoff, and Contreras, 2005). The weighted mean gives an IQ of 88.

Morocco. All the samples are of Moroccan immigrants in the Netherlands.

New Zealand. The median IQ of the three studies of the Europeans is 101. These comprised 85 percent of the population in the 2001 census. 14.3 percent of the popualtion were Maoris with an IQ of 90 obtained as the mean of 12 studies (Lynn, 2005). The IQ of the total population is therefore 99.

Peru. The UNESCO study gives an IQ of 83. The two studies of Native Americans and mestizos, who comprise 88 percent of the population, give IQs of 87 and 85. Europeans comprise 12 percent of the population. Their IQ is unknown but is assumed to be 95, the same as Europeans in Brazil and Columbia. Weighting by the proportions of the population gives an IQ of 87. The average of the two results is 85.

Singapore. A study of 147 ethnic Chinese had an IQ of 106 and of 190 ethnic Malays an IQ of 90.5 (Lynn, 1977b). The population of Singapore consists of 76 percent Chinese, 14 percent Malay, and 7 percent Indian. The IQ of the ethnic Indians is assumed to be 82, the same as that in India. Weighting the IQs of the three ethnic groups by their proportions of the population gives an IQ for Singapore of 103. Lim's (1994) study gives an IQ for Singapore of 114. The average of the two studies gives an IQ of 108 for Singapore.

South Africa. The population consists of 14 percent of Europeans with an IQ of 94; 9 percent of Coloreds, IQ 83; 2 percent of Indians, IQ 86; and 75 percent of Africans, IQ 65. This gives an IQ of 72 for the population

United States. The four studies are calculated for the total population. The mean IQ of whites in the United States is 100, i.e., the same as that of the whites in Britain. The mean IQ of blacks (approximately 12 percent of the population) is 85 (Lynn, 2005). Weighting the IQs of the two races by their proportions in the population gives an IQ for the United States of 98.

Vietnam. The IQ of 94 is given by Flynn (1991) for Vietnamese immigrants in the United States.

UNESCO (1998) gives data for approximately 4,000 10-year-olds in each of 11 Latin American countries (Argentina, Bolivia, Brazil, Chile, Columbia, the Dominican Republic, Honduras, Mexico, Paraguay, Peru, and Venezuela) given in the table. The tests were verbal and mathematical abilities and are averaged to give IQs calibrated against an IQ of 88 for Mexico.

Appendix 2

The adult literacy rate in 2002, the gross enrollment ratio at the tertiary level of education, PPP-GNI per capita in US dollars in 2002, and life expectancy at birth (LE) in 2002 in 192 Countries are shown on the following pages.

	Country	Adult literacy 2002	Tertiary enrollment 1998–2002	PPP-GNI per capita 2002	St. PPP-GNI pc 2002	Life expectancy 2002	St. LE 2002
1	Afghanistan	36.0[1]	2	700[1]	2.0	43.0[1]	26.0
2	Albania	98.7	15	4,960	14.2	73.6	87.2
3	Algeria	68.9	15[1]	5,530	15.8	69.5	79.0
4	Andorra	99.0[1]	29*	19,000[1]	54.3	83.5[2]	100.0
5	Angola	42.0	1	1,840	5.3	40.1	20.2
6	Antigua and Bar.	85.8	14*	10,390	29.7	73.9	87.8
7	Argentina	97.0	57	10,190	29.1	74.1	88.2
8	Armenia	99.0	26	3,230	9.2	72.3	84.6
9	Australia	99.0	65	27,440	78.4	79.1	98.2
10	Austria	99.0	57	28,910	82.6	78.5	97.0
11	Azerbaijan	97.0	23	3,010	8.6	72.1	84.2
12	Bahamas	95.5	25*	15,960[3]	45.6	67.1	74.2
13	Bahrain	88.5	21[1]	16,190	46.3	73.9	87.8
14	Bangladesh	41.1	6	1,720	5.1	61.1	62.2
15	Barbados	99.0	36[1]	14,660	41.9	77.1	94.2
16	Belarus	99.0	62	5,500	15.7	69.9	79.8
17	Belgium	99.0	58	28,130	80.4	78.7	97.4
18	Belize	76.9	18*	5,490	15.7	71.5	83.0
19	Benin	39.8	4	1,060	3.0	50.7	41.4
20	Bermuda	98.0[1]	62[1]	36,000[1]	100.0	77.6[2]	95.2
21	Bhutan	47.0	2*	1,969[2]	5.6	63.0	66.0
22	Bolivia	86.7	39	2,390	6.8	63.7	67.4
23	Bosnia and Herz.	94.6	15	5,800	16.6	74.0	88.0
24	Botswana	78.9	5	7,740	22.1	41.4	22.8

	Country	Adult literacy 2002	Tertiary enrollment 1998–2002	PPP-GNI per capita 2002	St. PPP-GNI pc 2002	Life expectancy 2002	St. LE 2002
25	Brazil	86.4	18	7,450	21.3	68.0	76.0
26	Brunei	93.9	13[1]	19,210[2]	54.9	76.2	92.4
27	Bulgaria	98.6	40	7,030	20.1	70.9	81.8
28	Burkina Faso	12.8	1	1,090	3.1	45.8	31.6
29	Burundi	50.4	2	630	1.8	40.8	21.6
30	Cambodia	69.4	3	1,970	5.6	57.4	54.8
31	Cameroon	67.9	5	1,910	5.5	46.8	33.6
32	Canada	99.0	59	28,930	82.7	79.3	98.6
33	Cape Verde	75.7	4[1]	4,920	14.1	70.0	80.0
34	Central African R.	48.6	2	1,170	3.3	39.8	19.6
35	Chad	45.8	1	1,010	2.9	44.7	29.4
36	Chile	95.7	37	9,420	26.9	76.0	92.0
37	China	90.9	13	4,520	12.9	70.9	81.8
38	Colombia	92.1	24	6,150	17.6	72.1	84.2
39	Comoros	56.2	1[1]	1,640	4.8	60.6	61.2
40	Congo-Zaire	62.7	2	630	1.8	41.4	22.8
41	Congo-Brazzaville	82.8	4	700	2.0	48.3	36.6
42	Cook Islands	95.0[1]	18*	5,000[1]	14.3	67.0*	74.0
43	Costa Rica	95.8	21	8,650	24.7	78.0	96.0
44	Cote d'Ivoire	49.7	3	1,450	4.1	41.2	22.4
45	Croatia	98.1	36[1]	10,000	28.6	74.1	88.2
46	Cuba	96.9	27	5,259[2]	15.0	76.7	93.4
47	Cyprus	96.8	22[1]	18,650	53.3	78.2	96.4
48	Czech Republic	99.0	30	14,920	42.6	75.3	90.6

	Country	Adult literacy 2002	Tertiary enrollment 1998–2002	PPP-GNI per capita 2002	St. PPP-GNI pc 2002	Life expectancy 2002	St. LE 2002
49	Denmark	99.0	59	30,600	87.4	76.6	93.2
50	Djibouti	65.5	1[1]	2,040	5.8	45.8	31.6
51	Dominica	76.4	9*	4,960	14.2	73.1	86.2
52	Dominican Rep.	84.4	20	6,270	17.9	66.7	73.4
53	Ecuador	91.0	20	3,340	9.5	70.7	81.4
54	Egypt	55.6	38[1]	3,810	10.9	68.6	76.0
55	El Salvador	79.7	17	4,790	13.7	70.6	81.2
56	Equatorial Guinea	84.2	3[1]	9,100	26.0	49.1	38.2
57	Eritrea	56.7	2	1,040	3.0	52.7	45.4
58	Estonia	99.0	59	11,630	33.2	71.6	83.2
59	Ethiopia	41.5	2	780	2.2	45.5	31.0
60	Fiji	92.9	19*	5,330	15.2	69.6	79.2
61	Finland	99.0	85	26,160	74.7	77.9	95.8
62	France	99.0	54	27,040	77.3	78.9	97.8
63	Gabon	71.0	7[1]	5,530	15.8	56.6	53.2
64	Gambia	37.8	2[2]	1,660	4.7	53.9	47.8
65	Georgia	99.0	36	2,270	6.5	73.5	87.0
66	Germany	99.0	46[1]	26,980	77.1	78.2	96.4
67	Ghana	73.8	3	2,080	5.9	57.8	55.6
68	Greece	97.3	61	18,770	53.6	78.2	96.4
69	Grenada	94.4	10*	6,600	18.9	65.3	70.6
70	Guatemala	69.9	8	4,040	11.5	65.7	71.4
71	Guinea	41.0	1	2,060	5.9	48.9	37.8
72	Guinea-Bissau	39.6	0	680	1.9	45.2	30.4

	Country	Adult literacy 2002	Tertiary enrollment 1998–2002	PPP-GNI per capita 2002	St. PPP-GNI pc 2002	Life expectancy 2002	St. LE 2002
73	Guyana	96.5	17*	3,940	11.3	63.2	66.4
74	Haiti	51.9	1	1,610	4.6	49.4	38.8
75	Honduras	80.0	14	2,540	7.3	68.8	77.6
76	Hong Kong	93.5	26[1]	27,490	78.5	79.9	99.8
77	Hungary	99.0	40	13,070	37.3	71.7	83.4
78	Iceland	99.0	48[1]	29,240	83.5	79.7	99.4
79	India	61.3	11	2,650	7.6	63.7	67.4
80	Indonesia	87.9	15	3,070	8.8	66.6	73.2
81	Iran	77.1	19	6,690	19.1	70.1	80.2
82	Iraq	58.0[2]	14	1,600[1]	4.6	62.0[1]	64.0
83	Ireland	99.0	47	29,570	84.5	76.9	93.8
84	Israel	95.3	53	19,000	54.3	79.1	98.2
85	Italy	98.5	50	26,170	74.8	78.7	97.4
86	Jamaica	87.6	17	3,680	10.5	75.6	91.2
87	Japan	99.0	48	27,380	78.2	81.5	83.0
88	Jordan	90.9	31	4,180	11.9	70.9	81.8
89	Kazakhstan	99.0	39	5,630	16.1	66.2	72.4
90	Kenya	84.3	4	1,010	2.9	45.2	30.4
91	Kiribati	86.0*	3*	800[1]	2.3	62.0[1]	64.0
92	Korea, North	99.0[1]	26*	1,000[1]	2.9	61.0[1]	62.0
93	Korea, South	97.9	82	16,960	485	75.4	90.8
94	Kuwait	82.9	21[1]	17,780	50.8	76.5	93.0
95	Kyrgyzstan	97.0	44	1,560	4.5	68.4	76.8
96	Laos	66.4	4	1,660	4.7	54.3	48.6

	Country	Adult literacy 2002	Tertiary enrollment 1998–2002	PPP-GNI per capita 2002	St. PPP-GNI pc 2002	Life expectancy 2002	St. LE 2002
97	Latvia	99.0	64	9,190	26.3	70.9	81.8
98	Lebanon	86.5	45	4,600	13.1	73.5	87.0
99	Lesotho	81.4	2	2,970	8.5	36.3	12.6
100	Liberia	55.9	3	1,000[1]	2.9	47.0[1]	34.0
101	Libya	81.7	58	7,570[2]	21.6	72.6	85.2
102	Lithuania	99.0	59	10,190	29.1	72.5	85.0
103	Luxembourg	99.0	28*	53,230	100.0	78.3	96.6
104	Macedonia	96.0	24	6,420	18.3	73.5	87.0
105	Madagascar	67.3	2	730	2.1	53.4	46.8
106	Malawi	61.8	1	570	1.6	37.8	15.6
107	Malaysia	88.7	26	8,500	24.3	73.0	86.0
108	Maldives	97.2	1*	4,798[2]	13.7	67.2	74.4
109	Mali	19.0	2	840	2.4	48.5	37.0
110	Malta	92.6	25[1]	17,710	50.6	78.3	96.6
111	Marshall Islands	93.7[1]	2.5*	1,600[1]	4.6	65.0[1]	70.0
112	Mauritania	41.2	3	1,790	5.1	52.3	44.6
113	Mauritius	84.3	11	10,820	30.9	71.9	83.8
114	Mexico	90.5	20	8,800	25.1	73.3	86.6
115	Micronesia	89.0[1]	4[1]	2,000[1]	5.7	68.0[1]	76.0
116	Moldova	99.0	29	1,600	4.6	68.8	77.6
117	Mongolia	97.8	35	1,710	4.9	63.7	67.4
118	Morocco	50.7	10	3,730	10.7	68.5	77.0
119	Mozambique	46.5	1	990	2.8	38.5	17.0
120	Myanmar (Burma)	85.3	11	1,027[2]	2.9	57.2	54.4

	Country	Adult literacy 2002	Tertiary enrollment 1998–2002	PPP-GNI per capita 2002	St. PPP-GNI pc 2002	Life expectancy 2002	St. LE 2002
121	Namibia	83.3	7	6,880	19.7	45.3	30.6
122	Nepal	44.0	5	1,370	3.9	59.6	59.2
123	Netherlands	99.0	55	28,350	81.0	78.3	96.6
124	New Caledonia	91.0	15*	21,960[3]	62.7	73.0[1]	86.0
125	New Zealand	99.0	72	20,550	58.7	78.2	96.4
126	Nicaragua	76.7	8	2,350	6.7	69.4	78.8
127	Niger	17.1	1	800	2.3	46.0	32.0
128	Nigeria	66.8	4	800	2.3	51.6	43.2
129	Northern Mariana	97.0	15**	12,500[1]	35.7	75.7[2]	91.4
130	Norway	99.0	70	36,690	100.0	78.9	97.8
131	Oman	74.4	7	13,000	37.1	72.3	84.6
132	Pakistan	41.5	11*	1,960	5.6	60.8	61.6
133	Panama	92.3	34	6,060	17.3	74.6	89.2
134	Papua New Guinea	64.6	3	2,180	6.2	57.4	54.8
135	Paraguay	91.6	18	4,590	13.1	70.7	81.4
136	Peru	85.0	30	4,880	13.9	69.7	79.4
137	Philippines	92.6	30	4,450	12.7	69.8	79.6
138	Poland	99.0	55	10,450	29.9	73.8	87.6
139	Portugal	92.5	50	17,820	50.9	76.1	92.2
140	Puerto Rico	94.1[1]	45	15,800[3]	45.1	76.0[1]	92.0
141	Qatar	84.2	23[1]	19,844[2]	36.7	72.0	84.0
142	Romania	97.3	27	6,490	18.5	70.5	81.0
143	Russia	99.0	68	8,080	23.1	66.7	73.4
144	Rwanda	69.2	2	1,260	3.6	38.9	17.8
145	Saint Kitts and N.	97.8	13*	10,750	30.7	70.0	80.0

	Country	Adult literacy 2002	Tertiary enrollment 1998–2002	PPP-GNI per capita 2002	St. PPP-GNI pc 2002	Life expectancy 2002	St. LE 2002
146	Saint Lucia	94.8	25[1]	4,950	14.1	72.4	84.8
147	Saint Vincent	83.1	11*	5,190	14.8	74.0	88.0
148	Samoa (Western)	98.7	7[1]	5,570	15.9	69.8	79.6
149	Sao Tome and Pr.	83.1	1[1]	1,317[2]	3.8	69.7	79.4
150	Saudi Arabia	77.9	22	12,660	36.2	72.1	84.2
151	Senegal	39.3	3	1,540	4.4	52.7	45.4
152	Serbia and Mont.	93.0[1]	36	2,300[1]	6.6	74.4[2]	88.8
153	Seychelles	91.9	32*	18,232[2]	52.1	72.7	85.4
154	Sierra Leone	36.0	2	500	1.4	34.3	8.6
155	Singapore	92.5	39[2]	23,730	67.8	78.0	96.0
156	Slovakia	99.0	30	12,590	36.0	73.6	87.2
157	Slovenia	99.0	61	18,480	52.8	76.2	92.4
158	Solomon Islands	76.6	1*	1,590	4.5	69.0	78.0
159	Somalia	37.8[1]	3	500[1]	1.4	47.0[1]	34.0
160	South Africa	86.0	15	9,810	28.0	48.8	37.6
161	Spain	97.7	57	21,910	62.6	79.2	98.4
162	Sri Lanka	92.1	5	3,510	10.0	72.5	85.0
163	Sudan	59.9	3	1,740	5.0	55.5	51.0
164	Suriname	94.0	12[1]	6,590[2]	18.8	71.0	82.0
165	Swaziland	80.9	5	4,730	13.5	35.7	11.4
166	Sweden	99.0	70	25,820	73.8	80.0	100.0
167	Switzerland	99.0	42	31,840	91.0	79.1	98.2
168	Syria	82.9	18	3,4700	9.9	71.7	83.4
169	Taiwan	96.1[1]	75*	23,400[1]	66.9	77.1[2]	94.2

	Country	Adult literacy 2002	Tertiary enrollment 1998–2002	PPP-GNI per capita 2002	St. PPP-GNI pc 2002	Life expectancy 2002	St. LE 2002
170	Tajikistan	99.0	15	930	2.7	68.6	77.2
171	Tanzania	77.1	1	580	1.7	43.5	27.0
172	Thailand	92.6	37	6,890	19.7	69.1	78.2
173	Timor-Leste	58.6	12[1]	500[1]	1.4	49.3	38.6
174	Togo	59.6	4	1,450	4.1	49.9	39.8
175	Tonga	98.8	4[1]	6,820	19.5	68.4	76.8
176	Trinidad and Tob.	98.5	7	9,000	25.7	71.4	82.8
177	Tunisia	73.2	23	6,440	18.4	72.7	85.4
178	Turkey	86.5	25	6,300	18.0	70.4	80.8
179	Turkmenistan	98.8	22	4,780	13.7	66.9	73.8
180	Uganda	68.9	3	1,360	3.9	45.7	31.4
181	Ukraine	99.0	57	4,800	13.7	69.5	79.0
182	United Arab Em.	77.3	9	24,030	68.7	74.6	89.2
183	United Kingdom	99.0	59	26,580	75.9	78.1	96.2
184	United States	99.0	71	36,120	100.0	77.0	94.0
185	Uruguay	97.7	38	7,710	22.0	75.2	90.4
186	Uzbekistan	99.0	9	1,640	4.8	62.5	79.0
187	Vanuatu	34.0	4[1]	2,850	8.1	68.6	77.2
188	Venezuela	93.1	18	5,220	14.9	73.6	87.2
189	Vietnam	90.3	10	2,300	6.6	69.0	78.0
190	Yemen	49.0	4	800	2.3	59.8	59.6
191	Zambia	79.9	2	800	2.3	32.7	5.4
192	Zimbabwe	90.0	4	2,180	6.2	33.9	7.8

Sources:

Adult literacy rate 2002 (% ages 15 and above)

If not otherwise noted, UNDP, *Human Development Report 2004,* Table 1 and Table 33. Cf. The World Bank, *World Development Indicators 2004,* Table 1.6 and 2.13.

1. CIA, *The World Factbook, 2004.* Online. Afghanistan, Andorra, Bermuda, the Cook Islands, North Korea, the Marshall Islands, Micronesia, Puerto Rico, Serbia and Montenegro, Somalia, and Taiwan.

2. CIA, *The World Factbook 2000,* p. 234.

* Kiribati, estimation (the Marshall Islands 93.7, Micronesia 89.0, and the Solomon Islands 76.6).

Gross enrollment ratio, tertiary 2001–02

If not otherwise noted, The World Bank, *World Development Indicators 2004,* Table 2.11. Data refer to 1990–91 in the cases of Afghanistan, Bosnia and Herzegovina, Congo-Zaire, the Dominican Republic, Ecuador, Guatemala, Guinea, Haiti, Liberia, Malawi, Nicaragua, Nigeria, Papua New Guinea, Peru, Puerto Rico, Senegal, Singapore, Somalia, Sri Lanka, Sudan, Syria, Turkmenistan, the United Arab Emirates, and Yemen. Cf. UNESCO Institute for Statistics, 2004. Online (Gross enrollment Ratio, Tertiary).

1. Unesco Institute for Statistics, 2004. Online. Data are from the period 1998–2002.

2. *Student Atlas of World Geography,* 2003, Table G. Data concern the year 1997.

* Gross enrollment ratios are estimated on the basis of the number of students per 100,000 inhabitants in such a way that percentages are calculated from 7,000 students per 100,000 inhabitants. Data on total populations are principally from the United Nations, *Demographic Yearbooks.*

Andorra, 1,335 students in 2000–01. *The Europa World Year Book 2004* (Europa 2004).

Antigua and Barbuda, 631 students in 1986. Europa 2004.

The Bahamas, 4,093 students in 1985–86. UNESCO, *Statistical Yearbook 1998,* 1999, Table II.7.

Belize, 2,853 students in 1997–98. Europa 2004.

Bhutan, 1,893 students in 2001/2002. UNESCO Institute for Statistics, 2004.

The Cook Islands, 360 students in 1980. Europa 2004.

Dominica, 461 students in 1995-96. Europa 2004.

Fiji, 10,704 students in 1999. Europa 2004.

Grenada, 651 students in 1993. Europa 2004.

Guyana, 8,965 students in 1996–97. UNESCO 1999, Table II.7. Cf. Europa 2004.

Kiribati, 198 students in 2001. Europa 2004.

North Korea, Kurian 1987, p. 1079.

Luxembourg, 8,645 students in 2001. Europa 2004.

Maldives, 171 students in 1999. Europa 2004.

Marshall Islands, 1,149 students in 1994. Europa 2004.

New Caledonia, 2,069 students in 2000. Europa 2003.

Pakistan, 1,044,712 students in 2001. Europa 2004.

Saint Kitts and Nevis, 394 students in 1992–93. UNESCO 1999, Table II.7.

Saint Vincent and the Grenadines, 904 students in 2000. Europa 2003.

Seychelles, 1,818 post-secondary students in 2000. Europa 2004.

Solomon Islands, 405 students in overseas centres in 1998. Europa 2004.

Taiwan, 1,187,225 students in 2001–02. Europa 2003.

** Northern Mariana Islands. Estimation (Marshall Islands 25, Micronesia 4).

PPP-GNI per capita income in US dollars 2002

If not otherwise noted, *World Development Indicators 2004,* Table 1.1 and Table 1.6. Cf. *World Development Report 2004,* Table 1 and Table 7.

1. CIA, *The World Factbook,* 2004. Online. Afghanistan, Andorra, Bermuda, the Cook Islands, Iraq, Kiribati, North Korea, Liberia, the Marshall Islands, Micronesia, the Northern Mariana Islands, Serbia and Montenegro, Somalia, Taiwan, and Timor-Leste.

2. *Human Development Report 2004,* Table 1 (PPP-GDP per capita in 2002, Bhutan, Brunei, Cuba, Libya, the Maldives, Myanmar, Qatar, Sao Tome and Principe, the Seychelles, and Suriname).

3. *World Development Report 2004,* Table 7 (the Bahamas, New Caledonia, and Puerto Rico).

St. PPP-GNI per capita

The values of PPP-GNI per capita income are transformed into a scale from zero to 100 by calculating the percentages of PPP-GNI per capita from $35,000. However, the upper limit for the standardized scale of PPP-GNI per capita is 100.

Life expectancy at birth 2002

If not otherwise noted, *Human Development Report 2004,* Table 1. Cf. *World Development Indicators 2004,* Table 2.19.

1. *World Development Report 2004,* Table 7 (data are for the year 2001, Afghanistan, Iraq, Kiribati, North Korea, Liberia, the Marshall Islands, Micronesia, New Caledonia, Puerto Rico, and Somalia). Cf. *World Development Indicators 2004,* Table 1.6.

2. CIA, *World Factbook 2004.* Online. Andorra, Bermuda, the Northern Mariana Islands, Serbia and Montenegro, and Taiwan.

*The Cook Islands, estimation (Kiribati 62.0, Samoa 69.8, and Tonga 68.4).

St. LE

The values of the life expectancy at birth variable (LE) are transformed into a scale from zero to 100 by the formula: St. LE = (LE − 30) x 2. This means that 30 years is subtracted from the actual years of life expectancy (LE) and the remainder is multiplied by 2. However, the upper limit for the standardized St. LE variable is 100.

Appendix 3

Data on the Index of Democratization (ID) and on its two components (Competition and Participation) in 2002 and on the Index of the Quality of Human Conditions (QHC) as well as data on latitude and annual mean temperature (MT) for 192 countries

	Country	Com. 2002	Part. 2002	ID 2002	St. ID 2002	QHC	Latitude	MT Celsius
1	Afghanistan	0	0	0	0	13.2	35	12.6
2	Albania	47.9	42.7	20.5	41.0	51.2	41	11.4
3	Algeria	37.6	27.7	10.4	20.8	39.9	28	22.5
4	Andorra	46.4	11.8	5.5	11.0	58.7	42*	7.6
5	Angola	0	0	0	0	13.7	11	21.5
6	Antigua and B.	47.4	51.5	24.4	48.8	53.2	17*	26.0
7	Argentina	51.5	50.7	26.1	52.2	64.7	39	14.8
8	Armenia	46.9	34.5	16.2	32.4	50.2	40	7.1
9	Australia	62.2	59.1	36.8	73.6	82.8	20	21.6
10	Austria	57.7	58.8	33.9	67.8	80.7	47	6.3
11	Azerbaijan	29.7	39.5	11.7	23.4	47.2	38	11.9
12	Bahamas	49.2	40.9	20.1	40.2	56.1	25	24.8

	Country	Com. 2002	Part. 2002	ID 2002	St. ID 2002	QHC	Latitude	MT Celsius
13	Bahrain	11.9	12.0	1.4	2.8	49.3	26*	27.1
14	Bangladesh	40.0	43.3	17.3	34.6	29.8	23	25.0
15	Barbados	35.0	47.9	16.8	33.6	60.9	13	26.0
16	Belarus	24.4	60.7	14.8	29.6	57.2	52	6.2
17	Belgium	70.0	61.2	42.8	85.6	84.1	51	9.6
18	Belize	40.7	34.0	13.8	27.6	44.2	18	25.3
19	Benin	32.9	22.0	7.2	14.4	20.5	10	27.5
20	Bermuda*	34.4	34.5	11.9	23.8	75.8	30	21.3
21	Bhutan	0	0	0	0	24.1	28	7.4
22	Bolivia	70.0	34.8	24.4	48.8	49.7	17	21.5
23	Bosnia and Her.	70.0	30.7	21.5	43.0	51.4	45	9.8
24	Botswana	43.0	20.9	9.0	18.0	29.4	23	21.5
25	Brazil	59.8	45.2	27.0	54.0	51.1	10	24.9
26	Brunei	0	0	0	0	50.8	4*	26.9
27	Bulgaria	50.0	55.2	27.6	55.2	59.1	44	10.5
28	Burkina Faso	12.5	21.2	2.6	5.2	10.7	11	28.2
29	Burundi	0	0	0	0	15.2	4	18.7
30	Cambodia	23.7	21.5	5.1	10.2	28.6	10	26.8
31	Cameroon	7.4	23.9	1.8	3.6	23.1	5	24.6
32	Canada	59.2	42.0	24.9	49.8	77.8	52	-5.2
33	Cape Verde	44.4	32.4	14.4	28.8	40.4	16*	23.3
34	Central African R.	45.5	24.5	11.1	22.2	19.1	5	24.9
35	Chad	36.8	31.1	11.4	22.8	20.2	15	26.5
36	Chile	48.7	47.2	23.0	46.0	59.5	32	8.5
37	China	0	0	0	0	39.7	38	6.9
38	Colombia	47.0	25.8	12.1	24.2	48.4	4	24.5
39	Comoros	0	20.0	0	0	24.6	12	25.5
40	Congo-Zaire.	0	0	0	0	17.9	5	24.0
41	Congo-Brazzaville	10.6	43.8	4.6	9.2	26.9	3	24.5
42	Cook Islands*	45.2	30.0	13.6	27.2	45.7	21*	24.6
43	Costa Rica	42.0	36.6	15.4	30.8	53.7	15	24.8
44	Cote d'Ivoire	49.0	11.7	5.7	11.4	18.1	7	26.4
45	Croatia	48.5	59.2	28.7	57.4	61.6	46	10.9
46	Cuba	0	67.5	0	0	46.5	22	25.2
47	Cyprus	65.3	53.3	34.8	69.6	67.6	36	18.4
48	Czech Republic	65.0	46.3	30.1	60.2	64.5	50	7.5
49	Denmark	68.8	64.3	44.2	88.4	85.4	55	7.5
50	Djibouti	21.4	14.7	3.1	6.2	22.0	12	28.0
51	Dominica	52.4	55.8	29.2	58.4	48.8	15*	22.3

	Country	Com. 2002	Part. 2002	ID 2002	St. ID 2002	QHC	Latitude	MT Celsius
52	Dominican Rep.	50.1	38.2	19.1	38.2	46.8	20	24.5
53	Ecuador	45.2	38.7	17.5	35.0	47.4	3	21.8
54	Egypt	13.1	23.0	3.0	6.0	37.3	23	22.1
55	El Salvador	55.5	19.3	10.7	21.4	42.6	15	24.4
56	Equatorial Guinea	0.5	44.8	0.2	0.4	30.4	3	24.5
57	Eritrea	0	0	0	0	21.4	16	25.5
58	Estonia	70.0	34.3	24.0	48.0	64.5	60	5.1
59	Ethiopia	12.1	29.2	3.5	7.0	16.7	8	22.2
60	Fiji	56.3	47.4	26.7	53.4	51.9	17	24.4
61	Finland	62.8	56.7	35.6	71.2	85.1	62	1.7
62	France	70.0	44.4	31.1	62.2	78.1	46	10.7
63	Gabon	31.0	22.1	6.9	13.8	32.2	2	25.0
64	Gambia	26.7	20.7	5.5	11.0	20.7	13	27.5
65	Georgia	34.8	39.5	13.7	27.4	51.2	42	5.8
66	Germany	61.5	58.1	35.7	71.4	78.0	50	8.4
67	Ghana	46.5	32.2	15.0	30.0	33.7	8	27.2
68	Greece	56.2	64.2	36.1	72.2	76.1	39	15.4
69	Grenada	37.8	42.8	16.2	32.4	45.3	12*	26.6
70	Guatemala	32.0	19.1	6.1	12.2	34.6	14	23.4
71	Guinea	34.6	39.0	13.5	27.0	22.5	10	25.7
72	Guinea-Bissau	45.4	32.4	14.7	29.4	20.3	12	26.7
73	Guyana	46.2	45.7	21.1	42.2	46.7	6	26.0
74	Haiti	8.0	35.9	2.9	5.8	20.4	18	24.9
75	Honduras	47.0	32.5	15.3	30.6	41.9	16	23.5
76	Hong Kong*	32.6	9.7	3.2	6.4	60.8	22*	22.6
77	Hungary	53.6	56.7	30.4	60.8	64.1	48	9.8
78	Iceland	59.3	59.1	35.0	70.0	80.0	64	1.7
79	India	45.5	37.6	17.1	34.2	36.3	23	23.7
80	Indonesia	31.2	25.7	8.0	16.0	40.2	2	25.8
81	Iran	11.7	25.2	2.9	5.8	40.2	30	17.2
82	Iraq	0	44.7	0	0	28.1	30	21.4
83	Ireland	58.5	58.3	34.1	68.2	78.5	54	9.3
84	Israel	70.0	54.0	37.8	75.6	75.3	31	19.2
85	Italy	57.5	64.0	36.8	73.6	78.9	42	13.4
86	Jamaica	47.6	27.6	13.1	26.2	46.5	18	24.9
87	Japan	51.5	47.3	24.4	48.8	71.4	35	11.1
88	Jordan	12.5	6.7	0.8	1.6	43.4	32	18.3
89	Kazakhstan	19.0	48.3	9.2	18.4	49.0	50	6.4
90	Kenya	39.4	18.8	7.4	14.8	27.3	0	24.7

	Country	Com. 2002	Part. 2002	ID 2002	St. ID 2002	QHC	Latitude	MT Celsius
91	Kiribati	47.7	31.4	15.0	30.0	37.1	1*	28.2
92	Korea, North	0	0	0	0	38.0	40	5.7
93	Korea, South	60.4	48.0	29.0	58.0	75.4	37*	11.5
94	Kuwait	36.0	2.2	0.8	1.6	50.0	29	25.3
95	Kyrgyzstan	23.6	38.6	9.1	18.2	48.1	40	1.6
96	Laos	1.0	45.4	0.5	1.0	24.9	20	22.8
97	Latvia	70.0	40.4	28.3	56.6	65.5	56	5.6
98	Lebanon	70.0	33.7	23.6	47.2	55.8	34	16.4
99	Lesotho	35.8	23.9	8.6	17.2	24.3	30	11.8
100	Liberia	24.0	21.6	5.2	10.4	21.2	6	25.3
101	Libya	0	0	0	0	49.3	27	21.8
102	Lithuania	68.9	39.8	27.4	54.8	65.4	56	6.2
103	Luxembourg	69.2	41.7	29.1	58.2	76.4	50	8.7
104	Macedonia	48.5	48.1	23.3	46.6	54.4	41	9.8
105	Madagascar	48.5	25.3	12.3	24.6	28.6	20	22.6
106	Malawi	47.6	43.8	20.8	41.6	24.3	13	21.9
107	Malaysia	43.4	29.3	12.7	25.4	50.1	3	25.4
108	Maldives	9.1	35.1	3.2	6.4	38.5	3*	27.6
109	Mali	35.0	9.7	3.4	6.8	13.4	17	28.2
110	Malta	48.2	70.0	33.7	67.4	66.4	36	19.2
111	Marshall Islands	45.4	30.6	13.9	27.8	44.2	9*	27.4
112	Mauritania	15.0	28.2	4.2	8.4	20.5	20	27.6
113	Mauritius	48.3	52.8	25.5	51.0	52.2	20*	22.4
114	Mexico	56.6	37.4	21.2	42.4	52.9	30	21.0
115	Micronesia	70.0	17.9	12.5	25.0	39.9	6*	27.0*
116	Moldova	29.7	34.8	10.3	20.6	46.2	49	9.4
117	Mongolia	48.4	36.7	17.8	35.6	48.1	45	-0.7
118	Morocco	42.3	12.1	5.1	10.2	31.7	34	17.1
119	Mozambique	47.3	24.1	11.4	22.8	18.0	19	23.8
120	Myanmar (Burma)	0	0	0	0	30.7	20	23.0
121	Namibia	23.5	31.6	7.4	14.8	31.1	20	19.9
122	Nepal	39.0	29.0	11.3	22.6	26.9	29	8.1
123	Netherlands	70.0	59.0	41.3	82.6	82.8	54	9.2
124	New Caledonia*	49.3	20.0	9.9	19.8	54.9	21	22.1
125	New Zealand	58.6	46.8	27.4	54.8	76.2	40	10.5
126	Nicaragua	43.7	41.7	18.2	36.4	41.3	10	24.8
127	Niger	41.1	18.4	7.6	15.2	13.5	10	27.1
128	Nigeria	37.2	27.4	10.2	20.4	27.3	8	26.8
129	Northern Mariana*	34.1	40.0	13.6	17.2	51.3	15*	27.3

	Country	Com. 2002	Part. 2002	ID 2002	St. ID 2002	QHC	Latitude	MT Celsius
130	Norway	70.0	56.0	39.2	78.4	89.0	62	1.5
131	Oman	0	0	0	0	40.6	20	25.6
132	Pakistan	20.3	28.0	5.7	11.4	26.2	25	20.2
133	Panama	55.2	45.3	25.0	50.0	56.6	10	25.4
134	Papua New Guinea	70.0	45.1	31.6	63.2	38.4	6	25.2
135	Paraguay	50.4	21.9	11.0	22.0	45.2	23	23.5
136	Peru	46.9	40.2	18.9	37.8	49.2	10	19.6
137	Philippines	60.1	35.8	21.5	43.0	51.6	15	25.8
138	Poland	52.6	39.7	20.9	41.8	62.7	54	7.8
139	Portugal	51.6	48.1	24.8	49.6	67.0	38	15.1
140	Puerto Rico*	52.0	40.0	20.8	41.6	63.6	18*	25.2
141	Qatar	0	0	0	0	45.6	25*	27.1
142	Romania	44.2	46.6	20.6	41.2	53.0	46	8.8
143	Russia	61.2	48.1	29.4	58.8	64.5	58	-5.1
144	Rwanda	0	0	0	0	18.5	3	17.9
145	Saint Kitts and Nevis	46.7	54.7	25.5	51.0	54.5	18*	24.5
146	Saint Lucia	45.8	39.9	18.3	36.6	51.1	13*	25.5
147	Saint Vincent	43.3	52.0	22.5	45.0	48.4	13*	26.8
148	Samoa (Western)	53.1	44.7	23.7	47.4	49.7	13*	26.7
149	Sao Tome and Principe	50.0	22.2	11.1	22.2	37.9	1*	23.7
150	Saudi Arabia	0	0	0	0	44.1	25	24.6
151	Senegal	41.5	17.4	7.2	14.4	21.3	15	27.9
152	Serbia and Mon.	51.0	43.9	22.4	44.8	53.8	44	9.9
153	Seychelles	32.4	64.6	20.9	41.8	60.6	4*	27.1
154	Sierra Leone	27.9	38.0	10.6	21.2	13.8	6	26.0
155	Singapore	26.3	15.6	4.1	8.2	60.7	1	26.4
156	Slovakia	59.4	53.9	32.0	64.0	63.2	50	6.8
157	Slovenia	53.6	53.2	28.5	57.0	72.4	47	8.9
158	Solomon Islands	60.0	39.6	23.8	47.6	41.5	7	25.6
159	Somalia	0	0	0	0	15.2	5	27.0
160	South Africa	33.7	37.1	12.5	25.0	38.3	30	17.8
161	Spain	54.8	57.8	31.7	63.4	75.8	38	13.3
162	Sri Lanka	51.6	45.2	23.3	46.6	47.4	8	26.9
163	Sudan	7.7	27.2	2.1	4.2	24.6	10	26.8
164	Suriname	52.4	44.1	23.1	46.2	50.6	5	25.7
165	Swaziland	0	0	0	0	22.2	26*	21.4
166	Sweden	60.2	59.6	35.9	71.8	82.9	62	2.1
167	Switzerland	70.0	57.6	40.3	80.6	82.2	47*	5.5
168	Syria	0.3	52.8	0.2	0.4	38.9	37	17.7

	Country	Com. 2002	Part. 2002	ID 2002	St. ID 2002	QHC	Latitude	MT Celsius
169	Taiwan	62.0	52.3	32.4	64.8	79.4	25	22.0*
170	Tajikistan	21.0	43.2	9.1	18.2	42.4	35	2.0
171	Tanzania	19.8	22.7	4.5	9.0	23.2	8	22.3
172	Thailand	37.8	32.0	12.1	24.2	50.3	15	26.3
173	Timor-Leste	27.4	49.3	13.5	27.0	27.5	7	26.0*
174	Togo	29.5	38.1	11.2	22.4	26.0	8	27.1
175	Tonga	11.1	14.0	1.6	3.2	40.5	20*	25.2
176	Trinidad and Tobago	49.3	46.5	22.9	45.8	52.0	9	25.7
177	Tunisia	4.5	33.8	1.5	3.0	40.6	34	19.1
178	Turkey	59.1	34.5	20.4	40.8	50.2	39	11.1
179	Turkmenistan	0	0	0	0	41.7	39	15.2
180	Uganda	30.7	32.7	10.0	20.0	25.4	3	22.8
181	Ukraine	58.7	51.4	30.2	60.4	61.8	53	8.3
182	United Arab Emirates	0	0	0	0	48.8	25	27.0
183	United Kingdom	59.3	44.9	26.6	53.2	76.7	54	8.4
184	United States	51.3	67.0	34.4	68.8	86.6	40	8.5
185	Uruguay	48.4	63.7	30.2	60.4	61.7	37	17.5
186	Uzbekistan	4.3	63.7	2.7	5.4	39.4	42	12.1
187	Vanuatu	44.2	38.0	16.8	33.6	31.4	15	24.0
188	Venezuela	43.1	27.4	11.8	23.6	47.4	5	25.3
189	Vietnam	10.3	60.0	6.2	12.4	39.5	10	24.4
190	Yemen	20.7	18.8	3.9	7.8	24.5	15	23.8
191	Zambia	62.0	15.6	9.7	19.4	21.8	15	21.4
192	Zimbabwe	46.0	19.5	9.0	18.0	25.2	20	21.0

Sources:

Competition, Participation, and ID

Data are from *FSD1289 Measures of Democracy 1810–2002* (2003). Cf. *The Polyarchy Dataset. Vanhanen's Index of Democracy* (2003).

* The values of democracy measures were separately calculated for Bermuda, the Cook Islands, Hong Kong, New Caledonia, the Northern Mariana Islands, and Puerto Rico.

St. ID

The Index of Democratization (ID) values are standardized into a scale from 0 to 100 by multiplying the original values by 2.

QHC

The five indicators of human conditions (adult literacy rate, gross enrollment ratio in tertiary education, standardized PPP-GNI per capita, standardized life expectancy at birth, and the standardized Index of Democratization) are combined into the Index of the Quality of Human Conditions (QHC) by calculating their arithmetic mean.

Latitude

If not otherwise noted, Allen, 2003, Part IX: Geographic Index.

* CIA, *The World Factbook 2000.*

Annual mean temperature

If not otherwise noted, TYN CY 1.1. Mitchell et al., 2003, a comprehensive set of climate scenarios for Europe and the globe. Online.

* Estimated for Micronesia, Taiwan, and Timor-Leste.

Appendix 4

Residuals produced by regression analyses of GNI PPP per capita 2002, adult literacy rate 2002, tertiary enrollment ratio, life expectancy at birth 2002, and the Index of Democratization (ID) 2002 on national IQ for single countries in the group of 192 countries

	Country	GNI PPP 2002	Literacy 2002	Tertiary enrollment	Life exp. 2002	ID 2002	Residuals + or -
1	Afghanistan	-8,049	-45.0	-20.9	-22.2	-15.3	-4
2	Albania	-6,960	10.8	-16.0	3.5	2.1	+3
3	Algeria	-2,727	-11.0	-6.5	5.0	-4.4	-4
4	Andorra	3,361	1.9	-12.8	7.0	-17.2	+3
5	Angola	965	-20.7	-0.3	-12.3	-6.8	-4
6	Antigua & Bar.	8,531	20.8	10.0	19.9	16.5	+5
7	Argentina	-2,988	5.6	22.0	1.6	6.1	+4
8	Armenia	-10,440	6.5	-10.4	-1.0	-4.4	-4
9	Australia	11,801	1.9	23.2	2.6	14.1	+5
10	Austria	12,287	-0.4	12.5	0.4	10.2	+4
11	Azerbaijan	-7,215	12.5	-3.9	4.4	-5.2	-3

	Country	GNI PPP 2002	Literacy 2002	Tertiary enrollment	Life exp. 2002	ID 2002	Residuals + or -
12	Bahamas	7,211	14.5	2.1	1.8	4.8	+5
13	Bahrain	7,933	8.6	-0.5	9.4	-13.4	+3
14	Bangladesh	-5,995	-37.7	-14.2	-2.6	3.1	-4
15	Barbados	7,880	22.5	18.5	15.0	3.6	+5
16	Belarus	-9,647	3.1	21.6	-5.8	-7.3	-3
17	Belgium	11,999	0.8	14.9	1.4	19.6	+5
18	Belize	-3,259	-4.1	-4.9	6.2	-1.5	-4
19	Benin	-799	-25.2	0.0	-3.3	-0.7	-4
20	Bermuda	24,298	10.1	31.0	7.5	-6.5	+4
21	Bhutan	-4,811	-29.5	-15.5	0.9	-13.2	-4
22	Bolivia	-7,835	2.2	12.1	-4.0	7.5	+3
23	Bosnia & Herz.	-5,902	6.7	-16.0	3.9	3.1	+3
24	Botswana	5,881	13.9	1.0	-12.6	1.1	+4
25	Brazil	-2,775	1.9	-8.9	0.3	10.1	+3
26	Brunei	7,016	4.8	-19.3	5.3	-19.0	+4
27	Bulgaria	-6,148	7.2	5.0	-1.6	7.6	+3
28	Burkina Faso	215	-49.9	-0.3	-6.6	-4.2	-4
29	Burundi	-737	-13.5	-0.6	-12.4	-7.4	-5
30	Cambodia	-10,224	-19.7	-29.3	-13.5	-13.9	-5
31	Cameroon	3,004	9.8	9.1	-2.4	-2.9	+3
32	Canada	12,799	0.8	15.9	2.0	1.7	+5
33	Cape Verde	108	3.8	-8.1	11.2	3.3	+4
34	Central African Rep.	2,264	-9.5	6.1	-9.4	6.4	+3
35	Chad	135	-16.9	-0.3	-7.7	4.6	-3
36	Chile	-2,282	7.8	6.0	5.9	4.6	+4
37	China	-14,564	-14.2	-38.2	-11.2	-26.4	-5
38	Cambodia	-2,599	11.1	1.1	6.8	-3.2	+3
39	Comoros	-3,614	-16.8	-12.4	1.0	-11.6	-4
40	Congo-Zaire.	1,231	3.4	4.8	-8.6	-5.3	+3
41	Congo-Brazzaville	1,804	24.8	8.1	-0.9	-0.1	+3
42	Cook Islands	-6,210	8.2	-11.6	-2.3	-4.3	-4
43	Costa Rica	-2,560	9.0	-8.6	8.7	-2.5	-3
44	Côte d'Ivoire	83	-14.2	0.4	-12.0	-1.7	-3
45	Croatia	-1,702	10.2	5.0	4.0	10.3	+4
46	Cuba	-3,982	14.7	2.8	10.6	-15.8	+3
47	Cyprus	6,456	7.7	-10.3	7.3	15.8	+4
48	Czech Republic	-719	1.9	-11.8	-1.2	7.4	-3

	Country	GNI PPP 2002	Literacy 2002	Tertiary enrollment	Life exp. 2002	ID 2002	Residuals + or -
49	Denmark	14,961	1.9	17.2	0.1	21.5	+5
50	Djibouti	1,165	2.8	-0.3	-6.6	-3.7	-3
51	Dominica	4,577	14.8	9.1	21.5	22.9	+5
52	Dominican Rep.	-1,495	5.6	-0.2	3.0	4.9	+3
53	Ecuador	-7,377	5.4	-8.3	2.2	0.1	+3
54	Egypt	-3,463	-22.0	19.2	5.7	-10.7	-3
55	El Salvador	-1,990	3.2	-0.5	8.5	-2.5	-3
56	Equatorial Guinea	12,664	31.8	13.9	3.9	-1.9	+4
57	Eritrea	165	-6.0	0.7	0.3	-6.8	+3
58	Estonia	-4,501	0.8	15.9	-5.7	0.8	+3
59	Ethiopia	1,874	-16.6	6.1	-3.7	-1.2	-3
60	Fiji	-3,911	10.7	-5.2	3.5	10.9	+3
61	Finland	10,129	0.8	41.9	0.6	12.4	+5
62	France	11,401	1.9	12.2	2.4	8.4	+5
63	Gabon	6,624	12.9	11.1	7.4	2.2	+5
64	Gambia	1,769	-22.6	3.4	3.1	-0.3	+3
65	Georgia	-11,400	6.5	-0.4	0.2	-6.9	-3
66	Germany	10,849	0.8	2.9	0.9	12.5	+5
67	Ghana	-271	7.6	-2.3	3.0	6.6	+3
68	Greece	6,084	7.1	27.3	6.5	16.6	+5
69	Grenada	4,249	28.2	4.7	10.5	7.8	+5
70	Guatemala	-2,248	-5.4	-8.1	4.4	-6.5	-4
71	Guinea	1,677	-20.6	1.1	-2.7	7.2	+3
72	Guinea-Bissau	297	-22.0	0.1	-6.4	8.4	+3
73	Guyana	-6,285	12.0	-9.9	-4.5	4.2	-3
74	Haiti	1,22	-9.7	1.1	-2.2	-3.4	-3
75	Honduras	-4,733	2.4	-4.8	5.7	1.6	+3
76	Hong Kong	6,930	-15.0	-29.3	-4.7	-24.7	-4
77	Hungary	-2,569	1.9	-1.8	-4.8	7.7	-3
78	Iceland	12,125	-1.5	2.2	0.8	10.8	+4
79	India	-5,115	-17.5	-9.2	0.0	2.9	-3
80	Indonesia	-7,155	3.4	-11.9	-1.1	-8.9	-4
81	Iran	-2,059	-3.9	-3.9	4.8	-12.4	-4
82	Iraq	-8,625	-26.5	-12.9	-5.7	-16.9	-5
83	Ireland	16,884	8.8	13.3	5.2	14.6	+5
84	Israel	4,838	1.6	15.3	5.0	16.7	+5
85	Italy	8,563	-3.2	2.8	-1.0	12.0	+3

	Country	GNI PPP 2002	Literacy 2002	Tertiary enrollment	Life exp. 2002	ID 2002	Residuals + or -
86	Jamaica	1,329	21.4	11.7	20.8	4.7	+5
87	Japan	8,296	-6.1	-3.2	-0.6	-2.0	-4
88	Jordan	-4,569	9.9	8.1	5.6	-14.5	+3
89	Kazakhstan	-8,040	6.5	2.6	-7.1	-11.4	-3
90	Kenya	-1,833	17.0	-2.7	-10.4	-1.5	-4
91	Kiribati	-8,441	3.8	-21.2	-4.1	-0.8	-4
92	Korea, North	-18,576	-7.3	-26.6	-21.9	-26.9	-5
93	Korea, South	-2,616	-8.4	29.4	-7.5	2.1	-3
94	Kuwait	8,047	-0.4	-4.6	9.6	-15.5	-3
95	Kyrgyzstan	-10,142	9.1	13.0	-1.7	-9.3	-3
96	Laos	-9,550	-20.4	-25.6	-15.0	-17.4	-5
97	Latvia	-6,449	1.9	22.2	-5.6	5.6	+4
98	Lebanon	-3,165	7.7	24.8	9.8	9.4	+4
99	Lesotho	2,587	19.8	2.1	-15.3	2.3	+4
100	Liberia	617	-5.7	3.1	-4.6	-1.1	-3
101	Libya	-687	1.8	36.5	8.1	-14.8	+3
102	Lithuania	-2,004	9.9	26.7	1.6	8.4	+4
103	Luxembourg	36,607	-0.4	-16.5	0.2	5.4	+3
104	Macedonia	-5,774	6.9	-8.3	2.6	4.3	+3
105	Madagascar	-7,035	-11.5	-18.2	-10.3	-1.9	-5
106	Malawi	-797	-2.1	-1.6	-15.4	13.4	-4
107	Malaysia	-4,186	-1.5	-7.7	1.3	-6.8	-4
108	Maldives	-2,475	19.6	-17.8	4.3	-10.5	-3
109	Mali	-527	-44.9	-0.6	-4.7	-4.0	-5
110	Malta	2,563	-3.3	-15.4	2.6	11.6	+3
111	Marshall Islands	-7,149	12.7	2.1	-0.3	-1.4	-3
112	Mauritania	-3,022	-30.7	-9.1	-6.5	-6.9	-5
113	Mauritius	-390	-2.5	-18.6	2.6	7.6	-3
114	Mexico	-1,917	4.9	-8.3	4.8	3.8	+3
115	Micronesia	-6,749	8.0	-18.9	2.7	-2.8	-3
116	Moldova	-13,055	4.2	-10.1	-6.1	-11.3	-4
117	Mongolia	-15,405	-2.7	-10.8	-15.2	-6.4	-5
118	Morocco	-5,019	-30.3	-12.9	3.2	-10.2	-4
119	Mozambique	2,084	-11.6	5.1	-10.7	6.7	+3
120	Myanmar	-9,198	0.8	-15.9	-10.5	-16.9	-4
121	Namibia	5,021	18.3	3.0	-8.7	-0.5	+3
122	Nepal	-4,426	-30.2	-9.8	-0.8	-0.8	-5
123	Netherlands	11,727	-0.4	10.5	0.2	17.6	+4

	Country	GNI PPP 2002	Literacy 2002	Tertiary enrollment	Life exp. 2002	ID 2002	Residuals + or -
124	New Caledonia	12,719	8.8	-9.2	6.9	-5.9	+3
125	New Zealand	4,419	0.8	28.9	0.9	4.2	+5
126	Nicaragua	-4,923	-0.9	-10.8	6.5	4.5	-3
127	Niger	-567	-46.8	-1.6	-7.2	0.2	-4
128	Nigeria	-567	2.9	1.4	-1.6	2.8	+3
129	Northern Mariana	5,227	19.4	-3.8	12.8	-0.1	+3
130	Norway	20,067	-0.4	25.5	0.8	15.5	+4
131	Oman	4,743	-5.5	-14.5	7.8	-14.8	-3
132	Pakistan	-6,789	-39.5	-11.9	-4.5	-9.6	-5
133	Panama	-2,689	11.3	11.1	9.3	9.7	+4
134	Papua New G.	-6,077	-15.3	-18.5	-7.1	16.8	-4
135	Paraguay	-4,159	10.6	-4.9	5.4	-4.3	-3
136	Peru	-4,361	2.8	5.8	3.6	3.1	+4
137	Philippines	-5,283	9.3	4.4	2.9	5.2	+4
138	Poland	-5,681	0.8	11.9	-3.5	-2.3	-3
139	Portugal	3,658	-1.2	12.3	2.0	3.7	+4
140	Puerto Rico	7,051	13.1	22.1	10.7	5.5	+5
141	Qatar	14,048	10.0	8.2	11.6	-12.1	+4
142	Romania	-7,180	4.8	-9.4	-2.8	0.0	-3
143	Russia	-7,067	3.1	27.6	-9.0	7.3	+3
144	Rwanda	-599	4.2	-2.0	-15.1	-7.9	-4
145	Saint Kitts & N.	10,367	36.2	13.1	18.4	19.2	+5
146	Saint Lucia	7,028	39.0	31.8	24.8	14.6	+5
147	Saint Vincent	2,839	16.9	5.7	19.2	14.1	+5
148	Samoa (Western)	-5,147	13.1	-21.3	1.3	6.3	+3
149	Sao Tome & P.	934	21.5	1.1	18.1	4.8	+5
150	Saudi Arabia	3,911	-3.1	-0.9	6.8	-15.3	-3
151	Senegal	1,649	-21.1	4.4	1.9	1.4	+4
152	Serbia and Mon.	-8,910	6.2	6.4	5.1	4.5	+4
153	Seychelles	8,499	8.6	6.4	5.8	4.6	+5
154	Sierra Leone	1,594	-22.1	6.1	-14.9	5.9	+3
155	Singapore	3,170	-16.0	-16.3	-6.6	-23.8	-4
156	Slovakia	-2,065	4.2	-9.1	-1.3	10.4	-3
157	Slovenia	3,825	4.2	21.9	1.3	6.9	+5
158	Solomon Islands	-7,159	-4.4	-21.9	3.7	8.5	-3
159	Somalia	-375	-24.9	1.7	-5.4	-6.8	-4
160	South Africa	6,967	18.7	8.3	-6.8	3.6	+4

	Country	GNI PPP 2002	Literacy 2002	Tertiary enrollment	Life exp. 2002	ID 2002	Residuals + or -
161	Spain	6,271	0.6	15.2	2.7	9.0	+5
162	Sri Lanka	-2,778	16.8	-11.1	11.2	10.7	+3
163	Sudan	-611	-6.3	-2.3	0.7	-6.3	-4
164	Suriname	-4,620	7.2	-17.6	1.7	5.2	+3
165	Swaziland	3,855	18.2	3.7	-16.7	-6.8	+3
166	Sweden	9,689	0.8	26.9	2.7	12.7	+5
167	Switzerland	14,725	-1.5	-3.8	0.2	16.1	+4
168	Syria	-4,787	3.0	-3.5	7.2	-14.6	-3
169	Taiwan	4,316	-9.0	23.8	-5.0	6.0	+3
170	Tajikistan	-9,295	14.5	-11.9	0.9	-7.8	-3
171	Tanzania	-2,263	9.8	-5.7	-12.1	-4.4	-4
172	Thailand	-5,304	3.5	4.7	-1.8	-6.9	-3
173	Timor-Leste	-9,725	-25.9	-14.9	-18.4	-3.4	-5
174	Togo	-409	-5.4	0.0	-4.1	3.3	-3
175	Tonga	-2,913	15.5	-21.6	1.5	-14.7	-3
176	Trinidad & Tob.	9,000	16.3	-17.2	5.3	7.1	+4
177	Tunisia	-1,817	-6.7	1.5	8.2	-13.3	-3
178	Turkey	-5,402	-1.4	-6.0	0.3	2.0	-3
179	Turkmenistan	-5,445	14.3	-4.9	-0.8	-16.9	-4
180	Uganda	-1,976	-9.5	-5.0	-10.7	0.5	-4
181	Ukraine	-10,347	3.1	16.6	-6.2	8.1	+3
182	United Arab Em.	15,281	-3.7	-13.9	9.3	-15.3	-3
183	United Kingdom	9,957	-0.4	14.5	0.0	2.9	+3
184	United States	20,481	1.9	29.2	0.5	11.7	+5
185	Uruguay	-6,945	2.9	-1.1	0.3	8.6	+3
186	Uzbekistan	-8,585	14.5	-17.9	1.8	-14.2	-3
187	Vanuatu	-5,899	-47.0	-18.9	3.3	1.5	-3
188	Venezuela	-3,529	12.1	-4.9	8.3	-3.5	-3
189	Vietnam	-11,370	-2.2	-26.4	-4.3	-14.4	-5
190	Yemen	-8,441	-33.2	-20.2	-6.3	-11.9	-5
191	Zambia	-1,551	13.7	-3.2	-22.1	1.3	-3
192	Zimbabwe	2,289	29.6	5.4	-16.9	3.2	+4

Appendix 5

The estimated data on per capita GDP for 1500 and for 2000 derived from Maddison (2003) in a group of 109 countries

	Country	Per capita GDP in 2000	Estimated per capita GDP in 1500	Regional group for 1500 (Maddison, 2003)
1	Afghanistan	1,467	565	Other Asia (Table 8cc)
2	Albania	2,651	496	Eastern Europe (Table 8c)
3	Algeria	2,792	430	Other North Africa (Table 6-2)
4	Andorra	19,401	612	13 small WEC (Table 1c)
5	Angola	789	400	Rest of Africa (Table 6-2)
6	Austria	20,097	707	
7	Belgium	20,742	875	
8	Benin	1,323	415	Sahel and West Africa (Table 6-2)
9	Bhutan	1,467	565	Other Asia (Table 8c)
10	Botswana	4,348	400	Rest of Africa (Table 6-2)
11	Bulgaria	5,365	496	Eastern Europe (Table 8c)
12	Burkina Faso	853	400	Rest of Africa (Table 6-2)
13	Burundi	577	400	Rest of Africa (Table 6-2)

	Country	Per capita GDP in 2000	Estimated per capita GDP in 1500	Regional group for 1500 (Maddison, 2003)
14	Cambodia	1,467	565	Other Asia (Table 8c)
15	Cameroon	1,115	400	Rest of Africa (Table 6-2)
16	Cape Verde	1,777	415	Sahel and West Africa (Table 6-2)
17	Central African Rep.	647	400	Rest of Africa (Table 6-2)
18	Chad	424	400	Rest of Africa (Table 6-2)
19	China	3,425	600	
20	Comoros	581	400	Rest of Africa (Table 6-2)
21	Congo-Zaire.	218	400	Rest of Africa (Table 6-2)
22	Congo-Brazzaville	2,214	400	Rest of Africa (Table 6-2)
23	Cote d'Ivoire	1,326	400	Rest of Africa (Table 6-2)
24	Cyprus	12,874	612	13 small WEC (Table 1c)
25	Czech Republic	9,047	496	Eastern Europe (Table 8c)
26	Denmark	23,010	738	
27	Djibouti	1,103	400	Rest of Africa (Table 6-2)
28	Egypt	2,920	475	
29	Equatorial Guinea	7,956	400	Rest of Africa (Table 6-2)
30	Eritrea	624	400	Rest of Africa (Table 6-2)
31	Ethiopia	624	400	Rest of Africa (Table 6-2)
32	Finland	20,235	453	
33	France	20,808	727	
34	Gabon	3,887	400	Rest of Africa (Table 6-2)
35	Gambia	895	415	Sahel and West Africa (Table 6-2)
36	Germany	18,596	688	
37	Ghana	1,280	415	Sahel and West Africa (Table 6-2)
38	Greece	12,044	433	
39	Guinea	572	415	Sahel and West Africa (Table 6-2)
40	Guinea-Bissau	681	415	Sahel and West Africa (Table 6-2)
41	Hungary	7,138	496	Eastern Europe (Table 8c)
42	Iceland	22,054	612	13 small WEC (Table 1c)
43	India	1,910	550	
44	Indonesia	3,203	565	Other Asia (Table 8c)
45	Iran	4,742	565	Other Asia (Table 8c)
56	Iraq	1,221	565	Other Asia (Table 8c)
47	Ireland	22,015	526	
48	Italy	18,740	1,100	
49	Japan	21,069	500	
50	Jordan	4,059	565	Other Asia (Table 8c)

	Country	Per capita GDP in 2000	Estimated per capita GDP in 1500	Regional group for 1500 (Maddison, 2003)
51	Kenya	1,020	400	Rest of Africa (Table 6-2)
52	Korea, North	1,467	565	Other Asia (Table 8c)
53	Korea, South	14,343	565	Other Asia (Table 8c)
54	Kuwait	10,210	565	Other Asia (Table 8c)
55	Laos	1,467	565	Other Asia (Table 8c)
56	Lebanon	3,409	565	Other Asia (Table 8c)
57	Lesotho	1,645	400	Rest of Africa (Table 6-2)
58	Liberia	847	415	Sahel and West Africa (Table 6-2)
59	Libya	2,322	430	Other North Africa (Table 6-2)
60	Luxembourg	37,138	771	West European average (Table 8c)
61	Madagascar	706	400	Rest of Africa (Table 6-2)
62	Malawi	679	400	Rest of Africa (Table 6-2)
63	Malaysia	7,872	565	Other Asia (Table 8c)
64	Mali	842	400	Rest of Africa (Table 6-2)
65	Malta	12,127	612	13 small WEC (Table 1c)
66	Mauritania	1,017	415	Sahel and West Africa (Table 6-2)
67	Mexico	7,218	425	
68	Morocco	2,658	430	
69	Mozambique	1,432	400	Rest of Africa (Table 6-2)
70	Namibia	3,795	400	Rest of Africa (Table 6-2)
71	Netherlands	21,591	761	
72	Niger	503	415	Sahel and West Africa (Table 6-2)
73	Nigeria	1,156	415	Sahel and West Africa (Table 6-2)
74	Norway	24,364	640	
75	Oman	6,893	565	Other Asia (Table 8c)
76	Philippines	2,385	565	Other Asia (Table 8c)
77	Poland	7,215	496	Eastern Europe (Table 8c)
78	Portugal	14,022	606	
79	Qatar	8,042	565	Other Asia (Table 8c)
80	Romania	3,002	496	Eastern Europe (Table 8c)
81	Russia	5,157	499	Former USSR (Table 8c)
82	Rwanda	830	400	Rest of Africa (Table 6-2)
83	Sao Tome & Principe	1,226	400	Rest of Africa (Table 6-2)
84	Saudi Arabia	8,002	565	Other Asia (Table 8c)
85	Senegal	1,433	415	Sahel and West Africa (Table 6-2)
86	Serbia & Montenegro	2,354	496	Eastern Europe (Table 8c)
87	Sierra Leone	379	415	Sahel and West Africa (Table 6-2)

	Country	Per capita GDP in 2000	Estimated per capita GDP in 1500	Regional group for 1500 (Maddison, 2003)
88	Somalia	863	400	Rest of Africa (Table 6-2)
89	South Africa	4,139	400	Rest of Africa (Table 6-2)
90	Spain	15,269	661	
91	Sri Lanka	3,645	565	Other Asia (Table 8c)
92	Sudan	991	415	Sahel and West Africa (Table 6-2)
93	Swaziland	2,606	400	Rest of Africa (Table 6-2)
94	Sweden	20,321	695	
95	Switzerland	22,025	632	
96	Syria	7,481	565	Other Asia (Table 8c)
97	Taiwan	16,642	565	Other Asia (Table 8c)
98	Tanzania	524	400	Rest of Africa (Table 6-2)
99	Thailand	6,336	565	Other Asia (Table 8c)
100	Togo	575	415	Sahel and West Africa (Table 6-2)
101	Tunisia	4,538	430	Other North Africa (Table 6-2)
102	Turkey	6,597	565	Other Asia (Table 8c)
103	Uganda	788	400	Rest of Africa (Table 6-2)
104	United Arab Emirates	16,560	565	Other Asia (Table 8c)
105	United Kingdom	19,817	714	
106	Vietnam	1,467	565	Other Asia (Table 8c)
107	Yemen	2,588	565	Other Asia (Table 8c)
108	Zambia	666	400	Rest of Africa (Table 6-2)
109	Zimbabwe	1,280	400	Rest of Africa (Table 6-2)

References

Abdel-Khalek, A. M. and Lynn, R. (2005). Sex Differences on a Standardisation of the Standard Progressive Matrices in Kuwait. *Personality and Individual Differences* (to appear).

Abul-Hubb, D. (1972). Application of Progressive Matrices in Iraq. In L. J. Cronbach and P. J. Drenth (Eds.), *Mental Tests and Cultural Adaptation.* The Hague: Mouton.

Adler-Karlsson, G. (2002). Ländernas framtid avgörs av medborgarnas IQ. *Aftonbladed,* September 2: 28.

Afzal, M. (1988). Consequences of consanguinity on cognitive behavior. *Behavior Genetics,* 18, 583–594.

Agrawal, N., Sinha, S. N., and Jensen, A. R. (1984). Effects of inbreeding on Raven matrices. *Behavior Genetics,* 14, 579–585.

Ahmed, R. A. (1989). The development of number, space, quantity, and reasoning concepts in Sudanese schoolchildren. In L. L. Adler (Ed.), *Cross Cultural Research in Human Development.* Westport, Conn.: Praeger.

Albalde Paz, E. and Muñoz, C. J. (1993). *El test PMS de Raven y los escolares de Galicia.* Universidade da Coruña: Servicio de Publicaciones.

Al-Heeti, K., Ganem, A., Al-Kubaldl, A., and Al-Nood, Y. (1997). Standardization of Raven's Coloured Progressive Matrices Scale on primary school children ages 6-11 in Yemen schools. *Indian Psychological Review,* 48, 49–56.

Allardt, E. (1995). Having, Loving, Being: An Alternative to the Swedish Model of Welfare Research. In M. C. Nussbaum and A. Sen (Eds.), *The Quality of*

Life. Oxford: Clarendon Press.

Allen, J. L. (2003). *Student Atlas of World Geography*. Third Edition. United States: The McGraw-Hill Companies.

Allen, T. and Thomas, A. (Eds.) (2000). *Poverty and Development into the 21st Century*. Oxford: Oxford University Press.

Alonso, O. S. (1974). Raven, *g* factor, age, and school level. *Havana Hospital Psiquiatrico Revista*, 14, 60–77.

Alvi, S. A., Khan, S. B., Vegeris, S. L., and Ansari, Z. A. (1986). A cross-cultural study of psychological differentiation. *International Journal of Psychology*, 21, 659–670.

Andreev, L. and Andreev, M. (2004). Analysis of Population Pyramids by a New Method for Intelligent Pattern Recognition. Scottsdale: Equicom, Inc. www.matrixreasoning.com/.

Angelini, A. L., Alves, I. C., Custodio, E. M., and Duarte, W. F. (1988). *Manual Matrizes Progressivas Coloridas*. Sao Paulo: Casa do Psicologo.

Ardila, A., Pineda, D., and Roselli, M. (2000). Correlation between intelligence test scores and executive function measures. *Archives of Clinical Neuropsychology*, 15, 31–36.

Aristotle. (1952). See *The Politics of Aristotle*.

Aristotle. (1984). *The Politics of Aristotle*. Translated and with an Introduction, Notes, and Glossary by Carnes Lord. Chicago: University of Chicago Press.

Ayittey, G. B. N. (1999). *Africa in Chaos*. New York: St. Martin's Griffin.

Badri, M. B. (1965a). The use of finger drawing in measuring the Goodenough quotient of culturally deprived Sudanese children. *Journal of Psychology*, 59, 333–334.

Badri, M. B. (1965b). Influence of modernization on Goodenough quotients of Sudanese children. *Perceptual and Motor Skills*, 20, 931–932.

Bagley, C., Iwawaki, S., and Young, L. (1983). Japanese children: group-oriented but not field dependent? In C. Bagley and G. K. Verma (Eds.), *Multicultural childhood, education, ethnicity, and cognitive styles*. Aldershot, UK: Gower.

Bajema, C. (1968). A note on the interrelations among intellectual ability, educational attainment, and occupational achievement. *Sociology of Education*, 41, 317–319.

Baker, D. P. and Jones, D. P. (1993). Creating gender equality; cross national gender stratification and mathematical performance. *Sociology of Education*, 66, 91–103.

Baker, L. A., Treloar, S. A., Reynolds, C. A., Heath, A. C., and Martin, N. G. (1996). Genetics of educational attainment in Australian twins: sex differences and secular changes. *Behavior Genetics*, 26, 73–102.

Barkow, J. H., Cosmides, L., and Tooby, J. (Eds.). *The Adaptive Mind: Evolutionary Psychology and the Generation of Culture.* New York: Oxford University Press.

Barnett, S. M. and Williams, W. (2004). National Intelligence and the Emperor's New Clothes. *IQ and the Wealth of Nations. Contemporary Psychology. APA Review of Books*, 49, 389–396.

Baron, R. A., Byrne, I. D., and Kantowitz, B. H. (1980). *Psychology: Understanding Behavior.* New York: Holt, Rinehart, and Winston.

Barro, R. J. (1999). *Determinants of Economic Growth: A Cross-Country Empirical Study.* Cambridge, Mass.: The MIT Press.

Barro, R. J. and Lee, J. W. (2001). International data on educational attainment: updates and implications. *Oxford Economic Papers*, 3, 541–563.

Bart, W., Kamal, A., and Lane, J. F. (1987). The development of proportional reasoning in Qatar. *Journal of Genetic Psychology*, 148, 95–103.

Bartels, M., Rietveld, M. J. H., van Baal, G. C., and Boomsma, D. I. (2002). Genetic and environmental influences on the development of intelligence. *Behavior Genetics*, 32, 237–249.

Bauer, P. T. 1981. *Equality, the Third World, and Economic Delusion.* Cambridge, Mass.: Harvard University Press.

Beaton, A. E., Mullis, I. V., Martin, M. O., Gonzalez, E. J., Kelly, D. L., and Smith, D. A. (1996a). *Mathematical Achievement in the Middle School Years.* Boston College, Chestnut Hill, Mass.: TIMSS International Study Center.

Beaton, A. E., Martin, M. O., Mullis, I. V., Gonzalez, E. J., Smith, T. A., and Kelly, D. L. (1996b). *Science Achievement in the Middle School Years.* Boston College, Chestnut Hill, Mass.: TIMSS International Study Center.

Beck, L. R. and St. George, R. (1983). The alleged cultural bias of PAT: Reading comprehension and reading vocabulary tests. *New Zealand Journal of Educational Studies*, 18, 32–47.

Behrman, J. and Taubman, P. (1989). Is schooling "mostly in genes"? Nature-nurture decomposition using data on relatives. *Journal of Political Economy*, 97, 1425–1446.

Behrman, J., Taubman, O., and Wales, T. (1977). Controlling for and measuring the effects of genetic and family environment in equations for schooling and labor market success. In P. Taubman (Ed.), *Kinometrics: Determinants of Socioeconomic Success within and between Families.* New York: North

Holland.

Bendix, R. and Lipset, S. M. (Eds.) (1969). *Class, Status and Power: Social Stratification in Comparative Perspective.* London: Routledge & Kegan Paul.

Berlioz, L. (1955). Etude des progressive matrices faite sur les Africains de Douala. *Bulletin du Centre Etude Recherce Psychotechnique,* 4, 33–44.

Berry, J. W. (1966). Temne and Eskimo perceptual skills. *International Journal of Psychology,* 1, 207–229.

Bhalla, S. S. (2002). *Imagine There's No Country: Poverty, Inequality, and Growth in the Era of Globalization.* Washington, D.C.: Institute for International Economics.

Bhogle, S. and Prakash, I. J. (1992). Performance of Indian children on the Colored Peogressive Matrices. *Psychological Studies,* 37, 178–181.

Binet, A. (1905). New methods for the diagnosis of the intellectual level of subnormals. *L'Annee Psychologique,* 12, 191–244.

Binnie-Dawson, J. L. (1984). Biosocial and endocrine bases of spatial ability. *Psychologia,* 27, 129–151.

Birdsall, N. (2001 [1998]). Life is Unfair: Inequality in the World. In R. J. Griffiths (Ed.), *Developing World 01/02.* Guilford, Conn.: McGraw-Hill/Duskin.

Bishop, J. H. (1989). Is the test score decline responsible for the productivity growth decline? *American Economic Review,* 79, 178–197.

Blackenau, W. F. and Simpson, N. B. (2004). Public education expenditures and growth. *Journal of Development Economics,* 73, 583–605.

Bleichrodt, N., Drenth, P. J. D., and Qierido, A. (1980). Effects of iron deficiency on motor and psychomotor abilities. *American Journal of Physical Anthropology,* 53, 55-67.

Bloom, D. E., Canning, D., and Sevolla, J. (2004). The effect of health on economic growth: A production transition. *World Development,* 32(1), 1–13.

Bodmer, W. F. (1995). Where Will Genome Analysis Lead Us Forty Years On? In D. A. Chambers (Ed.), *DNA: The Double Helix. Perspective and Prospective at Forty Years.* New York: New York Academy of Sciences.

Boissiere, M., Knight, J. B., and Sabot, R. H. (1985). Earnings, schooling, ability, and cognitive skills. *American Economic Review,* 75,1016–1030.

Boivin, M. J. and Giordani, B. (1993). Improvements in cognitive performance for schoolchildren in Zaire following an iron supplement and treatment for intestinal parasites. *Journal of Pediatric Psychology,* 18, 249–264.

Boivin, M. J., Giordani, B., and Bornfeld, B. (1995). Use of the tactual performance test for cognitive ability testing with African children. *Neuropsychology*, 9, 409–417.

Boivin, M. J., Giordani, B., Crist, C. L., and Chounramany, C. (1996). Validating a cognitive ability testing protocol with Lao children for community development applications. *Neuropsychology*, 10, 588–599.

Botstein, D. (1999). Of Genes and Genomes. In D. C. Grossman and H. Valtin (Eds.), *Great Issues for Medicine in the Twenty-first Century. Ethical and Social Issues Arising Out of Advances in Biomedical Sciences*. New York: New York Academy of Sciences.

Bouchard, T. J. (1993). The genetic architecture of human intelligence. In P. A. Vernon (Ed.), *Biological Approaches to the Study of Human Intelligence*. Norwood, N.J.: Ablex.

Bouchard, T. J. (1997). Whenever the Twain Shall Meet. *The Sciences*, 37(5), 52–57.

Bouchard, T. J. (1998). Genetic and environmental influences on adult intelligence and special mental abilities. *Human Biology*, 70, 257–279.

Bouchard, T. J., Lykken, D. T., McGrue, M., Segal, N. L., and Tellegren, A. (1990). Sources of human psychological differences: the Minnesota study of identical twins reared apart. *Science*, 212, 223–250.

Bourdier, G. (1964). Utilization and nouvel etalonnage du P.M. 47. *Bulletin de Psychologie*, 235: 39–41.

Bourguignon, F. and Morrison, C. (2002). Inequality among World Citizens, 1820–1992. *The American Economic Review*, 92, 727–744.

Brock, D. (1995). Quality of Life Measures in Health Care and Medical Ethics. In M. C. Nussbaum, and A. Sen (Eds.),*The Quality of Life*. Oxford: Clarendon Press.

Brody, N. (2003). Jensen's genetic interpretation of racial differences in intelligence: critical evaluation. In H. Nyborg (Ed.), *The Scientific Study of General Intelligence*. Amsterdam: Elsevier.

Bross, D. S. and Shapiro, S. (1982) Direct and indirect association of five factors with infant mortality. *American Journal of Epidemiology*, 115, 78–91.

Brown, W. W. and Reynolds, M. O. (1975). A model of IQ, occupation, and earnings. *American Economic Review*, 65, 1002–1007.

Buj, V. (1981). Average IQ values in various European countries. *Personality and Individual Differences*, 2, 168–169.

Carr, A. (1993). Twenty years a growing: a research note on gains in the intelligence test scores of Irish children over two decades. *Irish Journal of Psychology*, 14, 576–582.

Carroll, J. B. (1994). *Human Cognitive Abilities*. Cambridge, U.K.: Cambridge University Press.

Cassidy, T. and Lynn, R. (1991). Achievement motivation, educational attainment, cycles of disadvantage, and social competence: some longitudinal data. *British Journal of Educational Psychology*, 61, 1–12.

Cattell, R. B. (1971). *Abilities: Their Structure, Growth and Action*. Boston: Houghton Mifflin.

Cavalli-Sforza, L. L. and Cavalli-Sforza, F. (1995). *The Great Human Diasporas: The History of Diversity and Evolution*. Reading, Mass.: Addison-Wesley Publishing Company.

Cavalli-Sforza, L. L., Menozzi, P., and Piazza, A. (1994). *The History and Geography of Human Genes*. Princeton, N.J.: Princeton University Press.

Cavalli-Sforza, L. L., Menozzi, P., and Piazza, A. (1996). *The History and Geography of Human Genes*. Abridged Paperback Edition. Princeton, N. J.: Princeton University Press.

Cawley, J., Heckman, J., and Vytlacil, E. (2001). Three observations on wages and measured cognitive ability. *Labor Economics*, 8, 419–442.

Central Intelligence Agency (CIA). (2000). *The World Factbook 2000*. Washington, D.C.: Brassey's.

Central Intelligence Agency (CIA). (2004) *The World Factbook*. www.cia.gov/cia/publications/factbook/index.html.

Chaim, H. H. (1994). Is the Raven Progressive Matrices valid for Malaysians? Unpublished.

Chakraborty, R., Kamboh, M. I., Nwamko, M., and Ferrell, R. E. (1992). Caucasian genes in American blacks. *American Journal of Human Genetics*, 50, 145–155.

Chan, J., Eysenck, H. J., and Lynn, R. (1991). Reaction time and intelligence among Hong Kong children. *Perceptual and Motor Skills*, 72, 427–433.

Chan, J. and Vernon, P. E. (1988). Individual differences among the peoples of China. In D. H. Irvine and J. W. Berry, *Human Abilities in Cultural Context*. Cambridge, U.K.: Cambridge University Press.

Chandra, S. (1975). Some patterns of response on the Queensland Test. *Australian Psychologist*, 10, 185–191.

Chen, C., Lee, S., and Stevenson, H. W. (1996). Long term prediction of academic achievement of American, Chinese, and Japanese adolescents. *Journal of Educational Psychology*, 98, 750–759.

Chisholm, M. (1982). *Modern World Development: A geographical perspective.* London: Hutchinson.

Chopra, S. L. (1966). Family size and sibling position as related to measured intelligence and academic achievement. *Journal of Social Psychology,* 70, 133–137.

Claassen, N. C. W. (1990). The comparability of General Scholastic Aptitude Test scores across different populations groups. *South African Journal of Psychology,* 20, 80–92.

Clague, C. (1997). *Institutions and Economic Development: Growth and Governance in Less-Developed and Post-Socialist Countries.* Baltimore: The Johns Hopkins University Press.

Clay, M. M. (1971). The Polynesian language skills of Maori and Samoan school entrants. *International Journal of Psychology,* 6, 135–145.

Cole, C. J. (1999). Commentary on the Genetic Session. In D. C. Grossman and H. Valtin (Eds.), *Great Issues for Medicine in the Twenty-first Century. Ethical and Social Issues Arising Out of Advances in Biomedical Sciences.* New York: New York Academy of Sciences.

Collier, P. and Gunning, J. W. (1999). Explaining African economic performance. *Journal of Economic Literature,* 37, 64–111.

Collins, F. S. (1999). The Human Genome Project and the Future of Medicine. In D. C. Grossman and H. Valtin (Eds.), *Great Issues for Medicine in the Twenty-first Century. Ethical and Social Issues Arising Out of Advances in Biomedical Sciences.* New York: New York Academy of Sciences.

Coon, C. S., Garn, S. M., and Birdsell, J. B. (1950). *Races.* Springfield, Ill.: Thomas.

Costenbader, V. and Ngari, S. M. (2000). A Kenya standardisation of the Coloured Progressive Matrices. *School Psychology International,* 22, 258–268.

Cottereau-Reiss, P. and Lehalle, H. (1988). Comparison des performances d'enfants Kanak et d'enfants francais dans une situation de jugements de morphismes: structuration spatiale et moulin a vent. *Archives de Psychologie,* 66, 3–21.

Counter, M. (2004). Personal communication.

Cox, M. V., Koyasu, M., Hranamaa, H., and Perara, J. (2001). Children's human figure drawings in the UK and Japan: the effects of age, sex, and culture. *British Journal of Developmental Psychology,* 19, 275–292.

Cox, M. V., Perara, J., and Fan, X. U. (1998). Children's drawing ability in the U.K. and China. *Psychologia,* 41, 171–182.

Craig., J. D. (1974). *A study of the education and abilities of young Australian male adults.* Australian Department of Labor Research Report. Canberra: Government Printing Service.

Cramer, J. C. (1987). Social factors and infant mortality. *Demography,* 24, 299–322.

Cropsey, J. (1987a). Adam Smith. In L. Strauss and J. Cropsey (Eds.), *History of Political Philosophy.* Third Edition. Chicago and London: The University of Chicago Press.

Cropsey, J. (1987b). Karl Marx. In L. Strauss and J. Cropsey (Eds.), *History of Political Philosophy.* Third Edition. Chicago and London: The University of Chicago Press.

Crouse, J. (1979). The effects of academic ability. In C. Jencks (Ed.), *Who Gets Ahead? The Determinants of Economic Success in America.* New York: Basic Books.

Dague, P., Garelli, M., and Lebettre, A. (1964). Recherches sur l'echelle de maturite mentale de Columbia. *Revue de Psychologie Applique,* 14, 71–96.

Daley, Y. C., Whaley, S. E., Sigman, M. D., Espinosa, M. P., and Neuman, C. (2003). IQ on the rise: the Flynn effect in rural Kenyan children. *Psychological Science,* 14, 215–219.

Daly, M. and Wilson, M. (1983). *Sex, Evolution, and Behavior.* Second Edition. Boston: P.W.S. Publishers.

Dan, L., Yu, J., Vandenberg, S. G., Yuemei, Z., and Caihong, T. (1990). Report on Shanghai norms of the Chinese translation of the Weschsler Intelligence Scale for Children - Revised. *Psychological Reports,* 67, 531–541.

Dawkins, R. (1988). *The Blind Watchmaker.* London: Penguin.

Deary, I. J. (2000). *Looking Down on Human Intelligence.* Oxford: Oxford University Press.

Deary, I. J. (2004). Intelligence Differences. In R. L. Gregory (Ed.), *The Oxford Companion to the Mind.* Oxford: Oxford University Press.

Deary, I. J., Whalley, L. J., Lemmon, H., Crawford, J. R., and Starr, J. M. (2000). The stability of individual differences in mental ability from childhood to old age: Follow-up of the 1932 Scottish Mental Ability Survey. *Intelligence,* 28, 49–56.

De Bertoli, L. and Creswell, J. (2004). *Australian Indigenous Students in PISA 2000.* Melbourne: Australian Council for Educational Research.

Dennis, W. (1957). Performance of Near Eastern children on the Draw-a-Man test. *Child Development,* 28, 427–430.

Diamond, J. (1998). *Guns, Germs, and Steel: A Short History of Everybody for the Last 13,000 Years.* London: Vintage.

Dickerson, R. E. (2004). Exponential Correlation of IQ and the Wealth of Nations. Unpublished manuscript.

Dobzhansky, T., Ayala, F. J., Stebbins, G. L., and Valentine, J. W. (1977). *Evolution.* San Francisco: W.H. Freeman and Company.

Dodge, P. R., Palkes, H., Fierro-Benitez, R., and Ramirez, I. (1969). Effect on intelligence of iodine in oil administration to young adult Andean children. In J. B. Stanbury (Ed.), *Endemic Goitre.* Washington, D.C.: Pan American Health Organization.

Dowrick, Steve. (2003). "Income-based Measures of Average Well-being." Paper presented at the UNU/WIDER conference on *Inequality, Poverty, and Human Well-being,* 30-31 May 2003, Helsinki, Finland.

Dowrick, S. and Akmal, M. (2003). Contradictory Trends in Global Income Inequality: A Tale of Two Biases. Paper presented at the UNU/WIDER conference on *Inequality, Poverty, and Human Well-being,* 30-31 May 2003, Helsinki, Finland.

Drèze, J. and Sen, A. (2002). *India: Development and Participation.* Second Edition. Oxford: Oxford University Press.

Dronkers, J. (1999). Jeugdige intelligentie en later succes in onderwijs en beroep (Children's intelligence and success in education and work later on). *Psychologie & Maatschappij,* 87, 152–165.

Duncan, O. D. (1968). Ability and achievment. *Eugenics Quarterly,* 15, 1–11.

Duncan, O. D., Fetherman, D. L., and Duncan, B. (1972). *Socio-economic Background and Achievement.* New York: Seminar Press.

Durbow, E. H., Schaefer, B. A., and Jimerson, S. (2002). Diverging academic paths in rural Caribbean Children. *School Psychology International,* 23, 155–168.

Easterlin, R. A. (1981). Why isn't the whole world developed? *Journal of Economic History,* 41, 1–18.

Easterly, W. (2002). *The Elusive Quest for Growth: Economists' Adventures and Misadventures in the Tropics.* Cambridge, Mass.: The MIT Press.

Economic Freedom of the World. See Gwartney and Lawson.

Economic Freedom of the World: 2004 Annual Report. (2004). The Fraser Institute. www.freetheworld.com/.

The Economist. (2003). If you consider people, not countries, global inequality is falling rapidly, August 23, p. 56.

El-Mneizel, A. F. (1987). Development and psychometric analysis of a Jordanian adaptation of the Kaufman Assessment Battery for Children. Ph.D. thesis, University of Alabama.

Engelbrecht, H. J. (2003). Human capital and economic growth: cross-sectional evidence from OECD countries. *The Economic Record*, 79, S40–S51.

Engels, F. (1985[1884]). *The Origin of the Family, Private Property, and the State*. Introduction by Michèle Barrett. Harmondsworth, England: Penguin Books.

Erikson, R. (1995). Description of Inequality: The Swedish Approach to Welfare Research. In M. C. Nussbaum and A. Sen (Eds.), *The Quality of Life*. Oxford: Clarendon Press.

Ervik, A. O. (2003). *IQ and the Wealth of Nations. The Economic Journal*, 113, No. 488, F406–F407.

Esterhuysen, P. (Ed.). (1998). *Africa A-Z. Continental and Country Profiles*. Pretoria, South Africa: Africa Institute of South Africa.

The Europa World Year Book. (1996–2004). London: Europa Publications.

Evans, E. M., Schweingruber, H., and Stevenson, H. W. (2002). Gender differences in interest and knowledge acquisition: the United States, Taiwan, and Japan. *Sex Roles*, 47, 153–167.

Eysenck, H. J. (1998). *Intelligence*. New Brunswick, N.J.: Transaction.

Fagerlind, I. (1975). *Formal education and adult earnings*. Stockholm: Almqvist and Wiksell.

Fahmy, M. (1964). Initial exploring of the intelligence of Shilluk children. *Vita Humana*, 7, 164–177.

Fahrmeier, E. D. (1975). The effect of school attendance on intellectual development in Northern Nigeria. *Child Development*, 46, 281–285.

Falconer, D. S. (1960). *Introduction to Quantitative Genetics*. London: Longman.

Farron, O. (1966). The test performance of coloured children. *Educational Research*, 8, 42–57.

Fatouros, M. (1972). The influence of maturation and education on the development of abilities. In L. J. Cronbach and P. J. Drenth (Eds.), *Mental Test and Cultural Adaptation*. The Hague: Mouton.

Faverge, J. M. and Falmagne, J. C. (1962). On the interpretation of data in intercultural psychology. *Psychologia Africana*, 9, 22–96.

Ferguson, D. M. and Horwood, L. J. (1997). Sex differences in educational achievement in a New Zealand birth cohort. *New Zealand Journal of Educational Studies*, 32, 83–95.

Fernandez, M. (2001). A study of the intelligence of children in Brazil. *Mankind*

Quarterly, 42, 17–21.

Fernandez-Bellesteros, R., Juan-Espinoza, M., Colom, R., and Calero, M. D. (1997). Contextual and personal sources of individual differences in intelligence. In J. S. Carlson (Ed.), *Advances in Cognition and Educational Practice.* Greenwich, Cnn.: JAI Press.

Fick, M. L. (1929). Intelligence test results of poor white, native (Zulu), colored, and Indian school children and the social and educational implications. *South Africa Journal of Science,* 26, 904–920.

Fields, G. S. (1980). *Poverty, Inequality, and Development.* Cambridge: Cambridge University Press.

Fierro-Benitez, R., Cazar, R., and Sandoval, H. (1989). Early correction of iodine deficiency and late effects on psychomotor capabilities and migration. In G. R. De Long, J. Robbins, and P. G. Condliffe (Eds.), *Iodine and the Brain.* New York: Plenum.

Firebaugh, G. (2003). *The New Geography of Global Income Inequality.* Cambridge, Mass.: Harvard University Press.

Fish, J. M. (Ed.) (2002). *Race and Intelligence.* Mahwah, N.J.: Lawrence Erlbaum.

Fisher, R. A. (1929). *The Genetical Theory of Natural Selection.* Oxford: Clarendon Press.

Flaherty, M. (1997). The validity of tests of visuo-spatial skills in cross-cultural studies. *Irish Journal of Psychology,* 18, 439–412.

Flores, M. B. and Evans, G. T. (1972). Some differences in cognitive abilities between selected Canadian and Filipino students. *Multivariate Behavioral Research,* 7, 175–191.

Flynn, J. R. 1987. Massive IQ gains in 14 nations: What IQ tests really measure? *Psychological Bulletin,* 101, 171–191.

Flynn, J. R. (1991). *Asian Americans: Achievement Beyond IQ.* Hillsdale, N.J.: Lawrence Erlbaum.

Foster, J., López-Calva, L. F., and Székely, M. (2003). Measuring the Distribution of Human Development: Methodology and an Application to Mexico. Paper presented at the UNU/WIDER conference on *Inequality, Poverty, and Human Well-being,* 30-31 May 2003, Helsinki, Finland.

Frank, A. G. (1967). *Capitalism and Underdevelopment in Latin America: Historical Studies of Chile and Brazil.* New York: Monthly Review Press.

Freedom House. (2002). *Annual Survey of Freedom Country Scores 1972–73 to 2001–2002.* www.freedomhouse.org/research/freeworld/2002.

Freedom House. (2004). *Freedom in the World 2004. The Annual Survey of Political Rights and Civil Liberties.* Edited by Aili Piano and Arch Puddington. New York: Rowman & Littlefield Publishers.

Freeedom in the World. See Freedom House.

Frydman, M. and Lynn, R. (1989). The intelligence of Korean children adopted in Belgium. *Personality and Individual Differences,* 10, 1323–1326.

FSD1216 Democratization and Power Resources 1850-2000. (2003). Finnish Social Science Data Archive. Tampere: University of Tampere. www.fsd. uta.fi.

FSD1289 Measures of Democracy 1810-2002. (2003). Finnish Social Science Data Archive. Tampere: University of Tampere. www.fsd.uta.fi.

Fulker, D. W. (1978). Some implications of biometrical genetic analysis for psychological research. In J. R. Royce and L. P. Mos (Eds.), *Theoretical Advances in Behavior Genetics.* Netherlands: Sijthoff Noordhoff.

Gagne, F. and St. Pere, F. (2002). When IQ is controlled, does motivation still predict achievement? *Intelligence,* 30, 71–100.

Galler, J. R., Ramsey, F., and Forde, V. (1986). A follow-up study of the influence of early malnutrition on subsequent development. *Nutrition and Behavior,* 3, 211–222.

Galton, F. (1869). *Hereditary Genius: An Inquiry into Its Laws and Consequences.* London: Macmillan.

Gardner, H. S. (1998). *Comparative Economic Systems.* 2nd Ed. Philadelphia: Dryden Press.

Gasper, D. (2003). Human Well-being: Concepts and Conceptualization. Paper presented at the UNU/WIDER conference on *Inequality, Poverty, and Human Well-being,* 30-31 May 2003, Helsinki, Finland.

Geary, D. C., Hamson, C. O., Chen, G. P, Liu, F., Hoard, M. K., and Salthouse, T. A. (1997). Computational and reasoning abilities in arithmetic: cross-generational change in China and the United States. *Psychonomic Bulletin and Review,* 4, 425–430.

Geary, D. C., Liu, F., Chen, G. P., Salts, S. J., and Hoard, M. K. (1999). Contributions of computational fluency to cross-national differences in arithmetical reasoning abilities. *Journal of Educational Psychology,* 91, 716–719.

Georgas, J. G. and Georgas, C. (1972). A children's intelligence test for Greece. In L. J. Cronbach and P. J. D. Drenth (Eds.), *Mental Tests and Cultural Adaptation.* The Hague: Mouton.

Georgas, J., Weiss, L. G., van der Vijver, F. J., and Saklofske, D. H. (2003). A cross-cultural analysis of the WISC-111. In J. Georgas, L. G. Weiss, F. van der Vijver, and D. H. Saklofske (Eds.), *Culture and Children's Intelligence.* Amsterdam: Academic Press.

Gernet, J. (2002). *A History of Chinese Civilisation.* Translated by J. R. Foster and C. Hartman. London: The Folio Society.

Ghiselli, E. E. (1966). *The Validity of Occupational Aptitude Tests.* New York: Wiley.

Giddens, A. (1995). *Sociology.* Second Edition. Cambridge: Polity Press.

Gill, P. and Byrt, E. (1973). *The standardization of Raven's Progressive Matrices and the Mill Hill Vocabulary Scale for Irish school children aged 6–12 years.* University College, Cork: MA Thesis.

Ginsburg, H. P., Choi, E., Lopez, L. S., Netley, R., and Chao-Yuan, C. (1997). Happy birthday to you: early mathematical thinking of Asian, South American, and U.S. children. In T. Nunes and P. Bryant (Eds.), *Learning and Teaching Mathematics: An International Perspective.* Hove, U.K.: Psychology Press.

Giordani, B., Boivin, M. J., Opel, B., Nseyila, D. N., and Lauer, R. E. (1996). Use of the K-ABC with children in Zaire. *International Journal of Disability, Development, and Education, 43,* 5–24.

Glewwe, P. and Jaccoby, H. (1992). *Estimating the determinants of Cognitive Achievement in Low Income Countries.* Washington, D.C.: World Bank.

Global Corruption Report 2004. See Transparency International Corruption Perceptions Index.

Globerson, T. (1983). Mental capacity and cognitive functioning: developmental and social class differences. *Developmental Psychology, 19,* 225–230.

Goa, Y., Qian, M., and Wang, D. (1998). Changes in intelligence over 10 years (in Chinese). *Chinese Journal of Clinical Psychology, 6,* 185–186.

Godman, A. (1964). *The attainments and abilities of Hong Kong primary IV pupils: a first study.* Hong Kong: Hong Kong University Press.

Goosens, G. (1952a). Etalonage du Matrix 1947 de J. C. Raven. *Revue Belge de Psychologie et de Pedagogie, 14,* 74–80.

Goosens, G. (1952b). Une application du test d'intelligence de R. B. Cattell. *Revue Belge de Psychologie et de Pedagogie, 14,* 115–124.

Gordon, R. H. (1976). Diagnostic compliance in Rorschach interpretation as a function of group member status. *Journal of Consulting and Clinical Psychology, 44,* 826–831.

Gottfredson, L. S. (1997). Editorial; Mainstream science on intelligence. *Intelligence, 24,* 13–24.

Gottfredson, L. S. (2004). Intelligence: is it the epidemiologists' elusive fundamental cause of social class inequalities in health? *Journal of Personality and Social Psychology*, 86, 174–199.

Grantham-McGregor, S. M., Powell, C., Walker, S. P., Chang, S., and Fletcher, P. (1994). The long-term follow-up of severely malnourished children who participated in an intervention program. *Child Development*, 65, 428–439.

Grigolenko, E. L. and Sternberg, R. J. (2001). Analytical, creative, and practical intelligence as predictors of self-reported adaptive functioning: a case study in Russia. *Intelligence*, 29, 57–73.

Grusky, D. P. (1994). Introduction. In D. P. Grusky (Ed.), *Social Stratification: Class, Race, and Gender in Sociological Perspective*. Boulder: Westview Press.

Gupta, G. C. and Gupta, S. (1966). Norms for Raven's Colored Progressive Matrices. *Manus*, 13, 87–89.

Gurr, T. R. and Jaggers, K. (1999). *Polity98 Project. Regime Characteristics 1800-1998*. www.bsos.umd.edu/cidcm/polity/.

Guthke, J. and Al-Zoubi, A. (1987). Kulturspezifische differenzen in den Coloured Progressive Matrices (CPM) und in einer lerntestvariante der CPM. *Psychologie in Erziehung und Unterricht*, 34, 306–311.

Gwartney, J. D. and Lawson, R. A. (2000). *Economic Freedom of the World: 2000 Annual Report*. Canada: The Fraser Institute.

Gwartney, J. D. and Lawson, R. A. (2004). *Economic Freedom of the World: 2004 Annual Report*. www.freetheworld.com/release.html.

Hadidjaja, P., Bonang, E., Suyardi, A., Abidin, A. N., Ismid, I. S., and Margono, S. S. (1998). The effect of intervention methods on nutritional status and cognitive function of primary school children with *ascaris lumbricoides*. *American Journal of Tropical Medicine*, 59, 791–795.

Hamers, J. H. M., Hessels, M. G. P., and Pennings, A. H. (1966). Learning potential of ethnic minority children. *European Journal of Psychological Assessment*, 12, 183–192.

Hansen, K. T., Heckman, J. J., and Mullen, K. J. (2004). The effect of schooling and ability on achievement test scores. *Journal of Econometrics*, 121, 39–98.

Hanusheck, E. A. and Kimko, D. D. (2000). Schooling, labor-force quality, and the growth of nations. *American Economic Review*, 90, 1184–1208.

Harkness, S. (2003). Social and Political Indicators of Human Well-being. Paper presented at the UNU/WIDER conference on *Inequality, Poverty, and Human Well-being*, 30-31 May 2003, Helsinki, Finland.

Harrison, L. E. and Huntington, S. P. (2000). *Culture Matters: How Values Shape Human Progress.* New York: Basic Books.

Hass, R. G., Chaudhary, N., Kleyman, E., Nussbaum, A., Pulizzi, A., and Tison, J. (2000). The Relationship Between the Theory of Evolution and the Social Sciences, Particularly Psychology. In D. LeCroy and P. Moller (Eds.), *Evolutionary Perspectives on Human Reproductive Behavior.* New York: New York Academy of Sciences.

Hause, J. C. (1971). Ability and schooling as determinants of lifetime earnings. *American Economic Review,* 61, 289–298.

Hauser, R. M., Sewell, W. H., and Alwin, D. F. (1973). High school effects on achievement. In W. H. Sewell, R. M. Hauser, and D. L. Featherman (Eds.), *Schooling and Achievement in American Society.* New York: Academic Press.

Heath, A. C., Berg, K., Eaves, L. J., Solas, H. M., Corey, L. A., Sundet, J., Magnus, P., and Nance, W. E. (1985). Educational policy and the heritability of educational attainment. *Nature,* 314, 734–736.

Helsingin Sanomat. (2004). Suomi päihitti muut OECD-maat matematiikan taidoissa, December 7, p. 6.

The Heritage Foundation. See *The Index of Economic Freedom.*

Herodotus. (1972). *The Histories.* Translated by Aubrey de Sélincourt, revised by A. R. Burn. Harmondsworth, England: Penguin Books.

Herrman, M. A. and Hogben, L. (1932). The intellectual resemblance of twins. *Proceedings of the Royal Society of Edinburgh,* 53, 105–129.

Herrnstein, R. J. and Murray, C. (1994). *The Bell Curve: Intelligence and Class Structure in American Life.* New York: The Free Press.

Hertzig, M., Birch, H. G., Richardson, S. A., and Tizard, J. (1972). Intellectual levels of school children malnourished during the first two years of life. *Pediatrics,* 49, 814–824.

Heyneman, S. P. (1997). The quality of education in the Middle East and North Africa. *International Journal of Educational Development,* 17, 449–466.

Heyneman, S. P. and Jamison, D. T. (1980). Student learning in Uganda. *Comparative Education Review,* 24, 207–220.

Hicks, D. (2003). Inequalities, Agency, and Well-being. Paper presented at the UNU/WIDER conference on *Inequality, Poverty, and Human Well-being,* 30-31 May 2003, Helsinki, Finland.

Hobbes, T. (1651) (reprinted 1985). *Leviathan.* London: Routledge.

Hohnen, B. and Stevenson, J. (1999). The structure of genetic influences on general cognitive, language, phonological, and reading abilities.

Developmental Psychology, 35, 590–603.

Holding, P. A., Taylor, H. G., Kazungu, S. D., and Mkala, T. (2004). Assessing cognitive outcomes in a rural African population: development of a neuropsychological battery in Kilifi district. *Journal of the International Neuropsychological Society*, 10, 246–260.

Holzinger, K. H. (1929). The relative effect of nature and nurture influences on twin differences. *Journal of Educational Psychology*, 20, 241–248.

Hsu, C.-C. (1971). Chinese children's responses to Raven's Colored Progressive Matrices. *Journal of the Formosan Medical Association*, 70, 579–593.

Hsu, C.-C., (1976). The learning potential of first graders in Taipei city as measured by Raven's Coloured Progressive Matrices. *Acta Pediatrica Sinica*, 17, 262–274.

Hsu, C.-C., See, R., and Lin, C.-C. (1973). Assessment of learning potential of Chinese children with Raven's Standard Progressive Matrices. *Journal of the Formosan Medical Association*, 72, 658–670.

Huarte, J. (1575). *Examen de Ingenios*. Amsterdam: Da Capo Press. Published in English in 1594 as *A Triall of Wits*. London: Richard Watkins.

Human Development Report. See UNDP.

Hunter, J. E. (1986). Cognitive ability, cognitive aptitudes, job knowledge, and job performance. *Journal of Vocational Behavior*, 29, 340–362.

Hunter, J. E. and Hunter, R. F. (1984). Validity and utility of alternative predictors of job performance. *Psychological Bulletin*, 96, 72–98.

Husen, T. (1951). The influence of schooling on IQ. *Theoria*, 17, 61–88.

Index of Economic Freedom. (2003). Washington, D.C.: Heritage Foundation. www.heritage.org/.

Ishikuma, T., Moon, S., and Kaufman, A. S. (1988). Sequential-simultaneous analysis of Japanese children's performance on the Japanese McCarthy scales. *Perceptual and Motor Skills*, 66, 355–362.

Itzkoff, S. W. (2000). *The Inevitable Domination by Man: An Evolutionary Detective Story*. Ashfield, Mass.: Paideia Publishers.

Jacobs, N., van Gestel, S., Derom, C., Thiery, E., Vernon, P., Derom, R., and Vlietinck, R. (2001). Heritability estimates of intelligence in twins: effect of chorion type. *Behavior Genetics*, 31, 209–216.

Jaworowska, A. and Szustrova, T. (1991). *Podrecznik Do Testu Matryc Ravena*. Warsaw: Pracownia Testow Psychologicznych.

Jencks, C. (1972). *Inequality*. New York: Basic Books.

Jencks, C. and Phillips, M. (1998). *The Black-White Test Score Gap*. Washington, D.C.: Brookings Institution.

Jensen, A. R. (1980). *Bias in Mental Testing*. London: Methuen.

Jensen, A. R. (1998). *The g Factor: The Science of Mental Ability*. Westport, Conn.: Praeger.

Johnson, D. L., Johnson, C. A., and Price-Williams, D. (1967). The Draw-a-Man test and Raven Progressive Matrices performance of Guatemalan boys and Latino children. *Revista Interamericana de Psicologia*, 1, 143–157.

Jones, S. (1992). Genetic diversity in humans. In S. Jones, R. Martin, and D. Pilbeam (Eds.), *The Cambridge Encyclopedia of Human Evolution*. Cambridge: Cambridge University Press.

Jordheim, G. D. and Olsen, I. A. (1963). The use of a non-verbal test of intelligence in the trust territory of the Pacific. *American Anthropologist*, 65, 1122–1125.

Joseph, A. and Murray, V. F. (1951). *Chamorros and Carolinians of Spain*. Westport, Conn.: Greenwood.

Judge, T. A., Higgins, C. A., Thoresen, C. J., and Barrick, W. R. (1999). The big five personality test, general mental ability, and career success across the life span. *Personnel Psychology*, 52, 621–652.

Juel-Nielson, N. (1980). *Individual and environment: monozygotic twins reared apart*. New York: International University Press.

Kagitcibasi, C. (1972). Application of the D-48 test in Turkey. In L. J. Cronbach and P. J. D. Drenth (Eds.), *Mental Tests and Cultural Adaptation*. The Hague: Mouton.

Kamarck, A. M. (1976). *The Tropics and Economic Development: A Provocative Inquiry into the Poverty of Nations*. Published for the World Bank. Baltimore: The Johns Hopkins University Press.

Karatnycky, A., Motyl, A., and Schnetzer, A. (Eds.). (2001). *Nations in transit 2001: Civil Society, Democracy and Markets in East Central Europe and the Newly Independent States*. New Brunswick, N. J.: Transaction Publishers.

Kaufman, A. S., McLean, J. E., Ishikuma, T., and Moon, S. B. (1989). Integration of literature on the intelligence of Japanese children and analysis of the data from a sequential-simultaneous perspective. *School Psychology International*, 10, 173–183.

Kayizzi-Mugerwa, S. (Ed.). (2003). *Reforming Africa's Institutions: Ownership, Incentives, and Capabilities*. Tokyo: United Nations University Press.

Kazanava, S. (2005). Income inequality and economic development have no effects on life expectancy net of national IQs in 126 countries. Unpublished.

Kazulin, A. (1998). Profiles of immigrant students' cognitive performance on Raven's Progressive Matrices. *Perceptual and Motor Skills,* 87, 1311–1314.

Keller, C. and Fetterly, K. (1978). Legitimacy and mother's education as risk factors in post neonatal mortality. Los Angeles: Proceedings of the American Public Health Association.

Keller, L. M., Bouchard, T. J., Arvey, R. D., Segal, N., and Dawis, R. V. (1992). Work values: genetic and environmental influences. *Journal of Applied Psychology,* 77, 79–88.

Kendall, I. M. (1976). The predictive validity of a possible alternative to the Classification Test Battery. *Psychologia Africana,* 16, 131–146.

Kennedy, W. A., Van der Reit, V., and White, J. C. (1963). A normative study of intelligence and achievement of Negro schoolchildren in the southeastern United States. *Monographs of the Society for Research in Child Development,* 28, no. 6.

Klasen, S. and Grün, C. (2003). Growth, Income Distribution, and Well-Being: Comparisons across Space and Time. Paper presented at the UNU/WIDER conference on *Inequality, Poverty, and Human Well-being,* 30-31 May 2003, Helsinki, Finland.

Klingelhofer, E. L. (1967). Performance of Tanzanian secondary school pupils on the Raven Standard Progressive Matrices test. *Journal of Social Psychology,* 72, 205–215.

Kothari, R. (1993). *Poverty: Human Consciousness and the Amnesia of Development.* London: Zed Books.

Kurian, G. T. (1987). *Encyclopedia of the Third World.* Third Edition. New York: Facts on File.

Kurth, E. von. (1969). Erholung der leistungsnormen bei den farbigen Progressiv Matrizen. *Zeitschrift für Psychologie,* 177, 85–90.

Kyöstiö, O. K. (1972). Divergence among school beginners caused by different cultural influences. In L. J. Cronbach and P. J. Drenth (Eds.), *Mental Tests and Cultural Adaptation.* The Hague: Mouton.

Lai, T. J., Guo, Y. L., Guo, N. W., and Hsu, C.-C. (2001). Effects of prenatal exposure to polychlorinated biphenyls on cognitive development in children: a longitudinal study in Taiwan. *British Journal of Psychiatry,* 178, 49–52.

Lancer, I. and Rim, T. (1984). Intelligence, family size, and sibling age spacing. *Personality and Individual Differences,* 5, 151–157.

Landes, D. S. (1998). *The Wealth and Poverty of Nations: Why Some Are So Rich and Some So Poor.* New York: W.W. Norton and Company.

Landman, J. (1988). *Appendix to the Manual of the Junior South African Individual Scales.* Pretoria: Human Sciences Research Council.

Laroche, J. L. (1959). Effets de repetition du Matrix 38 sur les resultats d'enfants Katangais. *Bulletin du Centre d'etudes et Reserches Psychotechniques,* 1, 85–99.

Latouche, G. L. and Dormeau, G. (1956). La foration professionelle rapide en Afrique Equatoriale Francaise. Brazzaville: Centre d'Etude des Problems du Travail.

Leftwich, A. (2000). *States of Development: On the Primacy of Politics in Development.* Cambridge: Polity Press.

Lenski, G. (1970). *Human Societies: A Macrolevel Introduction to Sociology.* New York: McGraw-Hill Book Company.

Lenski, G., and Lenski, J. (1987). *Human Societies: An Introduction to Macrosociology.* Fifth Edition. New York: McGraw-Hill Book Company.

Lewontin, R. (1982). *Human Diversity.* New York: Scientific American Books.

Li, C. C. (1975). *Path Analysis–A primer.* Pacific Grove, Cal.: Boxwood Press.

Li, X., Sano, H., and Merwin, J. C. (1996). Perception and reasoning abilities among American, Japanese, and Chinese adolescents. *Journal of Adolescent Research,* 11, 173–193.

Lichtenstein, P., Pedersen, N. L., and McClearn, G. E. (1992). The origins of individual differences in occupational status and educational level: a study of twins reared apart and together. *Acta Sociologica,* 35, 13–25.

Lieblich, A. and Kugelmass, S. (1981). Patterns of intellectual ability of Arab school children in Israel. *Intelligence,* 5, 311–320.

Lim, T. K. (1994). Gender-related differences in intelligence: application of confirmatory factor analysis. *Intelligence,* 19, 179–192.

Liu, J., Raine, A., Venables, P. H., Dalais, C., and Mednick, S. A. (2003). Malnutrition at age 3 years and lower cognitive ability at age 11 years. *Archives of Pediatric and Adolescent Medicine,* 157, 593–600.

Llanos, Z. M. (1974). *El funcionamiento intelectuel de los ninos en las zones marginales de Lima.* Montevideo, Uruguay: Instituto Americano de Nino.

Lloyd, J. and Barenblatt, L. (1984). Intrinsic intellectuality: Its relations to social class, intelligence, and achievement. *Journal of Personality and Social Psychology,* 46, 646–654.

Lowenthal, D. (1987). Montesquieu. In L. Strauss and J. Cropsey (Eds.), *History of Political Philosophy.* Third Edition. Chicago and London: The University of Chicago Press.

Lubinski, D., Benhow, C., Webb, R. M., and Bleske-Rechek, A. (2005). Tracking exceptional human capital over two decades. *Psychological Science* (in press).

Lubinski, D. and Humpreys, L. G. (1996). Seeing the forest from the trees: when predicting the behavior or status of groups, correlate means. *Psychology, Public Policy, and Law*, 2, 363–376.

Lynn, R. (1977a). The intelligence of the Japanese. *Bulletin of the British Psychological Society*, 30, 69–72.

Lynn, R. (1977b). The intelligence of the Chinese and Malays in Singapore. *Mankind Quarterly*, 18, 125–128.

Lynn, R. (1979). The social ecology of intelligence in the British Isles. *British Journal of Social and Clinical Psychology*, 18, 1–12.

Lynn, R. (1980). The social ecology of intelligence in France. *British Journal of Social and Clinical Psychology*, 19, 325–331.

Lynn, R. (1981). The social ecology of intelligence in the British Isles, France, and Spain. In M. P. Friedman, J. P. Das, and N. O'Connor (Eds.), *Intelligence and Learning*. New York: Plenum.

Lynn, R. (1990). The role of nutrition in secular increases of intelligence. *Personality and Individual Differences*, 11, 273–285.

Lynn, R. (1991a). Race differences in intelligence: a global perspective. *Mankind Quarterly*, 31, 254–296.

Lynn, R. (1991b). The evolution of race differences in intelligence. *Mankind Quarterly*, 32, 99–121.

Lynn, R. (1991c). Intelligence in China. *Social Behavior and Personality*, 19, 1–4.

Lynn, R. (1994a). The intelligence of Ethiopian immigrant and Israeli adolescents. *International Journal of Psychology*, 29, 55–56.

Lynn, R. (1994b). Sex differences in brain size and intelligence: a paradox resolved. *Personality and Individual Differences*, 17, 257–271.

Lynn, R. (1994c). Some reinterpretations of the Minnesota Trans-racial Adoption Study. *Intelligence*, 19, 21–28.

Lynn, R. (1997). Intelligence in Taiwan. *Personality and Individual Differences*, 22, 585–586.

Lynn, R. (2001). Intelligence in Russia. *Mankind Quarterly*, 42, 151-154.

Lynn, R. (2002a). Racial and ethnic differences in psychopathic personality. *Personality and Individual Differences*, 32, 273–316.

Lynn, R. (2002b). Skin color and intelligence in African Americans. *Population and Environment*, 23, 365–375.

Lynn, R. (2003). The Geography of Intelligence. In H. Nyborg (Ed.), *The Scientific Study of General Intelligence. Tribute to Arthur R. Jensen.* Amsterdam: Pergamon.

Lynn, R. (2004). The intelligence of American Jews. *Personality and Individual Differences,* 36, 201–207.

Lynn, R. (2006). *Race differences in Intelligence: An Evolutionary Analysis.* Augusta, Georgia: Washington Summit Publishers.

Lynn, R. (2005a). The heritability of earnings. Unpublished.

Lynn, R., Allik, J., Pullman, H., and Laidra, J. (2002). A Study of the IQ in Estonia. *Psychological Reports,* 95, 611–612.

Lynn, R., Backhoff, E., and Contreras, L. A. (2005). Ethnic and Racial Differences in the Standard Progressive Matrices in Mexico. *Journal of Biosocial Science,* 37, 107–113.

Lynn, R., Chan, J. W. C., and Eysenck, H. J. (1991). Reaction times and intelligence in Chinese and British children. *Perceptual and Motor Skills,* 72, 443–452.

Lynn, R. and Chan, P. W. (2003). Sex differences on the Progressive Matrices: some data from Hong Kong. *Journal of Biosocial Science,* 35, 145–154.

Lynn, R. and Dziobon, J. (1980). On the intelligence of the Japanese and other Mongoloid peoples. *Personality and Individual Differences,* 1, 95–96.

Lynn, R. and Hampson, S. L. (1986). The rise of national intelligence: Evidence from Britain, Japan, and the USA. *Personality and Individual Differences,* 7, 230–332.

Lynn, R. and Hampson, S. (1986a). The structure of Japanese abilities: an analysis in terms of the hierarchical model of intelligence. *Current Psychological Research and Reviews,* 4, 309–322.

Lynn, R. and Hampson, S. (1987). Further evidence on the cognitive abilities of the Japanese: Data from the WPPSI. *International Journal of Behavioral Development,* 10, 23–36.

Lynn, R., Hampson, S., and Bingham, R. (1987a). Japanese, British, and American adolescents compared for Spearman's g and for the verbal, numerical and visuo-spatial abilities. *Psychologia,* 30, 137–144.

Lynn, R., Hampson, S. L., and Iwawaki, S. (1987b). Abstract reasoning and spatial abilities among American, British, and Japanese adolescents. *Mankind Quarterly,* 27, 397–434.

Lynn, R., Hampson, S., and Lee, M. (1988). The intelligence of Chinese children in Hong Kong. *School Psychology International,* 9, 29–32.

Lynn, R., Hampson S., and Magee, M. (1984). Home background, intelligence, personality, and education as predictors of unemployment in young people. *Personality and Individual Differences*, 5, 547–549.

Lynn, R. and Hattori, K. (1990). The heritability of intelligence in Japan. *Behavior Genetics*, 20, 545–546.

Lynn, R. and Holmshaw, M. (1990). Black-white differences in reaction times and intelligence. *Social Behavior and Personality*, 18, 299–308.

Lynn, R. and Kazlauskaite, V. (2002). A study of IQ in Lithuania. *Perceptual and Motor Skills*, 95, 354.

Lynn, R., Mylotte, A., Ford, F., and McHugh, M. (1997). The heritability of intelligence and social security in four to six year olds: a study of Irish twins. *Irish Journal of Psychology*, 18, 439–443.

Lynn, R. and Owen, K. (1994). Spearman's hypothesis and test score differences between whites, Indians, and blacks in South Africa. *Journal of General Psychology*, 121, 27–36.

Lynn, R., Pagliari, C., and Chan, J. (1988). Intelligence in Hong Kong measured for Spearman's *g* and the visuospatial and verbal primaries. *Intelligence*, 12, 423–433.

Lynn, R., Paspalanova, E., Stetinsky, D., and Tzenova, P. (1998). Intelligence in Bulgaria. *Psychological Reports*, 82, 912–914.

Lynn, R., Pullman, H., and Allik, J. (2003). A new estimate of the IQ in Estonia. *Psychological Reports*, 97, 662–664.

Lynn, R. and Song, J. M. (1994). General intelligence, visuospatial, and verbal abilities of Korean children. *Personality and Individual Differences*, 16, 363–364.

Lynn, R. and Vanhanen, T. (2002). *IQ and the Wealth of Nations*. Westport, Conn.: Praeger.

MacArthur, R. S., Irvine, S. H., and Brimble, A. R. (1964). *The Northern Rhodesia Mental Ability Survey*. Lusaka: Rhodes Livingstone Institute.

Mackintosh, N. J. (1998). *IQ and Human Intelligence*. Oxford: Oxford University Press.

McCall, R. B. (1977). Childhood IQs as predictors of adult educational and occupational status. *Science*, 197, 482–483.

McDaniel, M. A. and Whetzel, D. L. (2004). IQ and the Wealth of Nations: Prediction of GDP Not Dependent on Precise *g* Estimates. Paper presented at the Fifth Annual Conference of International Society for Intelligence Research. New Orleans. December, 2004.

McGillivray, M. (2003a). Composite Indices of Human Well-being: A Review. Paper presented at the UNU/WIDER conference on *Inequality, Poverty, and Human Well-being,* 30–31 May 2003, Helsinki, Finland.

McGillivray, M. (2003b). Capturing non-Economic Dimensions of Human Well-being. Paper presented at the UNU/WIDER conference on *Inequality, Poverty, and Human Well-being,* 30–31 May 2003, Helsinki, Finland.

McIntyre, G. A. (1938). *The Standardisation of Intelligence Tests in Australia.* Melbourne: University Press.

Maddison, A. (1995). *Monitoring the World Economy 1820-1992.* Development Centre Studies. Paris: Development Centre of the Organisation for Economic Co-operation and Development.

Maddison, A. (1999). *Chinese Economic Performance in the Long Run.* Development Centre Studies. Paris: Development Centre of the Organisation for Economic Co-operation and Development.

Maddison, A. (2001). *The World Economy: A Millenium Perspective.* Development Centre Studies. Paris: Development Centre of the Organisation for Economic Co-operation and Development.

Maddison, A. (2003). *The World Economy: Historical Statistics.* Paris: Development Centre of the Organisation for Economic Co-operation and Development.

Majumdar, P. K. and Nundi, P. C. (1971). Raven's Standard Progressive Matrices in two different populations. *Journal of the Indian Academy of Applied Psychology,* 8, 30–33.

Maller, J. B. (1933). Vital indices and their relation to psychological and social factors. *Human Biology,* 5, 94–121.

Malthus, T. R. (1960). *On Population.* The complete text of the first edition together with major portions of the seventh edition, edited and introduced by Gertrude Himmelfarb. New York: Random House.

Manley, D. R. (1963). Mental ability in Jamaica. *Social and Economic Studies,* 12, 51–77.

Mann, M. (1986). *The Sources of Social Power: A history of power from the beginning to A.D. 1769.* Cambridge: Cambridge University Press.

Mann, V. A., Sasanuma, S., Sakuma, N., and Masaki, S. (1990). Sex differences in cognitive abilities: a cross cultural perspective. *Neuropsychologia,* 28, 1063–1077.

Marinovich, R. I., Sparosvich, H. F., Santana, M. C. D., Game, J. H., Gomez, C. C., and Murinkovich, D. I. (2000). Estudio de la capacidad intellectuel (test de Matrices Progressivas de Raven) en escolares Chilenos de 5 a 18 anos. *Revista de Psicologia General y Aplicada,* 53, 5–30.

Martin, N. G. (1975). The inheritance of scholastic abilities in a sample of twins 11. *Annals of Human Genetics,* 39, 219–229.

Martinelli, V. and Lynn, R. (2005). Sex differences on verbal and non-verbal abilities among primary school children in Malta. Unpublished.

Marx, K. and Engels, F. (1969). *Selected Works in three volumes.* Moscow: Progress Publishers.

Mayer-Foulkes, D. (2003). Global Divergence. Paper presented at the UNU/WIDER conference on *Inequality, Poverty, and Human Well-being,* 30–31 May 2003, Helsinki, Finland.

Mehryar, A. H., Shapurian, R., and Bassiri, T. (1972). A preliminary report on a Persian adaption of Heim's AH4 test. *Journal of Psychology,* 80, 167–180.

Mehryar, A. H., Tashakkori, A., Yousefi, F., and Khajavi, F. (1987). The application of the Goodenough-Harris Draw-a-Man test to a group of Iranian children in the city of Shiraz. *British Journal of Educational Psychology,* 57, 401–406.

Miller, E. (2002). Differential Intelligence and National Income. A review of *IQ and the Wealth of Nations. Journal of Social, Political & Economic Studies,* 27, 413–524.

Miller, P., Mulvey, C., and Martin, N. (1995). What do twin studies reveal about the economic returns to education? *American Economic Review,* 85, 586–599.

Miron, M. (1977). A validation study of a transferred group intelligence test. *International Journal of Psychology,* 12, 193–205.

Misawa, G., Motegi, M., Fujita, K., and Hattori, K. (1984). A comparative study of intellectual abilities of Japanese and American children on the Columbia Mental Maturity Scale. *Personality and Individual Differences,* 5, 173–181.

Mitchell, T. D., Hulme, M., and New, M. (2001). Climate data for political areas. *Observations* 109. www.cru.uea.av.uk/.

Mitchell, T. D., Hulme, M., and New, M. (2003). *A comprehensive set of climate scenarios for Europe and the globe.* www.cru.uea.ac.uk/.

Modiano, N. (1962). Mental testing among Tzeltal and Tzotzil children. *Proceedings of the 35th International Congress of Americanists.* Mexico City, Mexico.

Mohanty, A. K. and Babu, N. (1983). Bilingualism and metalinguistic ability among Kond tribals in Orissa, India. *Journal of Social Psychology,* 121, 15–22.

Montesquieu, C. de. (1961[1748]). *De l'Esprit des lois.* Texte ètabli avec une introduction, des notes et des variantes par Gonzague Truc. Paris: Editions Garnier Fréres.

Montesquieu, C. de. (1989). *The Spirit of Laws*. Translated and edited by Anne M. Cohler, Basia Carolyn Miller, and Harold Samuel Stone. Cambridge: Cambridge University Press.

Moon, S. B. (1988). A Cross Cultural Study of the Kaufman Assessment Battery for children with Korean children. Ph.D. thesis, University of Alabama.

Moyles, E. W. and Wolins, M. (1973). Group care and intellectual development. *Developmental Psychology*, 4, 370–380.

Murnane, R., Willett, J. B., Braatz, M. J., and Duhaldeborde, Y. (2001). Do different dimensions of male high school students' skills predict labour market success a decade later? Evidence from the NLSY. *Education Economic Review*, 20, 311–320.

Murray, C. (1997). IQ and economic success. *Public Interest*, 128, 21–35.

Murray, C. (1998). *Income inequality and IQ*. Washington, D.C.: AEI Press.

Murray, L. S. (1983). Nutritional status and development of St. Lucian preschool children. M.Sc. Thesis. U.W.I, Mona.

Nafziger, E. W. (1997). *The Economics of Developing Countries*. 3rd Ed. Upper Saddle River, N.J.: Prentice Hall.

Natalicio, L. (1968). Aptidatao general, status social e sexo: um estudio de adolescentes Brasileiros e norte-Americanos. *Revista Interamericanas de Psicologia*, 2, 25–34.

Nathawal, S. S. and Puri, P. (1995). A comparative study of MZ and DZ twins on Level I and Level II mental abilities and personality. *Journal of the Indian Academy of Applied Psychology*, 21, 545–546.

Neal, D. A. and Johnson, W. R. (1996). The role of pre-market factors in black-white wage differences. *Journal of Political Economy*, 104, 98–123.

Nechyba, T. (2004). Review of *IQ and the Wealth of Nations*. *Journal of Economic Literature*, 42, 220–221.

Neisser, U. (1996). Intelligence: Knowns and Unknowns. *American Psychologist*, 51, 77–101.

Nettle, D. (2003). Intelligence and class mobility in the British population. *British Journal of Psychology*, 94, 551–561.

The New Encyclopaedia Britannica, Volume 18, *Macropaedia*. (1985). Chicago: Encyclopaedia Britannica.

Newman, H. H., Freeman, F. M., and Holzinger, K. J. (1937). *Twins: A Study of heredity and Environment*. Chicago: University of Chicago Press.

Nisbett, R. E. (1998). Race, genetics, and IQ. In C. Jencks and M. Phillips (Eds.),

The Black-White Test Score Gap. Washington, D.C.: Brookings Institution Press.

Nissen, H. W., Machover, S. and Kinder, E. F. (1935). A study of performance tests given to a group of native African Negro children. *British Journal of Psychology*, 25, 308–355.

Nkaye, H. N., Huteau, M., and Bonnet, J. P. (1994). Retest effect on cognitive performance on the Raven Matrices in France and in the Congo. *Perceptual and Motor Skills*, 78, 503–510.

Notcutt, B. (1950). The measurement of Zulu intelligence. *Journal of Social Research*, 1, 195–206.

Nussbaum, M. C. and Sen, A. (Eds.). (1995). *The Quality of Life*. Oxford: Clarendon Press.

Nyborg, H. and Jensen, A. R. (2001). Occupation and income related to psychometric g. *Intelligence*, 29, 45–55.

OECD. (2003). *The PISA 2000 Study*. Paris: OECD.

OECD Programme for International Student Assessment (PISA). (2004). www.pisa.oecd.org.

Olson, M. (1996). Big Bills Left on the Sidewalk: Why Some Nations are Rich, and Others Poor? Distinguished Lecture on Economics in Government. *Journal of Economic Perspectives*, 10(2), 3–24.

Olson, M. (2000). *Power and Prosperity: Outgrowing Communist and Capitalist Dictatorships*. New York: Basic Books.

Ombredane, A., Robaye, F., and Robaye, E. (1952). Analyse des resultats d'une application experimentale du matrix 38 a 485 noirs Baluba. *Bulletin Centre d'etudes et Reserches Psychotechniques*, 7, 235–255.

Oppenheimer, S. (2003). *Out of Eden: The peopling of the world*. London: Constable.

Ortar, G. (1952). Standardization of the Wechsler Test for Intelligence for children in Israel. *Megamot*, 4, 87–100.

Osberg, L. and Sharpe, A. (2003). Human Well-being and Economic Well-being: What Values are Implicit in Current Indices? Paper presented at the UNU/WIDER conference on *Inequality, Poverty, and Human Well-being*, 30–31 May 2003, Helsinki, Finland.

O'Toole, B. I. and Stankov, L. (1992). Ultimate validity of psychological tests. *Personality and Individual Differences*, 13, 699–716.

Oven, K. (1992). The suitability of Raven's Progressive Matrices for various groups in South Africa. *Personality and Individual Differences*, 13, 149–159.

Paine, P., Dorea, J. G., Pasquali, L., and Monteiro, A. M. (1992). Growth and cognition in Brazilian school children: a spontaneously occurring intervention study. *International Journal of Behavioral Development*, 15, 169–183.

Pal, S., Shyam, R., and Singh, R. (1997). Genetic analysis of general intelligence *g*: a twin study. *Personality and Individual Differences*, 22, 779–780.

Palairet, M. R. (2004). Book review, *IQ and the Wealth of Nations*. *Heredity*, 92, 361–362.

Parker, P. M. (2000). *Physioeconomics. The Basis for Long-Run Economic Growth*. Cambridge, Mass.: The MIT Press.

Passé-Smith, J. T. (2003). Could It Be That the Whole World Is Already Rich? A Comparison of RGDP/pc and GNP/pc Measures. In M. A. Seligson and J. T. Passé-Smith (Eds.), *Development and Underdevelopment: The Political Economy of Global Inequality*. Third Edition. Boulder and London: Lynne Rienner Publishers.

Pederson, N. L., Plomin, R., Nesselroader, I. R., and McClearn, G. E. (1992). A quantitative genetic analysis of cognitive abilities during the second half of the life span. *Psychological Science*, 3, 346–353.

Persaud, G. (1972). *The performance of two samples of primary school children on two culture-free and two culture-bound tests of intelligence*. University of Stockholm: Institute of Applied Psychology.

Petrogiannis, K. S., Bardos, A. N., and Randou, E. (1999). Performance of Greek and American students on the Matrix Analogies Test. *School Psychology International*, 20, 233–238.

Philip's World Atlas. (1996). London: Chancellor.

Pieke, F. N. (1988). The social position of the Dutch Chinese: an outline. *China Information*, 3, 12–23.

Pind, J., Gunnarsdóttir, E. K., and Jóhanssesson, H. S. (2003). Raven's Standard Progressive Matrices: new school age norms and a study of the test's validity. *Personality and Individual Differences*, 34, 375–386.

Plomin, R. (1994). *Genetics and experience: The interplay between nature and nurture*. Thousands Oaks, Cal: Sage.

Plomin, R., DeFries, J. C., and McClearn, G. E. (1990). *Behavioral Genetics*. New York: Freeman.

Plomin, R., Loehlin, J. C., and DeFries, J. C. (1985). Genetic and environmental components of 'environmental' influences. *Developmental Psychology*, 21, 391–402.

The Politics of Aristotle or a Treatise on Government. (1952). Translated by William Ellis. London: J.M. Dent & Sons.

Pollitt, E., Hatgirat, P., Kotchabhaldi, N., Missell, L., and Valyasevi, A. (1989). Iron deficiency and educational achievement in Thailand. *American Journal of Clinical Nutrition*, 50, 687–697.

The Polyarchy Dataset. Vanhanen's Index of Democracy. (2003). www.prio.no/ cwp/vanhanen/.

Pons, A. L. (1974). Administration of tests outside the cultures of their origin. *26th Congress of the South African Psychological Association.*

Prifitera, A., Lawrence, L. G., and Saklofske, D. H. (1998). The WISC-111 in context. In A. Prifitera and D. H. Sakfloske (Eds.), *WISC-111 Clinical Use and Interpretation.* San Diego, Cal: Academic.

Proctor, B. E., Kranzler, J. H., Rosenbloom, A. L., Martinez, V., and Guevara-Aguire, J. (2000). An initial investigation of validation of the Matrix Analogies Test-Expanded Form in Ecuador. *Psychological Reports*, 86, 445–453.

Rabinowitz, M. B., Wang, J. D., and Soong, W. T. (1991). Dentine lead and child intelligence in Taiwan. *Archives of Environmental Health*, 46, 351–360.

Rahman, A., Macbool, E., and Zuberi, H. S. (2002). Lead-associated deficits in stature, mental ability and behavior in children in Karachi. *Annals of Tropical Paediatrics*, 22, 301–311.

Rahman, T., Mittelhammer, R. C., and Wandschneider, P. (2003). Measuring the Quality of Life Indicators across Countries: A Sensitivity Analysis of Well-being Indices. Paper presented at the UNU/WIDER conference on *Inequality, Poverty, and Human Well-being*, 30–31 May 2003, Helsinki, Finland.

Raine, A., Reynolds, C., Venables, P. H., and Mednick, S. A. (2002). Stimulation seeking and intelligence: a prospective longitudinal study. *Journal of Personality and Social Psychology*, 82, 663-674.

Rao, S. N. and Reddy, I. K. (1968). Development of norms for Raven's Coloured Progressive Matrices on elementary school children. *Psychological Studies*, 13, 105–107.

Raveau, F. H. M., Elster, E., and Lecoutre, J. P. (1976). Migration et acculturation differentiale. *International Review of Applied Psychology*, 25, 145–163.

Raven, J. (1981). *Irish and British Standardisations.* Oxford: Oxford Psychologists Press.

Raven, J. and Court, J. H. (1989). *Manual for Raven's Progressive Matrices and Vocabulary Scales.* London: Lewis.

Raven, J. C., Court, J. H., and Raven, J. (1995). *Coloured Progressive Matrices.* Oxford: Oxford Psychologists Press.

Raven, J. C., Court, J. H., and Raven, J. (1996). *Standard Progressive Matrices*. Oxford: Oxford Psychologists Press.

Raven, J. C., Court, J. H., and Raven, J. (1998). *Advanced Progressive Matrices*. Oxford: Oxford Psychologists Press.

Raven, J. (2000). The Raven's Progressive Matrices: Change and stability over culture and time. *Cognitive Psychology*, 41, 1–48.

Raven, J., Raven, J. C., and Court, J. H. (2000). *Standard Progressive Matrices*. Oxford: Oxford Psychologists Press.

Ray, D. (1998). *Development Economics*. Princeton, New Jersey: Princeton University Press.

Redmond, M. and Davies, F. R. (1940). *The Standardisation of Two Intelligence Tests*. Wellington: New Zealand Council for Educational Research.

Ree, M. J. and Earles, J. A. (1994). The ubiquitous predictiveness of *g*. In M. G. Ramsey, C. B. Walker, and J. H. Harris (Eds.), *Personal Selection and Classification*. Hillsdale: Erlbaum.

Reed, T. E. (1971). The population variance of the proportion of genetic admixture in human intergroup hybrids. *Proceedings of the National Academy of Science*, 68, 3168–3169.

Reid, N. and Gilmore, A. (1989). The Raven's Standard Progressive Matrices in New Zealand. *Psychological Test Bulletin*, 2, 25–35.

Reitman, R., Angleitner, A., and Strelau, J. (1997). Genetic and environmental influences on personality: a study of twins reared together using the self and peer report NEO-FFI scales. *Journal of Personality*, 65, 449–475.

Resing, W. C. M., Bleidhrody, N., and Drenth, P. J. D. (1986). Het gebruit van de RAKIT bij allochtoon etnische groeben. *Nederlands Tijdschrift voor de Psychologie*, 41, 179–188.

Richards, M. (2002). *IQ and the Wealth of Nations. Intelligence*, 30, 174–175.

Rimoldi, H. J. (1948). A note on Raven's Progressive Matrices Test. *Educational and Psychological Measurement*, 8, 347–352.

Risso, W. L. (1961). *El test de Matrice Progressivas y el test Domino*. Proceedings of the 1961 Conference of the Psychological Society of Uruguay.

Ritter, H. (1981). *Humangenetik: Grundlagen – Erkenntnisse – Entvicklungen*. Freiburg: Herder.

Roberts, J. T. and Hite, A. (Eds.). (2000). *From Modernization to Globalization: Perspectives on Development and Social Change*. Malden, Mass.: Blackwell Publishers.

Robin, R. W. and Shea, J. D. C. (1983). The Bender Gestalt visual motor test in

Papua New Guinea. *International Journal of Psychology*, 18, 263–270.

Rodd, W. G. (1959). A cross-cultural study of Taiwan's schools. *Journal of Social Psychology*, 50, 30–36.

Rousseau, J. J. (1974[1754]). *Discourse On the Origin and Basis of Inequality among Men*. In *The Essential Rousseau*, translated by Lowell Bair. New York: A Mentor Book, New American Library.

Rowe, D. C. (1994). *The Limits of Family Influence*. New York: Guildford.

Rowe, D. C., Vesterdal, W. J., and Rodgers, J. L. (1998). Herrnstein's syllogism: genetic and shared environmental influences on IQ, education, and income. *Intelligence, 26, 405–423*.

Rushton, J. P. (1995). *Race, Evolution, and Behavior: A life history perspective*. New Brunswick: Transaction Publishers.

Rushton, J. P. (2000). *Race, Evolution, and Behavior*. 2nd Special Abridged Edition. Port Huron, Mich: Charles Darwin Research Institute.

Rushton, J. P. (2003). The bigger bell curve: intelligence, national achievement, and the global economy. *Personality and Individual Differences*, 34, 367–372.

Sadek, A. A. M. (1972). A factor analytic study of musical abilities of Egyptian students taking music as a special subject. Ph.D. dissertation, University of London.

Sahin, N. and Duzen, E. (1994). Turkish standardisation of Raven's SMP. *Proceedings of the 23rd International Congress of Applied Psychology*, Madrid, Spain.

Salgado, J. S., Anderson, N., Moscoso, S., Bertua, C., de Fuyt, F., and Rolland, J. P. (2003). A meta-analytic study of general mental ability validity for different occupations in the European community. *Journal of Applied Psychology*, 88, 1068–1081.

Salkind, N. J., Kojima, H., and Zelniker, T. (1978). Cognitive tempo in American, Japanese and Israeli children. *Child Development*, 49, 1024–1027.

Sandoval, J., Zimmerman, B., and Woo-Sam, D. (1983) Cultural differences on WISC-R verbal items. *Journal of Social Psychology*, 21, 49–55.

Santos, T. dos. (1993[1970]). The Structure of Dependence. In M. A. Seligson and J. T. Passé-Smith (Eds.), *Development and Underdevelopment: The Political Economy of Inequality*. Boulder and London: Lynne Rienner Publishers.

Saunders, P. (1995). Might Britain be a meritocracy? *Sociology*, 29, 23–41.

Savage, S. W. (1946). Intelligence and infant mortality in problem families. *British Medical Journal*, 19 Jan., 86–87.

Scarr, S. and McCartney, K. (1988). Far from home: an experimental evaluation of the mother-child home program in Bermuda. *Child Development,* 59, 531–543.

Schmidt, F. L. and Hunter, J. E. (1998). The validity and utility of selection methods in psychology: practical and theoretical implications of 85 years of research findings. *Psychological Bulletin,* 124, 262–274.

Schmidt, F. L. and Hunter, J. E. (2004). General mental ability in the world of work: occupational attainment and job performance. *Journal of Personality and Social Psychology,* 86, 162–173.

Scottish Council for Research in Education. (1933). *The Intelligence of Scottish Children.* London: University of London Press.

Scottish Council for Research in Education. (1949). *The Trend of Scottish Intelligence.* London: University of London Press.

Seligson, M. A. and Passé-Smith, J. T. (Eds.). (1998). *Development and Underdevelopment: The Political Economy of Global Inequality.* Boulder and London: Lynne Rienner Publishers.

Seligson, M. A. and Passé-Smith, J. T. (Eds.). (2003). *Development and Underdevelopment: The Political Economy of Global Inequality.* Third Edition. Boulder and London: Lynne Rienner Publishers.

Sewell, W. H., Haller, A. O., and Ohlendorf, G. V. (1970). The educational and early occupational attainment process. *American Sociological Review,* 35, 1014–1027.

Sewell, W. H., Hauser, R. M., and Wolf, W. C. (1980). Sex, schooling, and occupational status. *American Journal of Sociology,* 86, 551–583.

Shields, J. (1962). *Monozygotic Twins brought up together and apart.* New York: Oxford University Press.

Shigehisa, T. and Lynn, R. (1991). Reaction times and intelligence in Japanese children. *International Journal of Psychology,* 26, 195–202.

Siebert, H. (1999). *The World Economy.* London and New York: Routledge.

Silber, J. and Ramos, X. (2003). Efficiency Analysis and the Dimensions of Human Development. Paper presented at the UNU/WIDER conference on *Inequality, Poverty, and Human Well-being,* 30–31 May 2003, Helsinki, Finland.

Silventoinen, K., Kaprio, J., and Lahelma, E. (2000). Genetic and environmental contribution to the association between body height and educational attainment: a study of adult Finnish twins. *Behavior Genetics,* 30, 477–485.

Simeon, D. T. and Gratham-McGregor, S. (1989). Effects of missing breakfast on the cognitive functions of school children of differing nutritional backgrounds. *American Journal of Clinical Nutrition*, 49, 464–653.

Simoes, M. M. R. (1989). Un estudo exploratorio com o teste das matrizes progressivas de Raven para criancas. *Proceedings of the Congress of Psychology*. Lisbon, Portugal.

Sinha, U. (1968). The use of Raven's Progressive Matrices in India. *Indian Educational Review*, 3, 75–88.

Skandinaviska Testforlaget. (1970). *Manual of the Swedish WISC*. Stockholm: Skandinaviska Testforlaget.

Smith, A. (1976 [1776]). *An Inquiry into the Nature and Causes of The Wealth of Nations*. Ed. Edwin Cannan. Chicago: The University of Chicago Press.

Smith, C. L. and Beals, K. L. (1990). Cultural correlates with cranial capacity. *American Anthropologist*, 92, 193–200.

Soewondo, S., Husaini, M., and Pollitt, E. (1989). Effects of iron deficiency on attention and learning processes in preschool children: Bandung, Indonesia. *American Journal of Clinical Nutrition*, 50, 667–674.

Solow, R. M. (1956). A contribution to the theory of economic growth. *Quarterly Journal of Economics*, 70, 65–94.

Sorokin, B. (1954). *Standardization of the Progressive Matrices test*. Unpublished Report.

Spearman, C. (1904). General intelligence, objectively determined and measured. *American Journal of Psychology*, 15, 201–293.

Speth, J. G. (1997). Foreword. In UNDP, *Human Development Report 1997*. New York: Oxford University Press.

Spicher, P. (1993). *Nouvel etalonnage du SPM*. Freiburg, Switzerland: University of Freiburg.

Sternberg, R. J., Grigorenko, E. L., Ngorosho, D., Tantufuye, E., Mbise, A., Nokes, C., Jukes, M., and Bundy, D. A. (2002). Assessing intellectual potential in rural Tanzanian school children. *Intelligence*, 30, 141–162.

Sternberg, R. J., Nokes, C., Geissler, P. W., Prince, R., Okatcha, F., Bundy, D. A., and Grigorenko, E. L. (2002). The relationship between academic and practical intelligence: A case study in Kenya. *Intelligence*, 29, 401–418.

Stevenson, H. W., Stigler, J. W., Lee, S., Lucker, G. W., Kitanawa S., and Hsu, C. (1985). Cognitive performance and academic achievement of Japanese, Chinese, and American children. *Child Development*, 56, 718–734.

Stewart, F. (2003). Everyone agrees we Need Poverty Reduction, but not what this Means: Does this Matter? Paper presented at the UNU/WIDER conference on *Inequality, Poverty, and Human Well-being*, 30–31 May 2003, Helsinki, Finland.

Stewart, N. (1947). AGCT scores of army personel grouped by occupation. *Occupations*, 26, 5–24.

St. George, A. (1974). Cross-cultural ability testing. Unpublished.

Strauss, M. A. (1954). Subcultural variation in Ceylonese mental ability: a study in national character. *Journal of Social Psychology*, 39, 129–141.

Student Atlas of World Geography. See Allen.

Sumner, A. (2003). Economic and non-Economic Well-being: A Review of Progress on the Measurement of Poverty. Paper presented at the UNU/ WIDER conference on *Inequality, Poverty, and Human Well-being*, 30–31 May 2003, Helsinki, Finland.

Sundberg, N. and Ballinger, T. (1968). Nepalese children's cognitive development as revealed by drawings of man, woman, and self. *Child Development*, 39, 969–985.

Sundet, J. M., Tambs, K., Magnus, O., and Berg, K. (1988). On the question of secular trends in the heritability of test scores: a study of Norwegian twins. *Intelligence*, 12, 47–59.

Takeuchi, M. and Scott, R. (1992). Cognitive profiles of Japanese and Canadian kindergarten and first grade children. *Journal of Social Psychology*, 132, 505–512.

Tambs, K., Sunder, J. M., Magnus, P., and Berg, K. (1989). Genetic and environmental contributions to the covariation between occupational status, educational attainment, and IQ: a study of twins. *Behavior Genetics*, 19, 209–222.

Tarnopol, L. and Tarnopol, M. (1980). Arithmetic ability in Chinese and Japanese children. *Focus on Learning Problems in Mathematics*, 2, 29–48.

Taubman, P. (1976). The determinants of earnings: genetics, family, and other environments. *American Economic Review*, 66, 858–870.

Taylor, J. M. and Radford, E. J. (1986). Psychometric testing as an unfair labour practice. *South African Journal of Psychology*, 16, 79–86.

Teasdale, T. W. (1979). Social class correlations among adoptees and their biological and adoptive parents. *Behavior Genetics*, 9, 103–114.

Teasdale, T. W., and Owen, D. R. (1984). Social class and mobility in male adoptees and non-adoptees. *Journal of Biosocial Science*, 16, 521–530.

Teasdale, T. W. and Sorensen, Y. I. (1983). Educational attainment and social class in adoptees: genetic and environmental contributions. *Journal of*

Biosocial Science, 15, 509–518.

Te Nijenhuis, J. and van der Flier, H. (1997). Comparability of GATB scores for immigrant and majority group members: Some Dutch findings. *Journal of Applied Psychology,* 82, 675–685.

Terman, L. M. (1925). *Genetic Studies of Genius.* Vol. 1. *Mental and Physical Traits of a Thousand Gifted Children.* Stanford, Cal: Stanford University Press.

Terman, L. M. and Oden, M. H. (1959). *Genetic Studies of Genius.* Vol. IV. *The Gifted Child Grows Up.* Stanford, Cal: Stanford University Press.

Tesi, G. and Young, B. H. (1962). A standardisation of Raven's Progressive Matrices. *Archive de Psicologia Neurologia e Pscichologia,* 5, 455–464.

Tewes, U. (2003). Germany. In J. Georgas, L. G. Weiss, F. van der Vijver, and D. H. Saklofske (Eds.), *Culture and Children's Intelligence.* Amsterdam: Academic Press.

The Economist. (2003). If you consider people, not countries, global inequality is falling rapidly. August 23, p. 56.

The Europa World Year Book. (1996–2004). London: Europa Publications.

The Heritage Foundation. See *The Index of Economic Freedom.*

The Index of Economic Freedom. (2003). The Heritage Foundation and the *Wall Street Journal.* www.heritage.org.

The New Encyclopaedia Britannica, Volume 18, *Macropaedia.* (1985). Chicago: Encyclopaedia Britannica.

The Politics of Aristotle or a Treatise on Government. (1952). Translated by William Ellis. London: J.M. Dent & Sons.

The Polyarchy Dataset. Vanhanen's Index of Democracy. (2003). www.prio.no/cwp/vanhanen/.

The World Bank. (1999-2004). *World Development Report.* New York: Oxford University Press.

The World Bank. (2002-2004). *World Development Indicators.* New York: Oxford University Press.

The World Dataset of Happiness. See Veenhoven.

The World Factbook. See Central Intelligence Agency (CIA).

Thienpont, K. and Verleye, G. (2003). Cognitive ability and occupational status in a British cohort. *Journal of Biosocial Science,* 36, 333–349.

Thomas, A. (2000). Meanings and views of development. In T. Allen and A. Thomas (Eds.), *Poverty and Development into 21st Century.* Oxford: Oxford University Press.

Thomas, R. M. and Shah, A. (1961). The Draw-a-Man test in Indonesia. *Journal of*

Educational Psychology, 32, 232–235.

Thompson, P. M., Cannon, T. D., Narr, K. L., van Erp, T., and Poutanen, V. P. (2001). Genetic influences on brain structure. *Nature Neuroscience,* 4, 1253–1258.

Tocqueville, A. de. (1963 [1835]). *Democracy in America.* The Henry Reeve Text as revised by Francis Bowen. Now further corrected and edited with introduction, editorial notes, and bibliographies by Phillips Bradley. New York: Alfred A. Knopf.

Todaro, M. P. (2000). *Economic Development.* 7th Ed. Reading, Mass.: Addison-Wesley.

Transparency International Corruption Perceptions Index 2003. (2004). www.transparency.org/cpi/2003/.

TYN CY 1.1. See Mitchell et al.

Tzuriel, D. and Caspi, N. (1992). Cognitive modifiability and cognitive performance of deaf and hearing preschool children. *Journal of Special Education,* 26, 235–252.

Ucman, P. (1972). A normative study of the Goodenough-Harris test on a Turkish sample. In L. J. Cronbach and P. J. D. Drenth (Eds.), *Mental Tests and Cultural Adaptation.* The Hague: Mouton.

UNDP (United Nations Development Programme). (1997–2004). *Human Development Report.* New York: Oxford University Press.

UNDP (United Nations Development Programme). (1998). *UNDP Poverty Report 1998: Overcoming Human Poverty.* New York: United Nations Development Program.

Unesco Institute for Statistics. (2004). *Statistical tables.* www.uis.unesco.org/.

Unesco. (1998). *Statistical Yearbook 1998.* Paris: Unesco Publishing & Bernan Press.

Unesco. (1999). *Statistical Yearbook 1999.* Paris: Unesco Publishing & Bernan Press.

United Nations. (1990–2000). *Demographic Yearbook.* New York: United Nations.

UNU/WIDER World Income Inequality Database, Version 2.0 beta, 3 December 2004. www.wider.unu.edu/wiid/wiid.htm.

Valentine, M. (1957). Psychometric testing in Iran. *Journal of Mental Science,* 105, 93–107.

Vanhanen, T. (1999). *Ethnic Conflicts Explained by Ethnic Nepotism.* Research in Biopolitics. Volume 7. Stanford, Conn.: Jai Press Inc.

Vanhanen, T. (2003). *Democratization. A comparative analysis of 170 countries.* London and New York: Routledge.

Veenhoven, R. (2003). Return of inequality in modern society? Test by dispersion of life-satisfaction across time and nation. Paper presented at the UNU/WIDER conference on *Inequality, Poverty, and Human Well-being*, 30–31 May 2003, Helsinki, Finland.

Veenhoven, R. (2004). *World Database of Happiness*, Distributional Findings in Nations. www.eur.nl/fsw/research/happiness.

Vejleskov, H. (1968). An analysis of Raven Matrix responses in fifth grade children. *Scandinavian Journal of Psychology*, 9, 177–186.

Verhagen, P. (1956). Utilite actuelle des tests pour l'etude psychologique des autochones Congolese. *Revue de Psychologie Appliquee*, 6, 139–151.

Vernon, P. A., Wickett, J. C., Bazana, P. G., and Stelmack, R. M. (2000). The neuropsychology and neurophysiology of human intelligence. In R. J. Sternberg (Ed.), *Handbook of Intelligence*. Cambridge: Cambridge University Press.

Vernon, P. E. (1969). *Intelligence and Cultural Environment*. London: Methuen

Vernon, P. E. (1982). *The Abilities and Achievements of Orientals in North America*. New York: Academic Press.

Volken, T. (2003). *IQ and the Wealth of Nations*. A Critique of Richard Lynn and Tatu Vanhanen's Recent Book. *European Sociological Review*, 19, 411–412.

Wadsworth, S. J., Corley, R. P., Hewett, J. K., and DeFries, J. C. (2001). Stability of genetic and environmental influences on reading performance at age 7, 12, and 16 years of age on the Colorado adoption project. *Behavior Genetics*, 31, 353-359.

Walberg, H. J. (1984). Improving the productivity of America's schools. *Educational Leadership*, 41, 19–27.

Waldron, L. A. and Gallimore, A. J. (1973). Pictorial depth perception in Papua New Guinea, Torres Straits, and Australia. *Australian Journal of Psychology*, 25, 89–92.

Waller, J. H. (1971). Achievement and social mobility: Relationships among IQ score, education, and occupation in two generations. *Social Biology*, 18, 252–259.

Wallerstein, I. (1993 [1975]). The Present State of the Debate on World Inequality. In M. A. Seligson and J. T. Passé-Smith (Eds.), *Development & Underdevelopment: The Political Economy of Inequality*. Boulder and London: Lynne Rienner Publishers.

Wallerstein, I. (2004). *World-Systems Analysis. An Introduction*. Durham and London: Duke University Press.

Wang, Z. (1993). Psychology in China: A Review Dedicated to Li Chen. *Annual*

Review of Psychology, 44, 87–116.

WDI. See the World Bank, *World Development Indicators*.

Weede, E. (1998). Why People Stay Poor Elsewhere. In M. A. Seligson and J. T. Passé-Smith (Eds.), *Development and Underdevelopment: The Political Economy of Global Inequality*. Boulder and London: Lynne Rienner Publishers.

Weede, E. and Kämpf, S. (2002). The Impact of Intelligence and Institutional Improvements on Economic Growth. *Kyklos*, 55, Fasc. 3, 361–380.

Wein, N. and Stevenson, B. (1972). *Pre-school education programme - Dominica: Pilot evaluation of 3 and 4 year olds*. Jamaica: Bernard Van Leer Foundation U.W.I, Mona.

Weinberg, R. A., Scarr, S., and Waldman, I. D. (1992). The Minnesota transracial adoption study: a follow-up of the IQ test performance at adolescence. *Intelligence*, 16, 117–135.

Whalley, L. J. and Deary, I. J. (2001). Longitudinal cohort study of childhood IQ and survival up to age 76. *British Medical Journal*, 322, 1–5.

White, K. R. (1982). The relation between socioeconomic status and academic achievement. *Psychological Bulletin*, 91, 461–481.

Whitehouse, D. (1992). Principles of genetics. In S. Jones, R. Martin, and D. Pilbeam (Eds.), *The Cambridge Encyclopedia of Human Evolution*. Cambridge: Cambridge University Press.

WIDER. (2003). *Inequality, Poverty, and Well-being, Booklet of Abstract and papers*. www.wider.unu.edu

Wilson, E. O. (1978). *On Human Nature*. Cambridge, Mass.: Harvard University Press.

Wilson, E. O. (1992). *The Diversity of Life*. Cambridge, Mass.: The Belknap Press of Harvard University Press.

Winkelmann, W. von. (1972). Normen für den Mann-Zeichen-Test von Ziler und die Coloured Progressive Matrices von Raven für 5–7 jahrige Kinder. *Psychologische Beitrage*, 17, 80–94.

Winnick, M., Meyer, K. K., and Harris, R. C. (1975). Malnutrition and environmental enrichment by early adoption. *Science*, 190, 1173–1175.

Winship, C. and Korenman, S. (1997). Does going to college make you smarter? The effect of education on IQ in *The Bell Curve*. In B. Devlin, S. Fienberg, D. Resnick, and K. Roeder (Eds.), *Intelligence, Genes, and Success: Scientists respond to The Bell Curve*. New York: Copernicus Press.

WMO No. 847. See World Meteorological Organization.

Wober, M. (1969). The meaning and stability of Raven's matrices test among

Africans. *International Journal of Psychology*, 4, 220–235.

Wolfensohn, J. D. (2001). Foreword. In the World Bank, *The World Development Report 2000/2001: Attacking Poverty*. Oxford: Oxford University Press.

The World Bank. (1999-2004). *World Development Report*. New York: Oxford University Press.

The World Bank. (2002-2004). *World Development Indicators*. New York: Oxford University Press.

The World Database of Happiness. See Veenhoven.

World Development Indicators. See the World Bank.

World Development Report. See the World Bank.

World Directory of Minorities. (1997). Edited by Minority Rights Group. London: Minority Rights Group International.

The World Factbook. See Central Intelligence Agency (CIA).

World Meteorological Organization (WMO). n.d. *Climatological normals (CLINO) for the period 1961-1990*. Geneva: WMO No. 847.

Yaish, M. (2001). Class structure in a deeply divided society: class and ethnic inequality in contemporary Israel. *British Journal of Sociology*, 52, 409–440.

Yousefi, F., Shahim, S., Razavieh, A., Mehryar, A. H., Hosseini, A. A., and Alborzi, S. (1992). Some normative data on the Bender Gestalt test performance of Iranian children. *British Journal of Educational Psychology*, 62, 410–416.

Yule, W., Gold, R. D., and Busch, C. (1982). Long-term predictive validity of the WPPSI: An 11-year follow-up study. *Personality and Individual Differences*, 3, 65–71.

Zahirnic, C., Girboveanu, M., Onofrei, A., Turcu, A., Voicu, C., Voicu, M., and Visan, O. M. (1974). Etolonarea matricelor progressive colorate Raven. *Revista de Psicologie*, 20, 313–321.

Zaj, P. J. (2002) Genetics, family structure, and economic growth. *Journal of Evolutionary Economics*, 12, 343–365.

Zak, P. J. and Park, K. W. 2002. Population Genetics and Economic Growth. *Journal of Bioeconomics*, 4, 1–37.

Zax, J. S. and Rees, D. L. (2002). IQ, academic performance, environment, and earnings. *The Review of Economics and Statistics*, 84, 600–614.

Zetterbaum, M. (1987). Alexis de Tocqueville. In L. Strauss and J. Cropsey (Eds.), *History of Political Philosophy*. Third Edition. Chicago and London: The University of Chicago Press.

Zhou, Z. and Boehm, A. E. (2001). American and Chinese children's knowledge of basic relational concepts. *School Psychology International*, 22, 5–21.

Zindi, F. (1994). Differences in psychometric performance. *The Psychologist*, 7, 549–552.

Zimmerberg, J. (2002). The Impact of Cognitive and Non-cognitive Ability on Earnings-Swedish Evidence. Mimeo. Stockholm: IFAU.

Name Index

Subject Index

ABOUT THE AUTHORS

RICHARD LYNN is Emeritus Professor of Psychology of the University of Ulster, Coleraine, Northern Ireland. He graduated in Psychology at the University of Cambridge and has held positions at the University of Exeter and the Economic and Social Research Institute, Dublin. Among his earlier books are *Dysgenics: Genetic Deterioration in Modern Populations (1996)* and *Eugenics: A Reassessment (2001)*, *IQ and the Wealth of Nations (Co-author, 2002), and Race Differences in Intelligence (2006)*.

TATU VANHANEN is Emeritus Professor of Political Science of the University of Tempere, Finland, and Emeritus Docent of Political Science of the University of Helsinki. He became Doctor of Social Sciences at the University of Tampere in 1968 and has held positions at the University of Jyväskylä, at the University of Tampere, and the University of Helsinki. Among his earlier books are *The Process of Democratization: A Comparative Study of 147 States, 1980–88 (1990)*, *On the Evolutionary Roots of Politics (1992), Prospects of Democracy: A study of 172 Countries (1997), Ethnic Conflicts Explained by Ethnic Nepotism (1999)*, and *IQ and the Wealth of Nations (Co-author, 2002)*.